Thomson's Delictual Liability

Thomson's Delictual Liability

Seventh Edition

Professor Stephen Bogle

Professor of Law and Interpersonal Justice, University of Glasgow

Dr Bobby WM Lindsay

Senior Lecturer in Private Law, University of Glasgow

Bloomsbury Professional

LONDON • DUBLIN • EDINBURGH • NEW YORK • NEW DELHI • SYDNEY

BLOOMSBURY PROFESSIONAL

Bloomsbury Publishing Plc

50 Bedford Square, London, WC1B 3DP, UK

1385 Broadway, New York, 10018, USA

Bloomsbury Publishing Ireland Ltd

29 Earlsfort Terrace, Dublin 2, D02 AY28, Ireland

First published in Great Britain 2025

British Library Cataloguing-in-Publication Data

A catalogue record for this book is available from the British Library.

ISBN: PB: 978 1 52653 229 9
ePDF: 978 1 52653 231 2
ePub: 978 1 52653 230 5

Typeset by Compuscript Ltd, Shannon

Preface

We are privileged to take on the custodianship of this book. Our overriding aim in this text is to provide the reader with an accessible, structured, and modern account of the law of delict in Scotland – an approach for which Professor Thomson's previous editions were rightly renowned.

We have endeavoured to present the law of delict as it is described and understood by the courts in Scotland, regardless of whether we agree with the analysis or the trajectory of the law. At points, this has required us to depart (with diffidence) from Professor Thomson's analysis. We deliberately have limited our own commentary on legal developments, offering opinion only where absolutely necessary – particularly where future litigation or legislative intervention appears likely.

For the most part, our account is based on opinions from the Outer and Inner Houses of the Court of Session, and judgments of the UK Supreme Court. The civil court reforms enacted in 2014 – with the creation of an All-Scotland Personal Injury Court, and a Sheriff Appeal Court – also has increased the prominence of shrieval decisions, enriching our understanding of how the law of delict is applied in practice. But English precedents and judicial insights continue to provide invaluable guidance to Scottish courts on a wide variety of issues, and are frequently referred to in this text where appropriate.

We have undertaken a comprehensive revision of the text, significantly updating both its content and structure to reflect contemporary developments. Given the evolving nature of delict, such substantial updates occasionally are necessary, as legislation and judicial decisions continue to reshape the liability landscape. As a result, we have reframed the presentation of numerous issues – most notably, the duty of care, but also breach, vicarious liability, and prescription and limitation.

While opinions will continue to differ on the role of policy in the development of delict, the Supreme Court's decision in *Robinson v Chief Constable of West Yorkshire Police* clarified that, at least in the context of negligent conduct, the prevailing judicial approach is to prioritise principle and precedent over policy. In previous editions, Professor Thomson emphasised the role of policy in the development of the law of delict. In this text, we have moderated that analytical approach to better reflect current judicial attitudes and how the law is presently expressed by courts.

We are grateful for the comments provided to us by David Johnston KC on Chapter 17 and Iain Hunter on aspects of social security deductions covered in Chapter 18. We would also like to thank Gordon Cameron for his encouragement and previous stewardship of this text. Furthermore, we wish to thank Paula O'Connell and Kate Firth for their superb assistance in preparing this edition. All errors remain our own.

Stephen Bogle

Bobby Lindsay

Stair Building, Glasgow
July 2025

Contents

Table of Statutes

[All references are to paragraph number]

Table of Statutory Instruments

[All references are to paragraph number]

Table of Cases

[All references are to paragraph number]

B

C

D

E

F

G

H

I

J

L

M

N

O

P

S

T

Introduction

The essence of the modern Scots law of delict is the obligation of a person, A, to compensate another person, B, for the losses B has sustained as a result of harm caused to B by the wrongful actions of A. This obligation to pay compensation is called reparation. The obligation to make reparation when loss has been suffered as a result of a person's wrongful actions is involuntary; it arises by virtue of the law regardless of the will of the wrongdoer. In this respect, delictual obligations differ from contractual obligations which arise as a result of the agreement of the parties to a contract, ie a voluntary obligation. However, a delictual obligation is similar to the obligation to reverse an unjustified enrichment, since the latter obligation also arises by operation of the law. But unlike unjustified enrichment the delictual obligation to make reparation arises only when the loss has arisen as a result of the wrongful act of the person who caused the harm. It is only when a person has been at fault that the obligation to make reparation arises. In Scots law we use the term '*culpa*' to describe fault. *Culpa* covers both intentional and unintentional conduct which causes harm to another but before there is liability the law must regard the conduct as wrongous. This is encapsulated in the brocard *damnum injuria datum*, ie harm caused by wrongous conduct.

Some examples will make the point clearer. If A intentionally assaults B, causing him harm, A is under a delictual obligation to compensate B for the losses he has sustained from his injuries: A's conduct is culpable, because he deliberately intended to harm B by assaulting him, which the law regards as a wrongous act. If A drives his car carelessly on a public highway and as a result injures B, a pedestrian, then A is under a delictual obligation to compensate B for the losses he has sustained from his injuries: A's conduct is culpable because of his careless driving which the law regards as a wrongous act. Thus, we can say that modern Scots law begins from the premise that there is an involuntary obligation on a person to make reparation to another who has sustained losses as a consequence of suffering harm as a result of the *culpa* or fault of the wrongdoer, ie the wrongdoer's intentional or unintentional, but careless, conduct, which caused the harm. Its function is corrective justice – to put the victim, so far as an award of damages can, into the position he would have been if the wrong had never taken place.

It is not the case that a person who suffers loss from harm caused by another's intentional or unintentional, but careless, conduct will always be entitled to reparation. The act which causes the harm must be regarded by the law as wrongful (*injuria*). For policy reasons, certain acts are not regarded as wrongful in this sense. So, for example, as we shall see,[1] A is free to undercut the prices of his competitor, B, even if B suffers economically; nor does it matter if A deliberately undercuts B's prices with the intention of putting B out of business. The reason for this is that, in our society, competition is to be encouraged even if persons suffer economically as a result. This is an example of *damnum absque injuria,* ie harm without wrongful conduct. The encouragement of competition, however, does not go so far as to allow two parties to conspire to drive a third out of business. Conspiracy is a delict.[2]

Before there is an obligation to make reparation, the victim must suffer harm. But, in addition, this harm must arise from an intrusion by the wrongdoer upon a right of the victim which is recognised by the law as reparable. One of the fascinating aspects of the law of delict is to see when the courts are prepared to recognise rights as reparable and when they are not.

For example, the law has long recognised as reparable a person's right to physical integrity so that if there is an intrusion of that right as a result of wrongful conduct, the wrongdoer must make compensation for pain and suffering, ie non-patrimonial loss and any patrimonial, ie economic, loss arising from the injuries sustained, such as loss of earning capacity. But the Scots law of delict has, hitherto, not recognised as a reparable right a person's privacy *per se*[3] although it has, for example, protected a person's confidential information.[4]

An area which has caused controversy is whether the law should recognise as a reparable right economic loss sustained by a person where the economic loss does not derive from injury to that person's body or damage to his property.[5] So, for example, if A carelessly damages an electric cable owned by B with the result that there is a loss of power to C's factory, should C be able to obtain compensation for his loss of production (pure economic loss) if the power cut did not cause any physical damage to the machinery in his factory? B, of course, can seek reparation from A in respect of the physical damage to B's cable.

1 See para 2.2 below.
2 See paras 2.13–2.15 below.
3 Although protection is secured via the Convention Rights incorporated under the Human Rights Act 1998: see paras 1.10–1.15.
4 Breach of confidence is discussed at para 2.8 below.
5 This matter is discussed at length in Chapter 5.

Scottish lawyers maintain that Scots law is based on principle rather than remedies. It is probably true to argue that the modern Scots law of delict is based on the general principle of an involuntary obligation to make reparation for loss sustained as a result of wrongful conduct.

Stair laid the basis for the general principle of delictual liability when he recognised that to cause damage by delinquence gave rise to an obediential obligation to make reparation for the damage caused: *damnum injuria datum*. This was a general innominate remedy based on the defender's *culpa* which included deliberate as well as careless conduct. *Stair* treated the nominate Scottish remedies as simply aspects of the general obligation to make reparation for loss caused by a wrong.[1] This general obligation was accepted by the later institutional writers.[2] In attempting this synthesis, reliance was, of course, placed on Roman law and in particular liability under the Lex Aquilia which included liability for unintentional, but careless, conduct.

Although the modern Scots law of delict can be traced back to the institutional writers, their treatment is not extensive. Instead, the principles of the law of delict are largely the creation of the courts. The judges have had to develop the law to take account of the increase of potential injury to persons and damage to property created by industrialisation, mass production and distribution of goods, easier access to information, and the motor car. At the same time, they have also appreciated that there must be limits on a person's liability, particularly for unintentional conduct, if that person is to continue to engage in conduct which is socially and economically desirable, even if it is potentially harmful. The traditional Scots law solution has been to restrict liability by insisting that it is only triggered by the defender's fault and by refusing to recognise certain kinds of harm as reparable rights. This book is largely concerned with the rules of common law and statute which have developed to achieve this balance. However, in some areas it has been considered socially and economically desirable that persons should recover compensation for losses resulting from physical injury or damage to property without the need to establish fault on the part of the defender. Accordingly, legislation has been necessary to introduce into Scots law what is known as strict liability, ie where a person can be liable in delict for harm for which they are deemed responsible without the need for the person who suffers loss from the injury or damage to establish fault.[3] An example of strict liability at common law is vicarious liability whereby employers may be held liable for the delicts of their employees while not being at fault themselves.[4]

1 *Stair* I, 9, 2.
2 See, for example, Erskine *Institute* III, 1.
3 For example, liability for defective products falls on the manufacturer or importer, see Chapter 13 below; liability for some injuries or damage caused by animals falls on the keeper of the animal: Animals (Scotland) Act 1987.
4 See Chapter 15 below.

The authors' primary intention is to focus on the common law principles underpinning delictual liability – namely, intentional and unintentional wrongdoing – alongside key pieces of legislation, which have shaped the law of delict in Scotland. In doing so, we concentrate on the case law of the Scottish courts and where appropriate, the leading jurisprudence of English courts. There have been times when these principles have become difficult to explain in a coherent fashion. While it has always been accepted that the imposition of a duty of care in novel situations involves the courts making decisions on grounds of legal policy, once that decision was made, precedent could be applied more or less mechanically to determine whether or not a duty would be recognised in the instant case. A developing tendency to apply a 'fair, just and reasonable' test, whenever the question of duty arose had the potential to undermine principle and reduce every determination to the level of policy.[1] That situation has largely been averted by the Supreme Court in *Robinson v Chief Constable of West Yorkshire*.[2] A return to orthodoxy is well under way.

The book begins with a study of delictual liability for intentionally harmful conduct; the second part contains an analysis of the general principles of liability for unintentional, but careless, conduct; the third part considers delictual liability in the context of some important social and economic relationships. Included in this part is a chapter on defamation and malicious publication which are now on a statutory footing. The book ends with chapters on vicarious liability, prescription and limitation, and damages.

1 See JM Thomson 'Principle as Policy' (2003) 56 CLP 123.
2 [2018] UKSC 8, [2018] AC 736.

CHAPTER 1

The Intentional Wrongs

INTRODUCTION

1.1 This chapter will consider delicts which protect personal and bodily integrity and personality rights from deliberate action. These delicts protect certain rights or interests which we hold simply by virtue of our humanity: the right not to be harmed, the right to liberty, the right to privacy, and so on.

PERSONAL AND BODILY INTEGRITY

(1) Assault

1.2 'Everyone who lives under the protection of the law has an absolute right to the safety of his person; and wherever this right is invaded there is in Civil law a provision for redress of injury, as well as in penal law a punishment for the crime.'[1]

There are three stages to the analysis of civil assault:

(1) Did the defender's conduct have the effect of invading the pursuer's physical and bodily integrity?

(2) Was the defender's conduct voluntary?

(3) Did the defender have a valid defence?

Before examining these stages, it should be noted that assault also constitutes a common law crime in Scotland. However, the crime of assault differs from the delict of assault. In respect of stage (2), the crime of assault requires the establishment of evil intent, or intention to injure, on the part of the accused, whereas there is no such requirement in delict. Moreover, the consent of the victim precludes any delictual claim, but does not prevent a criminal prosecution for assault being brought against the assailant. There also are differences arising from the generic distinction between civil and criminal proceedings: for example, civil assaults need only be proved on the 'balance of probabilities', whereas the higher 'beyond reasonable doubt' standard applies to criminal assault. This means that it is possible to bring a successful civil action for assault even where the defender has been found not guilty or not proven in a prior criminal trial.[2]

1 Bell, *Principles*, para 2028. For a detailed treatment of this delict see E Reid, *Personality, Confidentiality and Privacy in Scots Law* (W Green & Son, 2010), Chapter 2; E Reid, *The Law of Delict in Scotland* (EUP, 2022), Chapter 16.

2 *Mullan v Anderson (No 2)* 1997 SLT 93 (OH) (murder); *C v G* [2017] CSOH 5, 2018 SC 47 (affirmed on appeal [2017] CSIH 72, 2018 SC 171); *AR v Coxen* 2018 SLT (Sh Ct) 335; *AB v Diamond* [2022] SC EDIN 4 (all concerning rape and sexual assault, cf the unsuccessful claim in *PW v KM* [2024] CSOH 85).

1.3 Most obviously, if the defender's conduct actually strikes the pursuer, then that will constitute an actionable invasion. But it remains the case that apprehension of the threat of immediate bodily harm will found a claim for damages even though the threat is not carried out or does not strike the pursuer.[1] For example, aiming a firearm at the pursuer, without pulling the trigger, will be sufficient to constitute an assault. So too will spitting at the pursuer if they are only a few feet away, even if the volley of spittle does not connect with the pursuer. The test is whether the defender's conduct is sufficient to place the pursuer in danger, or in reasonable alarm as to their physical integrity. The physical proximity between the defender and the pursuer may be a relevant factor in assessing the reasonableness of the pursuer's state of alarm.[2]

If the assault does not result in serious physical harm to the pursuer, the damages awarded will not be substantial despite any insult caused.[3] The flow of complaints based on affront without any physical invasion has not persisted to the present day.[4] However, an assailant is not entitled to think the victim is in good health. The thin skull rule operates. The defender will be liable to the full extent of damage suffered even though injury is exacerbated by the pursuer's health condition.[5]

1 See eg *Ewing v Earl of Mar* (1851) 14 D 314 (IH).

2 *Ewing* at 315 per Lord President Boyle.

3 See eg *Downie v Chief Constable of Strathclyde Police* 1997 SCLR 603 (OH) (the pursuer was awarded £1,500 in respect of an assault by two policemen; the victim had recovered without the need of medical treatment).

4 For discussion see E Reid, *Personality, Confidentiality and Privacy in Scots Law*, paras 2.19ff; E Reid, *The Law of Delict in Scotland*, paras 16.19–16.21. See the unsuccessful action in *McCallum v Morrison* [2023] SAC (Civ) 23, 2023 SLT (SAC) 119 (failure to observe professional hygiene standards not an assault).

5 *MacGregor v Shepherd* 1946 SLT (Sh Ct) 42 (defender struck the pursuer in the jaw; pursuer had a septic jaw so consequence of blow was much more severe than if his jaw had been healthy. Nevertheless, defender held fully liable for consequences).

1.4 If the conduct of which complaint is made crosses this threshold, the defender's state of mind must then be investigated. The intention to inflict hurt or injury is perfectly apparent in most assaults, but even where harm is not the object of the conduct the defender will nevertheless be liable if they acted in the knowledge that harm was likely to occur, or acted recklessly, disregarding the possibility of harm.[1] In other words, unlike with criminal assault, there is no need to establish the specific intent to injure the pursuer (so-called 'evil intent'). So where A playfully attacked B in order to make B engage in sport, it nevertheless constituted an actionable wrong even although it was done 'for a lark'.[2] If A throws a hammer at B, but the hammer strikes C, C should be able to pursue A in civil assault.[3] What matters is that the act which invaded the pursuer's bodily integrity was a voluntary one. Pure accidents, such as a police officer throwing an old woman to the ground as a reflex action, are not actionable as assaults,[4] but may give rise to a claim in negligence.[5]

1 E Reid, *Personality, Confidentiality and Privacy in Scots Law*, para 2.10.
2 *Reid v Mitchell* (1885) 12 R 1129 (IH).
3 The outcome in *Somerville v Harsco Infrastructure Ltd* [2015] SC EDIN 71 is consistent with this proposition.
4 See eg *Hall v Watson* (1896) 12 Sh Ct Rep 117.
5 See eg *Robinson v Chief Constable West Yorkshire* [2018] UKSC 4, [2018] AC 736. Negligence is discussed in chapters 3–9.

1.5 Unlike in criminal law, the consent of the victim prevents delictual liability for assault from arising.[1] This explains why there is no liability for assault in sports involving physical contact: boxing, rugby, football etc. Players consent to the 'risks incident to being a player' and will only be able to claim in the event of 'undue violence or unfair play' far outside the rules of the sport,[2] for instance if a rugby player punches, as opposed to tackles, an opponent. Sporting injury claims are more usually litigated in negligence, where similar principles of consent apply.[3]

In the medical context, the basis for medical intervention is the informed consent of the patient.[4] Any procedure carried out without the consent of an adult patient[5] is actionable as an assault.[6] The patient can obtain reparation not only for any resulting patrimonial loss but also for the insult suffered as a result of the non-consensual invasion of bodily integrity. The fact that the procedure was carried out for the patient's benefit is irrelevant.[7] However, again, negligence tends to be the usual basis for proceeding against a medical professional who operates without the informed consent of the patient.[8]

1 The place of consent in the delict of assault is not yet settled. It is unclear whether a lack of consent is part of the requirements of assault which must be established by a pursuer, or if the presence of consent is a defence to be established by the defender. The distinction matters for the allocation of the burden of proof. The former approach has been adopted by parties in sexual assault claims (see eg *C v G* [2017] CSOH 5, 2018 SC 47 at paras 269–271), but is not self-evidently correct.
2 *Reid v Mitchell* (1885) 12 R 1129 (IH) at 1132 per Lord Young.
3 See eg *Sharp v Highlands and Islands Fire Board* 2005 SLT 855 (OH) (football tackle); *Czernuszka v King* [2023] EWHC 380 (KB), [2023] 4 WLR 26 (rugby tackle).
4 *Montgomery v Lanarkshire Health Board* [2015] UKSC 11, 2015 SC (UKSC) 63.
5 A person under the age of 16 will have legal capacity to consent if the doctor or dentist is of the view that the young person is capable of understanding the nature and probable

consequences of the medical treatment or procedure: Age of Legal Capacity (Scotland) Act 1991, s 2(4). For adults with incapacity, see the Adults with Incapacity (Scotland) Act 2000, ss 47–48.

6 See *Thomson v Devon* (1899) 15 Sh Ct Rep 209 at 217. In an emergency if the patient is, for example, unconscious, a doctor may proceed without the patient's consent if it is *necessary* for the patient's wellbeing to do so: see *Montgomery* at para 88.

7 'Even when his or her own life depends on receiving medical treatment, an adult of sound mind is entitled to refuse it': *St George's Healthcare NHS Trust v S* [1998] 3 WLR 936 (CA) at 685 per Judge LJ.

8 See para 11.4 below.

1.6 Even if the defender's voluntary, non-consensual conduct constitutes a *prima facie* assault, the defender may avoid liability, in full or in part, by successfully establishing a defence. Here, the complete defences of self-defence and justification, and the partial defence of provocation, will be considered.

If the defender's use of force was in response to a perceived threat on the part of the pursuer, then self-defence may arise. This defence has two components. First, the defender must show that their response was in proportion to the threat presented by the pursuer. Use of a weapon when the pursuer is unarmed,[1] or a forceful blow when the pursuer is older and more infirm than the defender,[2] may defeat the defence, but it depends on the circumstances of the particular case. Secondly, the defender must show that the use of force was necessary in the circumstances. If the defender makes an unreasonable mistake as to the existence or extent of the threat posed by the pursuer, then the defence will fail.[3]

There are circumstances where the use of force is justified by the office or role held by the defender. Most cases concern police officers, but there are other officials (eg transport officers) for whom use of some degree of force also may be justifiable. Justification will fall away, however, if the officer acts outside the scope of their powers, such as if the order they are attempting to enforce is unlawful, or if the use of force is unnecessary because the pursuer was willing to comply with the order, or if the force used is excessive in the circumstances.[4]

In contrast to self-defence and justification, provocation is only a partial defence: if established, it reduces the defender's liability (and correspondingly the amount of damages awarded to the pursuer). Provoking acts may include physical threats or conduct insufficient to trigger self-defence,[5] abusive language,[6] or even attacking the defender's pet.[7]

1 *Marco v Merrens* 1964 SLT (Sh Ct) 74.

2 *Lane v Holloway* [1968] 1 QB 379 (CA).

3 *R (Officer W80) v Director General of the Independent Office for Police Conduct* [2023] UKSC 24, [2023] 1 WLR 2300; following *Ashley v Chief Constable of Sussex Police* [2008] UKHL 25, [2008] 1 AC 962.

4 *Mason v Orr* (1901) 4 F 220 (OH) at 223 per Lord M'Laren. On excessive force, see *Dawson v Threadgold* [2025] SC EDIN 38.

5 *Ashmore v Rock Steady Security* 2006 SLT 207 (OH).
6 *Anderson v Marshall* (1835) 13 S 1130 (IH); *MacGregor v Shepherd* 1946 SLT (Sh Ct) 42.
7 *Ross v Bryce* 1972 SLT (Sh Ct) 76.

(2) Unjustified detention

1.7 If the pursuer's right to liberty is interfered with without valid justification, then compensation must follow,[1] via the delict of unjustified detention. As Stair stated: 'Next to life is liberty; and the delinquence against it are restraint and constraint. And though liberty itself be inestimable, yet the damages sustained through these delinquencies are reparable.'[2]

A slight infringement of liberty is prima facie actionable: so, for example, where a lady was alleged to have been detained against her will for a quarter of an hour by a hotel manager, her action in delict was held to be relevant.[3] Any constraint on the pursuer's freedom of physical movement will suffice: this may even include a non-physical prohibition, such as a curfew breach of which attracts criminal penalty.[4]

Given this breadth of what may be an actionable constraint, the question of justification is key. Whereas, in other jurisdictions, justification operates as a defence (and therefore must be established by the detainer),[5] the position in Scotland would seem to be that the pursuer must establish that their detention was without justification.[6] While the location of the burden of proof may rarely be decisive, the fact that Scots law adopts a pro-detainer position as a starting point may not reflect the importance accorded to liberty by Stair.

There is a most unfortunate lack of clarity when it comes to justification. There is no direct authority as to when detention by a private citizen (a so-called 'citizen's arrest') will be justified. The criminal law considers such an arrest lawful where the citizen has a 'moral certainty' that a crime has been committed by the detainee.[7] That test could also sensibly be applied in delict, so that a detainer who is morally certain that the detainee has committed a crime will not be liable for unjustified detention, so long as the detainee is handed over to the authorities without delay.[8]

The most important class of defender for this delict is the police. Where a police officer detains a suspect pursuant to a warrant, the warrant supplies clear justification.[9] The police also may exercise relatively wide statutory powers of arrest without a warrant.[10] But there is conflicting authority as to what a pursuer must establish if they allege that they were detained unlawfully in circumstances where those powers of arrest did not actually arise. On one view, all that a pursuer needs to establish is that the conditions giving rise to the statutory powers of arrest were not satisfied, and therefore the detaining officer acted without justification.[11] On the other view, even if the pursuer can establish that the statutory powers were not engaged, it still must be established that the detaining officer acted maliciously and without probable cause.[12] The latter approach has been favoured in the most recent judicial consideration of the question,[13] but it has been contended that this places too high a burden on the citizen, resulting from confusion with the wrong of malicious prosecution, and is not a requirement found in other legal systems from which Scots law typically draws inspiration.[14]

Certain other public officials have power to detain persons if relevant criteria are met: for instance, transport officers[15] and immigration officials.[16] A person may be legitimately detained in a mental health hospital following examination by an approved medical professional.[17] Justices of the Peace may also be liable if they impose a custodial sentence maliciously and without probable cause.[18]

1 See Article 5(5) of the European Convention on Human Rights and eg *McCaffer v Lord Advocate* 2015 SLT (Sh Ct) 44.

2 Stair, *Institutes* I, 9, 4. For fuller coverage of this topic see E Reid, *Personality, Confidentiality and Privacy in Scots Law*, Chapter 5; E Reid, *The Law of Delict in Scotland*, Chapter 17.

3 *Mackenzie v Cluny Hill Hydropathic Co* (1908) SC 200 (IH).

4 *R (Jalloh) v Secretary of State for the Home Department* [2020] UKSC 4, [2021] AC 262. Moreover, even a partial physical constraint, such as handcuffing of limbs, may be actionable: *Henderson v Chief Constable, Fife Police* 1988 SLT 361 (OH).

5 See eg for English law *R (Lumba) v Secretary of State for the Home Department* [2011] UKSC 11, [2012] 1 AC 245 at para 65.

6 For recent *obiter* consideration, see *Scott v Police Investigations and Review Commissioner* [2024] SAC (Civ) 3, 2024 SC (SAC) 99 at paras 46–53.

7 *Wightman v Lees* 2000 SLT 111 (HCJAC).

8 *Lundie v MacBrayne* (1894) 21 R 1085 (IH) at 1090 per Lord McLaren.

9 Theoretically, the pursuer would be able to defeat that justification if it can be established that the police officer nevertheless acted maliciously and without probable cause in effecting the detention (cf *Sheppeard v Fraser* (1849) 11 D 446 (IH)). But such cases are exceedingly rare and unlikely to succeed on proof.

10 Criminal Justice (Scotland) Act 2016, s 1.

11 *McKinney v Chief Constable Strathclyde Police* 1998 SLT (Sh Ct) 80; *Louden v Chief Constable of Police Scotland* 2014 SLT (Sh Ct) 97.

12 *Woodward v Chief Constable of Fife* 1998 SLT 1342 (OH); *Whitehouse v Gormley* [2018] CSOH 93, 2020 SCLR 27.

13 *Whitehouse*.

14 B Lindsay, 'Relegated No Longer? The Role of Malice in the Delictual Protection of Liberty' (2019) 23 *Edinburgh Law Review* 75; E Reid, 'Liability for Wrongful Deprivation of Liberty: Malice and Police Privilege' (2020) 24 *Edinburgh Law Review* 175.

15 *Coutts v MacBrayne Ltd* 1910 SC 386 (ship captains); Regulation of Railways Act 1889, s 5(2) (railway officers).

16 Immigration Act 1971, Sch 2, paras 16–18B; see eg *S v Secretary of State for the Home Department* [2014] CSIH 91, 2015 SC 295.

17 Mental Health (Care and Treatment) (Scotland) Act 2003, s 36 (emergency 72-hour detention); s 44 (short-term 28-day detention). The police may remove a person to a place of safety for 24 hours pending examination by a medical practitioner: 2003 Act, s 297. Private individuals may retain a narrow common law power to detain: *B v F* 1987 SLT 681 (IH).

18 Criminal Procedure (Scotland) Act 1995, s 170. Other judges enjoy absolute immunity from suit: *McCreadie v Thompson* (1907) 15 SLT 216 (IH); *Russell v Dickson* 1997 SC 269 (OH).

1.8 Unjustified detention must be distinguished from the delict of malicious prosecution. This latter delict is concerned with the complaint that the defender has wrongfully initiated legal proceedings against the pursuer. While there is no authority that this generally extends to civil proceedings in Scots law,[1] there have been recent high-profile cases affirming its applicability to criminal proceedings. Crucially, it has been held that the Lord Advocate, and officers prosecuting under her authority as chief public prosecutor, no longer enjoy absolute immunity from suit, and may be held liable for malicious prosecution if it is established that they acted with malice and without probable cause.[2] Malice effectively means an 'improper purpose or motive',[3] whereas probable cause is a more involved question with objective and subjective elements.[4] Damages may be sought for legal expenses, *solatium* for distress, anxiety, humiliation and loss of reputation, and for consequential economic loss, but it may be difficult to establish causation between such losses and the prosecution itself.[5]

As malicious prosecution requires the defender to have actually executed criminal proceedings against the pursuer, no action lies against officials such as police officers or witnesses providing evidence.[6] However, a police officer who, maliciously and without probable cause, provides the prosecutor with false information, may be liable under a separate delict, but causation may be difficult to establish given the independent role of the prosecution service.[7]

1 Authority supports delictual liability for malicious institution of bankruptcy proceedings (see eg *J&W Kinnes v John Adam and Sons* (1882) 9 R 698 (IH)) and the wrongful use of diligence (see eg *Advocate General for Scotland v Galbraith Trawlers Ltd* [2021] SAC (Civ) 15, 2021 SLT (Sh Ct) 211). In English law, the tort of malicious prosecution extends to civil actions generally (*Willers v Joyce* [2016] UKSC 43, [2018] AC 779), but successful actions are rare.
2 *Whitehouse v Lord Advocate* [2019] CSIH 52, 2020 SC 133, overruling *Hester v Macdonald* 1961 SC 370 (IH).
3 *Grier v Lord Advocate* [2022] CSIH 57, 2023 SC 116 at para 118.
4 *Whitehouse* at para 108; *Grier v Lord Advocate* [2022] CSOH 2, 2022 SLT 199 at paras 66–71.
5 *Ahmad v Lord Advocate* [2024] CSOH 23.
6 *Grier* at para 135; cf *McKie v Strathclyde Joint Police Board* 2004 SLT 982 (OH) at para 28.
7 *Grier* at para 136; *MacGregor v Chief Constable of Police Scotland* [2024] CSOH 109, 2025 SLT 355.

(3) Harassment

1.9 The Protection from Harassment Act 1997 provides that every individual has a right to be free from harassment,[1] and creates a delictual action to protect that right. This delict has five steps to consider:

(1) Did the defender embark on a course of conduct?

(2) Did that course of conduct have the effect of harassing the pursuer?

(3) Did the defender intend for that course of conduct to harass the pursuer, or was that course of conduct objectively harassing?

(4) Does the defender have a valid defence?

(5) What remedy should the pursuer claim?

First, it must be established that the allegedly harassing conduct (which may include speech) occurred on at least two occasions:[2] liability under the statutory delict exists for a course of conduct, not a single instance of conduct.[3]

Harassment is not defined within the 1997 Act, but specifically includes causing the pursuer 'alarm or distress'.[4] It has been said that when:

> 'the quality of the conduct said to constitute harassment is being examined, courts will have in mind that irritations, annoyances, even a measure of upset arise at times in everybody's day-to-day dealings with other people. Courts are well able to recognise the boundary between conduct which is unattractive, even unreasonable, and conduct which is oppressive and unacceptable'.[5]

Even if the conduct is not directly targeted at the pursuer, it will still amount to harassment of him or her if it was targeted at a third party, and it was foreseeable that harassment of that third party could directly affect the pursuer.[6]

While it is possible for the pursuer to offer to prove the subjective harassing intention of the defender, they can also simply establish that the contact was objectively harassing, in the sense that the conduct occurred 'in circumstances where it would appear to a reasonable person that it would amount to harassment' of the pursuer.[7] This means that the reasonable person would consider the conduct to cross the line into what is 'oppressive and unacceptable'. Objectively harassing conduct may include stalking an ex-partner,[8] persistent and unwanted social media contact and encouraging a 'pile-on',[9] a campaign of workplace bullying,[10] placing the pursuer under physical or digital surveillance,[11] and repeatedly making unjustified threats of legal action,[12] but the concept of harassment is so open-textured that it may embrace many forms of conduct. In terms of journalism and the press, only a conscious abuse of media freedom would amount to harassment.[13]

It is a defence to an action of harassment that the course of conduct was authorised by law,[14] or was pursued for the purpose of preventing or detecting crime,[15] or was reasonable in the particular circumstances of the case.[16]

If the action is successful, the court can award damages:[17] these can include compensation for anxiety and financial loss caused by the harassment.[18]

The court can also grant interdict or a non-harassment order.[19] Breach of a non-harassment order is a criminal offence.[20] Typically, a pursuer will seek an interim interdict to preclude the defender from harassing the pursuer (while the action is pending) and then, if successful at the conclusion of the action, have the court substitute that interim interdict for a permanent non-harassment order.

1 Protection from Harassment Act 1997, s 8(1). This formulation means that a company may not sue for harassment on its own behalf: *Smithkline Beecham v Avery* [2009] EWHC 1488 (QB). The Scottish provisions of the Act (ss 8–11) are similar to the English provisions (ss 1–7), albeit the English provisions directly create a crime of harassment.

2 1997 Act, s 8(3). This requirement is removed in situations involving domestic abuse (s 8A), but it is possible that a new separate delict of domestic abuse will be introduced and this aspect of the 1997 Act will be repealed. See Scottish Law Commission Discussion Paper 178 on Civil Remedies for Domestic Abuse (2024).

3 So long as the separate instances are similar in content, a large gap in time between occurrences will not prevent them forming part of the same course of conduct: *Marinello v Edinburgh City Council* [2011] CSIH 33, 2011 SC 736. Repetition of identical or similar actions will constitute a course of conduct: *Wilson v Mendelsohn* [2023] EWHC 231 (KB).

4 1997 Act, s 8(3).

5 *Majrowski v Guy's and St Thomas's NHS Trust* [2006] UKHL 34, [2007] 1 AC 224 per Lord Nicholls at para 30, followed in Scotland in *Dickie v Flexcon Glenrothes* 2009 GWD 35-602 (Sh Ct).

6 *Levi v Bates* [2015] EWCA Civ 206, [2016] QB 91.

7 1997 Act, s 8(1).

8 See eg *Dew v Mills-Nanyn* [2022] EWHC 1925 (QB).

9 See eg *Davies v Carter* [2021] EWHC 3021 (QB).

10 As in *Majrowski* and *Dickie*.

11 *Shehabi v Bahrain* [2024] EWCA Civ 1158.

12 See eg *Ferguson v British Gas* [2009] EWCA Civ 46, [2010] 1 WLR 785; *Worthington v Metropolitan Housing Trust Ltd* [2018] EWCA Civ 1125.

13 *Sube v News Group Newspapers* [2020] EWHC 1125 (QB). For a successful action against a citizen 'journalist', see *Hibbert v Hall* [2024] EWHC 2677 (KB).

14 1997 Act, s 8(4)(a). See also s 12.

15 1997 Act, s 8(4)(b). To succeed, the defender must show that the conduct was rationally connected to the prevention of crime, so the defence may fall away if the allegations have been investigated and rejected by the authorities: *Hayes v Willoughby* [2013] UKSC 17, [2013] 1 WLR 935.

16 1997 Act, s 8(4)(c). This defence is broad enough to take into account human rights considerations eg freedom of assembly (*Canada Goose v Persons Unknown* [2019] EWHC 2459 (QB), [2020] 1 WLR 417).

17 1997 Act, s 8(5)(a). For procedural purposes, an action of damages for non-harassment is not an action for personal injuries: *G v S* [2006] CSOH 88, 2006 SLT 795 (OH).

18 1997 Act, s 8(6). See eg *Manson-Smith v Arthurworrey* [2021] EWHC 2137 (QB).

19 1997 Act, s 8(5)(b). Although an interim interdict is competent, an interim non-harassment order is not: *Heenan v Dillon* 1999 SLT (Sh Ct) 32. On the relationship of non-harassment orders with other court orders, see, for example, *McCann v McGurran* 2002 SLT 592; *McGuire v Kidston* 2002 SLT (Sh Ct) 66.

20 1997 Act, s 9.

(4) Privacy

1.10 The protection of privacy is a developing area of the law, prompted by the Human Rights Act 1998 and the need to give effect to

Article 8 ECHR. This section will discuss informational privacy: the law on protection of privacy more generally remains to be developed.[1]

The courts in England have adapted and extended the equitable doctrine of breach of confidence to cover the dissemination of private information thus giving effect to Article 8 rights. This has given rise to two causes of action: breach of confidence and the tort of misuse of private information. The former protects confidential information, the latter, private information. While both actions may overlap, and may arise from the same set of facts, this book will restrict its consideration of breach of confidence to information arising in the commercial sphere.[2]

This section will focus on the protection of personal information. It will consider liability for misuse of private information, and therefore on 'the right to control the dissemination of information about one's private life and the right to the esteem and respect of other people'.[3] It should be noted, however, that personal information may also be protected under the Data Protection Act 1998 or the law of copyright.[4]

1 See eg E Reid, *The Law of Delict in Scotland*, paras 20.82–20.88; J Ainslie 'Intrusion of Privacy and the *Actio Iniuriarium*' [2023] *Juridical Review* 139.
2 See para 2.8 below for discussion of breach of confidence.
3 *Campbell v MGN* [2004] UKHL 22, [2004] 2 AC 457 at para 51 per Lord Hoffmann.
4 See eg *HRH Duchess of Sussex v Associated Newspapers* [2021] EWHC 273 (Ch), [2021] 4 WLR 35.

1.11 The vast majority of litigation on privacy is in the English jurisdiction. While there was discussion at one time that Scots law could develop its own approach, it seems that English and Scots law on this point are converging.[1] This seems inevitable as a result of the common application of the Human Rights Act 1998, and the Convention Rights thereby incorporated.

In *C v Chief Constable of Police Scotland*[2] the Lord Ordinary (Bannatyne) went further than the English courts in appearing to recognise a common law right to privacy. While there was no reclaiming motion on this point, Lady Dorian and Lord Menzies in the Inner House cast doubt on whether the development of the law had reached this position.[3]

1 See *C v Chief Constable of Police Scotland* [2020] CSIH 61, 2020 SLT 1021 at para 83 *per* the Lord Justice Clerk (Lady Dorrian). For discussion see E Reid, *Personality, Confidentiality and Privacy in Scots Law* paras 12.24–12.27; E Reid, *The Law of Delict in Scotland*, paras 20.12–20.13 and 20.16–20.19.
2 [2019] CSOH 48.
3 [2020] CSIH 61, 2020 SLT 1021 at paras 75–86 and 124.

1.12 In determining whether there has been a misuse of private information, the court will consider two stages:

(1) Does the pursuer have a reasonable expectation of privacy in respect of the information?

(2) Does the defender's freedom to impart that information outweigh the pursuer's reasonable expectation of privacy?

This effectively involves a balance between the pursuer's Article 8 ECHR right to respect for their private life and the defender's Article 10 ECHR right to freedom of expression. Neither right takes precedence, and neither is absolute.[1] Article 8 is subject to the rights and freedoms of others, including the right of others to impart and receive information. Similarly, Article 10 is subject to restrictions imposed for the protection of the rights of others, including the right to privacy and to prevent disclosure of confidential information.

If the pursuer has a reasonable expectation of privacy in respect of the information, then their Article 8 rights will be engaged. The second stage involves a balance between that right of the pursuer's and the defender's freedom of expression rights. If the balance comes down in favour of the defender, then dissemination of the information will not be an actionable misuse. But if the pursuer's rights prevail, then publication will constitute a misuse of private information.

1 *In Re S* [2004] UKHL 47, [2005] 1 AC 593.

1.13 The first step, therefore, is asking whether the pursuer enjoyed a reasonable expectation in respect of the particular information. This is an objective test, asking what 'a reasonable person of ordinary sensibilities would feel if she was placed in the same position as the claimant and faced with the same publicity.'[1] This expectation does not end at the pursuer's front door: there is a 'zone of interaction of a person with others, even in a public context' which will give rise to a reasonable expectation of privacy.[2] The test involves considering objective factors as well as any signals the pursuer has made regarding how they would wish the information to be treated.[3] Relevant factors may include:[4]

- The particular attributes of the pursuer.
- The nature of the activity which is the subject of the information.
- The location, nature, and purpose of any intrusion to obtain the information.
- Any absence of consent on the part of the pursuer.
- The effect which disclosure would have on the pursuer.
- The purposes for which the information came into the hands of the defender.

While much will turn on the facts of individual cases, some broad propositions can be outlined. Information about a pursuer's medical condition or treatment[5] or financial situation[6] will usually attract a reasonable expectation of privacy. Information about sexual activity and relationships, especially if detailed, will engage a reasonable expectation.[7] A photograph will more readily engage a reasonable expectation than a written description,[8] and unauthorised photographs of a celebrity's children will invariably attract protection.[9] A person under suspicion of having committed a criminal offence will enjoy a reasonable expectation of privacy up until the point they are charged with this offence,[10] but information clearly implicating the pursuer in abhorrent conduct will not usually benefit from a reasonable expectation that it will be kept private.[11] Recklessness will not automatically remove a reasonable expectation,[12] but the pursuer's conduct may be such as to demonstrate they could not reasonably believe that it would be kept private.[13] The truth of the information is not relevant: disclosure of false information about a celebrity's private life still has the potential to invite unwanted scrutiny about intimate aspects.[14]

1 *Campbell v MGN* [2004] UKHL 22, [2004] 2 AC 457 at para 99 per Lord Hope.
2 *Von Hannover v Germany (No 1)* (2006) 43 EHRR 7 (ECtHR) at para 50.
3 NA Moreham, 'Unpacking the Reasonable Expectation of Privacy Test' (2018) 134 *Law Quarterly Review* 651.
4 *Murray v Express Newspapers plc* [2008] EWCA Civ 446, [2009] Ch 481 at para 36.
5 *Campbell*.
6 *Bekoe v London Mayor of Islington* [2023] EWHC 1668 (KB).
7 *Mosley v News Group Newspapers Ltd* [2008] EWHC 1777 (QB); *PJS v News Group Newspapers Ltd* [2016] UKSC 26, [2016] AC 1081; *BVC v EWF* [2019] EWHC 2506 (QB); *Reid v Price* [2020] EWHC 594 (QB).
8 *Campbell* at para 72 per Lord Hoffmann.
9 *Murray*; *Weller v Associated Newspapers* [2015] EWCA Civ 1176, [2016] 1 WLR 1541.
10 *ZXC v Bloomberg LP* [2022] UKSC 5, [2022] AC 1158, approving *Richard v BBC* [2018] EWHC 1837 (Ch), [2019] Ch 169.
11 Although not specifically cases on misuse of private information, this proposition regarding Article 8's application may be taken from *Sutherland v HMA for Scotland* [2020] UKSC 32, [2021] AC 427 and *C v Chief Constable Police Scotland* [2020] CSIH 61, 2020 SLT 1021.
12 *Ferdinand v MGN* [2011] EWHC 2454 (QB).
13 See eg *Stoute v News Group Newspapers* [2023] EWCA Civ 523.
14 *McKennitt v Ash* [2006] EWCA Civ 1714, [2008] QB 73 at para 86.

1.14 If the pursuer establishes a reasonable expectation of privacy, then this expectation must be balanced against the free expression rights of the defender. The factors to be taken into account include:[1]

- whether disclosure of the information would contribute to a debate of public interest;
- the role or functions of the pursuer and their prior conduct;
- the nature of activities with which the information is concerned;
- the method of obtaining the information and its veracity;
- the content, form and consequences of the publication; and
- the severity of the sanction imposed for misuse of private information.

The key question will be whether the information contributes to a debate of public interest. This requirement will not be met by the publication of salacious gossip. In *PJS v News Group Newspapers*, the UK Supreme Court considered the balancing test in the context of a story concerning a celebrity's extramarital sexual activities. It concluded that such stories lay 'at the bottom end of the spectrum of importance', regardless of the fact that sensationalist-minded members of the public may wish to know more about the story.[2] Also relevant was the negative impact that unlimited publication of the story would have on the celebrity's children.[3] That was sufficient to favour the claimant's Article 8 rights even though their identity was widely available on the internet and had been revealed by newspapers in other jurisdictions.[4]

Even if the information would contribute to a debate of general interest, the balancing exercise may still favour the pursuer on consideration of the other factors. For example, in *Richard v BBC*, it was accepted that the investigation of historic child sex abuse was a debate of general interest. However, the trial judge observed that it was not necessary to name the claimant as the subject of the police investigation to further that debate.[5] The fact that information that the claimant's house was to be raided had been improperly obtained from a police source, and the fact that the BBC then broadcast the raid live, filmed from a helicopter, tilted the balance in favour of the claimant.[6]

If the pursuer occupies an important position where they may be a 'role model', and publication of the information would highlight hypocrisy on their part, the court may be more inclined to uphold the publisher's Article 10 rights and reject the pursuer's claim in misuse of private information.[7] Publication of wide information about the pursuer may be a disproportionate means of 'putting the record straight' in respect of a minor inaccuracy, whereas publication of more limited information to correct that inaccuracy may well be justified.[8]

1 *Von Hannover v Germany (No 2)* (2012) 55 EHRR 15.
2 [2016] UKSC 26, [2016] AC 1081 at para 24 per Lord Mance.
3 *PJS* at para 72–74 per Baroness Hale.
4 *PJS* at para 35 per Lord Mance, cf the dissent of Lord Toulson at para 86.
5 *Richard v BBC* [2018] EWHC 1837 (Ch), [2019] Ch 169 at paras 280–282.
6 *Richard* at paras 288–302.
7 *Ferdinand v MGN* [2011] EWHC 2454 (QB).
8 *Duchess of Sussex v Associated Newspapers* [2022] EWCA Civ 1810, [2022] 4 WLR 81 at para 95.

1.15 If the balancing exercise favours the pursuer, a remedy will follow. If publication has not yet taken place, the pursuer may apply for an interim interdict to prohibit publication pending the resolution of their claim at trial. However, as this constitutes a severe interference with the defender's freedom of expression rights, the pursuer must meet special conditions before the court will grant an interim remedy.[1] If the pursuer succeeds at trial, they may crave a final interdict (to prohibit publication on penalty of contempt of court)[2] and damages. It is thought that the approach of English law to damages will be followed, where damages are awarded to compensate for distress caused, and for the loss of the right to control how the private information is used.[3] It should be noted that while aggravated damages may be awarded in England,[4] Scots courts may achieve the equivalent effect through increased awards of solatium.[5]

1 Human Rights Act 1998, s 12: these include notification of the respondent (unless court is satisfied that notification should not take place) and that the pursuer would be likely to succeed at full trial. There is no reported (or unreported) instance of the Scottish courts granting a 'super-interdict' (ie an interdict that prohibits reporting of the fact that an interdict is in place). On superinjunctions in English law, see eg *Donald v Ntuli* [2010] EWCA Civ 1276, [2011] 1 WLR 294.

2 The general criteria for granting interdict must, of course, be present: see eg *Waste Systems International Inc v Eurocare Environmental Services Ltd* 1999 SLT 198 (OH).

3 *Gulati v MGN* [2015] EWCA Civ 129, [2017] QB 149; applied in eg *FGX v Gaunt* [2023] EWHC 419 (KB).

4 See eg *Richard v BBC* [2018] EWHC 1837 (Ch), [2019] Ch 169.

5 See J Bailey, 'Aggravated Damages or Additional Solatium: A Distinction Without a Difference?' (2018) 22 *Edinburgh Law Review* 29.

CHAPTER 2

The Economic Wrongs

INTRODUCTION

2.1 This chapter will consider several delicts which protect the pursuer's economic interests from concerted action by the defender.[1] The extent to which negligent infringements of those interests are actionable will be considered in a later chapter.[2]

This chapter will first explain the general unwillingness of the law to impose liability for the infliction of economic loss by one person on another. It then will consider the exceptions which exist to that general reticence. First, the two-party[3] economic wrongs will be considered: the delict of fraud, and of passing off. This also is a convenient place to consider the wrong of breach of confidence in the context of the protection of commercially sensitive information. The chapter will then consider the more complicated three-party economic wrongs: inducement of breach of contract, causing loss by unlawful means, and conspiracy.

1 That is not to say that these wrongs *exclusively* protect economic interests, but that is the role to which these delicts are pressed most frequently in litigation.
2 See Chapter 5, below.
3 In some situations, these delicts may arise in situations involving three or more parties. But they are discussed under the heading of 'two-party' delicts as the involvement of a third party is not a necessary component of the wrongdoing.

THE GENERAL PRINCIPLE: ECONOMIC LIBERALISM

2.2 In a free market, competition is regarded as essential and in the public interest. In most markets, the success of Competitor A will inevitably entail a lack of success for Competitor B. Competitor A's desire to succeed necessarily, if indirectly, involves a desire to stop customers and business flowing to Competitor B, invariably to the latter's loss. Private law has no interest in intervening in this situation: there is no infringement of Competitor B's rights, and no relevant intention to injure on the part of Competitor A.[1]

Many of the early cases in this area concern labour relation disputes, between an employer, a trade union, and, occasionally, non-union employees. The basic principle is still that laid down by the House of Lords in the famous case of *Allen v Flood*.[2] The plaintiffs were shipwrights employed to repair woodwork on certain ships. Members of the boilermakers' union discovered that the shipwrights had previously been employed, by another employer, to repair ironwork on ships, which was perceived to have taken away work from boilermakers. Incensed, a trade union representative approached the current employer of the shipwrights and informed him that unless he dismissed the plaintiffs, his other employees who were members of the union would strike. This was done maliciously, to punish the plaintiffs. The employer dismissed the plaintiffs, who brought the action against the trade union representative.

Three points should be emphasised. First, the case proceeded on the basis that there was no conspiracy, ie no agreement among the boilermakers that they would strike; it was simply the individual trade union representative who said that there would be a strike. Second, if there had been a strike, the employees would have terminated their contracts of employment lawfully, as labourers were engaged on a day-by-day basis.[3] Third, when the employer dismissed the plaintiffs, he did so by lawfully terminating their contracts as, again, there was no long-term employment contract which such a decision would breach. In other words, the individual trade unionist used lawful means (the threat of a lawful strike) to compel the employer to use lawful means (the lawful dismissal) to harm the plaintiffs economically (the loss of their employment). In these circumstances, the House of Lords held that no wrong was committed even though the defendant had acted maliciously.

Accordingly, *Allen v Flood* is authority that an individual, A, can wield economic pressure to force B to act to his own or another's economic harm provided the means used by A are lawful. If, as in this case, the means used are lawful, no wrong is committed even if A acts maliciously to harm B or another person rather than to further A's economic interests. This result, while harsh, is an inevitable consequence of a free market economy.

The delicts we will consider in this chapter arise where a competitor or other economic actor deliberately uses unlawful means. But the general principle of economic liberalism is so strong that the law is keen to keep the boundaries of these exceptional strands of liability tightly drawn. As was explained in a modern conspiracy case:[4]

> 'The reason for the general rule is that, contract apart, common law duties to avoid causing pure economic loss tend to cut across the ordinary incidents of competitive business, one of which is that one man's gain may be another man's loss. The successful pursuit of commercial self-interest necessarily entails the risk of damaging the commercial interests of others. Identifying the point at which it transgresses legitimate bounds

is therefore a task of exceptional delicacy. The elements of the … economic [wrongs] are carefully defined so as to avoid trespassing on legitimate business activities or imposing any wider liability than can be justified in principle'.

1 See eg *Mogul Steamship v McGregor, Gow & Co* [1892] AC 25 (HL). Outside of the law of delict, anti-competitive practices may be a concern for competition law: see the Competition Act 1998, ss 2 and 18.

2 [1898] AC 1 (HL).

3 Cf *Rookes v Barnard* [1964] AC 1129 (HL), where the employees were engaged on contracts with a lengthy notice period. As the threat to strike therefore was an anticipatory breach of those contracts, the trade union official in *Rookes* was held liable.

4 *JSC BTA Bank v Khrapunov* [2018] UKSC 19, [2020] AC 727 at para 6 per Lords Sumption and Lloyd-Jones.

TWO-PARTY WRONGS

(1) Fraud

2.3 Fraud is the paradigm of an intentional delict in Scots law. It has been defined as 'a machination or contrivance to deceive'.[1] Fraud will usually cause pure economic loss to the pursuer. As we shall see, this provides a stark contrast to the situation where unintentional conduct results in pure economic loss; there the courts have traditionally been unwilling to allow damages in negligence for pure economic loss. But it should be noted that fraud is not restricted to economic loss. If A lies to B when A tells B that B's wife and children have been seriously injured, with the result that B suffers distress or a psychiatric disorder, B can recover damages from A.[2]

Although the institutional writers had a flexible view of the concept of fraud, because of developments in the nineteenth century fraud as a wrong was confined to a relatively narrow range of situations where the defender *intended* to harm the pursuer. In effect, the Scots wrong of fraud was equated with the English tort of deceit.[3]

Before delictual liability arises for fraud, there must be a positive act by the defender which causes loss to the pursuer. This will often take the form of a misrepresentation by words. But positive conduct can amount to a fraudulent misrepresentation, for example supplying reconditioned as opposed to new cash registers[4] or selling reproduction furniture 'got up' to look like antiques.[5] As a general rule, non-disclosure does not amount to a misrepresentation unless there is a fiduciary relationship between the parties or the contract is a contract *uberrimae fidei* ('of the utmost good faith').[6]

1 Erskine *Institute* III, 1, 16.

2 In English law, there is a specific tort, sometimes named after the case of *Wilkinson v Downtown* [1897] 2 QB 57 (QB), of the intentional infliction of psychological harm. See, for the limits placed on this tort in the modern age, *O (A Child) v Rhodes* [2015] UKSC 32, [2016] AC 219. For possible Scottish adoption, see *Robertson v The Scottish Ministers* [2007] CSOH 186.
3 On the development of fraud generally, see D Reid, Fraud in Scots Law, PhD Thesis, University of Edinburgh, 2013.
4 *Gibson v National Cash Register Co Ltd* 1925 SC 500 (IH).
5 *Patterson v H Landsberg & Son* (1905) 7 F 675 (IH).
6 For example, a contract of insurance.

2.4 Before there is liability for fraud, the pursuer must establish that the defender had the requisite mental element. In other words, the pursuer must show that at the time of the misrepresentation the defender's state of mind was such that he did not, or could not, believe his statement was true. It is, of course, extremely difficult to prove this mental element:[1]

> 'Fraud is not something to be lightly inferred. Nor should it be lightly averred. It is for the party alleging fraud to prove it and, in order to do so, to set out in specific terms the basis upon which the court will be invited to infer that the party against whom fraud is alleged did not honestly believe that the representation was true'.

Consequently, the law has developed liability for negligent – as opposed to fraudulent – misrepresentation where the defender's conduct can be tested objectively.[2]

What, then, will constitute the *mens rea* of fraud? There are three alternative states of mind which have been accepted as providing the necessary mental state for fraud. It may arise where the defender:[3]

(1) positively knows the statement is false; or

(2) positively believes the statement is false even though he does not positively know it is false: liability if in fact untrue; or

(3) does not positively believe the statement is true even though he does not positively know or believe it is false: liability if in fact untrue, provided both parties have an interest in what has been said.

The first situation arises where the defender makes a statement which he knows is false. For example, A tells B there is a gold seam in A's garden when A knows that no seam is there. In these circumstances, A is lying.

The second situation arises where the defender makes a statement which he does not positively *know* is false but which he positively *believes* to be false. For example, A tells B there is a gold seam in A's garden; A has not dug up his garden and therefore does not know that there is no gold seam but A believes no gold seam is there. If in fact there is no gold seam, then A can be sued by B for fraud. B will have great difficulty in proving that

A believed his statement was false if A maintains he believed it was true. However, the court will infer fraud if the statement was destitute of all reasonable grounds for believing it was true or the least inquiry would immediately correct.[4]

The final situation arises where the defender makes a statement which he does not positively know is false and does not positively believe is false but is recklessly indifferent to whether it is true or false. If the matter is of no importance to speaker and listener, this is not dishonesty. But if it is a matter of importance between them, it is fraud since the speaker has attempted to induce a belief in the listener, ie that the statement is true, which the speaker does not actually entertain.[5] For example, A tells B there is a gold seam in A's garden. A has done tests which establish that the strata are not inconsistent with a gold seam but A, nevertheless, has serious doubts whether a gold seam is actually there. Assuming B has an interest in the statement, although A does not positively know that the statement is false and does not positively believe that it is false, if he does not care whether it is true or false, he is liable in fraud to B if in fact there is no gold seam in the garden.[6] Proof of the requisite *mens rea* in this situation will be difficult but, again, will be inferred if there were no reasonable grounds for believing the statement to be true, or if the truth of the matter was easily discoverable.

There can, therefore, be no liability in fraud if the defender positively believes that the statement is true. In these circumstances, if he did not take reasonable care in making the statement, there may be liability for negligent misrepresentation. This narrow formulation of intention is the necessary control mechanism to avoid fraud cutting across the general principles in relation to economic loss discussed above. But an adviser may become liable to a third party for its client's fraud if it does not dissociate from the fraud and alert the potential victim.[7]

If the effect of the fraudulent misrepresentation has been to induce the pursuer to enter into a contract, it is important to separate out the contractual consequences of fraud from its delictual consequences.[8] In respect of the latter, because fraud is an intentional delict, the pursuer is entitled to recover damages for all the losses directly arising from the fraud – even if the losses are not reasonably foreseeable by the defender.[9]

1 *Zurich v Gray and Kellas* [2007] CSOH 91 at para 24 per the Lord Ordinary (Brodie).
2 On these developments, see paras 5.10–5.17 below.
3 These are drawn from the speech of Lord Herschell in *Derry v Peek* (1889) 14 App Cas 337 at 374. Although an English appeal, the impact of this case on Scots law was significant.
4 *Western Bank of Scotland v Addie* (1867) 5 M (HL) 80.
5 *Lees v Tod* (1882) 9 R 807 (IH).

6 *H & J M Bennet (Potatoes) Ltd v Secretary of State for Scotland* 1986 SLT 665 (OH) (reversed on another point 1988 SLT 390 (IH)).

7 *Frank Houlgate Investment Co Ltd v Biggart Baillie LLP* [2014] CSIH 79, 2015 SC 187, although the Inner House was not clear precisely through which mechanism the solicitor became liable in that case!.

8 For the contractual consequences, see HL MacQueen, *MacQueen and Thomson on Contract Law in Scotland* (6th edn, Bloomsbury Professional, 2024) at paras 5.3–5.11 and 5.52–5.63.

9 In *Barry v Sutherland* 2002 SLT 413, the pursuers bought a pub as a result of the seller's fraudulent misrepresentation concerning the business accounts. The Lord Ordinary (Eassie) held that the pursuers were able to recover damages for trading losses they had incurred when running the business: they were not restricted to compensation for the difference in the price paid as opposed to the true price of the pub. In other words, they were entitled to recover for the losses which directly flowed from entering into the sale and running the business.

(2) Passing off

2.5 Passing off protects the 'goodwill' of a business, ie the distinctive identifying marks and branding which a customer instinctively associates with the products and services of the pursue and distinguishes them from those of its competitors.[1] It arises where a competitor misleadingly suggests through the presentation of its products that they are associated with, or of a similar quality to the products of the pursuer. In such a case, the competitor may be said to be attempting to 'pass off' its product or service as being made by, endorsed by, or similar to those offered by, the pursuer, resulting in confusion among consumers. This delict offers common law protection to the pursuer's goodwill, but more extensive protection can be obtained by registering aspects of that goodwill as a trademark. Nowadays, passing off claims are commonly raised as an adjunct to trademark infringement claims:[2] only the former will be considered here.[3]

The most common formulation of passing off has three elements:[4]

(1) The pursuer must establish that its product has acquired 'goodwill' in the market, so that those products have become associated with some distinctive mark.

(2) The defender must use a device which has led, or is likely to lead, to the belief that its products are associated in some way with the products of the pursuer, resulting in the confusion of customers. That misrepresentation need not be intentional.

(3) That misrepresentation must result in loss to the pursuer.

The goodwill of a business can be a very valuable asset. Important elements of goodwill are the marketing devices used to enable customers to recognise the product and distinguish it from the products of competitors. Before there is an action for passing off it must be established that there is a close association between the pursuer and the particular device which identifies the product or services for existing or potential customers, ie that the device is part of the goodwill of the trader.

Most obviously, the name of a product or business may form part of its goodwill. A distinctive name which is clearly associated with the pursuer's product will likely be protected.[5] On the other hand, a descriptive product name will only be protected if it is shown that customers associate that descriptive name with the product of the pursuer (eg 'Pot Noodle'),[6] and slight alterations to descriptive product names will be sufficient to avoid confusion in most cases.[7] Logos,[8] branding,[9] and colour schemes[10] may also be sufficiently distinctive to form part of a business's goodwill. A website domain name may be sufficient to attract goodwill.[11] A product's packaging may be sufficiently distinct to be synonymous with the pursuer's products in the minds of consumers, such as a yellow Jif lemon bottle[12] or a distinctive 'dimple' whisky bottle.[13]

An individual may be sufficiently recognisable to have goodwill in their own image. Celebrities therefore may bring a claim against parties using that image to suggest the individual endorses their products,[14] or has authorised them to sell merchandise using that image.[15]

Goodwill may also exist in marks which denote the quality of a class of product. A manufacturer of products within that class may bring a claim for so-called 'extended passing off' if a competitor seeks to use that mark in relation to products which are not of the same quality or origin. So, for example, a manufacturer of Scotch whisky can bring a claim in passing off against the distiller of a 'Scotch' whisky which is in fact blended on the Isle of Man.[16] The term Scotch is not only an indicator of geographical origin, but also a hallmark of quality, and therefore the term is protected as forming part of the extended goodwill of distillers of Scotch whisky.[17]

Before a claim in passing off can succeed, it must be shown that the pursuer has goodwill in the jurisdiction, in the sense of having customers in Scotland who use their products and services in Scotland, even if the business is abroad.[18] So a foreign hotel which allows Scottish customers to book rooms from Scotland over the internet might plausibly have goodwill in Scotland;[19] but a foreign television provider whose customers only use the service outside of Scotland will not have goodwill in Scotland even if its customers subsequently move here.[20]

1 See further C Wadlow, *The Law of Passing Off* (6th edn, Sweet & Maxwell, 2021); E Reid, *The Law of Delict in Scotland*, paras 21.82–21.106.

2 See eg *William Grant & Sons Irish Brands Ltd v Lidl Stiftung & Co KG* [2021] CSIH 38, 2021 SLT 889. If a pursuer succeeds in both claims, the rule against double recovery means that only one set of damages will be recoverable.
3 For the law under the Trade Marks Act 1994, see eg D Keeling et al, *Kerly's Law of Trade Marks and Trade Names* (17th edn, Sweet & Maxwell, 2023).
4 *Reckitt & Colman (Products) v Borden* [1990] 1 WLR 491 (HL).
5 See eg *Phones 4U v Phone4U.co.uk Internet Ltd* [2006] EWCA Civ 244, [2007] RPC 5 ('phones4u'); cf *Tartan Army v SETT* 2017 SLT 532 (pursuer could not show that 'Tartan Army' was associated with its particular business, and not Scotland National Team football fans generally).
6 Compare *Cellular Clothing v Maxton & Murray* (1899) 1 F (HL) 29 ('Cellular Clothing' held not to have acquired protected secondary meaning) with *Powell v Birmingham Vinegar Brewery Co* [1897] AC 710 (HL) ('Yorkshire Relish' held to be exclusively associated with plaintiff's products).
7 See eg *Salon Services (Hairdresser Supplies) v Direct Salon Services* 1988 SLT 414 (OH) ('*Direct* Salon Services' sufficiently distinct from 'Salon Services').
8 See eg *Enterprise Holdings v Europcar Group* [2015] EWHC 17 (Ch).
9 For a case where polo-themed branding was held to be insufficiently distinct to attract goodwill, because of the crowded market for such branding, see *Lifestyle Equities v Royal County of Berkshire Polo Club* [2023] EWHC 1839 (Ch).
10 See eg *Lidl Great Britain Ltd v Tesco Stores Ltd* [2024] EWCA Civ 262 (Lidl's blue and yellow sufficiently distinctive to prevent Tesco for using same colours for Clubcard promotional offers).
11 Compare *Media Agency Group v Space Media Agency* [2019] EWCA Civ 712 with *Argos v Argos Systems* [2017] EWHC 231 (Ch).
12 *Reckitt and Colman.*
13 *John Haig & Co Ltd v Forth Blending Co Ltd* 1954 SC 35 (OH).
14 *Irvine v Talksport* [2002] EWHC 367 (Ch), [2002] 1 WLR 2355.
15 *Fenty v Arcadia Brands* [2015] EWCA Civ 3, [2015] 1 WLR 3291.
16 See eg *Scotch Whisky Association v Glen Kella Distillers* [1997] ETMR 470 (Ch D).
17 See also eg *Erven Warmink v J Townend & Sons (Hull)* [1979] AC 731 (HL) (Advocaat liqueur); *Taittinger SA v Allbev Ltd* [1993] FSR 461 (CA) (champagne); *Fage UK v Chobani UK* [2014] EWCA Civ 5 (Greek yoghurt).
18 *Hotel Cipriani Srl v Cipriani (Grosvenor Street) Ltd* [2010] EWCA Civ 110.
19 *Starbucks (HK) Ltd v British Sky Broadcasting Group* [2015] UKSC 31, [2015] 1 WLR 2628 at para 52.
20 *Starbucks (HK).*

2.6 Once it is established that the pursuer has goodwill, it must be shown that the defender's use of a particular device constitutes a 'misrepresentation', in the sense of that use being likely to confuse customers. The test used here is that of the reasonable customer.[1] If only a 'moron in a hurry' would be misled or confused by the defender's use of the device, then that is insufficient.[2] It must be shown that a reasonable customer would conclude from the defender's use of the device that its products were in some way associated with those of the pursuer. Context here is important. The manner in which particular product is stocked or displayed may increase the likelihood of consumer confusion.[3] A budget supermarket's own products may look very similar to that of a premium competitor, but the fact that the former's products are sold at a lower cost in that budget supermarket should make it clear to the reasonable customer that the product they are purchasing is not the premium one, but a budget copycat.[4] And the fact that a professional could distinguish between competing businesses is insufficient to avoid liability if a normal customer without special knowledge would confuse the defender's business with that of the pursuer.[5]

At one time it was thought that passing off was simply a particular aspect of the delict of fraud. This is no longer thought to be sound – at least if the only remedy sought is interdict as opposed to damages. Although the misrepresentation which constitutes passing off must be 'calculated to injure' the pursuer's business or goodwill, it is enough if this is a reasonably foreseeable consequence of the misrepresentation.[6] In other words, the question of misrepresentation is objectively ascertained: subjective intention to mislead need not be established.

1 As was memorably put in one Scottish case (*Dunlop Pneumatic Tyre Co v Dunlop Motor Co* (1907) SC HL 15 at 17), the 'average citizen of Kilmarnock would [not] be deceived' into thinking that a local garage operated by a Mr Dunlop was associated with the multinational tyre company.

2 *Morning Star Co-Operative Society v Express Newspapers* [1979] FSR 113 (Ch D) (only a 'moron in a hurry' would confuse the new *Daily Star* tabloid newspaper with the established *Morning Star* socialist newspaper, so the launch of the former involved no passing off).

3 See eg *Reckitt & Colman (Products) v Borden* [1990] 1 WLR 491 (HL) at 500–503 (likelihood of confusion enhanced by fact that supermarkets would only stock limited varieties of lemon juice, and even a reasonable customer would pay limited attention to labels affixed to bottles as attempt to distinguish goods from those of the pursuer); *John Haig & Co Ltd v Forth Blending Co Ltd* 1954 SC 35 (OH) (customers in a bar may be unable to see labels on bottles, and therefore defender's use of distinctive bottle associated with pursuer's product liable to mislead). See also *Montgomery v Thompson* [1891] AC 217 (HL) at 225 per Lord Macnaghten: 'thirsty folk want beer, not explanations'.

4 *William Grant & Sons Irish Brands Ltd v Lidl Stiftung & Co KG* [2021] CSIH 38, 2021 SLT 889 (Lidl's £16 Hampstead gin could not be confused with Hendricks gin despite similarities in bottle and labelling). The court held, however, that there had been an infringement of the pursuer's trademarks, demonstrating the wider protection that may following from registering a trademark.

5 See eg *Wise Property Care Ltd v White Thomson Preservation Ltd* [2008] CSIH 44 at paras 39–43.

6 See *Erven Warnink BV v J Townend & Sons (Hull) Ltd* [1979] AC 731 (HL) at 742 per Lord Diplock.

2.7 The final stage is establishing that the misrepresentation has caused, or is likely to cause loss, to the pursuer. While the precise calculation of loss in terms of loss of custom, potential custom, and goodwill may be difficult, a pursuer who is able to show at least some likelihood of diversion of custom will succeed.

If a pursuer establishes goodwill, misrepresentation, and loss, the remedy most often sought is interdict, to prevent or halt the use of the misleading device. An interim interdict may be granted to prohibit the release of a product or service pending full trial, but the pursuer must establish a *prima facie* case of passing off and that the balance of convenience favours the pursuer.[1] Damages assessed by reference to the pursuer's loss may be awarded, but the difficulty of quantification has already been mentioned.

Alternatively, if the defender has profited from use of the misleading device, the pursuer may seek an account of those profits.[2]

1 See eg *Wise Property Care Ltd v White Thomson Preservation Ltd* [2008] CSIH 44.
2 That a pursuer cannot seek *both* damages and an account of profits was confirmed in *Treadwell's Drifters v RCL Ltd* 1996 SLT 1048 (OH).

(3) Breach of confidence

2.8 Breach of confidence involves the wrongful dissemination of confidential information in breach of a duty of confidence. In chapter one, we discussed the protection of personal private information through the wrong of misuse of private information.[1] That wrong grew out of the wrong of breach of confidence, and while it remains competent to raise an action of breach of confidence in respect of private information alongside a claim in misuse of private information, this section will discuss breach of confidence in respect of commercial information.

Long accepted in Scots law,[2] this species of wrongdoing has three elements:[3]

(1) The information must have the necessary quality of confidence.

(2) The information must have been imparted in circumstances which gave rise to an obligation of confidence.

(3) There must be actual or threatened disclosure of the information.

It has been held that the law in Scotland and England follows similar lines in relation to these requirements.[4]

To have the 'necessary quality of confidence', information must not be in the public domain, must be 'sufficiently certain' so as to be capable of close replication,[5] and must be 'inaccessible' in the sense of not being obvious or readily ascertainable.[6] Cases frequently concern 'trade secrets', ie proprietary information known to a company which derives commercial value from its secrecy (for instance, the blend of 11 herbs and spices that make up the coating on Kentucky Fried Chicken, or the recipe for (classic) Irn Bru).[7]

Secondly, the circumstances in which the defender came to know the information must have been clear that the pursuer reasonably expected that information to be kept confidential. Most obviously, an express agreement between the parties will give rise to an obligation of confidence.[8] An obligation of confidence will also arise between parties to certain classes of relationships even absent an express contractual undertaking, eg solicitor and client.[9] The employer/employee relationship features frequently in cases, raising considerations such as how long the obligation persists after the employee leaves their post.[10] But there is no need for the parties to stand in some pre-existing relationship. If the defender knows or ought to know from the nature of that information that it is fairly and reasonably to be regarded as confidential, then the law will impose an obligation of confidence.[11]

If the defender threatens to disclose confidential information while bound by an obligation of confidence, then the pursuer may seek an interdict to prevent disclosure. If disclosure has been made, then the pursuer may seek damages. It may be possible for the defender to show that, for some reason, their obligation of confidence has been limited and should not be enforced by the court. This may arise where disclosure would be in the public interest.[12]

1 See para 1.10–1.15 above. Misuse of private information does not depend on showing the information was imparted in circumstances which gave rise to an obligation of confidence.

2 See eg E Reid, *The Law of Delict in Scotland*, Chapter 19 and E Reid, 'Breach of Confidence: Translating the Equitable Wrong into Scots Law' [2014] *Juridical Review* 1.

3 *Coco v AN Clark* [1968] FSR 415 (Ch D), followed in eg *Levin v Caledonian Produce (Holdings) Ltd* 1975 SLT (Notes) 69 (OH).

4 See eg *Lord Advocate v Scotsman Publications* 1989 SC (HL) 122 at 164 per Lord Keith of Kinkel.

5 See eg *Bailey v Graham* [2011] EWHC 3098 (Ch) (recipe for 'Reggae Reggae' sauce that left substantial latitude to the implementing chef was too imprecise to be 'confidential', and in any event would have to be disclosed in large part on food standards labelling on product).

6 Compare *Force India Formula One Team Ltd v Aerolab Srl* [2012] EWHC 616 (Ch) (detailed technical specifications concerning aerodynamic design of an F1 car could only be derived by detailed reverse engineering, so sufficiently inaccessible to be confidential) with *Racing Partnership v Sports Information Services* [2020] EWCA Civ 1300, [2021] Ch 233 (individual horse racing results could be accessed with the relevant television coverage, so were not confidential, but a database of those results compiled for betting odds calculation purposes could be confidential). Information which is in the public domain therefore is not protected.

7 The common law protection of trade secrets is fortified by the Trade Secrets (Enforcement, etc) Regulations 2018 (SI 2018/597).

8 On the interpretation of the extent of such an agreement, see eg *Vestergaard Frandsen S/A v Bestnet Europe Ltd* [2013] UKSC 31, [2013] 1 WLR 1556.

9 See eg *Munro v Fraser* (1858) 21 D 103 (IH).

10 See *Faccenda Chicken v Fowler* [1987] Ch 117 (CA): the duration of the obligation of confidentiality will depend on the nature of the information and other factors. See eg *Pursuit Marketing v Thomson* [2023] CSOH 22.

11 See eg *Lord Advocate v Scotsman*, following *Attorney General v Guardian Newspapers* [1990] 1 AC 109 (HL). If the defender receives information from a third party, who warrants to the defender that they have obtained the necessary authorisation from the pursuer in respect of that information, may not be liable if they go onto use that information where such authorisation was not in fact granted: *Racing Partnership*.

12 See eg *Lion Laboratories v Evans* [1985] QB 526 (CA) (in public interest to disclose technical issues with breathalyser machines made by plaintiffs); *Response Handling Ltd v BBC* [2007] CSOH 102, 2008 SLT 51 (public interest justified disclosure of security issues at call centre handling debit and credit card information).

THREE-PARTY WRONGS

(1) Inducing breach of contract[1]

2.9 If A induces B to break his contract with C, C can sue B for breach of contract. Alternatively, C may be able to sue A in *delict* for inducing B to break his contract with C. This actionable wrong was recognised as part of Scots law in *British Motor Trade Association v Gray*, where Lord Russell approved counsel's concession that:[2]

> 'by the law of Scotland an actionable wrong is committed by one who intentionally and without lawful justification induces or procures someone to break a contract made by him with another, if damage has resulted to that other, provided the contract creates contractual relations recognised by law'.

In *OBG Ltd v Allan*,[3] the House of Lords emphasised that inducement of breach of contract is an example of accessory liability: A is only liable if B breaks his contract with C as a consequence of A's acts: A's liability in *delict* for inducement of breach of contract is therefore *accessory* to B's breach of his contract with C. There is no liability if A's conduct simply makes B's performance of its contract with C more onerous without there being a breach.

The wrong can be represented by the following diagram.

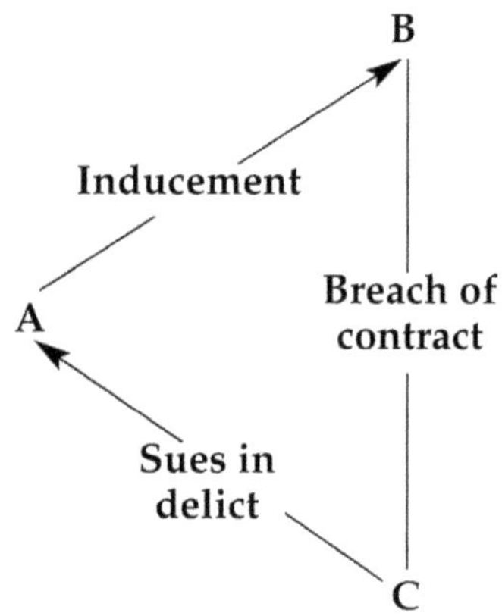

1 See Reid, *The Law of Delict in Scotland*, paras 21.04–21.32. For the argument that this delict is part of a broader principle of liability which protects personal rights in Scots law, see J Macleod, *Fraud and Voidable Transfer* (2020), Chapter 7.

2 1951 SC 586 (IH) at 603. The classic English case is *Lumley v Gye* (1853) 2 E&B 216. Until *BMTA v Gray*, liability for inducing a breach of contract had been recognised in some contexts in Scots law, but not as generally applicable across all types of contracts.
3 [2007] UKHL 21, [2008] 1 AC 1.

2.10 In *Global Resources Group v Mackay*,[1] Lord Hodge, following the analysis in *OBG*, said that inducement of breach of contract has five characteristics:

(1) **B must *breach* the contract with C:** interference with B's performance of the contract, which does not result in a breach of contract by B, will not suffice.[2]

(2) **A must *know* that his acts will result in B breaching his contract with C.**

Therefore, A must be aware of the existence of the contract between B and C, and at least the generalities of the terms of that contract.[3] Where A has received equivocal legal advice to the effect that its actions will result in no breach of contract by B, then A is entitled to rely on that advice.[4] If A reasonably suspects that B is bound by a contractual term towards C, and deliberately does not enquire further as to whether such a term does exist, then A's 'turning a blind eye' may constitute sufficient knowledge.[5]

(3) **A must *intend to induce the breach of contract* either as an end in itself or as the means by which he achieves some further end.**

Mere recklessness is insufficient, unless such recklessness is so pronounced it can be treated as tantamount to intention.[6] There is no need to establish that A intended to harm C:[7] intention to procure a breach of B's contract with C is 'necessary and sufficient.'[8] But the mere fact that it is foreseeable that A's acts might cause B to break his contract with C is insufficient: A must actually intend for its acts to secure that result.[9]

(4) **A must in *fact induce* B to break the contract by persuading, encouraging or assisting him to do so.**

A's inducement must take the form of positive conduct which is directed at B.[10] There is no need for the inducement to constitute unlawful means.[11] Typical examples may include a bribe or other financial inducement, a threat, or entering into dealings with B which are knowingly inconsistent with its dealings with C.[12]

A's conduct must be 'capable of influencing a choice by B whether or not to breach the contract', ie it must 'operate on the mind or will of B'.[13] Liability still arises if it is B who suggests the contract-breaking scheme to A:[14] their acceptance of B's offer amounts to positive conduct directed towards B influencing their decision to go ahead with the scheme.

Mere inaction – sitting back and saying nothing while B breaches its contract with C – is insufficient to give rise to liability.[15]

(5) **A may have a defence of justification.** A will have a defence if the inducement of the breach is justified. That justification may be supplied by public policy, for example inducing female artists to break their contracts of employment to obtain a living wage and so that they did not have to supplement their earnings by resorting to an 'immoral life'.[16] The defender may also be justified if, in inducing the breach of contract, they are acting to protect a right which is 'equal or superior' to the pursuer's contractual right.[17] The police and other public officials may have a defence of justification where their investigation of a crime induces a breach of contract.[18] Finally, statutory justification exists to protect trade unions in the event of authorised strike actions; otherwise, a call for its members to strike would be an inducement for those members to breach their employment contracts.[19]

Where A is the employee or director of a company (B), and A brings about a breach by B of its contract with C, A will not normally be liable in inducement of breach of contract, unless A acts in bad faith outside the scope of the authority conferred by B.[20]

1 [2009] CSOH 148, 2009 SLT 104 at paras 11–14.

2 In *OBG Ltd v Allan* [2007] UKHL 21, [2008] 1 AC 1, the House of Lords signalled that the decision to the contrary in *Merkur Island Shipping Corporation v Laughton* [1983] 2 AC 570 (HL) should no longer be followed.

3 See eg *Rossleigh Ltd v Leader Cars Ltd* 1987 SLT 355 (OH) (lease with unusual 'plenishing' clause).

4 *Allen v Dodd & Co Ltd* [2020] EWCA Civ 258, [2020] QB 781.

5 *Global Resources Group* at para 11 (*obiter*). The point was left open in *Rossleigh*. 'Blind-eye' knowledge has been accepted in Scots law in relation to unlawful means conspiracy: *Kidd v Lime Rock Management LLP* [2024] CSOH 28, 2024 SLT 347 at para 58, not dissented from on appeal [2025] CSIH 11.

6 See eg *Rossleigh* at 360.

7 *Global Resources Group* at para 12.

8 *OBG* at para 8 per Lord Hoffmann.

9 In *OBG* the House of Lords overruled the contrary decision of the Court of Appeal in *Millar v Bassey* [1994] EMLR 44: A and B had a contract to make an album; B enlisted C as musicians for that album, but had to disengage when A was no longer willing to record that album. While A's actions foreseeably would cause B to breach its contracts with C, that no longer is sufficient for liability.

10 The equivalent of this statement in the 3rd edition of this book was approved in *Global Resource Group* at para 13.

11 *OBG* at para 8 per Lord Hoffmann.

12 See eg *Northamber plc v Genee World Ltd* [2024] EWCA Civ 428, [2024] 1 WLR 4826 (A placed order with B which had exclusive supply agreement with C); *Rickless v United Artists Corporation* [1988] QB 40 (CA) (A used footage of C in new film made with B, when contract between B and C only permitted use of footage in original film).

13 *Kawasaki Kisen Kaisha Ltd v James Kemball Ltd* [2021] EWCA Civ 33 at para 33 per Popplewell LJ.

14 See eg *Aviva Insurance v Oliver* [2019] EWHC 2824 (Comm).

15 'Failing to stop a breach is not enough': *Calor Gas Ltd* v *Express Fuels (Sc) Ltd* [2008] CSOH 13, 2008 SLT 123 at para 47 per Lord Malcolm.
16 *Brimelow v Casson* [1924] 1 Ch 302 (Ch D).
17 *Edwin Hill and Partners v First National Finance Corporation* [1989] 1 WLR 225 (CA). A held mortgage over property owned by B. It required B to dismiss C to protect the value of B's land (and therefore its security). This inducement was justified as A's mortgage was superior to C's contractual right. C still had a claim in breach of contract against B.
18 This perhaps is suggested by *Forefront Scaffolding Hire & Sales Ltd* [2024] SAC (Civ) 39 at para 33 (albeit the claim there also lacked the requisite intention).
19 Trade Union and Labour Relations (Consolidation) Act 1992, s 219(1)(a).
20 *Said v Butt* [1920] 3 KB 497. For rationale, see *Lifestyle Equities CV v Ahmed* [2024] UKSC 17, [2025] AC 1 at paras 50–55.

(2) Intentional infliction of harm by unlawful means

2.11 In *OBG Ltd v Allan*, the House of Lords recognised the existence of an actionable wrong of causing loss by unlawful means.[1] The classic form of this wrong involves three parties:[2] A, with the intention of harming C, uses unlawful means against B, a third party in which C has an economic interest, in order to cause economic harm to C.

In this situation, A's delictual liability is primary: it is not dependent on B committing a wrong, such as a breach of contract, against C. But, as we shall see, it is dependent on A committing a wrong vis-à-vis B. What the delict of causing loss by unlawful means does is to allow C effectively to 'piggyback' on the wrongdoing suffered by B, and claim the losses which have resulted to C from A's conduct towards B.

This delict is conceptually difficult, so we will begin with an example:

> B supplies C with goods which are a fundamental part of C's business. A threatens B with publication of a defamatory statement unless it ceases selling to C. B gives into that threat, and C loses business as a result. Assume that there is no supply contract between B and C.

B's actions are not a breach of any contract with C, and therefore A's actions are not an inducement of breach of contract. A has, however, threatened to defame B. B, of course, could sue A in defamation, but that is of no use to C. Instead, as A has threatened B with unlawful means (defamation, which is actionable by B), and the intention in using those means was to restrict B's freedom to deal with C (by constraining B's willingness to continue to sell to C), C can pursue A for causing loss by unlawful means if A's intention can be established.

1 [2007] UKHL 21, [2008] 1 AC 1, adopted in Scotland in eg *McLeod v Rooney* [2009] CSOH 158, 2010 SLT 499.
2 Before *OBG*, intimidation was treated as a separate actionable wrong: on intimidation see the 3rd edn of this book at pp 44–46. In *OBG*, Lord Hoffmann suggested that it now could be conceptualised as a two-party version of the causing loss by unlawful means delict.

2.12 The characteristics of the actionable wrong are:

(1) **A must use *unlawful means* against B.** In *OBG Ltd v Allan* Lord Hoffmann, for the majority, held that 'unlawful means' were restricted to conduct which amounted to a civil wrong actionable at the instance of B.[1] Therefore, any of the other delicts considered in this book are capable of constituting unlawful means, as are breaches of contract.[2] For this delict, the definition of 'unlawful means' does not extend to wrongdoing which is criminal and which does not afford B a private law right of action.[3] In *OBG*, Lord Hoffmann suggested that this requirement would be met even if B itself had suffered no loss, and so could not bring a claim itself in respect of A's wrongdoing; the fact that C had thereby suffered loss through the effect of A's conduct on B is sufficient.[4]

(2) **Those unlawful means must *restrict B's freedom to deal with* C.** If the effect of B's actions is simply that it becomes less profitable for B to deal with C, then that will be insufficient.[5] Where the effect of A's conduct is that B is no longer willing to engage with C,[6] or to provide a platform for C,[7] then this requirement will be made out. B's will need not be completely displaced by A's conduct;[8] it is sufficient that A's conduct has impaired B's exercise of a choice in favour of C.[9] This 'dealing' requirement is an important control mechanism which keeps the scope of this delict in check.[10]

(3) **A must *intend* to harm C.**[11] Most obviously, if A intends directly to harm C, then this requirement will be met. But the requirement will also be met if A intends to bring about some end which necessarily involves harm to C: there is, in other words, no need to show malice or a desire that C should suffer.[12] Sometimes, A's gain will be inextricably linked with C's gain. For instance, if A and C are competitors, and A desires a monopoly of the market, steps taken toward that goal necessarily also involve harming C. If A knows that the only way for it to gain is at C's expense, then A's intention to profit will be treated as an intention to harm C.[13] On the other hand, the fact that loss to C was objectively likely, or reasonably foreseeable, to A is insufficient. An appreciation that *someone* will suffer loss – not specifically C, either individually or as a member of a particular group – does not constitute the requisite intention.

If C is able to establish these three criteria, then it must still show that A's conduct has caused it loss.[14] No authority exists as to whether there is a defence of justification to this delict, which would only arise where A believes that it is legally entitled to use the means in question against B.

1 [2007] UKHL 21, [2008] 1 AC 1 at para 49. Lady Hale and Lords Walker and Brown agreed with Lord Hoffmann. Lord Nicholls of Birkenhead adopted a wider formulation which embraced also purely criminal acts.

2 See eg *Roche Diagnostics Ltd v Greater Glasgow Health Board* [2024] CSOH 55, 2024 SLT 880 at para 113.

3 *OBG* at para 57. The position with unlawful means conspiracy is, as we shall see, different: para 2.14 below.

4 *OBG* at para 49. See eg *Costa v Dissociadid* [2022] EWHC 1934, where A made false content takedown requests to YouTube. YouTube relied on these requests and removed videos uploaded by C. Although it suffered no loss, all other elements for a claim in fraud would have been made out by YouTube. C was therefore able to bring a claim in causing loss by unlawful means against A.

5 *OBG* at paras 129 and 298; *RCA Corporation v Pollard* [1983] Ch 135 (CA); *McLeod v Rooney* [2009] CSOH 158, 2010 SLT 499; *Future Investments SA v FIFA* [2010] EWHC 1019 (Ch).

6 See eg *Rookes v Barnard* [1964] AC 1129 (HL) (B dismissed C as employee).

7 As occurred in *Costa v Dissociadid*.

8 See *Roche Diagnostics* at para 120: it need not be shown that B is formally prevented from contracting or otherwise dealing with C.

9 This may be because of a supposed factual hurdle created by A: see eg *Domestic & General Group Ltd v Premier Protect Holdings* [2024] EWHC 2654 (KB) at paras 221–226 (A induced B, customers of C, to enter into alternative insurance coverage plans by pretending to be associated with C. To avoid being subject to two plans, customers either cancelled direct debits with A, or, once the deception came to light, decided to stick with the plan taken out with A. It was held that in both instances the customers' freedom to deal with C had been constrained by A's deception). But it may also be because A creates a belief in B that it is subject to a legal obligation which obliges it to deal with C in a way which causes it loss: *Barclay Pharmaceuticals v Waypharm* [2012] EWHC 503 (Comm) (fraudulent presentation of invoice by A to bank created belief it was under an obligation to debit C's account).

10 *Secretary of State for Health v Servier Laboratories* [2021] UKSC 24, [2022] AC 959 at paras 94–95. The UK Supreme Court refused to remove the dealing requirement in this case.

11 See *OBG* at paras 62–64 per Lord Hoffmann and paras 164–167 per Lord Nicholls of Birkenhead.

12 See eg *Moray Offshore Renewable Power Ltd v Bluefloat Energy UK Holdings Ltd* [2023] CSOH 29, 2023 SLT 623 at paras 52–55 (A wished to succeed in B's tendering process, and harm to C (and other limited rival bidders) was means to achieve that end when allegedly fraudulent bid submitted).

13 See eg *Roche Diagnostics* at paras 122–124 (A and C only two bidders in tendering process, so A's gain obviously at C's expense).

14 See eg *Moray Offshore* at paras 67–69 (no evidence that B would have offered contract to C had A not misrepresented matters in tendering process, so causation of loss not established).

(3) Conspiracy

2.13 Unlike the previous two delicts, which involve the defender injuring the pursuer by constraining the will or freedom of a third party, conspiracy necessarily involves the third party as a participant in the wrongdoing which injures the pursuer. It arises where two or more parties reach an agreement (whether express or tacit) to carry into effect acts with the object of injuring the pursuer.[1]

Conspiracy comes in two forms: unlawful means conspiracy and lawful means conspiracy. The distinction turns on whether or not the implementation of the conspiracy would involve the commission of a civil or criminal wrong by (at least one) of the conspirators. The importance of the distinction is that different tests of intention are used for each form. If the means are unlawful, then all that must be shown is an intention to injure the pursuer. But if the means are lawful, then it must be shown that their *predominant* intention was to injure the pursuer. This is an exceedingly strict requirement.

This distinction will be explored further below. For both forms of conspiracy, it should be emphasised that the conspiratorial agreement need not be explicit: it may be tacitly inferred from the words or conduct of the alleged conspirators.[2] Once it is established that the defender in question was a party to the agreement, then there is no further requirement to show individual wrongdoing: 'The precise role played by each conspirator, whether active or passive, in itself wrongful or lawful, is not the true touchstone of liability'.[3] To become liable, a conspirator must 'be sufficiently aware of the surrounding circumstances and share the same object for it properly to be said that they were acting in concert at the time of the acts complained of'.[4]

The rationale of the wrong of conspiracy is that while the pursuer can be expected to withstand the harmful but lawful acts of another, it cannot be expected to withstand the harm caused by a combination or conspiracy of persons.[5] This rationalisation has been doubted, for a multinational conglomerate or oil company may exercise far greater economic power than a combination of small businesses.[6]

1 See eg *Roche Diagnostics v Greater Glasgow Health Board* [2024] CSOH 55, 2024 SLT 880 at para 87.
2 For a failed attempt to establish a tacit agreement, see *Kidd v Lime Rock Management* [2024] CSOH 28, 2024 SLT 347 at paras 103–111, upheld on appeal [2025] CSIH 11, 2025 SLT 651.
3 *Mex Group Ltd v Ford and Others* [2024] CSOH 86 at para 37 per Lord Sandison.
4 *Kuwait Oil Tanker Co SAK v Al Bader (No 3)* [2000] 2 All ER (Comm) 271 (CA) at para 111 per Nourse LJ. It is likely that some divergence of object will be tolerated.
5 *Mogul Steamship Co Ltd v McGregor, Gow & Co* (1889) 23 QBD 598 (CA) at 616 per Bowen LJ.
6 *Lonrho Ltd v Shell Petroleum Co Ltd (No 2)* [1982] AC 173 at 189 per Lord Diplock; see also *Crofter Hand Woven Harris Tweed Co Ltd v Veitch* 1942 SC (HL) 1 at 8 per Viscount Simon LC.

Unlawful means conspiracy

2.14 Unlawful means conspiracy is the only form of conspiracy claim encountered in modern commercial litigation. If the defender, along with at least one other party, uses unlawful means, with an intention to harm the pursuer, then the pursuer may sue the defender (and any co-conspirators) for unlawful means conspiracy. Two questions therefore arise: (a) what amounts to unlawful means for the purposes of the conspiracy delict, and (b) what degree of intention to injure must be established?

We have seen that, for the purposes of the delict of causing loss by unlawful means, it is a necessary condition that the 'unlawful means' be civilly actionable by the third party.[1] Such unlawful means also suffice for this delict. So, for instance, if C and B combine to cause loss to A by making defamatory statements about A, then A may sue B and C in unlawful means conspiracy, with the delict of defamation constituting the 'unlawful' means.[2] A breach of contract also may constitute unlawful means, so that if B and C agree that one of them will breach their contract with A, that also may constitute unlawful means conspiracy.[3]

However, in *Total Network v Revenue and Customs Commissioners*,[4] the House of Lords, perhaps unhelpfully, held that the definition of 'unlawful means' for conspiracy was wider than that in causing loss by unlawful means. That case involved a mass VAT fraud perpetrated by several parties. While the UK tax-registered companies could be pursued for unpaid VAT under UK tax legislation, the defendant company was Spanish tax-registered so fell outside the scope of the statutory recovery mechanism. The Revenue and Customs Commissioners brought a claim in unlawful means conspiracy against the Spanish company, arguing that it and the other conspirators had conspired to commit the criminal offence of cheating the revenue. Total contended that, as this was a crime that did not also involve a breach of a private law duty owed to the claimant, it did not satisfy the definition of 'unlawful means' set out in *OBG*. The House of Lords held that there was no reason why the definition of 'unlawful means' needed to be identical between the two forms of wrongdoing, and that 'unlawful means' had a wider meaning in the context of conspiracy, which was capable of embracing conduct which was criminal and involved no private law wrongdoing at the suit of any party.[5]

Criminal offences, therefore, constitute unlawful means even if no civil right of action is afforded to the victim of the crime. Despite the awkwardness of having two different definitions of 'unlawful means' across two related delicts, the UK Supreme Court confirmed the *Total Network* definition for conspiracy in *JSC BTA Bank v Khrapunov*.[6] In that case, the former chairman of a Kazakh bank had been found liable by the English courts in a multi-billion pound judgment. To aid in the enforcement of that judgment, the English courts made worldwide freezing orders, freezing assets of the debtor. The debtor, with the assistance of his son-in-law (Khrapunov), instructed those companies to transfer assets, so as to defeat the effectiveness of those freezing orders. The creditor contended that this scheme constituted an unlawful means conspiracy. The Supreme Court agreed with that contention: the removal of assets in breach of the ordered constituted a contempt of court which constituted sufficient unlawful means. In the course of its judgment, the Supreme Court confirmed the continuing existence of a separate delict of conspiracy and rejected the argument that its definition of unlawful means should be aligned with *OBG v Allan*.[7]

Therefore, a wide range of conduct may constitute 'unlawful means' for conspiracy. The knowing making of false statements, which do not themselves constitute an actionable fraudulent misrepresentation, will suffice.[8] So too may conduct which is unlawful under foreign law.[9] But it does not extend to conduct which breaches a regulatory statute which does not also result in civil or criminal liability on the part of the defender.[10]

The unlawful means must be the mechanism through which harm is caused to the pursuer: it is not enough that they play 'part of the story'.[11] The illustration frequently given is of a pizza delivery business which instructs its drivers to break the speed limit and ignore red lights.[12] Loosely, this could be said to be a conspiracy to use unlawful means, and a rival pizza business which loses business from its inability to deliver pizza at the same pace, could be said to thereby suffer loss. But the unlawful means here are just 'part of the story'; they are not the direct instrument through which the rival pizza business is caused loss.[13] If, however, the pizza delivery business and its drivers decided to assault the drivers of their competition, to nullify its delivery service, then the unlawful means of assault there clearly are the mechanism through which the pursuer's loss is caused.

The question of whether the conspirator must know that the means used are unlawful are not yet firmly settled. In *Racing Partnership v Sports Information Services* it was held that proof of knowledge of unlawfulness was not a necessary component of the delict,[14] with the dissenting judge of the opinion that such knowledge would be necessary where the unlawful means relied upon were civil, and not criminal, wrongs.[15] Subsequently, without much elaboration, the Inner House has opined, in *obiter* comments, that the dissenting view in *Racing Partnership* was 'wholly convincing'.[16] The point therefore is ripe for further examination: while a requirement of knowledge aligns conspiracy with inducement of breach of contract,[17] it is perhaps telling that no knowledge requirement was mentioned in *Total Network* or *Khrapunov*.

The requirement of intention for this delict is identical to that discussed in relation to causing loss by unlawful means:[18] the defender must either intend to harm the pursuer as an end in itself, or as a means to an end, and sometimes the pursuit of gain may knowingly and necessarily involve the infliction of loss, but mere foreseeability of harm will not suffice. No authority clearly supports the existence of a defence of justification.[19]

1 See para 2.12 above.
2 Although there is authority which suggests that a pursuer cannot recover damages for injury to reputation or feelings in a conspiracy claim: *Lonrho v Al-Fayed (No 5)* [1993] 1 WLR 1489 at 1496B-E (CA).
3 See eg *Racing Partnership v Sports Information Services* [2020] EWCA Civ 1300, [2021] Ch 233; *Roche Diagnostics v Greater Glasgow Health Board* [2024] CSOH 55, 2024 SLT 880.
4 *Revenue and Customs Commissioners v Total Network* [2008] UKHL 19, [2008] 1 AC 1174.
5 *Total Network* at paras 89–104 per Lord Walker of Gestingthorpe, at paras 113–126 per Lord Mance, and paras 220–226 per Lord Neuberger of Abbotsbury.
6 [2018] UKSC 19, [2020] AC 727.
7 *Khrapunov* at paras 9 and 11–16 These two points may be revisited in future: see *Secretary of State for Health v Servier Laboratories* [2021] UKSC 24, [2022] AC 959 at para 102 per Lord Sales.
8 *Moray Offshore Renewable Power Ltd v Bluefloat Energy UK Holdings* 2023 SLT 623 at para 71.
9 See eg *Loreley Financing (Jersey) No 30 Ltd v Credit Suisse Securities (Europe) Ltd* [2023] EWHC 2759 (Comm) at paras 489–493.
10 *Digicel (St Lucia) v Cable & Wireless* [2010] EWHC 774 (Ch) at Annexe I, para 62.
11 *Total Network* at para 95.
12 *OBG* at paras 160 and 266; *Total Network* at para 119; *Khrapunov* at para 14.
13 *Racing Partnership* at paras 154 and 172.
14 *Racing Partnership* at paras 106–144 per Arnold LJ. Phillips LJ expressly agreed with this analysis at para 171.
15 *Racing Partnership* at paras 213–265 per Lewison LJ.
16 *Kidd v Lime Rock Management* [2025] CSIH 11, 2025 SLT 651 at para 82; compare the first instance judgment ([2024] CSOH 28, 2024 SLT 347) at para 58(v).
17 In *Racing Partnership*, the fear was expressed (at paras 142 and 240–245) that, without such a requirement, conspiracy may undermine the requirements of the inducement delict.
18 See *Constatin Medien AG v Ecclestone* [2014] EWHC 387 (Ch) at para 333 and 336; and see para 2.12 above. For an exploration see eg *Kidd v Lime Rock Management* (IH) at paras 78–86 (no intention to injury when, in conflict of interest, conspirator thought it was acting to benefit both parties to a transaction).
19 For authority against, see eg *Seneschall v Trisant Foods Ltd* [2023] EWHC 1029 (Ch) at para 152–160.

Lawful means conspiracy

2.15 This delict was recognised in *Crofter Hand Woven Harris Tweed Co Ltd v Veitch*.[1] Mill owners on the Island of Lewis who made and sold tweed cloth from yarn spun on the island were unable to agree a 100 per cent union membership agreement ('closed shop') with the Transport and General Workers' Union (TGWU) because of competition from rival producers on the island (the pursuers) who obtained cheaper yarn from the mainland, wove it into cloth and sold it at a lower price than the mill owners. The TGWU and the mill owners came together. They instructed the members of the TGWU who were employed at the port to refuse to handle the yarn being imported by the pursuers to the island from the mainland. The case proceeded on the basis that the dockers were not in breach of their contracts of employment with the port authority in refusing to handle the imported yarn. The question was whether the combination amounted to an actionable conspiracy.

The House of Lords held that since no unlawful means were used, the conspiracy would be wrongful only if the pursuers could establish that the *predominant* motive or intention of the conspirators was to harm the pursuers. In this case, the predominant motive or intention was to further the union's legitimate interests, ie 100 per cent union membership. Harm to the pursuers was not their primary intention: it was only incidental to achieving their goal. Accordingly, the defenders were not liable.

As such, claims in lawful means conspiracy rarely succeed. If lawful means are used, and the predominant motive or intention of A and B is not to harm C but to further their own legitimate interests, the conspiracy is not wrongful even though C suffers economic loss as a result of the actions of A and B. The presence of a legitimate motive will negate a predominant intention to injure. For example, in *Scala Ballroom (Wolverhampton) Ltd v Ratcliffe*[2] it was held to be legitimate for trade union officials to organise a boycott among their members from playing at a dance hall which operated a colour bar; although this objective did not bring any financial benefits to the members of the union, it was genuinely thought by them to be in the interests of the union. Only if those interests were 'entirely lost sight of' would liability arise.[3]

Whereas unlawful means conspiracy is a fixture of modern litigation, lawful means conspiracy is not. It often is seen as anomalous: why should lawful acts suddenly become unlawful just because they are carried out by a combination of persons? The high level of intention required means it is extremely difficult to fix a conspirator with liability where no unlawful means have been used.

1 1942 SC (HL) 1.

2 [1958] 1 WLR 1057 (CA).

3 This was held to be the case in one of the very few claims for lawful means conspiracy to succeed: *Huntley v Thornton* [1957] 1 WLR 321 (Ch D) at 339–342. See also *Quinn v Leathem* [1901] AC 495 (HL) (noting that, in *Rookes v Barnard* [1964] AC 1129 (HL) at 1216, Lord Devlin noted that he was 'not at all sure that it can be said even now with certainty what *Quinn v Leathem* decided'.

CHAPTER 3

The Duty of Care

INTRODUCTION

3.1 In the introduction, we discussed that, in theory, the modern law of delict in Scotland is based on the principle that if individuals cause harm by *culpa* (fault), whether intentionally or unintentionally, they have a compulsory obligation to make reparation. Until now, this book has focused on intentional wrongs, situations where the harm is said to have been deliberately caused by the defender. We now shift our attention to unintentional delicts, where *culpa* is shown by demonstrating that the defender's actions were careless. In such situations, the pursuer must establish that this unintentional carelessness was legally significant, ie, that the defender owed it a duty of care, and the defender fell below the reasonable standard of care expected of adults with the basic capacity to control their actions.

The law here is concerned with legally irresponsible behaviour that results in legally recognised losses. It is not concerned with providing redress for each and every accident which befalls the pursuer. Unless there has been legislative intervention, it is for the courts to decide, guided by principle and precedent, what is legally significant carelessness.

At the outset, it is important to note that modern courts do not often use the language of *culpa* or describe the conceptual structure of intentional or unintentional wrongs. Nor is the term 'carelessness' a technical one. In contrast, as we will see, the term 'duty of care' has a specific technical meaning within the law of delict. It is far more common to find courts using the language of *negligence* when considering unintentional culpable conduct (which might informally be called carelessness). Nonetheless, the meaning of these expressions is effectively the same: an unintentional delict is the result of someone neglecting their duty to take reasonable care to prevent causing injury or harm to another. Simply put, negligence is the neglect of a duty of care.

THE BUILDING BLOCKS OF NEGLIGENCE

3.2 To successfully retrieve damages for negligence, a pursuer needs to establish four things, ie that:

(1) the defender owed them a duty of care;

(2) the defender breached that duty of care;

(3) the defender suffered a recoverable loss or harm; and

(4) the breach of the duty of care caused the pursuer's loss.

Each step will be explained in more detail, but some preliminary comments may be helpful at this stage. It may be counterintuitive to ask to whom the duty is owed, as part of step one, before examining what is reasonable care (ie whether the duty was breached), at step two. Both questions are intimately related, but courts expect a pursuer to first establish that they were owed a duty of care by the defender. It is on this basis that a pursuer can then justify their expectation of a reasonable standard of care. This determination can vary depending on the context of the injury suffered and other matters. This chapter outlines the basic duty of care inquiry, while Chapters 4–7 consider its application in certain contexts. Step two is considered in Chapter 8, and step four is considered in Chapter 9 alongside relevant defences which may remove or reduce the defender's liability.

INTRODUCING THE DUTY OF CARE

3.3 If A acts in a careless manner, ie its conduct fails to meet the standard of care demanded by society of a person in his position, then *prima facie* A is liable to anyone who suffers harm as a result of such conduct.[1] Of course, in abstract, and perhaps morally, this principle suggests that defenders must compensate a potentially large number of people if they are negligent. Certainly, if you consider the so-called butterfly effect then the consequences of careless behaviour are unpredictable and far reaching. Hence, in order to *limit* A's potential liability in delict, the law has developed restrictions on the identity of persons who can claim damages for harm incurred by A's unintentional, but careless, conduct.

Over the years, the law has offered different justifications for the limitation of liability and utilised various legal doctrines to implement those limitations.[2] The modern Scots law accepts as a general principle that A will be liable for careless conduct only if he owed a duty of care to the person harmed by his actions. This duty of care must pre-exist the careless conduct. Whether a duty of care is owed by A to a particular person or class of persons is ultimately a question of law to be determined by the courts. In deciding whether to recognise the existence of a duty of care in particular circumstances, the courts are influenced by issues of policy as well as legal principle. By recognising – or refusing to recognise – the existence of a duty of care, the courts in effect set the parameters of delictual liability for unintentional, but careless, conduct.

It is only once a duty of care is established that the pursuer can proceed to submit that the defender failed to take reasonable care. It also follows that the existence of a duty of care is just the start of the investigation: steps two, three, and four above must still be considered (and adjudicated in favour of the pursuer, or conceded by the defender) for the pursuer's claim to succeed.

It cannot be emphasised enough that even though there is a duty of care, which has been breached, delictual liability under the common law of Scotland only arises when the pursuer has sustained *harm*. There must be a concurrence of *damnum* (harm sustained) and *injuria* (breach of the duty of care) before delictual liability arises, linked together by causation (*datum*): *damnum injuria datum*.[3] If the pursuer does not suffer harm as a result of the defender's breach of a duty of care which he owes to the pursuer, then there is no delictual liability. Harm to the pursuer is a constituent of, as well as a consequence of, negligence.

1 Cardozo J's phrase 'liability in an indeterminate amount for an indeterminate time, to an indeterminate class' elegantly summarises the point: *Ultramares Corpn v Touche* (1931) 255 NY 170 at 179.

2 For example, by developing a doctrine of proximate causation before A will be liable, or by use of the doctrine of remoteness.

3 See eg *Watson v Fram Reinforced Concrete Co (Scotland) Ltd and Winget Ltd* 1960 SC (HL) 92. Thus, for example, the prescriptive period will only begin to run from the date that the pursuer suffers harm, not the date of the breach of duty: see Chapter 16. On what amounts to harm, compare *Rothwell v Chemical and Insulating Co Ltd* [2007] UKHL 39, [2008] 1 AC 281 (pleural plaques not actionable damage, reversed in Scotland by the Damages (Asbestos-Related Conditions) (Scotland) Act 2009) with *Dryden v Johnson Matthey plc* [2018] UKSC 18, [2019] AC 403.

WHEN WILL A DUTY OF CARE ARISE?

(1) The previous approach and the modern approach

3.4 Previously, textbooks such as this would have discussed the recognition of a duty of care as a methodical process. Like a chemical reaction, a duty of care would be said to arise if necessary elements were present on the facts of any given case. Those necessary elements were said to be reasonable foreseeability of harm, a proximate relationship between the parties, and (in some cases) that it would be fair, just and reasonable to impose a duty in the circumstances.[1] The judgment of Lord Reed in *Robinson v Chief Constable of West Yorkshire Police* made it abundantly clear that this approach is mistaken.[2] In most cases, the examination of whether or not a duty of care arises does not involve a return to first principles, investigating foreseeability, proximity, and policy. Most cases, instead, arise in situations where decided cases have already found for, or against, the existence of a duty of care in that situation. It is only if the case before the court is a 'novel' one that policy and proximity should be openly considered, and, even then, usually only as comparators to assess which previous case, if any, provides the best analogy.[3]

Nevertheless, an understanding of reasonable foreseeability and proximity grounds our understanding of the duty of care. All cases which have decided that A owes a duty of care to B have done so because it is considered, in that situation, that harm to B is reasonably foreseeable to A, and that A and B are in a sufficiently proximate relationship. There is necessarily an overlap between these concepts: if A and B are physically (or otherwise) proximate, it usually will be reasonably foreseeable that B could be harmed by the actions of A. Similarly, if it is not reasonable for A to foresee that its actions may harm B, then it may also be likely that the parties are insufficiently proximate. We should not be alarmed by this; the courts are well aware of this overlap,[4] and in any event do not usually insist on a scientific approach to the imposition of a duty of care. Therefore, while recognising that, in many cases, the determination of whether A owes B a duty of care is one of precedent, not (directly) principle and policy, we will now turn to consider the principle underpinning duty determinations. Our focus here will be on foreseeability and proximity; we will return to the (very limited) role of express consideration of policy factors in Chapter 7.

1 These factors were often labelled the 'tripartite' test, or the *Caparo* test, named after *Caparo Industries v Dickman* [1990] 2 AC 605. This is despite Lord Bridge in *Caparo* being very clear, at 617–618, that these were not limbs of a practical test, but merely labels to identify different features to permit comparisons to be made with previous case law.
2 [2018] UKSC 4, [2018] AC 736.
3 The approach to 'novel' cases is discussed further in Chapter 7.
4 See *Sutradhar (FC) v National Environmental Research Council* [2006] UKHL 33, [2006] PNLR 36 at para 32 per Lord Hoffmann; *Customs and Excise Commissioners v Barclays Bank plc* [2006] UKHL 28, [2007] 1 AC 181 at paras 36–37 per Lord Hoffmann.

(2) The 'neighbourhood principle'

3.5 The starting point of any discussion of the duty of care in Scots law is *Donoghue v Stevenson*.[1] One Sunday evening, Mrs Donoghue went to visit a friend in Paisley. They went to the Wellmeadow café at Wellmeadow Place, Paisley. The café was owned by Mr Minchella. They decided to have 'iced drinks', ie ice cream over which was poured lemonade. Mrs Donoghue's friend bought the ice cream and a bottle of 'ginger'.[2] The case proceeded on the assumption that Mrs Donoghue's friend had, in fact, bought ginger beer which would have been in an opaque bottle. The friend poured some of the ginger beer over Mrs Donoghue's ice cream; but when, later in the evening, the friend poured the rest of the ginger beer over Mrs Donoghue's melting ice, out floated the decomposing remains of a snail. The sight of the snail and her consumption of the snail-tainted iced drink resulted in Mrs Donoghue becoming ill. Mrs Donoghue sued Stevenson, the manufacturer of the ginger beer, in delict. The question before the courts was whether the manufacturer was liable to Mrs Donoghue in delict even if she could prove the facts alleged and Stevenson had, in fact, been careless.

1 1932 SC (HL) 31. The literature on this case is voluminous but see, in particular, AF Rodger 'Mrs Donoghue and Alfenus Varus' (1988) 41 Current Legal Problems 1.

2 In the West Coast of Scotland, 'ginger' is a generic term covering all kinds of aerated drinks. But it seems likely that the case did indeed involve ginger beer.

3.6 It was held by a majority[1] of the House of Lords that Mrs Donoghue was entitled to sue Stevenson in delict because he owed her a duty of care: if he had *in fact* broken his duty towards her by his careless conduct and she had suffered harm,[2] then she would succeed. In other words, the relationship between the pursuer and defender was sufficiently proximate that the majority was prepared to hold that Stevenson owed Mrs Donoghue a duty of care for the purpose of liability in delict. Lord Atkin concluded:[3]

> '... a manufacturer of products, which he sells in such a form as to show that he intends them to reach the ultimate consumer in the form in which they left him, with no reasonable possibility of intermediate examination, and with the knowledge that the absence of reasonable care in the preparation or putting up of the product will result in an injury to the consumer's life or property, owes a duty to the consumer to take that reasonable care'.

Lord Macmillan had:[4]

> 'no hesitation in affirming that a person, who for gain engages in the business of manufacturing articles of food and drink intended for consumption by members of the public in the form which he issues them, is under a duty to take care in the manufacture of these articles. That duty, in my opinion, he owes to those whom he intends to consume his produce ...'.

At its most specific level, *Donoghue v Stevenson* is authority that a manufacturer of food and drink, which he intends to be used by the ultimate consumer without the opportunity of inspection or interference before use, owes a duty of care to the ultimate consumer to prevent him sustaining harm to his person or property as a result of the manufacturer's carelessness when manufacturing the product. In other words, the relationship between manufacturer and ultimate consumer was sufficiently proximate in these circumstances that the court was prepared to impose a duty of care on the manufacturer towards the ultimate consumer. Today, however, *Donoghue v Stevenson* is the authority for a more general principle that a manufacturer of *any* product owes a duty of care to the ultimate consumer not to cause harm to his person or property as a result of a latent defect in a product which could not be discovered by inspection before use and was intended by the manufacturer to be used by the ultimate consumer in the same condition as it left the manufacturer.[5]

1 Lord Atkin, Lord Thankerton and Lord Macmillan; Lord Buckmaster and Lord Tomlin dissented.
2 After the decision of the House of Lords on the relevancy point, the case was settled, so the facts were never established at proof.
3 1932 SC (HL) 31 at 57.
4 1932 SC (HL) 31 at 71. On the genesis of Lord Macmillan's speech, see *AF Rodger* (1992) 168 *Law Quarterly Review* 236.
5 See eg *Grant v Australian Knitting Mills Ltd* [1936] AC 85 (PC, Australia).

3.7 However, *Donoghue* is not simply important for the law on product liability. In deciding in favour of Mrs Donoghue, Lord Atkin made several remarks in relation to the duty of care more generally, which have proved influential in the development of the concept.

Having posed the question, 'Who, then in law, is my neighbour?', Lord Atkin answered it thus:[1]

> 'persons who are so closely and directly affected by my act that I ought reasonably to have them in contemplation when I am directing my mind to the acts or omissions which are called into question'.

For Lord Atkin, therefore, a duty of care arises when it is reasonably foreseeable by the defender that a person in the position of the pursuer would be closely and directly affected by the defender's acts or omissions. This often is referred to as 'the neighbourhood principle'.

It serves well enough in commonplace situations where there is a risk of physical injury to persons in the vicinity if sufficient care is not taken. To take the paradigmatic example, a driver owes a duty of care to other road users because it is reasonably foreseeable that if he drives carelessly, he may harm other road users. Cases of physical injury to person and property rarely, at the duty stage, cause any difficulties: if such harm is reasonably foreseeable, then a duty will be owed to take reasonable care to prevent such harm arising.[2]

1 1932 SC (HL) 31 at 44.
2 See eg *Robinson v Chief Constable of West Yorkshire Police* [2018] UKSC 4, [2018] AC 736.

3.8 Where circumstances are less usual, however, such as where losses are purely economic or where harm is caused by the criminal act of a third party, the need to avoid overwhelming liability, plus a judicial commitment to predicable development of the law means that the issue of proximity comes necessarily to the fore. Proximity addresses the issue of how a boundary is to be drawn around those persons who ought reasonably to be within my contemplation.[1] Which persons should be excluded?

Considering the fundamental importance of these questions for the rights and duties of companies, charities, individuals, etc – not to mention the multiple billion-pound insurance industry in the UK – makes it tempting to examine proximity from a wider perspective, asking if it is fair, just and reasonable to hold someone responsible for another's losses. However, this is not how courts determine civil liability for wrongfully caused losses. Rarely will a court extend the duty of care to a new class of persons not previously recognised. Today courts are guided by precedent – established categories of liability recognised by or nascent within case law – and are mindful of their institutional limitations. They are a court, which applies the law, not a legislator, which makes the law. This can lead to results which might, *prima facie*, appear unjust from a moral or political perspective.

In practice, therefore, the duty of care is far less expansive than Lord Atkin's description in *Donoghue v Stevenson* might have first suggested. For example, in *Sutradhar (FC) v National Environmental Research Council*[2] the defendant carried out tests on ground water systems in Bangladesh for the purpose of discovering whether the water might contain toxic trace elements. At the time standard procedures for testing ground water did not include tests for arsenic. The defendant was not asked and did not test for arsenic. Their report made it clear that they had not done so. Four million shallow hand-pumped wells were installed to supply drinking water. The water was contaminated with arsenic, affecting over 140 million people. The claimant was one of the thousands to suffer from arsenic poisoning. The House of Lords held that the defendant, who had prepared the report, did not owe the claimant a duty of care on the ground that there was no proximity between the parties.

As Lord Macmillan remarked in *Bourhill v Young*:[3] 'The duty to take care is not owed to the world at large, but to those to whom injury may reasonably and probably be anticipated if the duty is not observed.' Duties can only be owed to identifiable persons or to persons within a reasonably well-defined class. In the absence of specific factors pointing to proximity, a population of 140.9 million is clearly too large a group to be owed a duty of care.

Proximity, in the law of delict, is about designating our *neighbours in law* rather than our social, political and morally determined neighbours. It is a key consideration in asking whether or not a duty of care has arisen. In many cases, this will be easy to satisfy,[4] but as we can see from *Sutradhar*, that will not always be so.

1 See eg the speech of Lord Goff in *Maloco v Littlewoods Organisation Ltd* 1987 SC (HL) 37, accepted as the correct approach in *Mitchell v Glasgow City Council* [2009] UKHL 11, 2009 SC (HL) 21.

2 *Sutradhar (FC) v National Environmental Research Council* [2006] UKHL 33, [2006] PNLR 36.
3 1942 SC (HL) 78 at 88.
4 See eg *Mitchell* at para 16 per Lord Hope of Craighead.

(3) Making things worse v not making things better

3.9 The cases we have considered so far have all been cases of positive action. But it is sometimes easy to reconceptualise positive action as an 'omission': the negligent preparation of a water safety report can just as easily be said to be a failure to provide an accurate safety report. The modern approach is to distinguish between cases where A has made B's situation worse, and cases where A has failed to confer a benefit on B.[1]

It is a fundamental principle of the law of delict that A is not liable to B in delict simply because A did not confer a benefit on B. This includes the benefit of A preventing B from sustaining harm, whether that be from A's conduct, or that of a third party. Merely because it is reasonably foreseeable to A that harm will happen to B does not of itself generate a duty on A to act to prevent B suffering that harm. The law does not compel us to be good Samaritans.[2]

But there may be additional factors present which make it fair for A to owe a duty of care to B in these circumstances. These factors may supply additional proximity which justifies the imposition of a duty on A. We will consider these in more detail in Chapter 6, but it is worth introducing them now.

Perhaps the most frequently-invoked additional factor is the notion that A has somehow assumed responsibility for B's welfare. We will elaborate on the content of this concept in Chapter 5 in the context of pure economic loss, but it can also, as we will see in Chapter 6, arise as an important consideration in personal injury cases. For example, if an adult naval airman voluntarily chooses to get cataclysmically drunk, then the Royal Navy has no duty of care to protect him in that drunken state: it is not liable for failing to confer the benefit of protection on him. However, as soon as other navy staff intervened, and returned the airman to his bunk, placing him in the recovery position, the Royal Navy had assumed responsibility for his well-being, and owed him a duty of care to protect him from the effects of his excessive drinking.[3] Absent that assumption, no duty of care would have arisen.

Proximity may also arise from status: where A has no duty to save B from drowning if B is a stranger, the position may be different where B is A's child.[4] Or A may somehow have control over the danger which causes injury to B which, in exceptional cases, may result in the imposition of a duty of care.[5]

As we will see in Chapter 6, the interpretation given to these 'additional factors' is often very restrictive. This makes it even more important to be clear whether the case is one of A making B's situation worse, or one of A failing to confer a benefit on B: A's liability is fairly easy to establish in the former; difficult in the latter.

1 See eg *GN v Poole* [2019] UKSC 25, [2020] AC 780 at para 28.
2 See eg *Vellino v Chief Constable of Greater Manchester Police* [2001] EWCA 1249, [2002] 1 WLR 218 at para 13.
3 [1995] 1 WLR 1217 (CA).
4 No authority supports this exact example. However, a school (which stands *in loco parentis*) may owe its pupils a duty of care to protect them from bullying: *Wands v Fife Council* 2009 GWD 30-477 (Sh Ct). It may also owe a duty to protect third parties from injuries caused by its pupils: *Carmarthenshire County Council v Lewis* [1955] AC 549 (HL).
5 See eg *Dorset Yacht Co Ltd v Home Office* [1970] AC 1004 (HL), discussed further in Chapter 6.

(4) Formulating the duty of care: the scope of the duty

3.10 We have said that the courts do not take a particularly scientific approach to the initial question as to whether or not a duty of care exists on the facts. Where the courts will be more scientific, however, is when ascertaining the exact scope or extent of the duty of care. This is crucial to determine what the defender has to do to fulfil that duty (and, therefore, in determining what the pursuer has to establish that the defender has *not* done to amount to a breach of the duty of care). We will consider this in more detail in Chapter 8, but we will introduce the point by discussing the leading case of *Muir v Glasgow Corporation*.[1] In this case, the House of Lords took the view that the defender could only be liable for the consequences that a reasonable person in her position would have had in contemplation in the circumstances of the case. The pursuer in that case was a child who was visiting a tearoom in premises operated by the defenders while on a church trip. The manageress of the tearoom allowed two members of the pursuer's party to carry an urn of hot water through the premises. For reasons unknown, one of the men dropped his side of the urn, causing the water to spill over the pursuer. There was no doubt that, in general, the defender owed the pursuer a duty of care: the pursuer, after all, was on the defender's property, which supplied the proximate relationship. However, the question which arose was the extent of that duty.

Lord Thankerton said:[2]

> '… it has long been held in Scotland that all that a person can be held bound to foresee are the reasonable and probable consequences of the

> failure to take care, judged by the standard of the ordinary reasonable man [sic]'.

Lord Wright considered that:[3]

> 'It is not, of course, a question of what she [the manageress] actually thought at the moment, but what the hypothetical reasonable person could have foreseen. That is the standard to determine the scope of her duty. This involves the question: Was the operation of carrying the tea-urn something which a reasonable person in [the manageress's] position should have realised would render the place in which it was performed dangerous to the children in the circumstances? This is the crucial issue of fact and the acid test of liability.'

The House of Lords held that a reasonable person in the position of the defender would not have foreseen as a possibility, let alone a probability, that the harm would occur as a result of their actions. It was not a *reasonable* and *probable* consequence of her allowing hot water to be carried into the tearoom that one of the men carrying the hot water would cause it to be spilled on a child.[4] The duty which arose was to take care to avoid reasonably foreseeable injury to the pursuer. the duty did not extend to protecting the pursuer from the consequences of a freak accident.

Where a duty of care arises, therefore, the defender will only owe a duty to take care in respect of injuries which were reasonably foreseeable. Generally, if the injury suffered by the pursuer is of a different nature to what could be reasonably foreseen, then the duty of care will not be breached if that unforeseen injury occurs because of the defender's conduct.[5]

1 1943 SC (HL) 3.
2 *Muir* at 8.
3 *Muir* at 15.
4 For instance, Lord Wright thought it would have been different if, for example, Mrs Alexander had allowed lions or tigers to be taken through the passage: 1943 SC (HL) 3 at 16.
5 See eg *Malcolm v Dickson* 1951 SC 542 (IH). Pursuer was a painter who accidentally set a house on fire. Defender suffered a heart attack while trying to save furniture from the fire. While it would have been reasonably foreseeable that the defender would have been injured by the fire or eg the effects of the smoke, it was not reasonably foreseeable that he would have injured himself through exertion in trying to save furniture.

3.11 However, it is not necessary to foresee the *extent* of the pursuer's injuries; it is enough that the injuries actually sustained by the pursuer are of a *kind* which would be foreseeable as a reasonable and probable consequence of the defender's careless conduct. Nor does every aspect of the accident have to be reasonably foreseeable. These points were settled by the House of Lords in the *Hughes v Lord Advocate*.[1] Two boys, upon seeing a tarpaulin shelter which had been left over an exposed manhole, took inside one of the paraffin lamps which had been left outside to warn of the exposed manhole. The pursuer slipped, dropped the lamp, causing an explosion, and fell into the manhole, suffering serious burns. The House of Lords held that it was foreseeable that a child could be induced to enter the unattended shelter with one of the lamps, and that injury by burning or falling could ensue. The fact that there had been an unforeseeable explosion and that the child's burns were therefore much worse than could have been reasonably anticipated was irrelevant. As Lord Morris of Borth-y-Gest explained:[2]

> 'The circumstances that an explosion as such could not have been contemplated does not alter the fact that it could reasonably have been foreseen that a boy who played in and about the canvas shelter and played with the things that were thereabouts might get hurt and might in some way burn himself. That is just what happened. The pursuer did burn himself, though his burns were more grave than would have been expected. The fact that the features and developments of an accident may not reasonably have been foreseen does not mean that the accident itself was not foreseeable. The pursuer was, in my view, injured as a result of the type or kind of accident or occurrence that could reasonably have been foreseen.'

Hughes v Lord Advocate is therefore authority that the scope of a duty of care will extend to the kind or type of injury which is a reasonable and probable consequence of the defender's careless act or omission; the fact that the injuries sustained are greater than could have been reasonably foreseen and/or that some of the causes of the accident were unforeseeable is irrelevant as long as the type of injury suffered by the pursuer and the fact that an accident could occur as a result of the defender's carelessness are reasonably foreseeable.[3]

1 1963 SC (HL) 31, 1963 SLT 150.
2 *Hughes v Lord Advocate* 1963 SC (HL) 31 at 43–44.
3 In other words, to use a concept we will return to in Chapter 17, the injuries suffered by the pursuer were not too remote as to render it unjust for the defender to make reparation for them.

SUMMARY

3.12 In general, and returning to first principles, it can be said that recognition of a duty of care requires first, that the pursuer is a person whom the defender ought to have had in their contemplation and second, that the harm complained of is of a type which ought to have been foreseeable to a reasonable person in the position of the defender. The two questions are inter-related. The duty will be owed in respect of harm that is foreseeable in the context of the relationship between the parties.

This may be a relatively straightforward matter, eg in cases involving death or personal injury or property damage caused by negligent driving. The driver will owe a duty of care to all other road users and pedestrians in the vicinity to guard against these forms of loss. The duty here arises out of physical or spatial proximity. The act of driving itself creates the necessary relationship with others walking or driving down the same street. By contrast, employers owe employees various duties of care, eg to provide a safe system of work. If a company based in Glasgow has failed to provide safety instructions, it may find itself in breach of a duty of care owed to an employee working in China at the time of the injury. In this case there is no physical proximity; proximity is nevertheless provided by the employment relationship and the harm that is foreseeable within the context of that relationship. In these cases, it should be noted that we are operating within established categories: a duty of care to prevent that injury will be owed, as a matter of precedent, if the harm which befalls the pursuer is reasonably foreseeable.

However, matters are not always straightforward. The type of loss may make it difficult to ascertain what is foreseeable and requisite proximity. We will see in Chapter 4 (psychiatric injury) and Chapter 5 (pure economic loss) that the duty of care is used to determine when injuries of those types will, or will not, be recoverable. In those contexts, specific tests have been developed to give rise to a duty to take reasonable care to avoid such injuries in exceptional cases. In Chapter 6, we will consider the problems posed where the defender is a public authority. We will see that the modern approach is a principled one, focussing on the distinction we have introduced between making a situation worse, and not making a situation better. Finally, in Chapter 7, we will consider what happens where established principles do not give us a clear answer as to whether A owes B a duty of care.

CHAPTER 4

Psychiatric Injury

INTRODUCTION

4.1 The law of delict in Scotland recognises in some instances an obligation of reparation where B's mental health has been harmed by the negligence of A. Indeed, the law has long recognised that A can owe a duty of care to prevent B suffering mental harm as a result of A's unintentional, but careless, conduct.[1] However, because of the nature of mental health and the complex ways by which it can be harmed, it has been necessary for the courts to develop tailored rules which adapt the general principles of negligence to the specific harm in question.[2] As this chapter demonstrates, the parameters of this specific duty of care are carefully defined by the courts. While modern medicine has made significant progress in identifying and explaining psychological and psychiatric conditions, the law has also advanced. Nevertheless, it remains a developing and challenging area for courts.[3] In cases involving claims for psychiatric or psychological injury, courts are seeking to strike a balance between the rightful acknowledgment of harm caused to someone's mental health whilst also ensuring that unreasonable burdens are not placed upon defenders.[4] As we shall see, this is not always an easy task for courts, but it is vital to ensure justice between individuals.

1 See para 4.4 below.

2 In *obiter* comments the Supreme Court has gone as far as to say that the rules discussed below relating to secondary victims are an *exception* to the principles of negligence, rather than simply a contextual adaption of the duty of care: *Paul v Royal Wolverhampton NHS Trust* [2024] UKSC 1, [2025] AC 459 at paras 2 to 5 per Lord Leggatt and Lady Rose.

3 For instance, after more than a century of jurisprudence on this matter, the UK Supreme Court could not reach a unanimous decision in *Paul*.

4 *McLoughlin v O'Brian* [1983] 1 AC 410 (HL) at 412–13 per Lord Wilberforce.

HARM TO MENTAL HEALTH

4.2 If a pursuer is seeking damages for a *negligently* caused injury to their mental health, ie psychiatric injury, it is first necessary to determine the type of harm for which they are seeking damages. It is possible to identify at least four different types of mental harm which are relevant in the law of delict. These, however, must be kept separate as the law's approach to each differs. Additionally, it must be borne in mind that there are different rules and remedies for cases of *intentionally* inflicted mental harm.[1] This chapter focuses on harm caused by negligence.

First, there is the pain and suffering experienced following a delict. In this situation, the harm caused to someone's mental health is derivative of the initial cause of their pain and suffering, ie their physical injury. Arguably, it is not a psychiatric injury because it is not a psychological disorder to experience pain and suffering upon sustaining a physical injury. Nonetheless, the law of delict compensates for this type of harm by awarding damages known as *solatium*, which is examined in Chapter 17.[2] It is important to remember, however, the primary injury is the physical injury, not the pain and suffering itself.

Second, there is the anguish we experience when our loved ones are killed by the wrongdoing of another. Historically, this has long been recognised in Scots law as giving rise to a standalone remedy for relatives. It has now been codified into a statutory remedy under the Damages (Scotland) Act 2011. Our mental health is, therefore, said to be impacted by the emotional upset of this tragedy at the time. But this remedy also acknowledges the consequences of this loss thereafter; that is, the long-term loss of the fellowship and societal support which our family member would have otherwise provided for us. We will return to this type of loss in more detail in Chapter 17.[3] Here, however, we must note that, by permitting damages for this type of harm, the law is acknowledging a natural occurrence subsequent to the loss of a relative (ie grief) and does not understand this to be a medically recognised disorder or psychiatric injury. Furthermore, it is a standalone right that a family member has; it is not related to whether they witnessed the death or suffered a psychiatric injury.

Third, there may be a series of experiences, relationships, and circumstances which over a period gradually impact upon our mental health. In such situations, we can experience a form of psychiatric injury which manifests in eg chronic stress, debilitating anxiety or severe depression. That injury is caused by a culmination of factors over a course of time. This type of psychiatric injury is rarely caused negligently in situations other than in the workplace. Hence, it is often employees who initiate such actions for damages, and workplace stress is dealt with in Chapter 10.[4] It differs from other types of mental harm in that (a) it is not the result of a single incident; (b) is a psychiatric injury rather than a natural response to busy and demanding employment conditions and (c) transpires almost exclusively within the employee-employer relationship.

Fourth, there are injuries caused to our mental health by virtue of either being involved in or witnessing an accident. Sometimes this is called 'pure psychiatric injury' because it is the primary injury for which damages are being claimed. In almost all modern cases involving this type of injury, the pursuer has not themselves suffered physical injury. Such pursuers are not seeking reparation for grief, workplace stress, or pain and suffering related to physical injury. Generally, this will arise in two broad situations. First, where the pursuer was involved in an accident, and while not physically injured, suffered a psychiatric/psychological injury as a result. Second, where the pursuer was not involved in the accident or a disaster, but witnessed it and subsequently suffered from a psychiatric injury. These two broad scenarios are the focus of this chapter.

1 Through, eg, the statutory delict of harassment (see para 1.9 above) or fraud or similar wrongdoing (para 2.3 above).
2 See para 17.11 below.
3 See para 17.29 below. A pursuer may make a claim on this basis alongside that discussed in this chapter: see eg *Young v MacVean* [2015] CSIH 70, 2016 SC 135.
4 See para 10.3 below.

RECOGNISED PSYCHOLOGICAL OR PSYCHIATRIC INJURY

4.3 To succeed in a negligence claim, the mental harm you suffer must amount to a recognised psychological or psychiatric disorder, not simply a fright or natural human reaction to a distressing incident. In the classic case of *McLoughlin v O'Brian*, Lord Wilberforce remarked that this requirement was necessary:

> 'either on the basis that … persons must be assumed to be possessed of fortitude sufficient to enable them to endure the calamities of modern life, or that defendants cannot be expected to compensate the world at large.'[1]

Thus, the law of delict will not offer compensation for the normal emotional distress that might be caused by a near miss accident. Or, if you witness an injury being caused to your loved one, and suffer anguish which naturally passes with time, or even grief which may not, you cannot seek damages for this disturbing experience.[2] Hence, courts stress that something you might naturally experience after being involved in an accident or witnessing an accident is not a recognised psychiatric/psychological injury. But if someone subsequently suffers eg from an anxiety disorder or reactive depression specifically related to the accident, these will be actionable. The key is that it needs to be a recognised psychological or psychiatric injury.[3]

The first challenge for a pursuer is to prove they have subsequently suffered from a recognised psychological or psychiatric illness, not grief or mere distress. Generally, to assist courts, parties now regularly refer to expert evidence and utilise authoritative medical texts, such as the American Diagnostic and Statistical Manual of Mental Disorders (DSM) or the International Classification of Mental Health and Behaviour Disorders

(ICD).[4] In medical handbooks such as these, parties can identify mental health disorders which go far beyond the normal day-to-day emotions of life. Common conditions which are recognised include: post-traumatic stress disorder, pathological grief disorder, major depressive disorder, or adjustment disorder. By using such handbooks, the language of the courts has been refined and updated, gaining a precision which the older case law lacked; for example, it is common to find phrases such as 'nervous shock' in many of the pre-1990s decisions.[5]

The distinction between psychological/psychiatric injury and physical injury is not factual; it is pragmatic. That is, it indicates that the pursuer needs to offer a specific type of evidence and averment when initiating their action, ie utilise expert opinion and the classifications found in the DSM and the ICD.[6] However, from a legal point of view, once it is demonstrated to be a medically recognised condition, very little if anything hinges on the fact that the injury was psychological/psychiatric rather than physical. For instance, in *Page v Smith*, the first instance judge decided that myalgic encephalomyelitis (also known as ME or chronic fatigue syndrome) was a recognised illness without necessarily determining if it was physical or psychological/psychiatric.[7] In this case, the debate was about whether the condition existed in the first place (which it was proven undoubtedly to be the case). Indeed, in situations such as this, where the condition is complex, the unscientific binary distinction used here – between physical and psychological/psychiatric injury – breaks down, rendering it somewhat meaningless. Yet, this is far from problematic. As the appellate courts often stress, the key question is whether the condition is more than a natural consequence of the events which proceeded its occurrence. In cases of physical injury, it is easier to determine if the consequence of someone's negligent actions caused an unnatural consequence – a leg is either fractured or not – whereas in instances of psychiatric injury, this can be more challenging – it is sometimes hard, for example, to differentiate natural grief from pathological grief disorder.[8] Hence the requirement for so-called psychological or psychiatric injuries to be medically recognised.

Some may criticise this approach, but there is no doubt that it is the law. It could be questioned whether it is always necessary to rely on expert medical evidence rather than judicial discretion. It is perhaps limiting for courts to be bound in this way when the facts of the case may present a strong case regardless. In Canada, for example, the courts have dispensed with this requirement. In *Saadati v Moorhead*, the appellant's case rested on evidence given by Saadati's friends to the effect that following the accident in question Saadati's personality had changed for the worse. The Supreme Court of Canada concluded that expert evidence could help determine if a mental injury had been demonstrated, but it was open to the court to ultimately determine if the condition of the victim was serious enough to warrant damages.[9] It was therefore open to the trial judge to find in Saadati's favour without the aid of expert evidence. In Canada, therefore, if a psychiatric diagnosis is not available, the decision-maker can still conclude, based on other evidence presented by the claimant, that the occurrence of mental injury has been proven on the balance of probabilities. In the UK, however, the Supreme Court has confirmed that it remains a requirement of the law: pursuers must show that the harm complained of amounts to a 'medically recognised condition'.[10] In practice, this means there will continue to be heavy reliance placed upon expert medical opinion, including the DSM and ICD.

1 *McLoughlin v O'Brian* [1983] 1 AC 410 (HL) at 423 per Lord Wilberforce.
2 *Alcock v Chief Constable of South Yorkshire Police* [1992] 1 AC 310 (HL) at 409 per Lord Oliver of Aylmerton.
3 See eg *Hinz v Berry* [1970] 2 QB 40 (CA); *Vernon v Bosley (No 1)* [1997] RTR 1 (CA); and *Young v MacVean*.
4 *Rorrison v West Lothian College* 2000 SCLR 245 (OH) at 252 per the Lord Ordinary (Reed).
5 *White v Chief Constable of South Yorkshire Police* [1999] 2 AC 455 (HL) at 489 per Lord Goff of Chieveley.
6 *Rorrison* at 252.
7 [1993] PIQR Q55 (QBD). The factual determination of the first instance judge was not appealed.
8 This was acknowledged by Lord Macmillan in *Bourhill v Young* [1943] AC 92 (HL) at 103. See also *White* at 464 per Lord Griffiths and *Paul v Royal Wolverhampton NHS Trust* [2024] UKSC 1, [2025] AC 459 at paras 28–29.
9 [2017] 1 SCR 543.
10 *Paul* at paras 31–32.

PRIMARY VICTIM: PURSUER IN HARM'S WAY

(1) *Wallace* and *Bourhill*: establishing the basics

4.4 In Scots law, the starting point is *Wallace v Kennedy*.[1] In this case, the pursuer was walking along a residential street, carrying their employer's infant child. As the defender's van careered along the street, a basket fell from the van's roof striking a lamppost, causing it to collapse. It narrowly missed the pursuer, causing her to leap aside to avoid physical injury. This incident, however, resulted in her experiencing (what the courts termed at this point) 'nervous shock' and related physical injuries, and she brought a claim in negligence. The defender argued that 'any injury sustained by the pursuer … resulted from a cause insufficient to affect injuriously a person of ordinary constitution' and that in any event her nervous shock was too remote to be considered the responsibility of the defender. Rejecting the defender's argument, the Lord Ordinary (Johnston) responded:[2]

> 'I am at a loss fully to understand, or at least appreciate, the defender's argument on this point. I think he maintained that there was no duty on

> him so to conduct himself … in the use of the roadway as not to frighten the pursuer in her use of the foot pavement.'

Furthermore, he dismissed the notion that the psychological consequences of the accident were too remote. Reflecting a willingness to accept nervous shock as a foreseeable consequence, he said:[3]

> 'Whether nervous shock causes disintegration or alteration in any of the delicate tissues which make up the human system or not, it cannot be doubted that such shock throws something in that system out of gear. And if such nervous shock occasions the physical or bodily consequence of disturbance of normal health which we call illness, that is sufficient.'

Despite its vintage, the facts of *Wallace* remain the paradigm example of when a pursuer is entitled to claim damages for psychological/psychiatric injuries.

1 (1908) 16 SLT 485 (OH), following *Dulieu v White & Sons* [1901] 2 KB 669 (KBD).
2 *Wallace* at 486.
3 *Wallace* at 486.

4.5 A key development in the law following *Kennedy* is the House of Lords decision in *Bourhill v Young*.[1] Young was a motorcyclist. Driving too fast, he overtook a stationary tramcar on its near side. He then crashed into a car which was turning right into a side street some fifty feet from the tramcar. Young was killed. It was accepted that the accident was caused by Young's careless driving. At the time of the accident, the pursuer, Mrs Bourhill, was on the far side of the tramcar, putting her creel on her back. She did not see the collision, but she heard the crash and saw blood on the road after Young's body had been removed. She maintained that, because of the accident, she suffered a 'nervous shock' which had caused her to miscarry. She sued Young's executor in delict. The question for the House of Lords was whether she could claim damages for what we would call today psychiatric injury.

In his speech, Lord Macmillan confirmed that 'it is now well recognised that an action will lie for injury by shock sustained through the medium of the eye or ear with direct contact.'[2] However, as Lord Thankerton explained, 'the injury must be within that which the cyclist ought to have reasonably contemplated as the area of potential danger which would arise as the result of his negligence …'[3] The central question was then whether Bourhill was within the area of potential danger. As Lord Porter observed, 'the defender was never herself in any bodily danger nor reasonably in fear of danger either for herself or others.'[4] At the time of the accident, Mrs Bourhill was 45–50 feet from the collision and on the far side of the tramcar. She was not within the area of risk of potential physical harm. In those circumstances, the House of Lords held that Young did not owe the pursuer a duty of care to prevent her suffering psychiatric injury as a result of his careless driving. It was accepted that a driver owes a duty of care to other road users or persons in premises adjoining the highway, but only when they were 'so placed' that they could reasonably be expected to be physically harmed by the defender's failure to take care. Lord Macmillan stated that:[5]

> 'The duty to take care is the duty to avoid doing or omitting to do anything the doing or omitting to do which may have as its reasonable and probable consequence injury to others, and the duty is owed to those to whom injury may reasonably and probably be anticipated if the duty is not observed.'

But while Young owed such a duty to the occupants of the motor car, he did not owe it to Mrs Bourhill because she was outwith the area of risk of potential physical harm. As Lord Wright observed, she 'was completely outside the range of the collision. She merely heard a noise which upset her ... She saw nothing of the actual accident, or indeed any marks of blood until later'.[6] However, if, like the pedestrian in *Wallace*, she was in the vicinity of potential harm, experienced shock, and suffered a psychiatric injury, she would have been eligible to claim damages from the defender.[7]

1 1942 SC (HL) 78. For a discussion of this case, see WW McBryde, '*Bourhill v Young*: the Case of the Pregnant Fishwife' in D Carey Miller and DW Meyers (eds), *Comparative and Historical Essays in Scots Law* (Butterworths, 1992) 66.
2 *Bourhill* at 87.
3 *Bourhill* at 83.
4 *Bourhill* at 98.
5 *Bourhill* at 88.
6 *Bourhill* at 93.
7 Compare with the pursuer in *Currie v Wadrop* 1927 SC 538 (IH).

(2) *Page* and subsequent cases: application and exceptions

4.6 Although *Bourhill* remains a landmark case, and has so far remained good law, Scottish and English courts have continued to refine its terminology and implications. In this regard, the next important case to consider is *Page v Smith*.[1] In this case, the House of Lords used the terminology of 'primary victim' to describe someone who was within the area of potential danger. The plaintiff was involved in a minor car accident and suffered no appreciable physical injury. He did, however, subsequently experience a relapse of his ME (or chronic fatigue syndrome). At proof, the judge decided that the negligence of the defendant was the cause of the development or prolongation of the plaintiff's symptoms.[2] As mentioned above, part of the argument in this case was whether this amounted to a recognised illness in the first place (which it was shown to be). Other arguments were made about whether it was right to impose a duty of care upon the defendant as the injury suffered could be said to be unforeseeable. In determining these issues, the House of Lords decided the following:[3]

(1) In situations where the defendant has put the plaintiff in the zone of potential physical harm, that is enough to demonstrate foreseeability of some sort of possible psychiatric harm. In other words, it is sufficient to demonstrate foreseeability of physical harm even if the eventual harm suffered was limited to psychiatric injuries.

(2) The defendant must take the plaintiff as they find them. It is not therefore appropriate to ask if the plaintiff was of ordinary fortitude. If you place someone at risk of physical harm due to your negligence, you must be prepared for them to suffer from a psychiatric injury as well. It does not matter whether the victim was more susceptible to developing a recognised psychiatric injury.

The key question is whether the pursuer has been exposed to physical danger:[4] in other words, whether the victim has been within the area of potential physical harm. Since *Page*, subsequent cases have tested the definition of 'potential harm'. Yet the courts have been unwilling to depart from the main tenor of *Page*. For example, persons who witnessed the death of fellow employees have been held not to constitute primary victims when they were not themselves in physical danger at the time of the accident.[5] Also of note is *Weddle v Glasgow City Council*.[6] In this case, a pedestrian witnessed a bin lorry collide with another vehicle. She then encountered the victims of the incident, including several dead bodies. Having failed to establish any reasonable belief that she was in danger of physical injury herself, her claim to be considered as a primary victim failed.

But there can be exceptional cases where a pursuer will be treated as a primary victim even though he was not at risk of physical harm. In these cases, pursuers have been able to establish foreseeability of injury, which is the most important element in any case dealing with negligently caused injury (whether that be physical or psychiatric). Here parties have established foreseeability due to the nature of the relationship or the context of the injury rather than the foreseeability of physical injury. These have included cases where the pursuer mistakenly thought that he had killed or injured a fellow employee;[7] parents who felt responsible for the sexual abuse of their children by a foster child introduced into their home by the defendant;[8] and parents whose dead children's organs were removed without permission.[9] On the other hand, a doctor or social worker does not owe a duty of care to a parent to prevent the parent from suffering mental harm if they mistakenly diagnose a child as having been abused by that parent.[10]

1 [1996] AC 155 (HL).
2 [1993] PIQR Q55 (QBD) at 74.
3 *Page* at 197 per Lord Lloyd of Berwick, with the concurrence of Lords Ackner and Browne-Wilkinson. The two Scottish law lords, Lord Keith of Kinkel and Lord Jauncey of Tulichettle, dissented, but the case has been accepted as representing Scots law: see eg *Simmons v British Steel Plc* [2004] UKHL 20, 2004 SC (HL) 94; *McCallum v Morrison* [2023] SAC (Civ) 23, 2023 SLT (SAC) 119 at para 21.
4 Or had reasonable grounds to believe that he was in danger: see, for example, *Hunter v British Coal Corpn* [1999] QB 140 (CA).
5 *Robertson v Forth Road Bridge Joint Board* 1995 SC 364 (IH) (pursuer saw fellow employee blown off lorry on Forth Road Bridge); *McFarlane v EE Caledonia Ltd* [1994] PIQR P154 (CA) (plaintiff witnessed Piper Alpha explosion from a supply ship); *Campbell v North Lanarkshire Council* 2000 SCLR 373 (OH) (proof before answer allowed to determine whether pursuer was in personal danger).
6 [2019] SC EDIN 42, 2019 SLT (Sh Ct) 206, affirmed [2021] SAC (Civ) 17, 2021 SLT (Sh Ct) 277.
7 *Salter v U B Frozen & Chilled Foods Ltd* 2003 SLT 1011 (OH) (pursuer actively involved in the accident which caused the death of a fellow employee for which the pursuer was blameless).
8 *W v Essex CC* [2001] 2 AC 592 (HL). See also *McLoughlin v Jones* [2001] EWCA Civ 1743, [2002] QB 1312 (plaintiff suffered a nervous breakdown having been wrongfully imprisoned as a consequence of his solicitor's negligence in preparing his defence; treated as a primary victim in his claim against the solicitor for negligence).
9 *Stevens v Yorkhill NHS Trust* [2006] CSOH 143, 2006 SLT 889 (OH); *AB v Leeds Teaching Hospital NHS Trust* [2004] EWHC 644 (QB), [2005] QB 506.
10 *D v East Berkshire Community Health NHS Trust* [2005] UKHL 23, [2005] 2 AC 373. In *Fairlie v Perth and Kinross Healthcare NHS Trust* 2004 SLT 1200 (OH) at paras 35–36 the Lord Ordinary (Kingarth) considered that the parent in such a case might have a remedy in defamation or breach of his Article 8 right to respect for private life. On the Article 8 ECHR point, see *B's Representative v NHS Grampian* [2024] CSOH 72.

SECONDARY VICTIM: PURSUER AS A WITNESS

4.7 If the pursuer was not in harm's way, but witnessed the negligently-caused accident, and thereafter suffered a recognised psychiatric injury, are they owed a duty of care? Here, we are considering the claim of someone who has *witnessed* a negligently caused traumatic event, disaster, or accident, yet who themselves were never in danger of being physically injured. In other words, can the bystander make a claim for psychological or psychiatric injury by virtue of witnessing, in effect, the breach of a duty of care not to cause physical harm which was owed to a third party?

In *Bourhill*,[1] Lord Wright addressed this very question. His Lordship confirmed the general principle that such witnesses *do not* have a right of action. Recalling the facts of *Bourhill*, he stated:[2]

> 'If, however, the Appellant has a cause of action it is because of a wrong to herself [ie a breach of the duty of care owed to her]. She cannot build on a wrong to someone else [ie the breach of a duty of care owed to someone

> else]. Her interest which was in her own bodily security, was of a different order from the interest of the owner of the car.'

In *Alcock*, Lord Oliver confirmed this:[3]

> '[t]he law in general provides no remedy, however severe the consequences of the distress or grief may be to the health or well-being of the third party and however close his relationship to the victim'.

In *Paul v Royal Wolverhampton NHS Trust*, the Supreme Court reaffirmed the general rule: in civil law, the death or injury of another person does not give rise to a right of action.[4]

However, there are some important qualifications to this general principle. We will examine one of these exceptions now, leaving the other to its more natural place in Chapter 17.[5]

1 See para 4.5 above.
2 *Bourhill v Young* 1942 SC (HL) 78 at 92.
3 *Alcock v Chief Constable of South Yorkshire* [1992] 1 AC 310 (HL) at 410.
4 *Paul v Royal Wolverhampton NHS Trust* [2024] UKSC 1, [2025] AC 459 at paras 2 and 252.
5 See Lord Carloway's discussion in *Paul* at paras 252–253.

(1) The *McLoughlin* exception

4.8 In *McLoughlin v O'Brian*,[1] the House of Lords authoritatively introduced an important exception to the general principle. In this case, the plaintiff's husband and three children were involved in a road accident at 4 pm. They were taken to hospital, where it was discovered that one child was dead. The plaintiff was told of the accident at 6 pm and immediately went to the hospital where she saw the primary victims and the extent of their physical injuries. She later suffered a psychiatric disorder. McLoughlin's case came before the House of Lords, who held that a duty of care did exist between the driver and the plaintiff, even though she had not been directly involved in the accident.

To understand the approach of the House of Lords in *McLoughlin*, it is important to remember that three additional factors were present in this case which provided the necessary degree of proximity between the negligent driver and the mother and wife, which generated a duty of care. First, the primary victims were close members of her family. Secondly, the plaintiff was with the victims shortly after the accident; accordingly, she had witnessed the immediate aftermath of the accident. Upon seeing her family at the hospital, she found them covered in oil, mud and blood, and distraught with pain – effectively the same condition they were in on the roadside. Thirdly, she had directly *seen* the effects of the accident on her family and had not simply learned of the accident by letter or on television or from a third party. These facts placed *McLoughlin* within a temporal vicinity of the accident, which gave the House of Lords good reason to consider her injury to be reasonably foreseeable to the driver.

In allowing this appeal, the House of Lords created the status of a secondary victim. It is a narrow category of persons who can claim damages as a secondary victim. Indeed, as noted, courts sometimes frame this as an exception to the general rule that you cannot claim damages for the death or injury of another person.[2] It is noteworthy that the secondary victim is not at any point within the zone of potential harm. However, based on *McLoughlin* a duty of care can still arise, and damages will be awarded, if the following is shown by the pursuer:

(1) They have suffered a psychiatric/psychological injury, as discussed above.

(2) They have suffered a *foreseeable* injury.

(3) That there is a 'close tie' between the victim of the accident, such as parent and child or husband and wife, and the pursuer.

(4) That they were proximate in time and space to the accident, meaning they had direct perception of the accident or immediate aftermath.

Hence, it follows from *McLoughlin* that a duty of care can be owed to someone not within the zone of potential physical harm. However, foreseeability and proximity, the fundamentals of a duty of care, must be established using the steps outlined above. If these factors are *not* present, the court will not impose a duty of care.

1 1942 SC (HL) 78.
2 *Paul v Royal Wolverhampton NHS Trust* [2024] UKSC 1, [2025] AC 459 at para 2.

(2) *Alcock* criteria: foreseeability of injury to relatives

4.9 *McLoughlin* was developed by the leading case of *Alcock v Chief Constable of South Yorkshire Police.*[1] Friends and relatives of Liverpool FC fans who died in the Hillsborough football ground disaster brought claims for psychiatric injuries, such as PTSD. Owing to the negligence of South Yorkshire Police, parts of the stadium were catastrophically overcrowded, culminating in 95 people being crushed to death (another two fans died years later from their injuries). The plaintiffs in this case were not within the zone of potential physical harm. However, they had witnessed the events unfold from parts of the stadium that were comparatively safe; heard of the events on the radio; viewed the disaster live on television; received news of the events and knew that their loved ones would have been within harm's way; and visited make shift morgues to identify the dead bodies of their friends and relatives only hours after the disaster. Understandably, these experiences caused the plaintiffs psychiatric and psychological injuries. The question for the House of Lords was whether the *McLoughlin* exception would allow recovery in these situations.

The House of Lords held that before a duty of care arose, it had to be reasonably foreseeable that the plaintiffs would suffer a psychiatric disorder. In taking this approach, they did not depart from the ratio of *McLoughlin*. From the perspective of a reasonable person, who, apart from the primary victim, could be said to be foreseeably affected by acts of negligence? Could it be said, following *McLoughlin*, that a defender should also have friends and extended family within their contemplation? Lord Oliver addressed this question, and his consideration merits full quotation:[2]

> 'As regards the class of persons to whom a duty may be owed to take reasonable care to avoid inflicting psychiatric illness through nervous shock sustained by reason of physical injury or peril to another, I think it sufficient that reasonable foreseeability should be the guide. I would not seek to limit the class by reference to particular relationships such as husband and wife or parent and child. The kinds of relationship which may involve close ties of love and affection are numerous, and it is the existence of such ties which leads to mental disturbance when the loved one suffers a catastrophe. They may be present in family relationships or those of close friendship, and may be stronger in the case of engaged couples than in that of persons who have been married to each other for many years. It is common knowledge that such ties exist, and reasonably foreseeable that those bound by them may in certain circumstances be at real risk of psychiatric illness if the loved one is injured or put in peril. The closeness of the tie would, however, require to be proved by a plaintiff, though no doubt being capable of being presumed in appropriate cases.'

Some important points should be noted. It is often wrongly assumed that *Alcock* created set categories of relatives who can or cannot claim damages. As is evident from Lord Oliver's speech, this is not the case. Rather, he offers a general principle that is illustrated by different types of relationship; that is, a close tie of love and affection. Further, the test here is a factual one and not a legal one. The burden rests on the pursuer to demonstrate that the substance of their relationship amounts to a close tie of love and affection. It may be presumed in favour of parent and child relationships, for example, but it thereafter remains possible for a defender to subsequently challenge it. Lastly, therefore, the list is not fixed. It is feasible for many different types of relationship to fulfil this requirement. Whether this has been realised in subsequent cases, however, is a different story.[3]

1 [1992] 1 AC 310 (HL).
2 *Alcock* at 398.
3 See *Robertson v Forth Road Bridge Joint Board* 1994 SC 364 (IH) and *McFarlane v EE Caledonia Ltd* [1994] PIQR P154 (CA).

(3) Further *Alcock* criteria: presence at the scene and direct perception

4.10 As we have already seen, *McLoughlin* stressed that proximity in time and space to the accident was necessary. Hence, *Alcock* reaffirmed that the plaintiff had to witness the calamity or its aftermath (for example, by being at the stadium). On that basis, for example, identifying a dead relative or friend eight hours after the event was not enough. Further, it is important that the pursuer was fully aware of what they were witnessing, and the response is directly related to that experience.[1] In *Young v MacVean*,[2] a mother on her way to meet her son passed the scene of the accident in which he had been killed. Only later, when he did not turn up at the rendezvous, did it gradually dawn on her what had happened. The Inner House held, on application of the *Alcock* criteria, that she was not owed a duty of care. On their analysis, she could not be said to have been present at the immediate aftermath of the accident, as she did not at that time have the awareness that her loved one had been involved.

Secondly, it was confirmed in *Alcock* that secondary victims must have seen or heard the accident: watching the event on television did not suffice, because they did not get sight of their relatives during the broadcast. Here we must be careful; often it is wrongfully said that *Alcock* determined that the mechanism of perception must be, in effect, with the naked eye. Rather, in *Alcock*, it was said that the defendant, the police, knew that the policy of the television company in such circumstances was to ensure that no specific person could be identified. It was not the television itself that was crucial, but rather the defendant's awareness that, in this instance, the relatives would not see their loved one's injury on screen. Hence, applying the principles of foreseeability it was said that the police should not have had in contemplation the relatives of the victims who were watching at home on television.[3]

Remote perception by a screen may, therefore, in some instances be foreseeable to the wrongdoer. Of note is that in *McLoughlin*, Lord Wilberforce left this possibility open in his judgment, and it was something which Lord Ackner did not rule out in *Alcock*. Lord Oliver in *Alcock* was more explicit: 'there may well be circumstances where the element of visual perception may be provided by witnessing the actual injury to the primary victim on simultaneous television.'[4] Of course, these observations are *obiter* but the ubiquity today of live streaming, video calls, and other visual communication devices means that there may be situations in the future which render a remote viewer a secondary victim.

1 *Young v Downey* [2025] EWCA Civ 177, [2025] 4 WLR 32.
2 [2015] CSIH 70, 2016 SC 135.
3 *Alcock v Chief Constable of South Yorkshire Police* [1992] 1 AC 310 (HL) at 421.
4 *Alcock* at 418.

(4) The nature of the event

4.11 In *Paul v Royal Wolverhampton NHS Trust*,[1] the Supreme Court considered three challenging medical negligence cases, where the claimants' psychological or psychiatric injuries resulted from witnessing the death of a close relative. They did not, however, witness an accident as such but rather the development of a medical condition over a period, which eventually resulted in the death of their loved ones. In these cases, the defendants had negligently failed to diagnose and treat the medical condition leaving the claimants to witness firsthand the consequences of their loved one's medical condition unfold resulting in their death. The court clarified several important points of law: here, we consider the court's definition of the *event* in question; that is, does it need to be a *singular* 'horrifying event', or can it be a distressing scenario that unfolds over days or even weeks?

Until *Paul*, it was conventional to follow Lord Ackner's description in *Alcock* of how the injury to a secondary victim must come about. It must be, according to *Alcock*, the result of a 'shock' which involves the sudden appreciation by sight or sound of a horrifying event. It is this that is said to 'violently agitate the mind' causing a psychiatric/psychological injury.[2] In *Alcock*, it was noted that an injury caused by accumulation over a period of more gradual assaults was not recoverable. The Supreme Court returned to this in *Paul*. In the majority decision, the court clarified that Lord Ackner's statements here were *obiter*. Further, the Supreme Court noted that this terminology was redolent of outdated conceptions of mental health, which were found in older definitions of psychiatric or psychological injury, such as 'nervous shock.' Additionally, it was observed that it was, strictly speaking, unnecessary in the law to demonstrate the precise neurological or psychological mechanism by which the injury came about. Hence, there was no need for the House of Lords to describe how the injury must come about. It was sufficient to demonstrate that it was medically recognised and caused by witnessing the event.

Some key points can be taken from *Paul*:

(1) There is no requirement on the claimant/pursuer to demonstrate that the event caused 'sudden shock to the nervous system'; it is

sufficient to demonstrate a causal link, using the established rules of causation, between the breach of the duty of care and the medically recognised condition.[3]

(2) The event does not need to be categorised as 'horrific' or 'horrifying' or 'terrifying'. It is necessary to demonstrate that it was reasonably foreseeable that the claimant/pursuer would suffer injury upon witnessing the event. There is no requirement to add any additional evaluative descriptor when determining if the circumstances gave rise to a duty of care.[4]

(3) The passage of time between the negligent act or omission and the accident does not necessarily preclude a right to recover damages for psychiatric injury caused by witnessing a person's death or injury.[5]

(4) 'An accident is, by definition, a discrete event in the ordinary sense of that word, meaning something which happens at a particular time, at a particular place, in a particular way.'[6] Following this, there is therefore a distinction to be made between witnessing an accident in contrast to witnessing someone suffer an ongoing or unfolding medical crisis.

In this case, the claimants failed to persuade the Supreme Court that they were secondary victims. Applying the above points, the court was unable to find that the claimants witnessed an 'accident', which is vital. The nature of the event must be an accident. In seeking to understand this decision it is useful to bear in mind that courts envisage a paradigm secondary victim scenario when considering difficult cases. Indeed, in *Paul* Lord Leggatt and Lady Rose gave the examples of a mother who sees her child knocked over by a car or a husband who rushes moments after an accident to find his wife badly injured.[7] These are situations where it is easy for us to envisage the subsequent psychological trauma and hard to sometimes determine exactly whether the pursuer is in fact a primary victim themselves. If a pursuer's situation is similar to these paradigms, they are likely to satisfy the criteria. Of course, subsequent cases will continue to explore what can be considered analogous to these paradigm examples of secondary victimhood. In resolving them, courts will continue to draw upon *Bourhill*, *McLoughlin*, *Alcock* and now *Paul*.

1 *Paul v Royal Wolverhampton NHS Trust* [2024] UKSC 1, [2025] AC 459.
2 [1992] 1 AC 310 (HL) at 402.
3 *Paul* at paras 71–74.
4 *Paul* at para 75.
5 *Paul* at para 79.
6 *Paul* at para 108.
7 *Paul* at para 109.

CONCLUSION

4.12 The law of delict in Scotland has long recognised that damages are recoverably if someone suffers psychological or psychiatric harm. As this chapter demonstrates, courts are, however, keen to set clear boundaries around the type of claim. Initially, these limits were set around the need to be within the zone of physical harm – something which is still a requirement – but the criteria have been refined over the years.

For example, due to concerns about the somewhat intangible nature of the injury, courts rely upon medical diagnosis to confirm the existence of a psychological or psychiatric injury. In taking this approach, courts wish to ensure that only the most serious conditions are afforded protection. Instances where someone has suffered upset, distress or natural grief are not considered sufficiently serious to damages.

Nevertheless, as we have seen, courts are prepared to allow the recovery of damages to those who witness a traumatic event or are present at the immediate aftermath. Here courts are concerned to award compensation to those supposedly within the reasonable contemplation of the defender. While primary victims are easily identifiable as falling within a zone of potential harm and thus foreseeable victims of carelessness, secondary victims are, admittedly, one step removed, being beyond the zone of personal physical harm. Nonetheless, as we have explored, for decades courts have acknowledged that relatives, friends or those with a close tie of love and affection should also be considered victims and taken into consideration.

Although difficult cases continue to arise in this area, the Supreme Court, in *Paul* emphasised that the leading authorities of *Bourhill*, *McLoughlin* and *Alcock* can continue to be used to guide the development of the law but also mark the boundaries of liability for psychological or psychiatric injury. It is upon these cases which the modern law was designed. Whether they offer a satisfactory system of compensation for those who suffer psychological or psychiatric injury is another question.

CHAPTER 5

Negligently-Caused Economic Loss

INTRODUCTION

5.1 With the discussion of psychiatric injury, we have seen how matters complicate when we move even slightly away from the paradigmatic case of negligently-inflicted physical injury. This is even more evident when there is no personal injury in the equation, and the pursuer is claiming in respect of economic losses. In this context, we can see the role played by the duty of care as effectively a 'threshold' device, determining when such losses will or will not be recoverable. We will start by explaining the law's general unwillingness to permit recovery of pure economic loss.

MAPPING THE RECOVERY OF ECONOMIC LOSS

(1) The general rule: no recovery of 'pure' economic loss

5.2 The starting point that the law adopts is that there is no delictual duty 'to avoid causing a purely economic loss unless it is parasitic upon some injury to person or property.'[1] In the first place, it can be difficult to grasp exactly what pure economic loss is. It is therefore important to first establish an understanding of what it is in contrast to other concepts covered in this book.

Pure economic loss is loss which flows from an injury to the pursuer's patrimony or wealth alone, unconnected to any injury to the pursuer's person or property. Such loss, generally, is not recoverable.

In Chapter 2, we encountered one major exception to that starting point: if the defender uses unlawful means, with the intention of causing the pursuer economic loss, then there may be liability under one of the economic delicts.[2] With deliberately inflicted economic harm, the need to prove the defender's malevolent intention operates as an important limiting principle.

When we turn to carelessly inflicted economic harm, there is no targeting of the pursuer to assist with justifying the imposition of liability. The implications of a general duty not to carelessly cause economic loss would be profound. Engaging in any activity could expose the negligent actor to potentially extensive liability, to a potentially limitless number of persons. Scots law calls upon the duty of care as the control device to keep liability for negligently-caused economic harm within acceptable boundaries, and to distinguish between pure economic loss which is recoverable, and that which is not. First, we should distinguish 'pure' economic loss from 'derivative' economic loss, and consider what is sometimes described as 'secondary' economic loss.

1 *JSC BTA Bank v Khrapunov* [2018] UKSC 19, [2020] AC 727 at para 6 per Lords Sumption and Lloyd-Jones.
2 See generally Chapter 2 above.

(2) Derivative economic losses: generally recoverable

5.3 Where economic loss has been caused by the breach of an established duty – for example, by physical or psychiatric injury or by damage to the pursuer's property in breach of duties not to cause such injury – then there is no difficulty at the duty stage. Such economic loss is 'derivative' of the primary injury, and therefore, if the pursuer's claim is within an established category, that 'derivative' or 'consequential' loss will be *prima facie* recoverable.

To take a simple example: imagine A negligently crashes into B's car. B's injuries mean that she is unable to attend work, and the damage to her car necessitates hire of a rental car. B's economic loss in the form of lost wages is derivative of the injury caused by A's breach of his duty not to cause B physical injury and may be recovered. Similarly, B's economic loss[1] in the form of the car rental fees is recoverable, as it derives directly from the damage caused to her car by A's breach of his duty not to damage B's property. So long as ordinary principles of causation and remoteness are satisfied,[2] such losses form part of the quantification of the damages owed to the pursuer to compensate for the loss caused by the defender's breach of duties, and do not require separate consideration.

1 Often the loss will actually be suffered by B's insurer, but nothing turns on this for present purposes.
2 That is, A's breach of duty must have caused the specific loss suffered by B, and that specific loss must be of a type which arises naturally and directly from A's breach of duty. See Chapters 9 and 17.

(3) Secondary economic loss: generally not recoverable

5.4 On the contrary, if the pursuer's economic loss is caused by breach of a duty owed to a *third* party, then the pursuer will not be able to recover such economic losses.[1] These sometimes are referred to as 'secondary economic losses'[2] or, in terms rejected by the UK Supreme Court, 'relational economic losses',[3] but in effect, they are simply pure economic losses in respect of which the law generally recognises no duty founding a right of recovery. Two examples will illustrate, the first pertaining to personal injury. *Reavis v Clan Line Steamers*[4] involved a claim by the leader of an orchestra which lost, through injury and death, several members when the ship they were travelling on sank as a result of the defender's negligence. The orchestra, which was moderately successful to that point, had to disband as a result. There was no doubt that the pursuer could recover for her own personal injuries, any damage to her own property, and (as discussed above) any economic losses reasonably consequential to those two injuries.[5] But the pursuer also claimed economic loss that resulted from the injuries to, and deaths of, the orchestra members. The Inner House rejected the pursuer's attempts to characterise this as an injury to her property, and refused the claim, holding that:[6]

> '[i]n the law of Scotland there is no such thing as a right or interest, in the nature of property, in the services of another; and a person claiming reparation for injury by another person's fault cannot go beyond the effects of such injury on his own person, his own health, his own business or other capabilities, and his own property'.

The injured orchestra members, and the relatives of the deceased members,[7] could, of course, bring personal claims in respect of their injuries suffered, and for any consequential economic loss.

1 It should be emphasised that this does not encompass the situation where the conduct which triggers the breach of the duty owed to the third party also breaches a duty owed to the pursuer, such as where physical injury to a third party causes the pursuer foreseeable psychiatric or psychological injury. See paras 4.7–4.11 above.

2 Which may be a short-hand way of saying 'economic losses suffered by a secondary victim'.

3 *Armstead v Royal & Sun Alliance Insurance Company* [2024] UKSC 6, [2025] AC 406 at para 27.

4 1925 SC 725 (IH).

5 Ibid at 738. Further proceedings on these injuries are reported at 1926 SC 215 (IH).

6 Ibid at 740 per the Lord President (Clyde), referring to *Allan v Barclay* (1864) 2 M 873 (IH).

7 For a statutory exception to the rule against recovering secondary economic loss, operating where the deceased provided a relative with personal services, see Damages (Scotland) Act 2011, ss 6–7, discussed further below at 17.29.

5.5 The second example pertains to damage to property. In *Dynamco Ltd v Holland and Hannen and Cubitts (Scotland) Ltd*,[1] the defender's excavator damaged an underground electric supply cable owned by the South of Scotland Electricity Board. As a result, there was a power cut at the pursuer's factory which lasted for over 15 hours, during which time production could not take place. The pursuer sued for the loss of profits incurred while the factory was closed. The court held that although the defender owed a duty of care to the electricity board not to damage its property, ie the cable, the defender did not owe a duty to the pursuer in respect of 'secondary' economic loss, even though such loss was reasonably foreseeable.[2] Such loss did not result from an infringement of any interest or property right of the pursuer, and therefore was not recoverable.

Some simple counterfactuals may assist further in illuminating this area. First, if the factory had a private electricity supply, and the pursuer owned the electricity cable severed by the defender's negligence, it would be able to recover the lost profits: those losses would arise directly and foreseeably from the damage to its property.[3] Secondly, reversing the ownership of the cable to the electricity board, it is conceivable that its severing interrupted the pursuer's manufacturing process in a manner which rendered a batch of the pursuer's products unfit for use and sale. In those circumstances, the pursuer may be able to recover in respect of (a) the damage to that batch and (b) losses consequent to that damage,[4] but would still be unable to sue for the lost profits caused by the factory downtime, as this involves no further damage to its property.[5] Thirdly, if the interruption of the power supply caused damage to the pursuer's machinery, and that damage halted production, any lost profits arising out of the time it takes to repair the machine may be recoverable, so long as it can be shown that the downtime was caused by damage to the machine (ie the pursuer's property) and not the severing of the cable itself (ie damage to a third party's property).[6]

1 1971 SC 257 (IH).
2 *Dynamco* at 267 per Lord Migdale and at 269 per Lord Cameron.
3 This follows from the emphasis placed by each member of the Inner House in *Dynamco* that the cable was owned by the electricity board, not the pursuer. Cf *Network Rail v Conarken* [2011] EWCA Civ 644 (where Network Rail owned the railway bridge which was damaged and could therefore recover consequential losses).
4 In *Coleridge v Miller Construction Ltd* 1997 SLT 485 (OH), the Lord Ordinary (MacLean) held that it would not be 'fair, just, and reasonable' to impose liability for (a) and (b) on a party who had caused the interruption of electricity supply to the pursuer. This case should not be followed: the use of policy considerations is out of line with the modern approach to the duty of care.
5 This counterfactual is borrowed from the facts of the famous English case of *Spartan Steel and Alloys Ltd v Martin & Co (Contractors) Ltd* [1973] QB 27 (CA). It is submitted that this decision is to be preferred to that in *Coleridge*.
6 This counterfactual is taken from *SCM (United Kingdom) v WJ Whittall & Son* [1971] 1 QB 337 (CA), which was cited in *Dynamco* at 270 and 272.

5.6 To fall outside the rule prohibiting the recovery of secondary economic losses, therefore, the pursuer must show they have a sufficient relationship with the property which has been damaged by the defender's negligence. The distinction is between 'ownership or a right of possession similar to that of an owner on the one hand' (which will suffice) and 'mere contractual rights to have the use or services of the chattel for certain limited purposes' (which will not).[1] What will amount to a 'right of possession similar to that of an owner' requires elaboration. A lease of heritable property which confers an exclusive right of possession in respect of those subjects confers title to sue in respect of damage to that property and any foreseeable consequential losses suffered by the tenant.[2] But a mere contractual right to enter a property to carry out works will be insufficient.[3] As for moveable property, it has been held that a party who had possession on its own behalf of a helicopter, which it leased from a finance company, had title to sue in respect of its destruction.[4] Possession of a corporeal moveable, in Scots law, is a real right, so a party with day-to-day use of an asset on its own behalf should be able to sue in respect of its damage or destruction even though its ownership resides with a third party.[5]

The distinctions drawn in this area may not seem entirely principled, and it is openly admitted that they are based on policy.[6] The law must draw the line somewhere, and direct and consequential losses stemming from damage to the pursuer's property seem at least a clear endpoint for what is recoverable.

1 *Nacap v Moffat Plant Ltd* 1987 SLT 221 (IH) at 223 per the Lord Justice-Clerk (Ross). The test is translated, not entirely happily, from the decision of the House of Lords in the English appeal of *The Aliakmon* 1986 AC 785 (HL). The fact that the helicopter was possessed on its own behalf, and not on behalf of a third party, distinguishes it from *Nacap*.

2 Compare *Mull Shellfish Ltd v Golden Sea Produce Ltd* 1992 SLT 703 (IH), *Hand v North of Scotland Water* 2002 SLT 798 (OH) and *Devon Angling Association v Scottish Water* [2018] SAC Civ 7, 2018 SC (SAC) 35; (exclusive possession) with *TCS Holdings Ltd v Ashtead Plant Hire Co Ltd* 2003 SLT 177 (OH) (no exclusive possession).

3 *Cruden Buildings and Renewals Ltd v Scottish Water* [2017] CSOH 98.

4 *North Scottish Helicopters Ltd v United Technologies Corporation Inc* 1988 SLT 77 (OH). Compare with *Blackburn v Sinclair* 1984 SLT 368 (OH), where a taxi driver who drove a taxi on hire purchase could not recover in respect of damage to that taxi. It is suggested that *Blackburn* does not fully acknowledge the nature of possession enjoyed by the taxi driver.

5 *Armstead v Royal & Sun Alliance Insurance Company* [2024] UKSC 6, [2025] AC 406, as discussed in relation to Scots law by C Anderson, 'Liability to a Hirer for Damage to Property' (2025) 182 Reparation Bulletin 3.

6 See eg *Spartan Steel and Alloys Ltd v Martin & Co (Contractors) Ltd* [1973] QB 27 (CA) at 36–39 per Lord Denning MR.

(4) Defining pure economic loss

5.7 Pure economic loss, as we have said, is loss which does not result from an injury to the pursuer's person or property. Some examples may assist.

As just discussed, loss which results from injury to another person or damage to another's property can be classified as pure economic loss.[1]

Incurring expenditure, extending credit, purchasing property, transferring money, or passing up an opportunity to make a profit on the basis of an assertion or representation made by another party, or as a result of their defective performance of a service, all involve pure economic loss. So, for example, in *MacDonald v FIFA*,[2] MacDonald had purchased match tickets, flights, and hotel accommodations to watch Scotland's Men's National Football Team play Estonia in Tallinn. FIFA rescheduled the match, and the Estonian team refused to take to the field, resulting in the game being abandoned. MacDonald's claim against FIFA failed on other grounds, but is clear that the money spent on tickets and accommodation on the expectation the match would take place as scheduled would be irrecoverable as it constituted pure economic loss.

Pure economic loss also arises where a builder or manufacturer supplies an inherently defective product. If we purchase a house, and a defect is discovered which causes injury to person or property, then losses flowing from those injuries will be recoverable as consequential economic loss. But if no further injury ensues, and the issue is solely with the defect inherent to the building, then our loss is purely an economic one: the defect has simply lowered the value of the building which we already own, leaving us with an asset worth less than first supposed. The cost of repairs to an inherently defective building cannot be recovered in delict.[3] The same is true if we buy a moveable asset, such as a car, which is defective when purchased.[4]

1 See paras 5.4–5.6.
2 1999 SCLR 59 (OH). The report at 1999 SLT 1129 omits this part of the opinion.
3 *Murphy v Brentwood District Council* [1991] 1 AC 398 (HL), overruling *Anns v Merton London Borough Council* [1978] AC 728 (HL).
4 This point, although not clearly established as a matter of authority at common law in Scotland, is carried over to the Consumer Protection Act 1987: s 5(2). The point was not taken by the helicopter manufacturer in *North Scottish Helicopters Ltd v United Technologies Corporation Inc* 1988 SLT 77 (OH), but that decision was a preliminary proof limited to the question of title to sue, which the Scottish courts have not always considered separately to the question of duty.

(5) Rationalising non-recovery of pure economic losses

5.8 Why does the law generally place these losses outside a defender's duty of care, rendering them irrecoverable? Three reasons are frequently offered.

First, the reluctance to allow recovery in delict for pure economic loss is to protect the defender from potentially indeterminate liability. It is one thing for the defender who carelessly severs an electricity cable to be liable for damage to the property of others which ensues; that liability would increase exponentially if the duty of care also extended to encompass any loss of profits suffered by businesses who have lost power.[1] So, where an electricity cable is severed, resulting in a loss of power to a restaurant's fridges, rendering the produce stored within inedible, it seems fair to make the negligent party liable for the cost of re-instating that food. But it seems less fair to hold that party liable for lost custom arising from the restaurant's decision to close until the power to its dining room is recovered.[2]

Secondly, the reluctance stems from autonomy and anti-paternalistic concerns. The law of contract is always available to parties to use to protect their own interests, in respect of which there is no rule preventing the recovery of pure economic loss.[3] If we seek advice from a financial adviser, it is always open (at least in theory) to us to enter into a contract with them, requesting that they take responsibility for any losses which might be suffered if the advice provided turns out to be bad. Of course, they can – and often do – say no, but if they agree, the risk which they thereby take on will no doubt be reflected in the price charged for their services. When we buy a car from a dealership, there is implied into that contract by law a term that the car must be of 'satisfactory quality', which will be breached if the car is defective.[4] And wherever there is a risk of economic loss, it is possible (again, in theory), for us to contract to insure against that risk eventuating.[5] It is important that the law of delict respects our freedom of contract and does not cut across contractual arrangements and allocations of risk.

Thirdly, as we have seen with the intentional economic wrongs, while damage to persons and property is not something society tolerates lightly, the infliction of economic loss is a necessary consequence of a capitalist society.[6]

These reasons are not always convincing, and do not apply to every case with equal force. It is therefore not surprising that exceptions to the general rule have arisen.

1 It has become a cliché to quote the dictum of Cardozo J in *Ultramares Corp v Touche* 255 NY 170 (1932) at 179: the law should not impose 'liability in an indeterminate amount for an indeterminate time to an indeterminate class'.

2 This example is taken from the Canadian decision in *Seaway Hotels Ltd v Gragg (Canada) Ltd and Consumer Gas Co* (1960) 21 DLR (2d) 264. The Canadian court's decision to allow recovery for the lost custom has been doubted. *SCM (United Kingdom) Ltd v WJ Whittall & Son Ltd* [1971] 1 QB 337 at 343 per Lord Denning MR.

3 See eg *Grant Estates Ltd v Royal Bank of Scotland plc* [2012] CSOH 133 at para 71 and 76–77 per the Lord Ordinary (Hodge); *Lifestyle Equities CV v Ahmed* [2024] UKSC 17, [2025] AC 1 at paras 57–58 per Lord Leggatt.

4 Consumer Rights Act 2015, s 9. For business-to-business sales, see Sale of Goods Act 1979, s 14. While there is no equivalent in the context of the purchase of heritable property, see the National House Building Council, which effectively provides a ten-year warranty for defective construction by registered builders.

5 For an argument to this effect, see *Murphy v Brentwood District Council* [1991] 1 AC 398 (HL) at 491–492 per Lord Oliver of Aylmerton.

6 See eg *McLoughin v Jones* [2001] EWCA Civ 1743, [2002] QB 1312 at para 58 per Hale LJ.

(6) Exceptional recovery of pure economic loss?

5.9 Although the starting point of the law of negligence is no recovery for pure economic loss, the courts have forged exceptions to that rule by developing the duty of care in particular situations. Those developments, and their relationship to the duty of care generally, are not always easy to explain or understand. The remainder of this chapter discusses how the duty of care operates in respect of pure economic loss cases in the post-*Robinson*[1] landscape.

1 [2018] UKSC 4, [2018] AC 736.

ASSUMPTION OF RESPONSIBILITY: CARELESS MISSTATEMENTS

(1) The importance of assumption of responsibility

5.10 Where a pursuer claims that the defender owes them a duty not to cause pure economic loss, the UK Supreme Court has stated that the 'foundation' of such liability is the device of the 'assumption of responsibility'.[1] Negligent misstatements, or negligent performance of services, in the context where the defender has assumed responsibility to the pursuer, is the most clearly established category.

A may make a statement to B which causes B physical harm or damage to B's property: for example A tells B that it is safe to drink contaminated water. A will owe B a duty of care if it is reasonably foreseeable that B will suffer physical harm or damage to his property if A's statement is made carelessly.[2] This is an established category where, in principle, a duty of care has been held to exist.[3]

But A may make a statement to B which causes B pure economic loss. For example, A tells B that B should enter into a contract with C. Relying on A's advice, B enters into the contract with C. As a result, B loses money. Can B sue A in delict for the pure economic loss B has sustained, if A's statement was made carelessly? The answer depends on whether A owes a duty of care to B not to make careless statements which cause B pure economic loss.

1 *NRAM Ltd v Steel* [2018] UKSC 13, 2018 SC (UKSC) 141 at para 24 per Lord Wilson.

2 The equivalent of this passage in the 4th edition of this book was approved in *United Central Bakeries Ltd v Spooner Industries Ltd* [2012] CSOH 111 at para 30 per the Lord Ordinary (Hodge).

3 The question of proximity, in the sense of the control which the statement-maker has over the danger, distinguishes cases where a duty has been recognised and where it has not. For personal injury, compare *Perrett v Collins* [1999] PNLR 77 (CA) (incorrect statement certifying plane as safe and permitting it to fly created foreseeable risk of injury, so duty of care owed to injured passenger by inspector and his association) with *Sutradhar v Natural Environment Research Council* [2006] UKHL 33, [2006] PNLR 36 (incorrect statement in report that water supply in Bangladesh did not contain arsenic, defendants had no control over that water and their generic report created no duty towards those drinking that water). For property damage, see *Spooner Industries* at paras 35–40, but see *Marc Rich & Co AG V Bishop Rock Marine Co Ltd* [1996] AC 211 (HL), where a duty was denied on policy grounds.

5.11 *Hedley Byrne v Heller and Partners*[1] established the potential for a duty of care in the context of a careless misstatement made to and acted upon by the pursuer in reliance on the accuracy of the information and which caused pure economic loss.

The plaintiffs, through their bankers, asked Easipower's bankers, the defendants, whether Easipower was a respectably constituted company. Easipower's bankers replied that they were creditworthy. On reliance of this statement, the plaintiffs became Easipower's advertising agents. Easipower later went into liquidation. As a result, the plaintiffs suffered pure economic loss. The facts of the case can be shown as follows:

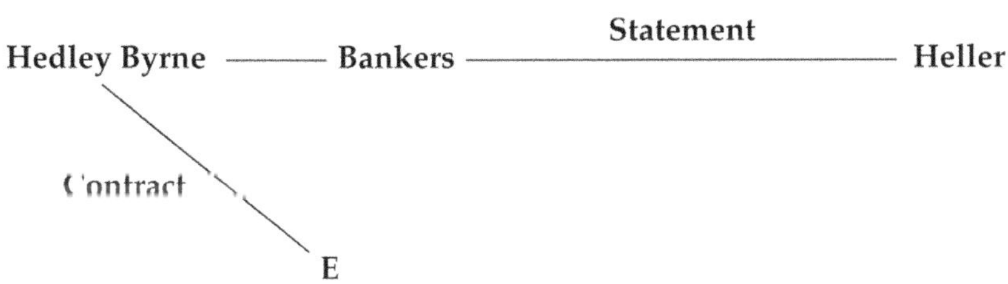

It will be clear that there was no contract between Hedley Byrne and Heller. The question was whether the plaintiffs could sue the defendants in delict. The House of Lords held that the defendants owed a duty of care to the plaintiffs if the defendants had undertaken responsibility for the accuracy of the statement and knew or ought to have known that the plaintiffs would rely on that statement. If the duty was broken as a result of the statement being made carelessly, the defendants could be liable for the plaintiffs' pure economic loss.

That duty would arise if there existed a 'special relationship' between the parties. The categories of 'special relationships' where this duty arose included not only contractual relationships (ie, where there was a contract between the parties) or fiduciary relationships (for example, principal and agent, trustee and beneficiary), but also relationships which were 'equivalent to contract'.[2] One example of this would be where the defender had voluntarily assumed responsibility for the accuracy of the statement and knew or ought to have known that the pursuer would rely on the information. As Lord Reid stated:[3]

> 'A reasonable man, knowing that he was being trusted or that his skill and judgment were being relied on, would, I think, have three courses open to him. He could keep silent or decline to give the information or advice sought: or he could give an answer with a clear qualification that he accepted no responsibility for it or that it was given without that reflection or inquiry which a careful answer would require: or he could simply answer without any such qualification. If he chooses to adopt the last course he must, I think, be held to have accepted some responsibility for his answer being given carefully, or to have accepted a relationship with the inquirer which requires him to exercise such care as the circumstances require.'

The House of Lords in *Hedley Byrne* therefore accepted that, in principle, a duty could arise where Heller assumed responsibility for Hedley Byrne's financial interests by providing a statement as to Easipower's creditworthiness which the latter foreseeably would rely upon.[4]

However, on the specific facts of the case, it was held that no duty arose because Heller's response contained a disclaimer to the effect that the information was provided 'without responsibility on the part of the bank'. That disclaimer was sufficient to avoid liability.[5] We will return to the effect of disclaimers below:[6] the importance of *Hedley Byrne* lies in its general statements as to the existence of a duty of care based on the defender's assumption of responsibility towards the pursuer.

1 [1964] AC 465 (HL). The literature on this case is immense. Its golden anniversary was commemorated with an edited collection: K Barker, R Grantham, and W Swain, *The Law of Misstatements: 50 Years on from Hedley Byrne v Heller* (Hart, 2015). See also K Barker, 'Unreliable Assumptions in the Law of Negligence' (1993) 109 *Law Quarterly Review* 46.

2 *Hedley Byrne* at 486 per Lord Reid; at 497 per Lord Morris of Borth-y-Gest; at 509 per Lord Hodson; at 528–529 per Lord Devlin.

3 *Hedley Byrne* at 486.

4 *Hedley Byrne* at 486 per Lord Reid; at 502–503 per Lord Morris of Borth-y-Gest; at 514 per Lord Hodson; at 528–529 per Lord Devlin; and at 539 per Lord Pearce. These formulations vary in minor ways.

5 *Hedley Byrne* at 493–493 per Lord Reid; at 504 per Lord Morris of Borth-y-Gest; at 511 per Lord Hodson; at 533 per Lord Devlin; and at 540 per Lord Pearce. Lords Morris (at 504) and Hodson (at 513) also would have found that, on the specific facts of the case, if a duty did arise, it was simply a duty to respond honestly.

6 See para 5.13 below.

5.12 The doctrine of assumption of responsibility plays a wide role across the law of negligence, but it is not always analysed consistently, with courts and commentators identifying different factors, or according different prominence to those factors.[1] This section will discuss the key factors seized upon by the courts as favouring, or countering, the imposition of a duty of care on the basis of an assumption of responsibility for a misstatement. The Privy Council has emphasised the objective nature of the assumption of responsibility enquiry and the relevance of three factors:[2]

(i) the purpose of the task or service and whether it is for the [pursuer]'s benefit;

(ii) the [defender]'s knowledge and whether it is or ought to be known that the [pursuer] will be relying on the [defender]'s performance of the task or service with reasonable care; and

(iii) the reasonableness of the [pursuer]'s reliance on the performance of the task or service by the [defender] with reasonable care.

It should be noted that we are only here discussing delictual aspects of a negligent misrepresentation; if such a representation induces a party to enter into a contract, then, aside from delictual damages for negligence, there may also be contractual consequences in the form of reduction.[3]

1 One excellent analysis, going beyond the economic loss context, is D Nolan, 'Assumption of Responsibility: Four Questions' (2019) 72 *Current Legal Problems* 123. For a discussion of the economic loss context specifically, by a Supreme Court Justice, see P Sales, 'Pure Economic Loss and Assumption of Responsibility' (2023) 23 *Professional Negligence* 113–118 and 122–127.

2 *JP SPC 4 v Royal Bank of Scotland* [2022] UKPC 18, [2023] AC 461 (Isle of Man) at paras [62]–[64].

3 See generally *MacQueen and Thomson: The Law of Contract in Scotland* (6th edn, 2024) at paras 5.52–5.62.

(2) The need for an objective assumption of responsibility

5.13 The hallmark of an assumption of responsibility is that the defender undertakes a task (ie, the provision of information) on behalf of the pursuer, and implicitly undertakes to perform that task carefully.

Whether or not responsibility is assumed in relation to a particular task is an objective question and is a conclusion reached regardless of the subjective intention of the defender. It is the undertaking of the task which gives rise to a duty to carry that task out carefully.[1] In assessing the existence and extent of that undertaking, 'the primary focus … must be on things said or done' by the defender in its dealings with the pursuer, in 'light of the relevant contextual scene'.[2]

The broader contextual scene may demonstrate that, objectively, the defender did not assume any responsibility towards the pursuer. This explains, for instance, why the disclaimer in *Hedley Byrne v Heller* negated an assumption of responsibility: it was a clear objective indication that the bank did not undertake any responsibility for the veracity of the information provided.[3] But it should be borne in mind that disclaimers are subject to statutory controls,[4] and a disclaimer which is struck down pursuant to those controls cannot negate an assumption of responsibility.[5] On the contrary, it has been held that the lack of a disclaimer may be a positive indicator that the defender did assume responsibility for the pursuer in relation to the task in question.[6]

Similarly, the parties may be in a contractual relationship, and that contract might make explicit provision for the allocation of risk and responsibility. That may then counteract any sense that the defender had assumed responsibility for the pursuer other than within the terms set out between them in the contract.[7] Conversely, the dynamic between the parties may be so informal and social that it would be unrealistic for an assumption of responsibility to spring forth from their interaction.[8]

The objective context also determines the scope of the assumption of responsibility: the defender may only assume responsibility for a particular task, or advice on a particular topic. For instance, if a client engages a solicitor on retainer, that creates a delictual duty of care usually co-extensive with the solicitor's contractual duties.[9] But, absent a retainer, if a solicitor offers advice on only a particular matter, they undertake no assumption of responsibility beyond what is reasonably incidental to that particular matter.[10]

1 *White v Jones* [1995] 2 AC 207 (HL) at 274 per Lord Browne-Wilkinson.
2 *Williams v Natural Life Health Foods Ltd* [1998] 1 WLR 830 (HL) at 835 per Lord Steyn.
3 See para 5.11 above. Compare also eg *Hadden v Glasgow District Council* 1986 SC 157 (OH) with *Martin v Bell-Ingram* 1986 SC 208 (IH).
4 In business-to-business contexts, see the Unfair Contract Terms Act 1977, s 16 (test of reasonableness). For business-to-consumer contexts, see now the Consumer Rights Act 2015, s 62 (test of fairness). See generally *MacQueen and Thomson: The Law of Contract in Scotland* (6th edn, 2024) at paras 8.57–8.95.
5 See eg *Smith v Eric S Bush* [1990] 1 AC 831 (HL) at 858–860 per Lord Griffiths; *Bank of Scotland v Fuller Peiser* 2002 SLT 574 (OH).
6 *Royal Bank of Scotland plc v Bannerman Johnstone Maclay* [2005] CSIH 39, 2005 1 SC 437 at para 63 per the Lord Justice-Clerk (Gill). It is submitted that this should not be a weighty consideration.
7 Compare eg *Scott Lithgow v GEC Electrical Projects* 1989 SC 412 (OH) at 426 per the Lord Ordinary (Clyde) with *Realstone Ltd v J&E Shepherd* [2008] CSOH 31 at paras 12 and 17–19 per the Lord Ordinary (Hodge).

8 In *Chaudhry v Prabhakar* [1989] 1 WLR 29 (CA), the defendant undertook to find a car for a family friend. An assumption of responsibility was conceded despite the social context, but May LJ questioned whether that concession was correctly made: at 38–39. See, more convincingly, *Burgess v Lejonvarn* [2017] EWCA Civ 254.

9 See para 11.1 below.

10 See eg *Miller v Irwin Mitchell LLP* [2024] EWCA 53, [2024] 4 WLR 27 (advice given on helpline about generalities of personal injury law did not assume responsibility to give specific practical guidance to safeguard insurance coverage).

(3) The purpose of providing the information must be its communication to the pursuer, who must be identified, or part of an identifiable group

5.14 It has been said that proximity is 'the foundation of the duty' which arises from an assumption of responsibility.[1] That is to say that, for a duty to arise by virtue of an assumption of responsibility:

> 'it is fundamental that the [defender] is assuming a responsibility to an identifiable (although not necessarily identified) person or group of persons, and not to the world at large or to a wholly indeterminate group'.[2]

If the defender is unaware of the existence of the pursuer, or unaware of the existence of the class of persons to which the pursuer belongs, then it cannot be said that the defender has assumed responsibility to the pursuer. It 'must be part of the statement's known purpose that it should be communicated and relied upon' by the pursuer.[3] In other words, the statement must be pursuer-specific: 'it must be given to the actual [pursuer] or to a member of a group, identifiable at the time the statement is made, to which the actual [pursuer] belongs'.[4]

These points were emphasised by the UK Supreme Court in *Playboy Club London Ltd v Banca Nazionale del Lavoro SpA*,[5] the facts of which are reminiscent of *Hedley Byrne*. The claimants operated a casino in London. It wished to establish that a client seeking credit was creditworthy. With the client's permission, a sister company of the casino contacted the client's bank to seek a credit reference.[6] The bank provided that reference, which turned out to be manifestly incorrect: the client did not even have an account with the bank at the time the reference was provided. The casino nevertheless extended undue credit to the client, who then absconded, owing the casino over £800,000. The UK Supreme Court held that the client's bank had not assumed responsibility to the casino in relation to the accuracy of the reference. The key point negating the existence of a duty was that the bank 'knew nothing' of the casino's involvement, and had no reason to suppose that the intermediary company was not enquiring on its own behalf.[7]

That is not to say, however, that the defender must know exactly whom the reference is for. In *Hedley Byrne v Heller*,[8] for instance, the bank which provided the reference did not know it specifically was for Hedley Byrne. But it did know that it was for a customer of the requesting bank, who was seeking assurances regarding the creditworthiness of Heller's customer in relation to an advertising contract. That was sufficient to give rise to the assumption of responsibility: Hedley Byrne were sufficiently identifiable. In *Playboy Club*, Lord Mance noted that, if the defendant bank knew that the reference was being sought on behalf of an unnamed party, a duty of care would have arisen.[9]

The important point is that the group to which the pursuer belongs must be sufficiently determined at the time when the information is provided. This will be relatively easy to establish in bipartite situations[10] and where the class of recipients is relatively small or ascertainable.[11] Contrastingly, where the information is made available to the world at large, it will be more difficult to show sufficient proximity for an assumption of responsibility to arise.[12]

1 *Playboy Club London Ltd v Banca Nazionale del Lavoro SpA* [2018] UKSC 43, [2018] 1 WLR 4041 at para 8 per Lord Sumption.
2 *Playboy Club* at para 7 per Lord Sumption.
3 *Playboy Club* at para 11 per Lord Sumption.
4 *Reeman v Department of Transport* [1997] PNLR 618 (CA) at 639 per the Lord Bingham CJ.
5 [2018] UKSC 43, [2018] 1 WLR 4041.
6 The interposition of the sister company was to attempt to secure discretion on the client's behalf, so that his bank did not know he was seeking a substantial line of credit for gambling purposes.
7 *Playboy Club* at para 16 per Lord Sumption.
8 [1964] AC 465 (HL) at 483 per Lord Reid; at 493–494 per Lord Morris of Borth-y-Gest. See para 5.11 above.
9 *Playboy Club* at para 25.
10 Even where, as in *Hedley Byrne*, the parties knowingly act through intermediaries.
11 See eg *Hagen v ICI* [2002] Pens LR 1 (QBD) (439 ex-employees of defendant sufficiently determined and identifiable group).
12 Although it will not be impossible: see eg *Patchett v Swimming Pool & Allied Trades Association Ltd* [2009] EWCA Civ 717 (statement on website that contractor had been approved potentially assumed responsibility to claimants as members of class of persons considering installation of swimming pool, but duty did not arise because of lack of foreseeable reliance); *Taberna Europe CDO II plc v Selskabet* [2016] EWCA Civ 1262, [2017] QB 633 (investor presentation had been uploaded to defendant's website to encourage investment, and claimant had been invited to consult this, but disclaimer effective to negate duty).

(4) The pursuer must use the information for the same purpose for which it was provided by the defender

5.15 As has been said: 'the statement must be purpose-specific: the statement must be made for the very purpose for which the actual [pursuer] has used it.'[1] Where the statement is provided under a retainer, or in response to a direct enquiry from or on behalf of an identified or identifiable pursuer, there usually is no issue here: the defender will be providing the statement to allow the pursuer to make an informed decision or adoption of a course of action. So, in *Hedley Byrne v Heller*, the defendant bank provided the reference as to its customer's creditworthiness so that Hedley Byrne could assess whether or not it should extend credit to that customer. That was another factor showing the 'special relationship' between the bank and Hedley Byrne.

But where there is a misalignment of purpose, that may be a strong indication that no assumption of responsibility was undertaken. *Caparo Industries v Dickman*[2] involved a claim by a shareholder of a company against that company's auditors. Prior to an annual general meeting of the company's shareholders, the defendants had been appointed to report on the company's accounts. The statutory purpose of that report was primarily to provide information to shareholders to enable them to fully participate in that general meeting. The plaintiffs were shareholders who received the defendant's report and used this as a basis to launch a takeover bid for the company, purchasing a majority of its shareholding. The report overestimated the profitability of the company, and the new majority shareholder argued that the auditors owed them a duty of care. The House of Lords denied the existence of a duty of care on the facts. There was a mismatch between the purpose for which the report was produced (to inform the body of shareholders as a whole as to the company's financial position to assist with their conduct of an imminent annual general meeting) and the purpose for which the defendant used it (as a basis for deciding whether to take over the company and to greatly increase its existing shareholding).[3] Moreover, the statement was not 'plaintiff-specific' – the report was provided to the shareholder in their capacity as an existing shareholder, not their capacity as an investor seeking to acquire further shares in the company in order to take overall control.[4] This demonstrates the interrelated nature of the factors which a court will take into account when assessing the existence, or otherwise, of an assumption of responsibility.

A further illustration of the relevance of the pursuer's purpose in using the information is *Reeman v Department of Transport*.[5] There, the plaintiffs bought a boat in a private sale on reliance on a certificate of seaworthiness that had been provided on behalf of the Department of Transport, but, on subsequent certification, the vessel failed a stability test, rendering it only valuable as scrap. The initial certificate was provided for the purpose of ensuring the vessel was safe to use on the water; it was not concerned with appraising its commercial value on the open market. Therefore, the fact that the plaintiff relied on the certificate for that latter purpose, contrary to that for which the certificate was provided, strongly indicated against the existence of a duty of care not to cause pure economic loss.[6]

1 *Reeman v Department of Transport* [1997] PNLR 618 (CA) at 640 per Lord Bingham CJ.
2 [1990] 2 AC 605 (HL). Compare with *Twomax Ltd v Dickson, McFarlane & Robinson* 1982 SC 113 (OH), which may now be decided differently.
3 See *Caparo* at 621 (Lord Bridge of Harwich), 629 (Lord Roskill) and 630–631 (Lord Oliver of Aylmerton).
4 See *Caparo* at 627 (Lord Bridge of Harwich) and 652 (Lord Oliver of Aylmerton).
5 [1997] PNLR 618 (CA).
6 See also *Seddon v Driver and Vehicle Licensing Agency* [2019] EWCA Civ 14, [2019] 1 WLR 4593 (incorrect classification of vehicle by DVLA as historic, which it later reversed, was for the purposes of licensing it for road use and establishing applicable road tax band, not a representation as to its age or value). *Seddon* and *Reeman* also involved certificates relied on by parties unknown to the relevant authorities and did not form part of an identifiable class. This again emphasises that this consideration will overlap with the identifiability of the pursuer.

(5) The defender must reasonably foresee that the pursuer would rely on the information

5.16 If the defender was not aware, and could not have foreseen, that its statement would be relied upon by the pursuer, then no duty of care will arise.[1] The test is not one of intended reliance;[2] it involves a consideration of whether it was reasonable for the pursuer to make use of the information provided by the defender without making independent enquiries.[3]

The UK Supreme Court considered this question in the appeal from the Inner House in *NRAM Ltd v Steel*.[4] Steel acted as the solicitor for clients who owned commercial units in Hamilton, the purchase of which was funded by a loan from NRAM secured against those units. In negotiating the subsequent sale of one of those units, the bank agreed to release it from its security in return for a partial loan repayment. However, when it came to securing that release, Steel emailed the band and represented that the full loan was being repaid, attaching deeds of discharge in respect of the security on all three units. The bank duly executed those deeds, rendering it unsecured in relation to the remainder of the loan.

NRAM brought a claim against Steel for negligent misrepresentation, arguing that she had assumed responsibility to carefully representing the extent of the loan repayment and the correlating extent of the securities to be discharged. The UK Supreme Court, however, accepted Steel's argument that the bank did not act reasonably in relying on her representation, and that such reliance was not foreseeable. It would have been obvious in comparing Steel's representations with the account file that total discharge was not what was contemplated. The lack of independent checks meant that the bank relied upon Steel's representation unreasonably. Correspondingly, Steel could not reasonably foresee that the bank would act solely on her representation, and no assumption of responsibility arose. Lord Wilson summarised the proposition neatly:

> 'a commercial lender about to implement an agreement with its borrower referable to its security does not act reasonably if it proceeds upon no more than a description of its terms put forward by or on behalf of the borrower.'[5]

Such reliance in an arms-length transaction would be 'presumptively inappropriate'.[6]

1 See *Hedley Byrne v Heller* [1964] AC 465 (HL) at 487 per Lord Reid; at 497 per Lord Morris of Borth-y-Gest; at 514 per Lord Hodson. Again, we see the relevant factors bleed into one another: if the defender is unaware of the pursuer's existence and/or unaware that they will be acting on the information for a divergent purpose, it is difficult to see how that reliance could nevertheless be foreseeable.
2 See *Royal Bank of Scotland plc v Bannerman Johnstone Maclay* [2005] CSIH 39, 2005 1 SC 437 at paras 47–50.
3 The cases also speak of the need for (i) the pursuer to rely on the information and (ii) for that reliance to be reasonable. But these factors post-date the initial duty, and more properly go to questions of breach or causation.
4 [2018] UKSC 13, 2018 SC (UKSC) 141.
5 *NRAM* at para 38.
6 *NRAM* at para 32.

5.17 The question is then when it would be reasonably foreseeable for the pursuer to have relied on the defender's statement or advice without obtaining independent advice. Of course, if the pursuer has specifically made an enquiry of, or commissioned advice from, the defender, it usually is clear that the pursuer will rely on that advice without further investigation.[1] Similarly, where the pursuer and defender are on opposite sides of contractual negotiations, the foreseeability of reliance is such that a duty of care will, absent a disclaimer, invariably be owed.[2]

But, where there is no request or negotiation, the situation and status of the pursuer may be a relevant factor in ascertaining reasonable foreseeability of reliance. In *Smith v Eric S Bush*,[3] the plaintiff paid a bank a fee in order to have a house she was intending to purchase valued for mortgage purposes.[4] The bank enlisted the defendant surveyors, whose valuation report did not detect severe structural issues with the chimneys. The plaintiff purchased the property on the basis of the report. When the structural issues were discovered, the cost of repairs were almost as much as the total purchase price of the house. The plaintiff sued the surveyor, contending that it had assumed responsibility to her to value the property with reasonable skill and care.[5] The House of Lords observed that, although the report was commissioned by the bank, the surveyor knew that the practice was to give intending purchasers sight of the report to inform their purchase.[6] Moreover, it was not realistic to expect the purchasers to commission independent valuation reports in respect of a 'modest' house purchase;[7] it was reasonably foreseeable that the report commissioned would be relied upon in informing that purchase. This can be contrasted with cases where the property was being purchased not for residential purposes, but for development and resale at profit[8] or to provide a rental income.[9]

Beyond the surveyor context, the claimant's situation was crucial to the foreseeability of reliance in *McClean v Thornhill*.[10] The defendant was a barrister who was instructed to report on the tax benefits which would follow from investment in particular schemes. Before investing, investors had to affirm that they sought and solely relied upon independent advice. When the tax benefits mooted in the reports failed to materialise, the investors sued the defendant as author of the report. The express undertaking as to independent advice, and the regulatory context which required investors to take independent advice meant that reliance on the barrister's report was not reasonably foreseeable.[11] Moreover:[12]

> 'it was reasonably to be expected that any person with sufficient wealth and potential tax liabilities to be a potential investor in a tax avoidance scheme of this kind, would seek and obtain specialist accountancy and/or taxation advice on a regular basis, and would thereby have easy and convenient access to independent advice'.

1 As, of course, occurred in *Hedley Byrne*. See also eg *Lennon v Commissioner of Police for the Metropolis* [2004] EWCA Civ 130, [2004] 1 WLR 2594. The fact the pursuer has requested the information or advice also should make the pursuer-specific and purpose-specific nature of the defender's response clear.

2 See *Cramaso LLP v Viscount Reidhaven's Trustees* [2014] UKSC 9, 2014 SC (UKSC) 121 at paras 38–42 per Lord Hodge. See also the decision to grant proof before answer in *Biffa Waste Services Ltd v The Scottish Ministers* [2025] CSOH 9.

3 [1990] 1 AC 831 (HL).

4 Conveyancing practice differs in Scotland: here, the *seller* of the property is obliged to commission a home report: Housing (Scotland) Act 2006, Part 3. Circumventing any difficulty of showing an assumption of responsibility by the surveyor to the ultimate purchaser in such circumstances, secondary legislation provides a right of damages to a purchaser who suffers material loss as a result of a careless home report: Housing (Scotland) Act 2006 (Consequential Provisions) Order 2008 (SI 2008/1889), Article 3.

5 In *Smith v Eric S Bush*, Lord Griffiths at 862 expressly disavowed use of an assumption of responsibility analysis, but Lords Templeman (at 845–848) and Jauncey of Tullichettle (at 866–873) employed the concept.

6 *Smith v Eric S Bush* at 847 per Lord Templeman; at 865 per Lord Griffiths; and at 871 per Lord Jauncey of Tullichettle. It should be noted that the Appellate Committee also heard the conjoined appeal in *Harris v Wyre Forest District Council*, where the loan was provided by the local authority who had an in-house surveyor. There was no evidence that in such arrangements the valuation reports were shown to intending purchasers. Nevertheless, the Appellate Committee found that a duty of care nevertheless was

owed to the purchasers in these circumstances: at 844 per Lord Templeman; at 865 per Lord Griffiths; and at 875 per Lord Jauncey of Tullichettle (who was more doubtful).

7 See *Smith v Eric S Bush* at 865 per Lord Griffiths and 870–872 per Lord Jauncey of Tullichettle. The Appellate Committee's reasoning on the unreasonableness of the attempted disclaimer also overlaps with this point: see at 852–853 per Lord Templeman and 858 per Lord Griffiths.

8 *Wilson v DM Hall & Sons* [2005] PNLR 22 (OH) at paras 143–146.

9 *Scullion v Bank of Scotland* [2011] EWCA Civ 693, [2011] 1 WLR 3212 at paras 48–54.

10 [2023] EWCA Civ 466, [2023] 1 WLR 3802.

11 *McClean* at paras 98–105.

12 *McClean* at para 104 per Simler LJ.

ASSUMPTION OF RESPONSIBILITY: CARELESS PERFORMANCE OF SERVICES

(1) The creation of the 'extended *Hedley Byrne*' principle

5.18 The *Hedley Byrne v Heller* duty of care was extended beyond statements and advice by the House of Lords in the case of *Henderson v Merrett Syndicates*.[1] Actions for damages were brought by Lloyd's 'names' against Lloyd's members' agents and managing agents of syndicates. Under contracts with their members' agents, the names gave the agents the exclusive right to undertake risks and reinsurance on their behalf. This was done directly through the members' agents or indirectly by the members' agents delegating the tasks to managing agents through a sub-agency contract. This can be illustrated as follows:

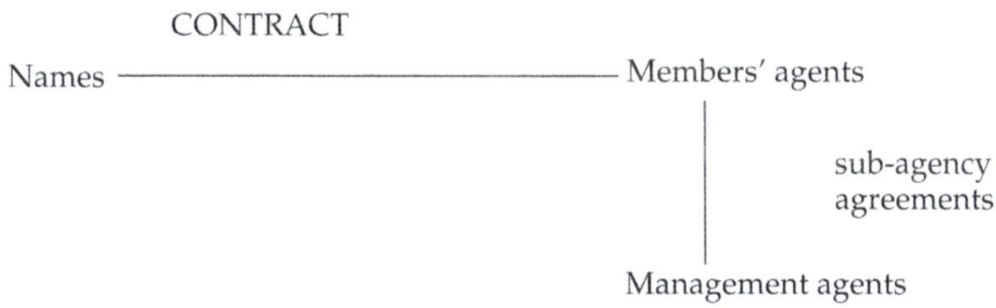

The 'names' alleged that they had suffered losses as a result of the negligence of the agents: the agent's management exposed the syndicate to excessive risks and liabilities. The obvious remedy was for the names to sue the members' agents for breach of contract. Unfortunately, this action was time-barred by rules of limitation. So, an action against them and the management agents could lie only in tort/delict. The question before the House of Lords was whether the management agents and the members' agents owed a duty of care to the names. Their Lordships held that they did.

Lord Goff of Chieveley maintained that a duty of care arises to prevent the plaintiff sustaining pure economic loss when the defendant has voluntarily assumed responsibility for the economic interests of the plaintiff with the knowledge that the plaintiff is relying on the defendant's expertise. This assumption of responsibility covers the provision of services as well as information; careless omissions as well as careless actions.[2] This has become known as the 'extended *Hedley Byrne* principle'.[3]

1 [1995] 2 AC 145 (HL).
2 *Henderson* at 180.
3 The term originated in *Williams v Natural Life Health Foods Ltd* [1998] 1 WLR 830 (HL) at 834–835 per Lord Steyn.

5.19 However, two House of Lords decisions falling either side of *Henderson v Merrett* potentially stretch the assumption of responsibility concept in a way which muddies understanding. *Spring v Guardian Assurance*,[1] which predated *Henderson*, demonstrates the malleability of the concept of reliance. The plaintiff's prospective employers asked his former employer for a reference. Regulatory rules which applied to both firms obliged the prospective employer to seek a reference and obliged the former employer to respond to that reference request. The plaintiff did not at any point ask his former employer to provide a reference. The reference which was provided was unfavourable, and the plaintiff did not secure employment. The plaintiff sued his former employer, including for negligence. The House of Lords held that a duty of care was owed in the circumstances, Lord Goff of Chieveley analysed the case as involving an assumption of responsibility.[2] The ex-employer had special information, and the purpose of providing that information was not only to assist the prospective employer, but also (it is said) the subject of the reference. Lord Goff thought it 'plain' that the employee relied upon the ex-employer 'to exercise due skill and care in the preparation of the reference' before submission to the prospective employer. But, on the facts, there was no actual reliance by the ex-employee: at the very most, it could be said that he applied for another job in a regulated industry where it was highly likely that prospective employers would ask his ex-employers for a reference. He simply would have to cross his fingers that the reference would be a positive one. It has been suggested that it may be more appropriate to see this as a case of 'dependence' as opposed to reliance.

White v Jones,[3] decided subsequent to *Henderson*, will be discussed further in the context of professional negligence.[4] Solicitors whose negligent failure to implement correctly the instructions of a testator were held to have 'assumed responsibility' to potential beneficiaries who did not inherit as a consequence. It will be noted that the task undertaken by the solicitor was for the benefit of the testator, not the beneficiaries. However, it is important to note that Lord Goff's speech did not proceed on the basis that the solicitor had assumed responsibility to the beneficiaries. The solicitor assumed responsibility towards the testator to draw up the will in accordance with his wishes with due skill and care. The intended beneficiaries had no remedy elsewhere, and Lord Goff thought that justice required finding that the law deemed that assumption of responsibility to extend to the beneficiaries.[5] In essence, the case involves a fictional assumption of responsibility imposed for policy reasons, and only provides a basis for analogy where there is a gap in the law that prevents a third party from having a remedy.

1 [1995] 2 AC 296 (HL).
2 *Spring* at 317–322.
3 [1995] 2 AC 207 (HL).
4 See paras 11.13–11.14 below.
5 *White v Jones* at 267–279.

(2) Applying the 'extended *Hedley Byrne*' principle

5.20 It now is useful to consider the application of the 'extended *Hedley Byrne*' principle to cases involving the negligent performance of services.

In *D v Victim Support Scotland*,[1] the defender was a charity which made an application to the Criminal Injuries Compensation Board on behalf of the pursuer. The charity did not explore the possibility of claiming in respect of lost earnings, with the result that the award which the CICB made to the pursuer was significantly less than it could have been. The defender had agreed to act as the pursuer's representative in making the application, holding itself out as an agency with expertise in making such applications with trained staff for that purpose. Alternative agencies were available to assist with making such claims, but the defender's taking on that service and making the incorrect application closed down the availability of those alternatives. Moreover, the charity did not pass on any further information about the CIC scheme, so the pursuer's reliance on their service was obvious. Sheriff Braid accordingly held that the defender had clearly assumed responsibility to the pursuer.[2] This is obviously correct: there was a clear objective undertaking to assess the pursuer's eligibility and make an application on his behalf. This undertaking was pursuer-specific, purpose-specific, and which evidently would be relied upon by the pursuer, who was in a position of vulnerability and had not been supplied information about the scheme.

The importance of the services rendered being pursuer-specific and person-specific can also be seen in *West Bromwich Albion v El-Safty*.[3] Michael Appleton signed for West Bromwich Albion FC, but suffered a knee injury in training. He was sent to the defendant, a private surgeon, for assessment. The defendant negligently recommended aggressive surgical treatment. Lesser intervention could have seen Appleton return by the end of the season; but his career was effectively ended post-surgery. Clearly, the surgeon owed Appleton a duty of care, which had been breached.[4] But his club had suffered pure economic loss in the form of the lost value of Appleton to their playing squad and the cost of having to replace him. The Court of Appeal denied that the surgeon owed the club a duty of care. The surgeon's concern was exclusively with Appleton's well-being, and the purpose of the surgeon's intervention was medical, not financial.[5] Moreover, we could also say that, as the paramount concern of the surgeon was the best interests of his patients, it would not be reasonably foreseeable for the club to have relied on his medical intervention in relation to its financial circumstances. Here we can see a failed attempt to deploy an assumption of responsibility to circumvent the rule prohibiting recovery of so-called secondary economic losses.

Banks owe their customers a duty to execute clear and unambiguous instructions, with a duty of skill and care arising only where it is faced with unclear instructions.[6] In *JP SPC 4 v Royal Bank of Scotland*,[7] the question for the Privy Council was whether the bank owed any duty to a third party who suffered loss as a result of frauds perpetrated on an account of one of the bank's customers. Lords Hamblen and Burrows held that no assumption of responsibility arose on the facts. The bank's undertaking was solely towards its customer, the purpose of the service provided by the bank in no way involved providing a benefit to third parties, and there was no evidence that the bank should have been aware that faith was being placed in them by the third party to detect fraudulent activity.[8]

The question of reliance may also arise in service cases, with the courts seemingly taking a more flexible approach than in misstatement cases. In *Coulter v Anderson, Anderson and Brown LLP*,[9] the pursuer was dismissed from his position as company director. This triggered a provision requiring the mandatory sale of his company shares to other shareholders. The defenders were appointed as auditors to value those shares; the pursuer contended that the figure arrived at by the defender considerably undervalued his shares. The Lord Ordinary (Braid) opined that reliance was not a necessary component of the claim, as it was not one relating to negligent misstatement. However, he was willing to find reliance, if necessary, in the fact that the pursuer had, when being appointed director, accepted the mandatory share mechanism.[10] The point could instead be put as one of 'dependence': the pursuer had no choice as to whether or not he was to sell his shares, and was wholly dependent on the defenders accurately valuing his shares to secure their market worth. The defenders knew the purpose for which the valuation was requested and knew the identity of the pursuer, so an assumption of responsibility had been properly pled on the facts.[11] However, a limitation clause in the contract between the defenders and the instructing company was highly relevant (and, on the facts of this case, determinative) in limiting the scope of the defender's liability to the pursuer.[12]

1 [2017] SC EDIN 85, 2018 SLT (Sh Ct) 91.
2 *D v Victim Support Scotland* at para 59–61.
3 [2006] EWCA Civ 1299.
4 See *Appleton v El-Safty* [2007] EWHC 631 (QB).
5 [2006] EWCA Civ 1299 at paras 58 and 81.
6 *Philipp v Barclays Bank UK Plc* [2023] UKSC 25, [2024] AC 346.
7 [2022] UKPC 18, [2023] AC 461 (Isle of Man).
8 *JP SPC 4* at paras 65–68 and 79. See also *Commissioners of Customs and Excise v Barclays Bank* [2006] UKHL 28 [2007] 1 AC 181 (no assumption of responsibility by bank towards customer's creditor when it failed to implement a freezing injunction, permitting removal of funds from that customer's account).
9 [2025] CSOH 32.
10 *Coulter* at para 24–25.
11 *Coulter* at para 26.
12 *Coulter* at paras 32–34 and 39.

DEFECTIVE PERFORMANCE BY BUILDERS AND SUBCONTRACTORS

5.21 When a buyer purchases property, the cost of remedying a defect which is discovered before it causes injury to person or other property is characterised as pure economic loss.[1] The contract of sale may provide a remedy in the case of goods,[2] but this is less likely in the case of heritable property such as land or a building.[3] And, absent an assumption of responsibility, such loss also is not recoverable in delict.[4]

As we have seen, a surveyor may be liable in the law of delict if, exercising reasonable skill and care, they ought to have detected the defect and observed it in a report it knew would be made available to the purchaser.[5] Similarly, if an architect or other professional has certified that the property is sound, there may be an assumption of responsibility towards the ultimate purchaser.[6]

What of the situation where the inherently defective fixture or product has been supplied by a sub-contractor? Previous editions of this book devoted substantial attention to the case of *Junior Books Ltd v Veitchi Co Ltd*.[7] The pursuers entered into a contract with Ogilvie (Builders) Ltd (the main contractor) for the construction of a factory. The pursuers' architects apparently nominated Veitchi, a floor specialist, to lay a floor in the factory. In other words, Veitchi was a nominated sub-contractor. However, Veitchi's contract to lay the floor was with the main contractor, not Junior Books. The floor laid was seriously defective and had to be replaced by the pursuers. There was no averment that the floor laid was dangerous so as to be likely to cause physical harm to any persons in the factory or any damage to the pursuers' property. The pursuers sought damages from the defenders for the cost of replacing the floor.

The House of Lords in *Junior Books* were able to find an assumption of responsibility.[8] But it frequently is said that the case was a decision on its own special facts,[9] which is usually a polite way of saying that the case should be ignored. The last Scottish case to consider its reasoning in detail was decided in 1990,[10] and since then senior Scottish judges have shown no great love for the case.[11] Much is made about the proximity brought about by the nomination of the sub-contractor, but one of the counsel involved in the case has since stated that such nomination did not, in fact, take place.[12]

Apex authority has closed down Professor Thomson's ingenious attempt to rationalise the case as an extension of inducement of breach of contract[13] or causing loss by unlawful means.[14] Moreover, the concept of a collateral warranty now has been developed, which provides a contractual mechanism for a purchaser or other third party to bring a claim against a sub-contractor.[15]

1 For a case demonstrating the difference between an inherent defect, and subsequent damage to the pursuer's property, see *Halvorson v Persimmon Homes Limited* [2018] SC EDIN 40.

2 If the pursuer has a contract with the seller, then a term as to quality or fitness for purpose will be implied by the Consumer Rights Act 2015, s 9 (business-to-consumer); Sale of Goods Act 1979, s 14 (business-to-business). No such term is implied in a private, consumer-to-consumer sale.

3 Scots property law does not imply any term as to the condition of the heritable property being transferred. Most residential purchases will use the Scottish Standard Clauses as a basis for the missives of sale. Clauses 2–5 and 8 contain warranties on specific matters (eg a working central heating system). See https://www.lawscot.org.uk/media/dggc12pg/1-scottish-standard-clauses-edition-6-extract-pdf-version.pdf (accessed 16 May 2025).

4 *Murphy v Brentwood District Council* [1991] 1 AC 398 (HL); *URS Corporation Ltd v BDW Trading Ltd* [2025] UKSC 21 at para 27. In limited cases, there may also be statutory liability: Building Safety Act 2022, ss 148 and 149.

5 See above, para 5.17.

6 Compare *McGhee v Alcorn & Friel* [2016] PNLR 25 (High Court of Ireland); *Stevenson v A&J Stephen (Builders) Ltd* 1996 SLT 140 (OH); and *Strathford East Kilbride Ltd v HLM Design Ltd* 1999 SLT 121 (OH).

7 1982 SC (HL) 244. See the 6th edition of this book at paras 4.22–4.24, and see also JM Thomson, 'A Prophet Not Rejected in His Own Land' (1994) 110 *Law Quarterly Review* 361.

8 Ibid at 277 per Lord Roskill.

9 See eg *D&F Estates v Church Commissioners for England* [1989] AC 177 at 202 per Lord Bridge of Harwich, who describes features of *Junior Books* as 'unique' three times in one paragraph.

10 *Parkhead Housing Association Ltd v Phoenix Preservation Ltd* 1990 SLT 812 (OH).

11 See eg *Landcatch Limited v The International Oil Pollution Compensation Fund* [1998] ECC 314 at para 122 per Lord Gill; *Realstone Ltd v J&E Shepherd* [2008] CSOH 31 at para 22 per Lord Hodge.

12 A Rodger, 'Some Reflections on *Junior Books*' in P Birks (ed) *The Frontiers of Liability: Volume 2* (1994) at 64–70.

13 See paras 2.9–2.10, above. It is now clear that this delict requires a positive intention to induce a breach of contract and is not engaged by conduct which merely foreseeably interferes with the performance of a contract.

14 See para 2.11–2.12, above. This delict requires an intention to restrict the third party's freedom to deal with the pursuer, which would not be met by careless performance of a subcontract which causes a ripple effect on the primary contract.

15 Of course, principal contractors have to agree to engage sub-contractors on terms which include such a warranty, and sub-contractors have to agree to be bound by them. See eg *British Overseas Bank Nominees Ltd v Stewart Milne Group Ltd* [2019] CSIH 47, 2020 SC 24.

CHAPTER 6

Public Authorities

INTRODUCTION

6.1 This chapter considers the question of when a public authority will owe a citizen a duty of care to prevent harm. There is no fixed definition of a public authority for our purposes: it embraces both Westminster and Scottish governments and their departments and agencies; local authorities; the emergency services; road authorities; and other bodies. Such authorities often exercise special statutory powers to fulfil specific public duties but may also enjoy common law powers. The range of duties fulfilled by such authorities captures the breadth of the modern welfare state: from road safety, to social services, to housing, to regulation, to the defence of the realm.

A citizen who is injured by a public authority may have several routes for compensation. If the public authority's conduct has violated a Convention right of the pursuer's, then they may bring a claim against the public authority seeking 'just satisfaction'.[1] Such claims are a matter of public, not private law, and are not discussed in this book.[2] If a public official has intentionally harmed the pursuer, then the ordinary principles of intentional wrongdoing will apply. In that context, we have seen that sometimes a special defence of 'justification' will apply to public officers, but, that aside, the general principles explored in Chapters 1 and 2 apply.

1 The 'Convention rights' are contained in Sch 1 to the Human Rights Act 1998, and judicial remedies are provided for by s 8. On the calculation of just satisfaction, and the rejection of any analogy with delictual damages, see eg *R (Faulkner) v Secretary of State for Justice* [2013] UKSC 23, [2013] 2 AC 254 at paras 24–40 and *Boyle v Greater Glasgow and Clyde Health Board* [2021] SC GLA 62 at paras 135–137.

2 See generally Lord Reed and J Murdoch, *Human Rights in Scotland* (4th edn, Bloomsbury Professional, 2017).

6.2 It is perhaps a matter of relief that intentional cases of wrongdoing by public authorities are rare. Allegations of negligent conduct arise much more regularly. If the public authority is under a statutory duty, and it can be demonstrated that Parliament intended the statute to be civilly actionable, and the damage and the pursuer falls within the protective scope of the statute, then an action for breach of statutory duty may be brought.[1] But far more common are actions based on common law duties of care, which is the concern of this chapter.[2]

The UK Supreme Court, in a series of recent cases, have emphasised that, in general, no special considerations apply, and public authorities will be liable in much the same circumstances as any other defender. That may legitimately prompt the question of why this book still has a separate chapter considering the liability of public authorities in negligence.

A partial answer is that the facts of such cases often present two specific fact patterns, and consideration of the public authority cases permits us to examine how the law of negligence deals with those fact patterns in general. These involve two general principles: the first being that we generally do not owe each other a duty to prevent injuries caused by third parties; the second being that we generally do not owe each other a duty to confer a benefit upon the other.

The first fact pattern is where A claims that B is liable for harm caused by C, a third party. Much of the apparatus of the modern state has a protective function, and where it fails to protect the pursuer from harm from a fellow citizen, it is natural for the pursuer to feel entitled to look to the state for compensation. But, as we shall see, the law only imposes a duty to protect the pursuer from injuries caused by a third party in limited circumstances.

The second fact pattern is where A contends that it has been injured by B's failure to confer a benefit, or, in other words, by B's omission in respect of A. The level of resources enjoyed by the state, combined with the sheer expanse of the modern welfare state, means that it is often well-situated to make its citizens better off. Essential state services – the police and the fire service, to take two obvious examples – exist to benefit the public. If they do not take action, and the pursuer is injured, then, again, the pursuer may rightly feel aggrieved. But the general position, as we shall see, is that the law of delict does not require us to improve the lives of others, even when they are evidently struggling. In other words, the law of delict does not usually require us to be good Samaritans: we will consider the limited exceptions to that principle in this chapter.

1 See E Reid, *The Law of Delict in Scotland* (2022), Chapter 24.
2 See also E Reid, *The Law of Delict in Scotland* (2022), Chapters 7 and 9; D Fairgrieve and D Squires, *The Negligence Liability of Public Authorities* (2nd edn, OUP, 2019).

THE EVOLVING APPROACH: A SUMMARY

6.3 The application of the law of negligence to public authorities has evolved considerably over the last few decades. In perhaps overly simplistic terms, three (to an extent overlapping) periods may be identified. The first period was typified by the frequent denial that public authorities owed citizens a duty of care. While a lack of proximity featured in the reasoning behind these decisions, the courts often relied on policy reasons (eg the fear that the imposition of liability would result in defensive practices carried out not for the public good but in order to avoid litigation; the resource burden created by the imposition of liability; the risk of undermining the newly-blossoming mechanism of judicial review) to deny the existence of a duty of care.[1] Such decisions coincided with the period where policy played a prominent role in the test for finding a duty of care, or where it was supposed that policy played such a role.[2] At various points during this period, it could appear that public authorities enjoyed a blanket common law immunity, protecting them from suit where they had acted, or omitted to act, negligently.

The second period coincided with the coming into force of the Human Rights Act 1998. Under its influence,[3] courts were initially wary of denying claims based on a blanket common law immunity, but instead considered whether it would be fair, just, and reasonable to impose a duty in the circumstances of the case.[4] That question was often overlaid, not entirely happily, with arguments based on the newly incorporated Convention rights.

1 See eg *Hill v Chief Constable of West Yorkshire* [1989] AC 53 (HL) and *X (Minors) v Bedfordshire County Council* [1995] 2 AC 633 (HL).

2 Eg the second limb of the test in *Anns v Merton London Borough Council* [1978] AC 728 (HL) and the 'fair just and reasonable' component of *Caparo Industries v Dickman* [1990] 2 AC 605 (HL).

3 Particularly the decision of the European Court of Human Rights in *Osman v United Kingdom* (2000) 29 EHRR 245, subsequently tempered in *Z v United Kingdom* (2002) 34 EHRR 3.

4 For cases imposing a duty, see eg *Barrett v Enfield London Borough Council* [2001] 2 AC 550 (HL) and *Phelps v Hillingdon London Borough Council* [2001] 2 AC 619 (HL). For cases denying a duty, see eg *D v East Berkshire Community Health NHS Trust* [2005] UKHL 23, [2005] 2 AC 373 and *Van Colle v Chief Constable of Hertfordshire* [2008] UKHL 50, [2009] 1 AC 225.

6.4 We will take the third, and present, period to start[1] from in *Robinson v Chief Constable of West Yorkshire Police*.[2] This clarified that:[3]

> 'public authorities are generally under a duty of care to avoid causing actionable harm in situations where a duty of care would arise under ordinary principles of the law of negligence, unless the law provides otherwise'.

Subsequently, in *GN v Poole*, Lord Reed expanded on the consequences of his judgment in *Robinson* for public authority liability, explaining that:[4]

> '(1) … public authorities may owe a duty of care in circumstances where the principles applicable to private individuals would impose such a duty, unless such a duty would be inconsistent with, and is therefore excluded by, the legislation from which their powers or duties are derived;
>
> (2) … public authorities do not owe a duty of care at common law merely because they have statutory powers or duties, even if, by exercising

their statutory functions, they could prevent a person from suffering harm; and

(3) … public authorities can come under a common law duty to protect from harm in circumstances where the principles applicable to private individuals or bodies would impose such a duty, as for example where the authority has created the source of danger or has assumed a responsibility to protect the claimant from harm, unless the imposition of such a duty would be inconsistent with the relevant legislation.'

Adoption of this framework may require the reanalysis, or even reconsideration, of previous decisions.[5]

In broad terms, we can say that a public authority will owe a duty of care if it has acted positively in creating a dangerous situation, or making a dangerous situation worse. On the other hand, there is generally no duty on a public authority to confer a benefit (eg, in the form of, rescue or intervention) unless it has assumed responsibility to the pursuer, or has a high degree of control over the dangerous situation and specific harm to the pursuer is reasonably foreseeable. Non-fulfilment of a statutory duty, or careless exercise of a statutory power, will not, without more, give rise to a duty of care.[6]

The framework set out in *Robinson* and *GN v Poole* promptly was adopted by the Inner House as representing the law of Scotland.[7] Before exploring it further, we should consider situations where statute or the wider constitutional context may deny a claim in negligence.

1 Foundations of the framework were laid down in *Gorringe v Calderdale Metropolitan Borough Council* [2004] UKHL 15, [2004] 1 WLR 1057 and *Michael v Chief Constable of South Wales* [2015] UKSC 2, [2015] AC 1732.
2 [2018] UKSC 4, [2018] AC 736.
3 *Robinson* at para 33 per Lord Reed.
4 [2019] UKSC 25, [2020] AC 780 at para 65.
5 *GN v Poole* at para 34.
6 See eg *Bonthrone v Secretary of State for Scotland* 1987 SLT 34 (OH) at 40–41; *Gorringe* at paras 23 and 32 per Lord Hoffmann; at para 71 per Lord Scott of Foscotte; and at paras 90–91 per Lord Rodger of Earlsferry.
7 *Adiukwu v Secretary of State for the Home Department* [2020] CSIH 47, 2021 SC 38 at paras 7–9 per the Lord Justice Clerk (Lady Dorrian); at para 52 per Lord Glennie; and at para 72 per Lord Woolman.

SITUATIONS WHERE NEGLIGENCE CLAIM PRECLUDED

6.5 As explicitly stated by Lord Reed in *Robinson* and *Poole* in the above quotations, a duty of care will not be owed by a public authority where this is excluded by legislation. Such exclusion may be express, such as where an immunity is conferred on a specific public authority in respect of its negligence. But examples are rare.[1] More commonly, there may be no express exclusion, but there may be a statutory basis for arguing that a common law duty would be inconsistent with the powers conferred on the authority, with the effect that the duty therefore is implicitly excluded by statute.[2] This often is treated as part of the 'fair, just and reasonable' consideration which arises where a novel duty is alleged: it will not be just or reasonable to impose a duty which undermines or cuts across a statutory regime.[3] It is, however, a question of degree and a matter of interpretation where the statute does not expressly exclude liability for damages in the event of negligence.

1 See eg Financial Services and Markets Act 2000, Schedule 1ZA, para 25 (Financial Conduct Authority and its officers not liable in damages for negligence in course of discharge of its functions); Legal Profession and Legal Aid (Scotland) Act 2007, s 44 (immunity of Scottish Legal Complaints Commission).

2 Compare *D v East Berkshire Community Health NHS Trust* [2005] UKHL 23, [2005] 2 AC 373 (duty allegedly owed by doctors to parents suspected of abusing children would conflict with statutory duty to act in child's best interests) and *Jain v Trent Strategic Health Authority* [2009] UKHL 4; [2009] 1 AC 853 (alleged duty to protect nursing home owner's economic interests when conducting investigation would conflict with regulator's statutory duty to protect nursing home residents) with *Biffa Waste Services Ltd v Scottish Ministers* [2025] CSOH 9 (no apparent conflict between alleged duty and statute requiring Scottish Ministers to seek statutory exclusion of goods from UK internal market principles).

3 See eg *Mitchell v Glasgow City Council* [2009] UKHL 21, 2009 SC (HL) 21 at para 63 per Lord Rodger of Earlsferry; *Aitken v Scottish Ambulance Service* [2011] CSOH 49, 2011 SLT 822 at paras 53–55 and 66–69. Concerns that a novel duty may conflict with the statutory context arise outside of the public authority context: see eg *Santander UK Ltd v CCP Graduate School Ltd* [2025] EWHC 667 (KB) at paras 48–49.

6.6 Secondly, a duty will not arise where the subject matter of the claim would put its adjudication beyond the constitutional competence of the courts. This often is referred to as a situation where the claim is 'non-justiciable', either because adjudication would offend against the separation of powers, or where there are no appropriate standards to adjudicate the claim.[1] Non-justiciability is a principle of judicial restraint which applies where determination of a claim places the court in uncomfortable territory. 'Non-justiciable decisions are thus policy decisions which involve the balancing of competing policy interests where typically financial, economic, social or political considerations are to the fore.'[2] It is inappropriate for the civil courts to adjudicate on how a public authority should spend its budget, especially given that such decisions will have ramifications far beyond the parties before the court.[3] If a citizen argues that a decision on resource allocation has caused her injury, that dispute is non-justiciable in private law.[4] The formulation of a defective policy (as opposed to the defective implementation of a policy) provides no remedy in negligence if it results in injury.[5] It also is beyond the province of judicial decision-making to determine, for instance, what is reasonable decision making in the heat of combat on a battlefield.[6] Nevertheless, such situations of outright non-justiciability are rare; but similar arguments will often be deployed to argue that the recognition of a duty in a novel case would not be 'fair, just, and reasonable'.[7]

1 On justiciability generally, see *Shergill v Khaira* [2014] UKSC 33, [2015] AC 359 especially at para 37–44. The leading case on its application to the law of negligence remains *Phelps v Hillingdon London Borough Council* [2001] 2 AC 619 (HL). This emphasised that the fact a discretionary decision was at play did not automatically render the case non-justiciable. *Phelps* was not cited in *Paton v Scottish Ministers* [2019] SAC (Civ) 31, which perhaps focused too much on the discretionary nature of the decision at issue.

2 *Santander Ltd Plc v Keeper of the Registers of Scotland* [2013] CSOH 24, 2013 SLT 362 at para 71 per the Lord Ordinary (Boyd of Duncansby).

3 See eg *Marcic v Thames Water Utilities Ltd* [2003] UKHL 66, [2004] 2 AC 42 at paras 63–64 per Lord Hoffmann.

4 See eg *Ryder v Highland Council* [2013] CSOH 95, 2013 SLT 847 at paras 51–52 (driver killed on icy patch of road; roads authority did not provide for 24-hour treatment of road in winter. Whether decision not to allocate sufficient resources was negligent was not one that the court was 'fit to determine').

5 On this distinction, see *Dorset Yacht v Home Office* [1970] AC 1004 (HL) at 1067H–1069B per Lord Diplock. See also eg *Miller v Greater Glasgow NHS Board* [2010] CSIH 40, 2011 SLT 131 at paras 40–41 (argument that hand-washing policy not followed by hospital was an issue of implementation which was justiciable; it was not an attack on the formulation of the policy itself).

6 *Smith v Ministry of Defence* [2013] UKSC 41, [2014] AC 52.

7 See eg *A v Essex County Council* [2003] EWCA Civ 1848, [2004] 1 WLR 1881 at para 33; *Smith* at para 83. The two questions are, however, analytically distinct, and the court should deal with the justiciability objection before turning to the existence of the duty of care.

CREATION OR EXACERBATION OF DANGER: DUTY OWED

6.7 It is now clearly accepted that, as with a private party, a public authority will owe a duty of care to prevent reasonably foreseeable physical injury where it has created the danger, or where it increases the danger posed by an already-dangerous situation. In other words, has the intervention by the public authority made matters worse? In this regard:

> 'the relevant comparison is with what would have happened if the [authority] had done nothing at all and had never embarked on the activity which has given rise to the claim … it is only if carrying out the activity makes another person worse off than if the activity had not been undertaken that liability can arise'.[1]

This is neatly illustrated by the facts of *Robinson*.[2] During an attempt to arrest a suspect, two officers physically apprehended him on a busy street. The three men struggled, and knocked over a passing elderly pedestrian, falling on top of her. She sued the Chief Constable in negligence, who denied that a duty of care was owed to her as the injury occurred in the midst of a police operation. The UK Supreme Court rejected that argument. It characterised the case as involving the creation of danger: the act of apprehending the suspect in a busy street created a reasonably foreseeable risk that a passing pedestrian could be physically injured.[3] A duty was therefore owed to Mrs Robinson on the basis that it was reasonably foreseeable that she could be harmed by the officer's conduct; the same basis on which she would have been owed a duty by a private citizen.[4] Had the police not intervened to arrest the suspect, the claimant would not have been injured.

On this basis, the driver of an emergency vehicle will owe the same duty to take reasonable care to prevent reasonably foreseeable personal injury as a normal driver.[5] A carelessly-driven police car constitutes a danger of the driving officer's making.[6] Similarly, the police were held to have created a danger when they allowed a probationary officer access to a revolver, which he later used off-duty to shoot his girlfriend and a suspected romantic partner.[7] This gave rise to a duty of care, owed to the public, to take reasonable care to ensure that officers with access to dangerous weapons are fit and proper persons to have such access.[8] A negligently-conducted social services investigation, which leads to a conclusion that the child should be placed with an abusive parent, also may fall into this category of case,[9] but a mere dilatory investigation that reaches no conclusion, or no harmful conclusion, cannot be characterised as a dangerous positive act.[10]

This principle also means that a public authority may be liable for careless misstatements on the same grounds on which a private may be held to assume a duty of care to take care to provide accurate information. Cases where it is alleged a public authority has caused pure economic loss will thus be analysed in much the same way as we have seen in Chapter Five; the only difference is that questions of justiciability and statutory coherence may be more prominent where a public authority is said to owe a duty not to negligently inflict pure economic loss.[11]

1 *Tindall v Chief Constable of Thames Valley Police* [2024] UKSC 33 at para 44(iii) per Lords Leggatt and Borrows. This case is discussed further below at para 6.9.
2 [2018] UKSC 4, [2018] AC 736.
3 *Robinson* at paras 71–73.
4 *Robinson* was followed in Scotland in *Gilchrist v Chief Constable Police Service of Scotland* [2022] SC EDIN 32, where it was held that police officers did not create any danger when an NHS clinical support worker was injured when a suspect was being restrained in a hospital emergency department. It is unclear why the pursuer did not instead sue her employers.
5 *Gilfillan v Barbour* 2003 SLT 1127 (OH). The existence of this duty was not contested, but Lord Reed (then a Lord Ordinary) noted that the standard of care owed by a police driver may not necessarily be that owed by a non-service driver: see paras 29–31 and 36–38.
6 The same holds true for fire engines (eg *Ward v London County Council* [1938] 2 All ER 341 (KBD)) and ambulances (eg *Griffin v Mersey Regional Ambulance* [1998] PIQR P34 (CA)).
7 *Hartwell v Attorney General of the British Virgin Islands* [2004] UKPC 12, [2004] 1 WLR 1273 (BVI).
8 *Hartwell* at para 39.
9 *AA and BB v CC* 2020 WL 07048894 at paras 95–98.
10 *Woodcock v Chief Constable of Northamptonshire Police* [2025] EWCA Civ 13 at paras 134–135.
11 See eg *Biffa Waste Services v Scottish Ministers* [2025] CSOH 9. Compare the outcome in *Santander Ltd Plc v Keeper of the Registers of Scotland* [2013] CSOH 24, 2013 SLT 362 (no duty where keeper registered forged discharge of standard security; where loss was

caused by criminal acts of pursuer's customer it would be unfair for their loss to fall on the public purse) with *Sebry v Companies House* [2015] EWHC 115 (QB), [2016] 1 WLR 2499 (duty where Companies Registrar registered winding up petition against wrong company, completely destroying its economic value).

6.8 Another illustration, which pre-dates *Robinson* but is consistent with its reasoning, is *Capital & Counties Plc v Hampshire County Council.*[1] This involved conjoined appeals in cases relating to three separate fires. A's property was destroyed after the fire service attended its property, turned off the sprinkler system, and then failed to extinguish the fire.[2] B's property was destroyed by fire several hours after a small explosion at a neighbouring property, which the fire service attended and left after giving the all clear.[3] And C's property was razed after the fire service attended the property but did not have a sufficient water supply to extinguish the fire.[4]

The Court of Appeal held that the respective fire services owed no duty to B or C. The fire service was not under a duty to answer the call for help,[5] nor did a duty arise when they attended the fire.[6] Their attendance did not create the fire which damaged the properties,[7] nor did it make those fires worse. Post-*Robinson*, we also could say that, as is the case with private individuals, public authorities generally are under no duty to confer a benefit on another. The fire services therefore were not under a duty to extinguish the fire at C's property; nor to investigate B's property for any possible sources of ignition from the explosion next door.[8]

But, in respect of A, the Court of Appeal held that the respective fire service *did* owe a duty of care. This is because, when they attended that fire, they made matters worse by turning off the sprinkler system.[9] It was accepted that, with the combined efforts of the sprinkler system and the fire service, the majority of the buildings would have been saved. Turning the sprinkling system off sped up the progress of the fire throughout the buildings. The intervention of the fire service in that case therefore exacerbated the damage, which was sufficient to impose a duty on that fire service.[10]

1 [1997] QB 1004 (CA).
2 Discussed in the judgment as 'The Hampshire Case'.
3 'The London Fire Brigade Case'.
4 'The West Yorkshire Case'.
5 *Capital & Counties* at 1026D–1030A.
6 *Capital & Counties* at 1030B–1038E.
7 If they did, a duty would have been owed: *Capital Counties* at 1031D–H.
8 On this basis, the Inner House held that a duty was not owed by a fire service to inspect a property after a fire had been extinguished with a thermal camera to prevent reignition: *AJ Allan (Blairnyle) Ltd v Strathclyde Fire Board* [2016] CSIH 3, 2016 SC 304.
9 *Capital & Counties* at 1034C–E and 1042E–F.
10 Another possible example, from Northern Ireland, is *Magill v Chief Constable of PSNI* [2022] NICA 49. The plaintiff was a member of an Orange Order march, which was stopped by the police and held in position for ten minutes near protestors, who threw missiles into the crowd. Arguably, the police either (a) created the danger by stopping

the march next to the protestors, or (b) made the danger presented by the protestors worse by holding the march in position for ten minutes.

6.9 The public authority may also make matters worse by interfering with the situation such as to deter another person from attempting to improve the pursuer's situation. In *Tindall v Chief Constable of Thames Valley Police*,[1] a car skidded off a road and into a ditch because of black ice. The driver, aware of the risk which the ice could pose to other drivers, started trying to wave down traffic. He then phoned emergency services, who deployed police to the scene. The police placed a 'slow' sign on the road, cleared it of debris, and requested the attendance of a gritter to clear the ice, but the urgency of that request was not communicated. The officers left about 25 minutes later, taking the 'slow' sign with them. Some time later, the claimant was driving on the same stretch of road, when an oncoming car slid on the black ice, and careered into the path of his vehicle. The claimant died in the collision.

The claimant's relatives contended that the police owed the deceased a duty of care because, by intervening, it had prevented the first driver from continuing trying to wave down traffic to warn them of the danger posed by the ice, which may have prevented the accident from occurring. The UK Supreme Court accepted that, in some circumstances, a public authority may make a danger worse by interfering with matters in a way that deterred a third party from intervening to prevent harm coming to the claimant.[2] But it must be reasonably foreseeable to the public authority that their intervention would have that consequence.[3] There was no evidence that the police had known, or should have known, that the first driver was seeking to warn other drivers of the danger, as opposed to trying to flag them down for help with his own injuries.[4] No duty of care was therefore owed to the deceased.

That a duty may be owed by a public authority where it can reasonably foresee that its conduct might deter an independent attempt to protect the pursuer might also explain the existence of a duty of care in cases involving the dispatch of ambulances. In *Aitken v Scottish Ambulance Service*,[5] the brother of a child experiencing an epileptic seizure phoned for an ambulance. The family lived a short distance away from the relevant hospital, but they were assured that an ambulance was on its way. The ambulance's dispatch was delayed by 21 minutes because of an alleged operational failure, and the child unfortunately died some time after arriving at hospital. The Outer House held that it was arguable that the ambulance service owed a duty to the child. One reason for this was that, had the family known the true arrival time of the ambulance, it was 'reasonable to assume' that other means of getting to the hospital would have been explored.[6] Following *Tindall*, we can say that the ambulance service could reasonably foresee that its intervention stopped the family making their own way to hospital. Perhaps more so than with other emergency services, it may be readily foreseeable that a party requiring medical attention may, independently or with the help of family or friends, attempt to get themselves to hospital were it not for the assurance of the prompt arrival of an ambulance. It is less likely that an independent firefighting venture, or risky vigilante or rescue attempt (in the case of the police), will be reasonably foreseeable.

1 [2024] UKSC 33.
2 *Tindall* at paras 50–57.
3 *Tindall* at para 58.
4 *Tindall* at paras 62–69.
5 [2011] CSOH 49, 2011 SLT 822. For an earlier English authority to similar effect, see *Kent v Griffiths* [2001] QB 36 (CA).
6 *Aitken* at para 61. See also *Kent v Griffiths* at para 49.

THIRD PARTIES AND OMISSIONS: NO GENERAL DUTY, BUT EXCEPTIONS

6.10 If the danger was not created, or made worse, by the public authority, then generally no duty arises. As with private citizens, this means that, in general, there is no duty to confer a benefit on another, and no duty to protect another from the acts of third parties. We have already seen this in our discussion of *Capital & Counties*. There are, as we shall see, exceptions to that starting point, but first we will begin with further illustrations of the general position.

The classic case is *East Suffolk Rivers Catchment Board v Kent*.[1] The plaintiffs owned and operated a farm on marshland adjacent to the River Deben. A seawall which separated the marshland from the river was breached during a storm, resulting in the flooding of the farm. The defendants had statutory power of repair in relation to walls adjoining the river. They undertook such repairs, but it took 150 days longer to complete the repairs than it should have done. The plaintiffs contended that they were owed a duty to take reasonable care to ensure the repair works were completed efficaciously. Had the defendants simply not undertaken the repair work, no duty would be owed: a classic case of a 'pure omission' or failure to confer a benefit.[2] But did the undertaking of the works give rise to a duty of care? A majority of the House of Lords held that no duty of care was owed in respect of the failure to promptly stem the flooding. The intervention of the defendants did not create new damage, make existing matters worse, or foreseeably deter anyone else from undertaking the repair works: they simply conferred a benefit at a slower rate than could have been done.[3] No duty of care arose from the mere exercising of a statutory power.[4]

In *Mitchell v Glasgow City Council*,[5] the pursuer was a tenant of the defender local authority. He was the victim of anti-social behaviour from his neighbour, also a local authority tenant. Complaints were made to the local authority, and early steps were taken towards ejecting the neighbour on anti-social behavioural grounds. The behaviour continued, and the neighbour was summoned to a meeting with the local authority, where he reacted angrily to being informed that further steps to seek his ejection would be taken. Around an hour after leaving that meeting, the neighbour assaulted the pursuer, resulting in his death. His relatives argued that the local authority owed the deceased a duty to be warned that the meeting was taking place. The House of Lords unanimously denied that a duty of care was owed by the local authority to protect the deceased against the actions of a third party.[6] This was even though the local authority was in a relationship with both the deceased and the third party, and even though it knew that the third party previously had expressed a desire to kill the deceased.[7] Absent some special factor, no duty was owed to protect the pursuer against the criminal actions of a third party.[8]

This also is emphasised by *Michael v Chief Constable of South Wales*.[9] The claimant made a 999 call which was answered by a call response handler. The claimant relayed that her ex-partner had attacked her in her home, and threatened to return and kill her. The response handler incorrectly classified the call as not involving a threat to life, so the police response was therefore delayed. The claimant then phoned again when her ex-partner re-appeared and screamed. The police immediately deployed to her house, where her body was discovered. Her relatives argued that the police owed her a duty, either as an identified person in respect of whom they were aware of a threat to safety, or on the basis of an assumption of responsibility. It will be observed that the relationship between the claimant and the police was much closer here than it was in *Tindall*: the police knew the identity of the claimant and the nature of the specific harm posed to her. Nevertheless, a majority of the UK Supreme Court rejected the existence of a duty of care on both grounds. We will return to consider assumption of responsibility shortly, as this is one route through which a pursuer may exceptionally argue that the public authority owed it a duty to confer a benefit or protect it from a third party.[10] In respect of the general duty of care argument, Lord Toulson emphasised that the police only owe a duty to the public at large.[11] Rather than relying on policy reasons, Lord Toulson emphasised, as later would be done in *Robinson* and *GN v Poole*, first principles of negligence: the general rule that we do not owe each other a duty in respect of third party actions and we are not obliged to confer a benefit by taking steps to stop such actions.[12]

1 [1941] AC 74 (HL).
2 *East Suffolk* at 83 per Viscount Simon LC; at 95 per Lord Thankerton; at 98 per Lord Romer; and at 104 per Lord Porter.
3 *East Suffolk* at 84–88 per Viscount Simon LC; at 102 per Lord Romer; at 104–105 per Lord Porter. Lord Thankerton decided the case on causation grounds; Lord Atkin dissented.

4 *East Suffolk* at 87 per Viscount Simon LC; at 94–95 per Lord Thankerton; at 102 per Lord Romer; and at 103 per Lord Porter.
5 [2009] UKHL 21, 2009 SC (HL) 21.
6 See particularly the speech of Lord Hope of Craighead at paras 14–29, and of Lord Rodger of Earlsferry at paras 49–63.
7 It could be argued that the local authority, by calling the meeting which enraged the neighbour, created or exacerbated the danger which he posed to the pursuer. With respect, House of Lords did not deal with this point entirely convincingly: see para 58 per Lord Rodger of Earlsferry.
8 *Mitchell* was followed by the UK Supreme Court in the key case of *GN v Poole Borough Council* [2019] UKSC 25, [2020] AC 780. The claimants were housed by the local authority. Their neighbours, who had previous complaints of anti-social behaviour, commenced a campaign of harassment against the claimants. The court unanimously concluded that no duty was owed.
9 [2015] UKSC 2, [2015] AC 1732.
10 See paras 6.12–6.15 below. Such an assumption did not exist on the facts of *Michael*: para 138.
11 *Michael* at para 33.
12 *Michael* at para 97.

6.11 The law, therefore, generally sets its face against imposing a duty otherwise than where the public authority has created, or intensified, the danger. The police therefore does not owe a duty to a potential victim of a crime to stop that crime from taking place.[1] The fire service owes no duty if it simply fails to respond to an emergency call. And, ordinarily, social services owe no duty of care if they fail to take a vulnerable child into its care. This is not because of any special immunity or policy factor,[2] but a result of the application general principles of the law of negligence.

Two exceptions, however, have been recognised, which may, in particular circumstances, give rise to a duty to prevent third party harm, or a duty to confer a benefit on the citizen. These are:

(a) where the defender has, through words or conduct, assumed responsibility for the pursuer's interests; and

(b) where the defender has a close level of control over a third party which inflicts the harm; and harm to the specific pursuer is reasonably foreseeable.

1 [2009] UKHL 11, 2009 SC (HL) 21.
2 See particularly the speech of Lord Hope of Craighead at paras 14–29, and of Lord Rodger of Earlsferry at paras 49–63.

ASSUMPTION OF RESPONSIBILITY

6.12 We have encountered the device of the assumption of responsibility as a mechanism to circumvent the general rule against the recovery of non-economic loss.[1] But the device was soon untethered from that context and applied to find a 'special relationship' justifying the existence of a duty of care in other situations, including those involving public authorities and going beyond economic interests.[2] The UK Supreme Court has now affirmed that the context plays a key role in the context of public authority liability, as a public authority may assume responsibility to confer a benefit on a citizen or to protect them from harm from a third party, thus circumventing the general rule that no duty is owed in such circumstances.[3]

It will be recalled that an assumption of responsibility arises where the defender objectively, through words or conduct, undertakes that they will perform a particular task for the pursuer carefully, it being reasonably foreseeable that the pursuer will rely on that undertaking. But questions arise as to how the device, forged in the context of economic loss, applies in the broad context of public authority liability. The UK Supreme Court has described the concept as 'elusive', and has observed that it 'possibly' may have 'different requirements in different contexts'.[4] For instance, it has been emphasised in this particular context that sometimes it may be inappropriate (eg in the case of vulnerable young children) to insist on actual reliance.[5] But questions may arise as to the scope of the assumption: precisely what has the authority undertaken to do carefully?

To understand the broader contours of the application of assumption of responsibility in this context, we will turn to consider cases where there has been an alleged undertaking by a public authority.

1 See paras 5.10–5.20, above.
2 See eg *Kirkham v Chief Constable of the Greater Manchester Police* [1990] 2 QB 283 (CA), and compare with the more doubtful views of its application to personal injury cases in *Gibson v Orr* 1999 SC 420 (OH) at 434–435 per the Lord Ordinary (Hamilton).
3 *GN v Poole* [2019] UKSC 25, [2020] AC 780; *HXA v Surrey County Council* [2023] UKSC 52, [2024] 1 WLR 335.
4 *Tindall v Chief Constable of Thames Valley Police* [2024] UKSC 33 at para 75.
5 *HXA* at para 108.

6.13 The pursuer must clearly aver the factual basis from which the asserted assumption of responsibility is said to arise, and also should set out the scope of that assumption.[1] Where a pursuer fails to do so, their claim may be dismissed as irrelevant on the basis that it discloses no arguable ground for the imposition of a duty of care and therefore is bound to fail.[2] If, however, sufficient basis is set out, the court may order a proof before answer to determine the facts before concluding whether the factual basis asserted by the pursuer had the effect of giving rise to an assumption of responsibility.[3] What, therefore, may indicate an assumption of responsibility in this context?

Many of the public authority cases will take place against a complicated statutory backdrop. While the existence of a statutory duty does not, by itself, confer a common law duty of care, steps taken in fulfilment of that statutory duty may give rise to an assumption of responsibility.[4] In other words, even where a public authority is obliged by statute to take steps, taking those steps may result in an assumption of responsibility even if the authority is not acting voluntarily but instead under statutory compulsion. The key point is that the authority must take such steps for there to be a factual basis for the contention that an assumption of responsibility exists; the assumption does not arise simply from the fact that a statute states that the authority ought to have acted in a particular way. So, for instance, where the Home Secretary has the statutory power to grant a person leave to remain, but delays in exercising that power, with the effect that the applicant is meanwhile unable to obtain employment or access benefits, no duty is owed to the applicant.[5] If all the Home Secretary does is delay in making a decision, there is no conduct of the Home Secretary capable of forming an assumption of responsibility and circumventing the general position that there is no duty to confer a benefit on another. The same is true if the public authority simply fails to take a decision altogether.[6]

1 *GN v Poole* [2019] UKSC 25, [2020] AC 780 at paras 82 and 89; *HXA v Surrey County Council* [2023] UKSC 52, [2024] 1 WLR 335 at para 91.

2 A plea to the relevancy is the procedural device within Scots law for bringing an end to unmeritorious claims before a full trial. It is similar, although not identical, to the English 'strike out' procedure.

3 See eg *Cruickshanks v Glasgow City Council* [2024] CSOH 35, 2024 SLT 526 (placing of pursuer's son in 'kinship care' with grandmother may have given rise to assumption of responsibility, but that depended on precise terms of the placement which was a matter for proof).

4 *GN v Poole at* paras 72–73.

5 *Adiukwu v Secretary of State for the Home Department* [2020] CSIH 47, 2021 SC 38 at paras 16, 58, and 74; followed in *FXJ v Secretary of State for the Home Department* [2023] EWCA Civ 1357, [2024] KB 371. Compare with *Husson v Secretary of State for the Home Department* [2020] EWCA Civ 329, where the assumption allegedly arose from an assurance made in the settlement of litigation.

6 See eg *Djennas v Glasgow City Council* [2023] SAC (Civ) 28, 2023 SLT (SAC) 109 at para 22 (statutory duty to provide homeless person with accommodation, but no facts demonstrating any assumption of responsibility to give rise to duty of care).

6.14 Prominent cases often concern the interaction between local authority social services departments and vulnerable children. There may be some obvious cases where an assumption of responsibility will arise.[1] Where a local authority exercises its powers to take a child into care,[2] or instructs a local authority educational therapist to assess a child's educational needs,[3] one can easily see the outline of an argument based on an assumption of responsibility. The local authority has undertaken a particular task (the provision of care and exercise of parental responsibilities; assessment of educational needs) in respect of the child. The child is in a position where it is reasonably foreseeable that it is dependent on the authority carrying out that task with reasonable care; this is even the case if, in the case of the educational psychologist, the report is prepared for internal local authority decision making purposes.

However, most cases will be less clear cut. As we have stated, the public authority must take some steps pursuant to their statutory functions before an argument about assumption of responsibility can be made; the mere existence of the statutory power or function is insufficient. Where the authority has taken some steps, the question is whether those steps do anything to confer a relevant assumption of responsibility. In *GN v Poole*, for instance, where the claimants were harassed by their neighbours, it was contended that the fact that the local authority monitored the claimant's situation, and investigated the allegations amounted to an assumption of responsibility obliging the authority to use its social services powers to safeguard the children by taking them into care. The UK Supreme Court disagreed; monitoring and investigation were not services proffered to the claimants.[4] The individual social workers did not provide advice the accuracy of which, nor a task or service the careful performance of which, the families foreseeably would rely upon.[5]

This was followed in *HXA v Surrey County Council*. Two claimant children (anonymised as HXA and YXA) alleged that their respective local authority social services department had a duty to intervene to protect them from abuse based on an assumption of responsibility. HXA alleged that this arose from assurances made after investigation about assessments and safeguarding instruction which were not followed up on, and YXA founded on the arrangement by the local authority of a schedule of respite care a few days each month away from the parental home. The Supreme Court held that no assumption of responsibility to safeguard the claimants' well-being from the abuse arose from these circumstances. The court emphasised the importance of ascertaining the scope of any assumption of responsibility.[6] In YXA's case, by arranging for periods of respite care, the authority assumed responsibility for protecting him from dangers arising from the sporadic placement with the foster parents. But that assumption did not extend to protecting YXA when at home with his birth parents.[7] HXA's case was effectively indistinguishable from *GN v Poole*: internal decisions made to gather information as to whether a care order should be obtained could not constitute an assumption of responsibility towards the child.[8]

1 See *GN v Poole* [2019] UKSC 25, [2020] AC 780 at paras 69 and 87.

2 See eg *Barrett v Enfield LBC* [2001] 2 AC 550 (HL) at 569B–H per Lord Slynn of Hadley and at 589H per Lord Hutton, refusing to strike out a claim in these circumstances. Such cases could also be explained on the basis that the care order confers parental rights and responsibilities on the local authority, and therefore their status and/or level of control over the child gives rise to a duty to protect the child.

3 See *Phelps v Hillingdon London Borough Council* [2001] 2 AC 619 (HL) at 654C–G per Lord Slynn of Hadley, at 675D per Lord Clyde, and at 677 per Lord Millett (claim not struck out).

4 *GN v Poole* at paras 80–83.
5 *GN v Poole* at paras 86–89.
6 *HXA v Surrey County Council* [2023] UKSC 52, [2024] 1 WLR 335 at para 91.
7 *HXA* at paras 97–100 and 107.
8 *HXA* at paras 93–95 and 101.

6.15 Pursuers also have frequently sought to set up an assumption of responsibility by emergency services. Answering a 999 call or attending the scene of an emergency do not, by themselves, constitute an assumption of responsibility in the case of the police[1] or the fire service.[2] However, the ambulance service, as part of the NHS, is treated differently; when dispatching an ambulance to the patient, it assumes responsibility to take reasonable care to ensure the ambulance arrives without unreasonable delay.[3] The bulk of the cases have concerned police conduct. The police will assume responsibility to take reasonable care for the safety of a prisoner when they are in police custody,[4] which extends to ensuring they are released into a safe environment.[5] The authority's undertaking may even extend to protecting the pursuer when it should have continued to detain them under its mental health powers.[6]

Beyond custodial situations, the police likely will only assume responsibility towards the pursuer where they 'make something in the way of a specific representation or promise [...] to take particular action' upon which the pursuer's reliance or dependence is reasonably foreseeable.[7] This requires a 'communication or interaction' between the police and the pursuer.[8] Absent such representation, the police owed no duty to a victim of domestic abuse to inform them that a neighbour had reported that the abusive ex-partner was loitering outside her house.[9] Contrastingly, when a mother phoned the police with concerns about her daughter who had been expressing suicidal ideations, an assumption of responsibility arguably arose from repeated assurances by a call handler that the police had been dispatched to check on her daughter, and that the mother should 'leave' with them the question of any transfer to hospital.[10]

The requirement for direct communication or interaction between the public authority and the pursuer for an assumption of responsibility to arise narrows the extent to which the doctrine can provide an exception to the general rule precluding liability for failing to protect the pursuer or make them better off.

1 See eg *Michael v Chief Constable of South Wales Police* [2015] UKSC 2, [2015] AC 1732 at para 138. The same seems to follow for Scots law in *Gibson v Orr* 1999 SC 420 (OH) at 432B–D, 433B: the duty there arose once control was taken of the hazard.
2 See eg *AJ Allan (Blairnyle) Ltd v Strathclyde Fire Board* [2016] CSIH 3, 2016 SC 304 at para 27 and 37; *Capital & Counties Plc v Hampshire County Council* [1997] QB 1004 (CA) at 1035–1036.
3 See eg *Aitken v Scottish Ambulance Service* [2011] CSOH 49, 2011 SLT 811 at para 63–65; *Kent v Griffiths* [2001] QB 36 (CA) at paras 45 and 49.

4 See eg *Reeves v Commissioner of Police of the Metropolis* [2000] 1 AC 360 (HL).

5 See eg *Wilson v Chief Constable of Lothian and Borders Constabulary* 1989 SLT 97 (OH) (police removed an exceptionally drunk man from his house, and then let him leave the police car in early morning winter conditions to wander off on himself, resulting in death by hypothermia).

6 *Dobson v Chief Constable of Leicestershire* [2025] EWHC 272 (KB) at para 76 and 96–104. In that case, the claimant was released after an adequate risk assessment by a medical professional, which displaced any post-release assumption of responsibility). See also *Magee v Chief Constable of Police Service of Northern Ireland* [2019] NIQB 83 at paras 43–50.

7 *Woodcock v Chief Constable of Northamptonshire Police* [2025] EWCA Civ 13 at para 121. See also eg *Holbeach v Chief Constable of the Police Service of Northern Ireland* [2024] NICA 45 (no assumption towards victim of Enniskillen bombing by security operation which did not discover explosive device).

8 *Tindall v Chief Constable of Thames Valley Police* [2024] UKSC 33 at para 76 per Lords Leggatt and Burrows.

9 *Woodcock* at para 122.

10 *Sherratt v Chief Constable of Greater Manchester Police* [2018] EWHC 1746 (QB) at para 83–84. See too *Bell v Commissioner of Police of the Metropolis* [2024] EWHC 379 (KB) at paras 309–314 (father assured by officer that son's passport would not be returned to mother who clearly intended to remove child to Brazil).

CONTROL AND REASONABLE FORESEEABILITY OF SPECIFIC HARM

6.16 If no specific responsibility has been assumed towards the pursuer, a duty may exceptionally be owed where the defender has a close level of control over a third party which inflicts the harm; and harm to the specific pursuer is reasonably foreseeable.

The leading case on this exception to the rule against liability for the acts of a third party is *Home Office v Dorset Yacht*.[1] Young offenders (known at this time as 'borstal boys') were working on an island off the Dorset coast under the custody and control of three prison officers. The officers went to bed, leaving the boys to their own devices. Seven boys decided to escape. They boarded a yacht moored off the island, which collided with the plaintiff's yacht, which they then vandalised. The House of Lords held that the borstal officers owed a duty of care to the plaintiff. The officers were legally responsible, under specific statutory provisions, for the boys. They were to ensure the implementation of the boys' terms of detention, including to guard them and prevent them from absconding. It was foreseeable as a reasonable and probable consequence of leaving the boys alone that they would try to escape. Since the only means of escape was by sea, it was also reasonably foreseeable as a probable consequence that they would steal a yacht and, being inexperienced mariners, collide with another vessel.[2]

The key aspects of this case, therefore, are: (i) the significant degree of control the officers had over the potential danger (the boys were legally detained and could be coerced) and (ii) that the risk to the third party was reasonably foreseeable to the officers (the boys were likely to steal and recklessly use property close to the island in the course of their escape from it).

The necessary degree of control and foreseeability is very high, and few cases have successfully engaged this exception as a result. One case which could be explained on this basis is *Kaizer v Scottish Ministers*,[3] where a prison authority was held to owe a duty of care to a prisoner assaulted by a fellow inmate who had previously expressed his intention to harm the pursuer to a prison officer. The level of control was no less than that in *Dorset Yacht*, and the harm was perhaps even more foreseeable than the risk posed to the yacht, given the specific threat by the third party.

Kaizer can be contrasted with *Thomson v Scottish Ministers*,[4] where a prisoner who was granted leave to visit his mother's house murdered his brother's girlfriend. The prison's control over the prisoner had effectively evaporated once he was disembarked from prison transport at the central bus station in Glasgow, and no specific threat had been made to the victim prior to the prisoner's temporary release. It was insufficient to say that the victim was someone with whom the prisoner may make contact during his release. *Thomson* was followed in *A v B Ltd*.[5] The assailant in that case had been placed in a residential care home and was assessed as posing a high risk of sexualised offending against other young people. He was mistakenly released on unsupervised leave for two hours. The assailant groomed a child at a primary school within walking distance of the residential home and subsequently assaulted him. Despite the close control (the assailant was only on a short period of leave close to the home), the reasonable foreseeability of harm coming to the pursuer (being a member of a class to whom the assailant was known to pose a risk) and the proximity of the school to the home (which places the case closer to *Dorset Yacht* than *Thomson*), no duty of care was held to arise on the facts.

1 [1970] AC 1004 (HL).

2 *Dorset Yacht* especially at 1070E–1071A. See also at 1030B–D per Lord Reid (viewing the matter as one of causation); at 1035D–G and 1039A–B per Lord Morris of Borth-y-Gest; at 1053H–1055G per Lord Pearson.

3 [2017] CSOH 110, affirmed [2018] CSIH 36, 2018 SC 491. The case perhaps could also be rationalised on the basis of an assumption of responsibility, or on the basis of a non-delegable duty to protect the prisoners within the prison. See, earlier, *Whannel v Secretary of State for Scotland* 1989 SLT 671 (OH).

4 [2013] CSIH 63, 2013 SC 628.

5 [2022] CSOH 34, 2022 SLT 577. This decision was not cited in *NM v Henderson* [2025] CSIH 22 which, although citing *Thomson v Scottish Ministers*, arguably adopts (at para 28) a much more generous approach to proximity than either earlier decision.

6.17 All these cases have concerned situations where it was alleged that the public authority had control over a third party (ie, another person) who harmed the pursuer. It is not yet settled law as to whether or not the exception extends beyond human agency to cover control over man-made or natural hazards.[1] As we have seen, cases involving the emergency services have held that proximity to a dangerous situation and the ability to intervene does not give rise to a duty of care.[2] Something else, such as making the situation worse or an assumption of responsibility, is required. One exceptional decision is that of the Outer House in *Gibson v Orr.*[3] A bridge carrying a public road collapsed. The police coned off the north side and positioned a police vehicle as a warning to drivers on the south side. After an hour, they left without having received confirmation that any barrier or warning was in place on the south side. The pursuer was injured when the car in which he was a passenger was driven onto the bridge from the south side and fell into the river. The Lord Ordinary (Hamilton) held, contrary to English authorities, and applying the *Caparo* 'test', that there was sufficient proximity between the police and the pursuer to give rise to a duty of care, arising from the police taking charge of the hazard.[4] His Lordship did not see a relevant distinction between human and inanimate hazards, fitting the case within the *Dorset Yacht* principle.[5] That duty extended 'not only to the manner of the exercise of that control' but also 'to the circumstances of the relinquishment of it'.[6]

In *AJ Allan (Blairnyle) Ltd v Strathclyde Fire Board*,[7] the Inner House questioned the continuing authority of *Gibson v Orr*. Lady Paton stated that the 'more restrictive approach currently approved and adopted by the UK Supreme Court must be followed by the Scottish courts',[8] giving *Gibson* as an example of a case expressing views contrary to that approach and then expressly disapproving the case.[9] However, her Ladyship then noted that 'it is possible that the result achieved was correct'. Lady Dorrian stated that *Gibson* could be explained as a case where the police's 'taking control of and then abandoning a known hazard was at least analogous with a situation where the authority created the damage or made the situation worse', it being relevant that only a 'limited class of individuals at particular risk' had been identified.[10] Lord Drummond Young was most clear in explaining *Gibson* as an example of the 'control' exception exemplified by *Dorset Yacht*, drawing an analogy with the treatment of roads authorities.[11]

While *Gibson* was not discussed by the Supreme Court in its decision in *Tindall*,[12] the court thought that it was 'untenable' to argue that:

> 'a duty of care could arise from the fact that the police took steps attending the scene with blue emergency lights flashing and putting up a sign to encourage motorists to slow down which temporarily reduced the risk of another accident but which were then terminated when the police left …',

concluding that:[13]

> 'taking steps which are ineffectual, whether because they are inadequate to begin with or because the [public authority] does not persist in them, cannot give rise to a duty of care'.

In so stating, their Lordships also approved of the reasoning and decision in one of the English authorities not followed by *Gibson*.[14] The Supreme Court, it is submitted, therefore would not follow *Gibson v Orr* were its facts to be repeated today. The *Dorset Yacht* principle involves a near-total level of control, and attempts to expand control to cover the situation in *Gibson v Orr* perhaps overlook this, instead falsely analogising with a generic sense of 'control'. Moreover, the lack of any direct interaction between the officers and the victim would – given the strict test adopted in *Tindall* – preclude any assumption of responsibility.

The narrowness of the control exception means that it rarely comes to the aid of a citizen injured by the negligent omission of a public authority. This furthers the importance of the assumption of responsibility; itself a doctrine of narrow application.

1 The point was left open in *Tindall v Chief Constable of Thames Valley Police* [2024] UKSC 33 at paras 78–84 (on the facts of that case, the danger which resulted in the claimant's death was 184 metres away from where the police had responded to the initial incident, so they could not be said to have been 'in control' of it).
2 See paras 6.8–6.9 above.
3 1999 SC 420 (OH).
4 *Gibson* at 433B. His Lordship declined the invitation to follow *Clough v Bussan* [1990] 1 All ER 431 (QBD), *Alexandrou v Oxford* [1993] 4 All ER 328 (CA), or *Ancell & Ancell v McDermott* [1993] 4 All ER 355 (CA).
5 *Gibson* at 433G–434A. This is perhaps lightly supported by the reasoning in *Tindall* at para 56 ('no material distinction' between deterring assistance by person and by object).
6 *Gibson* at 435D–E.
7 [2016] CSIH 3, 2016 SC 304.
8 *AJ Allan* at para 26.
9 *AJ Allan* at para 33.
10 *AJ Allan* at para 50.
11 *AJ Allan* at para 62.
12 In the Court of Appeal ([2022] EWCA Civ 25, [2022] 4 WLR 104), Stuart-Smith LJ considered that *Gibson* did not reflect English law, and was inconsistent with *Robinson* and *GN Poole* (at paras 62 and 65). Contrary to what Lady Dorrian suggested in *AJ Allan*, the police's intervention did not make the situation any worse: the situation before and after their intervention was exactly the same (at para 64). Finally, there could be no assumption of responsibility on the facts (at para 65).
13 *Tindall* at para 84.
14 *Ancell & Ancell*.

ROAD AUTHORITIES: AN EXCEPTIONAL PUBLIC AUTHORITY?

6.18 We must briefly consider the position of roads authorities.[1] Alongside a duty not to create or exacerbate danger by its own actions,[2] it long has been recognised in Scots law that roads authorities owe a duty to confer benefits on road users in the form of repairing hazards which would not be spotted by a reasonably careful and skilful driver.[3] A roads authority which unreasonably does not repair or remove such a non-obvious hazard will breach a duty of care owed to the road user; it is no argument for them to say that they merely failed to act to make the pursuer better off. This duty extends to hazards created by third parties,[4] and may even extend, unlike in England, to implementing road safety improvements if there is evidence of a particularly dangerous locus.[5]

It is true that the liability of roads authorities has not been reconsidered in Scotland following the UK Supreme Court's modern approach to the liability of public authorities. But the generous position towards users has long been held, and it is suggested that the Scottish courts likely will seek to make it fit into the new framework rather than switching to a general stating point of no duty in respect of a failure to repair. Moreover, in English law, the duty to proactively maintain and repair is a statutory one, breach of which is civilly actionable.[6] It therefore stands aside from the common law framework; it would be most undesirable for that framework to compel more limited protection in Scotland.

Happily, it is submitted that liability of roads authorities in Scotland can be made to fit within, or at least alongside, the modern framework of public authority liability. Roads authorities have a monopoly on authorising repairs to public roads.[7] With limited exceptions, a person who carries out work on a public road without the permission of the road authority commits a criminal offence.[8] The roads authority therefore is in a position of exclusive control; it alone can bring about the amelioration of any hazard due to the state of the road, either by conducting the repairs itself or by giving permission for those repairs to be carried out. The UK Supreme Court has repeatedly endorsed the suggestion that the status of the particular public authority may provide a 'special reason' for finding liability for failure to confer a benefit; albeit it has not provided much guidance on when this exception would be engaged.[9] It has also, as we have seen, accepted that control by the public authority may provide another exceptional route to liability, although the application of that exception to inanimate, non-human hazards is not yet clear.[10] It could easily be argued that the monopolistic powers of the roads authority are sufficient to engage the 'status' exception, and the total level of control would justify engaging the 'control' exception. The duty arises from the fact of their management and physical control of the road and effectively is a duty analogous to that owed by the occupier of land, which includes a proactive duty to repair hazards.[11]

1 See eg E Reid, *The Law of Delict in Scotland* (2022), Chapter 8.

2 See eg *MacDonald v Comhairle Nan Eilean Siar* [2015] CSOH 132 at para 148.

3 See eg *MacDonald v Aberdeenshire Council* [2013] CSIH 83, 2014 SC 114 and *Bowes v Highland Council* [2018] CSIH 38, 2018 SC 499.

4 See eg *Innes v Magistrates of Edinburgh* (1798) Mor 13189 (IH); *McKnight v Clydeside Buses Ltd* 1999 SLT 1167 (OH).

5 A duty of this sort was asserted in *MacDonald v Aberdeenshire Council*, but the Inner House denied it existed on the facts. Lady Paton did not think that sufficient reasonable

foreseeability existed, as no other accidents had occurred on account of the faded road markings: at paras 43–48. Lord Drummond Young held (at paras 84–87) that, absent the road markings, the danger posed by the junction nevertheless would be obvious to a careful driver, and therefore this was not a 'hazard' within the scope of the roads authority's duty of care. See too *Murray v Nicholls* 1983 SLT 194 (OH). Therefore, absent evidence of particular danger posed to careful and skilful drivers, the result in such cases tends to be similar to English law, where no such duty exists at common law: *Stovin v Wise* [1996] AC 923 (HL); *Gorringe v Calderdale Metropolitan Borough Council* [2004] UKHL 15, [2004] 1 WLR 1057.

6 Highways Act 1980, ss 41 and 58, as discussed in *Stovin* and *Gorringe*.

7 See Roads (Scotland) Act 1984, s 56; New Roads and Street Works Act 1991, ss 108–109.

8 See 1984 Act, s 56(6); 1991 Act, s 110.

9 See eg *Robinson v Chief Constable of West Yorkshire Police* [2018] UKSC 4, [2018] AC 736 at para 34; *GN v Poole Borough Council* [2019] UKSC 25, [2020] AC 780 at para 76; *HXA v Surrey County Council* [2023] UKSC 52, [2024] 1 WLR 335 at para 88; *Tindall v Chief Constable of Thames Valley Police* [2024] UKSC 33 at paras 42, 74, and 85–87, all citing S Tofaris and S Steel, 'Negligence Liability for Omissions and the Police' [2016] *Cambridge Law Journal* 128.

10 See para 6.17 above.

11 This is not to argue that roads authorities are occupiers in the sense of the Occupiers' Liability (Scotland) Act 1960: this is often assumed not to be the case (see eg *Syme v East Lothian Council* 2012 Rep LR 66, compare with Reid, The *Law of Delict in Scotland* at para 25.19). But the level of control enjoyed by roads authorities justifies the analogy, as it is arguably the source of their duty: *Gibson v Orr* 1999 SC 420 (OH) at 435. See on occupiers' liability generally paras 12.13–12.19 below.

CONCLUSION

6.19 The UK Supreme Court has placed the liability of public authorities in negligence on a principled basis. If the actions of the public authority positively damage the pursuer, or exacerbate an existing danger created by somebody or something else, then a duty of care will be owed. But there is no general duty to make the pursuer better off by intervening to protect them from danger not created by the public authority, unless an assumption of responsibility or the 'control exception' can be established on the facts. This no longer can be considered a 'developing' area of law.

At the very least, this provides a clear framework to assist us in predicting the outcome of cases. That being said, one cannot help but read these decisions and feel uncomfortable, even outraged, with the results that follow application of these principles.[1] The exceptional approach to finding a duty to intervene or rescue, combined with a narrow formulation of assumption of responsibility, may be appropriate for private individuals, but the decision to also adopt that approach for public authorities is at core a policy one. It might therefore be ironic that the effect of that decision has been to marginalise policy considerations in all cases save those where the existence of a novel duty is alleged.[2]

It is not surprising that the Scottish courts have swiftly adopted this framework. The interconnectedness of the welfare state and other public services within the UK makes it hard to justify any significant divergence. But it must always be borne in mind that the structure of Scottish public authorities may differ,[3] as may their statutory functions, powers, and duties.[4] This means that English cases should always be considered with care before deciding to follow them in respect of Scottish public authorities.[5] And, in any event, those authorities are only persuasive, and it remains open to the Scottish courts to create new exceptions to the non-liability for failure to confer benefits, or to interpret existing exceptions differently.[6] In that regard, notable doubts persist about the scope and application of the assumption of responsibility doctrine in this context; the scope of the 'control' exception, and the content – if any – of the 'status' exception. But continuing convergence likely will remain the norm.

1 See eg S Tofaris and S Steel, 'Negligence Liability for Omissions and the Police' [2016] *Cambridge Law Journal* 128.

2 See eg *NM v Henderson* [2024] CSOH 84, 2025 SLT 35, cf the analysis on appeal at [2025] CSIH 22. See generally Chapter 7 below.

3 Eg the existence of a single police authority and fire service under the Police and Fire Reform (Scotland) Act 2012.

4 As demonstrated by the position of roads authorities: see para 6.18 above.

5 See D Brodie, 'Pursing the police and the assumption of responsibility: *Tindall v Chief Constable of Thames Valley*' [2022] *Juridical Review* 100 at 105.

6 Although adoption of the Supreme Court's framework makes it unlikely that Scottish courts will be able to take up Lord Drummond Young's suggestion, in *AJ Allan (Blairnyle) Ltd v Strathclyde Fire Board* [2016] CSIH 3, 2016 SC 304 at paras 97–99, to develop the law in the direction of a duty to rescue, limited to dangers to the physical safety of another person which would not unduly place the rescuer in physical jeopardy.

CHAPTER 7

Novel Duties of Care

INTRODUCTION

7.1 Previous chapters on the duty of care have considered situations where the imposition of a duty of care has been accepted as a matter of authority: so-called 'established categories'. If a case falls within such an 'established category', then the court simply applies the test which has been developed within that category to ascertain whether a duty of care is owed. The court must not, in such cases, embark on a holistic consideration of whether a duty arises on the facts of the case, and especially should not enquire whether the imposition of a duty would be 'fair, just, and reasonable'.[1] Such a course may result in the court falling into error, and may well invite criticism from an appellate court.[2] The point was put thus by Lord Reed in *Robinson v Chief Constable of West Yorkshire Police*:[3]

> 'Where the existence or non-existence of a duty of care has been established, a consideration of justice and reasonableness forms part of the basis on which the law has arrived at the relevant principles. It is therefore unnecessary and inappropriate to reconsider whether the existence of the duty is fair, just and reasonable (subject to the possibility that this court may be invited to depart from an established line of authority). Nor, a fortiori, can justice and reasonableness constitute a basis for discarding established principles and deciding each case according to what the court may regard as its broader merits. Such an approach would be a recipe for inconsistency and uncertainty …'.

This chapter considers the approach to be taken where it is established that the situation before the court genuinely is a 'novel' one.

1 As was thought to be required by *Caparo Industries v Dickman* [1990] 2 AC 605 (HL).
2 See eg *Finlayson v Alban Wine Ltd* [2024] CSIH 32, where the Inner House castigated the Lord Ordinary for applying the *Caparo* tripartite test to assess whether a duty of care arose in an ordinary personal injury action, rather than applying the established rule that such a duty is owed where injury is reasonably foreseeable.
3 [2018] UKSC 4, [2018] AC 736 at para 26.

7.2 The overall process when a court is 'faced with a question as to whether or not a duty of care exists' has been explained by the Sheriff Appeal Court in the following terms:[1]

(1) First, the court should, by identifying the legally significant features of the case before it, and of previous cases, ask itself whether the case is novel.

(2) If the answer to that is no, then, second, the court should decide the case in accordance with established principles, without resorting to *Caparo*.

(3) However, if the case is novel, then, third, the court must consider which of the previous cases provides the closest analogy.

(4) Having done that, then, fourth, the court must decide whether to extend the law, so as to provide for a duty of care in the case before it, taking care to maintain the coherence of the law and to avoid inappropriate distinctions. In carrying out this task, the court must weigh up the reasons for and against imposing liability and ask whether the imposition of a duty of care would be just and reasonable.

It will be noted that, even when the court is considering whether or not to impose a new duty, it does not consider the matter from first principles or start from a blank slate. It reasons by analogy, taking the closest cases as a starting point and enquiring as to whether an extension of those cases would be sustainable or desirable.

1 *Commodity Solution Services Ltd v First Scottish Searching Services Ltd* [2019] SAC Civ 4, 2019 SC (SAC) 41 at para 31 per Sheriff Braid (numbering added).

WHEN DOES THE NOVELTY WEAR OFF?

7.3 The first question, therefore, is whether the case is a novel one. In *Robinson*, Lord Reed considered a 'novel' case to be one where 'established principles do not provide an answer'[1] and where 'the question whether a duty of care arises has not previously been decided'.[2] The case before the court, involving a passer-by physically injured as the police sought to arrest a suspect, was not treated as novel, but instead as turning on the application of established principles. The difficulty becomes, however, working out exactly how the categories are drawn. At its broadest, *Robinson* could be said to be a case where a positive act has caused physical injury. More narrowly, it could be said to be a case where a positive act *by the police* has caused physical injury. Even more narrowly still, it could be said that it was a case where a positive act by the police has caused physical injury *in the course of attempting to effect an arrest*. The level of abstraction at which the category should be formulated is not self-evident: Lord Reed seemed to adopt the broadest categorisation (where the identity of the defendants as police officers was irrelevant),[3] Lord Hughes seemed to adopt the intermediate categorisation (finding relevant the fact that the defendants were police officers)[4] and Lord Mance seems to have adopted the narrowest categorisation (finding relevant the fact that the defendants were police officers and the injury occurred during the arrest of a suspect).[5]

None of these categorisations is obviously correct. Here, we can see the close analogy with the ordinary judicial techniques employed when dealing with precedent. When a judge is unable to distinguish a previous binding case from the facts before her, then *stare decisis* dictates that she must follow that case. But if the prior case can be distinguished there is no obligation to follow it; the judge may decide whether or not to do so.

This involves the same process as determining whether or not a duty is a novel one; if the factors material to the formulation of a duty of care in a previous case are present in the case now before the court, then the court is not dealing with a novel case.[6] The question is: which factors are material, and which are immaterial, to the formulation of an existing duty of care?

1 [2018] UKSC 4, [2018] AC 736 at para 27 per Lord Reed.
2 *Robinson* at para 29 per Lord Reed.
3 *Robinson* at paras 32, 68, 70 and 74.
4 *Robinson* at para 98.
5 *Robinson* at paras 95 and 97.
6 See the algebraic expression of this point by Lord Diplock in *Dorset Yacht v Home Office* [1970] AC 1004 (HL) at 1058–1060.

7.4 The exhortation that courts should take care 'to maintain the coherence of the law and to avoid inappropriate distinctions …'[1] applies just as much to the designation of a case as novel as it does to the formulation of a new duty. A common-sense approach should be taken. For instance, where a patient with a head injury decides to leave hospital after an erroneous statement by an NHS receptionist as to waiting times, and suffers an aggravated injury as a result, the duty of care could be formulated in at least two ways. The first is to ask whether a hospital receptionist owes a duty of care to accurately give information about waiting times. The second is to ask whether an NHS accident and emergency hospital owes a duty to take reasonable care of patients presenting with an injury. The broader second formulation, obviously, is more likely to have antecedents in the case law than the narrower first formulation. The first formulation introduces distinctions that are unnecessary: the receptionist is just one aspect of the casualty department provided by the NHS to receive and treat patients. When the Court of Appeal searched for a duty using the first formulation, the UK Supreme Court was highly critical and opted instead for the second, well-established formulation.[2] Lord Lloyd-Jones observed that the duty of care must be 'considered in the round',[3] and that where the case fell under an established broad category 'it is not necessary to address, in every instance where the precise factual situation has not previously been the subject of a reported judicial decision, whether it would be fair, just and reasonable to impose a duty of care'.[4] This cautions against taking too fine-grained an approach when considering the novelty of a duty of care.[5]

It has been made clear that, even if the parties agree that the alleged duty is a 'novel' one, the court must still make that assessment for itself.[6] The danger, however, is that with an underinclusive selection of authority by counsel,[7] a busy first-instance judge may not be fully abreast of all relevant authority.[8] It may also be difficult to distinguish between a case alleging a novel duty, and a case which falls into an 'established category' where it is established beyond doubt there that no duty of care arises.[9] Once a novel duty is recognised, it goes without saying that it forms a new established category, which should be followed by a subsequent court (unless a superior court overrules the decision that a duty of care exists in such circumstances).[10]

It is impossible to provide firm guidance on when a case or situation will be a novel one. As will be seen below, the courts have treated as novel alleged new duties in respect of, among others, foreseeable physical harm, foreseeable psychological harm, and economic loss. The insignia of novelty may vary widely, and it is difficult to make general observations. Instead, it is hoped that a discussion of some of these cases, besides illustrating the process of reasoning used when deciding whether or not to extend a duty of care, will give a flavour of when the courts will consider a duty to be novel.

1 *Robinson v Chief Constable of West Yorkshire Police* [2018] UKSC 4, [2018] AC 736 at para 27 and 29 per Lord Reed.
2 *Darnley v Croydon Health Services NHS Trust* [2018] UKSC 50, [2019] AC 831 at paras 15–19.
3 *Darnley* at para 19.
4 *Darnley* at para 16.
5 Arguably, such an approach was taken in *Coulter Property Ltd v Coulter* [2022] SC EDIN 10 and *4U2 Ltd v Glasgow City Council* [2025] SC GLA 10. These were quintessential cases of pure economic loss (with the latter involving the exercise of a statutory power), a well-established category requiring an assumption of responsibility for a duty to be owed. Although each case arguably adopted the wrong starting point in deciding that the duty was novel, their analyses of assumption of responsibility and conclusions are undoubtedly correct. On the latter case, see D Brodie, 'Administrative Decisions and *Hedley Byrne*' [2025] Reparation Bulletin 6.
6 *Commodity Solution Services* at para 33.
7 See eg *SJ v CALA Management Ltd* 2019 SCLR 873 (Sh Ct) at paras 114–115, where only two authorities were cited by the pursuer's representatives. However, the sheriff was able to dispense with the case on a pleading point as insufficient notice of the pursuer's common law case had been given to the defender.
8 In this respect, it should be noted that, in the Court of Session, unless the permission of the court is given, each side can only lodge five authorities: Practice Note No 3 of 2017, para 30.
9 See eg *Spark v Western Isles NHS* [2019] 7 WLUK 592, where a patient's wife claimed the health board owed her a duty of care to take reasonable care not to cause distress after failing correctly to diagnose her husband's condition. The sheriff accepted this was a novel duty (at para 30), but with respect it should have been seen as a hopeless

attempt to extend the principles regarding recovery as a secondary victim in respect of psychiatric injury (which the sheriff dealt with separately at paras 32–35).

10 Eg the recognition that a parent company may owe a duty to those injured by the actions of its subsidiary in *Chandler v Cape plc* [2012] EWCA Civ 525, [2012] 1 WLR 3111 is to be treated as an established category: *Lungowe v Vedanta Resources plc* [2019] UKSC 20, [2020] AC 1045.

THE INCREMENTAL APPROACH TO NOVEL DUTIES OF CARE

7.5 That being said, it must be admitted that the difficulty in ascertaining whether or not a case is novel is of limited practical consequence. If the court does conclude that the situation before it is a novel one, then that does mean that it may construct a duty of care out of thin air and ignore any previous authority. The process by which a duty determination is made in novel situations is said to be an 'incremental' one, in the sense that:[1]

> '[i]n cases where the question whether a duty of care arises has not previously been decided, the courts will consider the closest analogies in the existing law … They will also weigh up the reasons for and against imposing liability, in order to decide whether the existence of a duty of care would be just and reasonable'.

The starting point, therefore, is not an abstract application of the concepts of reasonable foreseeability, proximity, and policy. Instead, the court should start from previously decided cases which share legally significant features with the case before it. If those previous cases have found the existence of a duty of care, the court must then ask whether extension to the present case is justified. If those previous cases have denied the existence of a duty of care, the court may ask whether there is something of significance in the present case, not present in the previous cases, which would justify imposing a duty of care. The concepts of reasonable foreseeability, proximity, and policy provide potentially useful lenses through which the instant case can be compared to previous cases. The result is that, even where the case is a novel one, the gravitational pull of previously decided cases is such that any newly-forged duty will usually be a justified extension from those decisions.[2]

The UK Supreme Court consider a novel situation very shortly after *Robinson* in *James-Bowen v Commissioner of Police of the Metropolis*.[3] The claimants were police officers who were involved in the arrest of a suspected terrorist, who later made allegations of police brutality in the arrest. While disciplinary proceedings were dismissed, the suspect brought a civil claim against the Metropolitan Police Commissioner. The claim was settled, with the Commissioner apologising for the 'excessive violence' of the claimants and issuing a press release which suggested they were at fault. The claimants argued that they were owed a duty to take reasonable care not to inflict economic and reputational harm in the course of defending the civil action, which the settlement and ensuing press release allegedly breached. This being a novel case,[4] and foreseeability of harm and proximity of relationship both being seen as at least arguable, attention swiftly turned to the 'fair, just and reasonable' question.[5]

The closet analogous case was *Calveley v Chief Constable of the Merseyside Police*, where it was held that the police force did not owe its officers a duty of care to avoid economic and reputational harm when conducting internal disciplinary proceedings. If no duty was owed in respect of an internal investigation, then it would logically follow that no duty also would be owed in respect of an external process over which the police force had limited control.[6] Lord Lloyd-Jones nevertheless proceeded to assess the alleged duty in policy terms. First, any such duty would give rise to conflicting interests: the interest of the police force favours efficient resolution of the claims brought against it, whereas the interest of the officers was in a full exploration of the claims to hopefully lead to their vindication.[7] The Commissioner's public duties might also be undermined if she had to respond to litigation in a manner that safeguarded the reputational and economic interests of her employees.[8] The supposed duty also would be inconsistent with the principle that a litigant should be free to conduct her defence as she sees fit[9] and eg the policy which encourages the settlement of disputes.[10] This all fortified the conclusion that no duty of care should be recognised.

To further illustrate the methodology involved in novel cases, we will consider cases involving physical injury, psychological injury, and economic loss.

1 *Robinson v Chief Constable of West Yorkshire Police* [2018] UKSC 4, [2018] AC 736 at 29 per Lord Reed.
2 If, however, the case is novel in the extreme, in that none of the previous case law provides a useful basis for an analogy, it is submitted that the court then is justified in considering the existence of a duty of care from a blank canvas. But considerations of foreseeability, proximity, and policy likely will still be partially guided by previous cases. See eg *Piepenbrock v London School of Economics and Political Science* [2022] EWHC 2421 (KB) (no duty of care owed to subject of publication to take care in accuracy of published text).
3 [2018] UKSC 40, [2018] 1 WLR 4021.
4 *James-Bowen* at para 23.
5 *James-Bowen* at para 22.
6 *James-Bowen* at para 26.
7 *James-Bowen* at paras 30–32.
8 *James-Bowen* at para 33.
9 *James-Bowen* at paras 35–36. Relatedly, the Commissioner may have had to disclose privileged information in respect to a claim by the officers under the supposed duty, which may undermine the defence of the action brought by the third party: para 46.
10 *James-Bowen* at para 36.

PHYSICAL INJURY

7.6 Although cases of physical injury are almost paradigmatic in the law of negligence, there may be features of the case which nevertheless justify use of the incremental approach.

In *Hughes v Turning Point Scotland*[1], the defender charity operated a facility to help treat alcohol withdrawal. The pursuer checked himself into that facility, and was assessed as needing medication. This was not kept onsite; rather, it had to be prescribed by one of two external doctors, neither of whom was immediately available. Although a prescription was eventually written, the pursuer died six hours after admission from a seizure induced by alcohol withdrawal before medicine could be administered. The deceased's relatives brought a claim in negligence against the defender, claiming that they owed a duty to provide a safe detox, and had failed to intervene to protect him from the seizure. The Lord Ordinary (Clark) observed that the defender's charitable status distinguished the case as novel.[2] Imposition of a holistic duty to ensure an in-patient's wellbeing on a fully-resourced hospital or health provider might be justified. Contrastingly, the defender had limited control over the pursuer and only assumed responsibility to consult with external doctors and provide him with prescribed medicine.[3] Extending the duty owed by a hospital to also cover a charitable provider would not be a desirable incremental extension. It also would be unfair, unjust, and unreasonable to impose any wider duty on the charity, as exposure to liability could destroy its ability and willingness to provide services to the vulnerable.[4]

1 [2019] CSOH 42, 2019 SLT 651.
2 *Hughes* at para 93.
3 *Hughes* at paras 95–99.
4 *Hughes* at para 94.

7.7 *Glasgow City Council v First Glasgow (No 1) Ltd*[1] arose out of the Glasgow bin lorry crash in December 2011, caused when the driver blacked out. The council, the driver's employer, settled a claim brought by the families of one of the deceased. The council claimed the driver's previous employer knew of a previous blackout but omitted to mention this in any employment reference. It sought to recover the settlement sum from the defenders under a statutory mechanism, operable where the defenders also owed a duty of care to the victim.[2] The Lord Ordinary (Ericht) accepted that any duty would be novel.[3] The closest analogy, *Spring v Guardian Assurance*,[4] recognised that a previous employer owed an employee a duty to take reasonable care not to give an inaccurate reference which may harm future employment prospects.

Adopting the incremental approach, would it be justified to extend the duty in *Spring* so that it could be owed to a third party, unknown to the defender, who was physically injured by their ex-employee? The Lord Ordinary thought not. While His Lordship thought harm was reasonably foreseeable, the proximity between the previous employer and their ex-employee in *Spring* was of a far closer degree than that which existed between the previous employer and the victim of the bin lorry crash. Unlike the employee in *Spring*, the victim would have been wholly unaware of the fact a reference had been given and placed no reliance on the reference, or that there was any assumption of responsibility.[5] A comparison was also made with *Mitchell v Glasgow City Council*: there, it was held that a landlord had no duty to warn its tenant of the risk of physical danger, a decision reached in the context of a much more proximate relationship than that in the instant case.[6] Imposition of a duty, further, would not be fair, just, and reasonable.[7] The driver's current employer owed the victim a duty, so the victim had a remedy elsewhere. Moreover, as in *Hughes*, imposition of a duty might undermine a socially (and, in this case, economically) desirable practice: few, if any, employers being willing to provide references if doing so exposed them to liability for physical injury to members of the public injured in course of their ex-employee's subsequent employment.

Subsequently, the council reframed its argument and contended that the defender had caused it pure economic loss (in the form of the money paid out to settle claims) and alleged a novel duty to take care to avoid such loss when providing a reference was owed.[8] But the court left this question open, as it concluded that no reference had been provided by the defender.

1 [2019] CSOH 101, 2020 SLT 75. Cf *NM v Henderson* [2025] CSIH 22, dubiously concluding that the duty contended for there was not novel.
2 Law Reform (Miscellaneous Provisions) Act 1940, s 3, discussed in *First Glasgow* at paras 16–21.
3 *First Glasgow* at para 26 and 40.
4 [1995] 2 AC 296, discussed in *First Glasgow* at paras 27–29.
5 *First Glasgow* at paras 41 and 43.
6 2009 SC (HL) 21, discussed in *First Glasgow* at paras 29–31 and 41.
7 *First Glasgow* at para 42.
8 [2022] CSOH 8 at para 2.

PSYCHOLOGICAL INJURY

7.8 We have already seen in Chapter 4 the tightly-drawn rules the courts have developed for recovery in relation to psychological injuries. But where those rules are not directly engaged, would-be primary or secondary victims may seek to use the incremental approach to argue for the existence of a duty of care.

One of the claimants in *Kerrigan v Elevate Credit International Ltd*[1] argued that their depression was aggravated when the defendant, a payday loan provider, agreed to loan him large sums of money. It was contended that the creditor owed the customer a duty, when assessing his creditworthiness and subsequently deciding to make the loan, to take care not to cause him psychiatric injury. No closely analogous authority existed.[2] The court considered the claim to be one for psychiatric injury which derived from the pure economic loss represented by the debt incurred by the customer, and therefore the pure economic loss context provided a useful comparator.[3] Unlike where recovery of pure economic loss is permitted under *Hedley Byrne* principles, the instant case involved no advice or statement, no holding out of expertise, no reliance, and no objective assumption to take reasonable care to prevent harm of the kind suffered.[4] Any extension would not be an incremental one, and the judge was not convinced that sufficient foreseeability or proximity existed to justify the imposition of a duty.[5] But even if so, a duty would be precluded on policy grounds.[6] Statute permitted the regulator to enact specific remedies for losses caused by infringements of financial regulatory rules.[7] Any decision to effectively extend this to psychiatric injury should be a decision for the regulator who was better placed to assess the competing public interests; the court should not second-guess this by extending a common law duty to cover losses not yet encompassed by the regulatory scheme.

1 [2020] EWHC 2169 (Comm).
2 *Kerrigan* at para 166, noting that the case was very different from those involving primary or secondary victims of accidents. The analogy with workplace stress cases or those involving psychiatric injuries suffered by prisoners was not thought particularly close: paras 167–168.
3 *Kerrigan* at para 169.
4 *Kerrigan* at paras 173–175.
5 *Kerrigan* at paras 176–177.
6 *Kerrigan* at paras 179–182.
7 These rules, promulgated under the Financial Markets and Services Act 2000, s 138D, apply only to financial losses. Breaches were found in *Kerrigan* at paras 128–131.

7.9 A novel duty to take reasonable care not to inflict psychiatric injury when giving advice relating to a licencing decision was considered in *Arshad v Wokingham Borough Council.*[1] Mr Arshad, a taxi driver, contacted his local authority to enquire if the Ford Galaxy he was considering would be suitable for use as a taxi, as there were specific accessibility requirements for his type of licence. A council employee responded that such a car was appropriate, once Mr Arshad proceeded to purchase it. However, council subsequently withdrew his licence on the basis that the Ford Galaxy was not, in fact, compliant with its requirements. He alleged that the loss of his licence (and therefore livelihood) caused a depressive disorder, and that the inaccurate advice breached a duty of care owed to him by the council. This being a novel duty, the court considered the closest analogy to be the economic loss case of *Welton v North Cornwall District Council*, where a council employee negligently instructed owners of a guest house to undertake substantial renovation of their property for licencing purposes.[2] There was a clear assumption of responsibility in that case, recognised in the context of a statutory licencing regime. The council knew the identity of Mr Arshad when it provided the advice, and clearly knew the purpose for which he would rely on that information.[3] Such a duty would be fair: Mr Arshad had no other redress, and the council's policy was 'opaque', and the advice was necessary for him to know how to comply with his terms.[4] If this was a case about economic loss, therefore, it is likely a duty would have been imposed on the facts. However, the court held on the facts that *psychiatric* injury to the claimant was not reasonably foreseeable: the council had no particular knowledge of a pre-existing vulnerability to depression, which is the control mechanism employed in other cases of 'pure' psychiatric injury.[5] This lack of foreseeability precluded the existence of a duty.

1 [2022] EWHC 2419 (KB).
2 [1997] 1 WLR 570 (CA), discussed in *Arshad* at paras 32–36.
3 *Arshad* at paras 27–30.
4 *Arshad* at paras 39–43.
5 *Arshad* at paras 56–62, referring to workplace stress cases (see para 10.4 below) and *Yapp v Foreign and Commonwealth Office* [2014] EWCA Civ 1512. See also *K v Police Scotland* [2020] CSIH 18, 2020 SC 399 at paras 125–130 (no duty to avoid causing psychiatric harm by conduct of investigation by one employee to another).

7.10 *Feder and McCamish v Royal Welsh College of Music and Drama*[1] was a claim brought by two students who alleged that their university negligently responded to their reporting of sexual assaults committed by a fellow student. For the judge, most aspects of the case were covered by established principles (the college had taken some positive acts which had exacerbated matters, and, analogously with *Phelps*, had assumed responsibility to support and protect the claimants).[2] However, one alleged duty – to take care to ensure confidential information relating to the disciplinary investigation was not disclosed – was, in the education context, novel. It was reasonably foreseeable, in the instance of a victim of sexual assault, that a negligently-conducted investigation resulting in disclosure of sensitive information could cause psychiatric injury.[3] There was close proximity between the college and its students, particularly where specific assurances that the disciplinary process would be carried out confidentially.[4] The imposition of a duty was justified in policy terms:[5] in effect, the legal duty of care would merely reflect normal practice in the higher education context and give legal underpinning to student expectations. It also would be unjust if there was no remedy for the college's negligence;[6] it was no answer to say that the students could sue their assailant.

1 Central London County Court, 5 October 2023, Cases G67YJ147 and G67YJ153.
2 *Feder and McCamish* at paras 491–496 and 538–560, discussing and applying *Phelps v Hillingdon London Borough Council* [2001] 2 AC 619 (HL).
3 *Feder and McCamish* at paras 564–565.
4 *Feder and McCamish* at paras 566–567.
5 *Feder and McCamish* at paras 569–571.
6 Compare, on this point, *Abrahart v University of Bristol* [2022] 5 WLUK 260, where the County Court Judge refused to recognise a novel general duty to take reasonable care for student's wellbeing. One key reason (at para 151) was that the claim arose from a failure to implement reasonable adjustments, which gave rise to liability under the Equality Act 2010. The equality law aspect of the case was upheld with limited discussion of the negligence point: [2024] EWHC 299 (KB).

ECONOMIC LOSS

7.11 The instinctive response of the law of delict when faced with a claim for pure economic loss is to grasp for the assumption of responsibility concept. Both careless advice/statements and performances of services form established categories where, if an assumption of responsibility exists on the facts, a duty of care to avoid causing pure economic loss will arise. In *NRAM v Steel*, after observing the foundational nature of assumption of responsibility to statement and services cases, Lord Wilson noted that the concept 'may require cautious incremental development in order to fit cases to which it does not readily apply'.[1] Apart from the case considered in the next paragraph, it should be noted there have been attempts to argue for novel duties to prevent economic loss in the employment context[2] and in the banking context.[3]

1 [2018] UKSC 13, 2018 SC (UKSC) 141 at para 24.
2 See eg *Rihan v Ernst and Young Global Ltd* [2020] EWHC 901 (QB) (novel, but limited, duty to ensure that audit conducted ethically recognised); *Benyatov v Credit Suisse Securities (Europe) Ltd* [2023] EWCA Civ 140, [2023] ICR 534 (novel duty to protect employee from economic loss arising from criminal prosecution arising out of exercise of functions not recognised).
3 See *Larsson v Revolut Ltd* [2024] EWHC 1287 (Ch) and *Santander UK Plc v CCP Graduate School Ltd* [2025] EWHC 667 (KB) (no novel duty on banks to prevent economic loss occasioned by fraudsters instructing payments into accounts held with that bank).

7.12 Perhaps the fullest consideration of the incremental approach post-*Robinson* comes from the pure economic loss case of *Commodity Solution Services Ltd v First Scottish Searching Services Ltd.*[1] The pursuer obtained an 'inhibition' against a recalcitrant debtor. When registered against the debtor, an inhibition prohibits them from selling or burdening their heritable property until the owed debt is paid. Solicitors for intending house purchasers routinely search the Register of Inhibitions; discovery of an inhibition against the seller will usually be fatal to a sale. In this case, the defenders had been instructed by a solicitor to search the register against the third party. Negligently, they did not report on the inhibition which was in place, and the third party sold their house to a buyer. As a result of statutory reforms to the law of inhibitions, that sale terminated the inhibition and substantially reduced the assets available to satisfy the pursuer's debt. The pursuer brought a claim against the defender in negligence, contending that its negligence caused it to lose the chance of recovering the debt owed to it by the third party.

It should be noted that there was no relationship between the pursuer and the defender, nor between the third party debtor and the defender. The defender was engaged by the solicitor of an intending purchaser. No prior authority directly bore on the question. This was therefore a novel situation. The defender contended that the closest analogy was *Customs and Excise Commissioners v Barclays Bank*.[2] There, the defendant received notice of a freezing injunction obtained by the claimants in respect of one of its customers but negligently allowed sums to leave the customer's account in violation of the injunction. No duty of care was owed in that case, which, the defenders submitted, made it even less likely a duty was owed in the present case: in *Barclays*, the defendants were aware of the claimant and the freezing order they had obtained, whereas there was no such knowledge in the instant case. The pursuer, instead, argued that *Ministry of Housing and Local Government v Sharp* was the better analogy.[3] There, an error by a clerk failed to discover the existence of a compensation notice imposed on a plot of land for planning purposes, meaning that the plaintiff could not recover that sum from a subsequent purchaser of that land. It was held that the clerk owed the creditor a duty of care. Like the present case, it concerned a negligent search of a registry which destroyed the utility of a protective device granted in favour of a creditor, of which and of whom the searcher was unaware.

The Sheriff Appeal Court agreed with the pursuer.[4] It observed that the key distinction was that the searcher in *Sharp* was a clerk for a local authority performing a public service, whereas the searcher in the instant case was a private firm operating for profit. Nevertheless, as in *Sharp*, the searchers could have been said, in a sense, to have assumed responsibility to creditors present on the register to take care to correctly discover the existence of their interest on the register. The searchers could not rely on their negligent failure to discover the existence of the pursuer's interest to deny the existence of a proximate relationship. This was therefore an incremental extension of *Sharp*,[5] and the court considered such an extension to be justified on policy grounds.[6] While Parliament could have, when reforming the law of inhibitions, legislated to provide a remedy to a creditor in these circumstances, the fact that it did not do so did not preclude the existence of a duty. There was no indication of parliamentary intention; the assumption may well have been that the system relied upon accurate searches by competent searchers. The existence of a duty would incentivise accuracy, provided the pursuer with a remedy, and placed no greater burden on searchers than existed prior to the statutory reform of the law of inhibitions.

1 [2019] SAC Civ 4, 2019 SC (SAC) 41.
2 [2006] UKHL 28, [2007] 1 AC 181, discussed at paras 35–36 of *Commodity Solution*.
3 [1970] 2 QB 223 (CA), discussed at paras 37–40 of *Commodity Solution*.
4 *Commodity Solution* at para 43.
5 *Commodity Solution* at paras 44–45.
6 *Commodity Solution* at paras 46–47.

CONCLUSION

7.13 In this chapter, we have surveyed the 'incremental' approach adopted by the courts where the answer to the question of whether a duty of care exists is not precisely provided by previous authority. Considerations of foreseeability, proximity, and especially policy provide comparators to evaluate the similarity between prior cases and that before the court.

As we have said, it is difficult to give a clear indication of when a situation will be deemed to be a 'novel' one. From the above discussion of a small number of cases, certain pointers emerge. The characteristics of the defender may make the case a novel one: for instance, the fact that the defender is a voluntary charitable organisation may justify treating the alleged duty of care as novel, even if there are previous cases holding that an NHS or private doctor would owe a duty in similar circumstances. Similarly, identity of the pursuer may also distinguish the duty as a novel one, such as where the pursuer stands in a more remote position from the defender than did the pursuers in previous cases where a duty has been held to exist. While the parameters of the alleged duty may be similar to that established in previous cases, the statutory context may be so distinct that it justifies treating the case as a novel one. Finally, it may be that a duty in similar cases to protect against a certain type of loss is well-established, but the instant case seeks to extend that duty to cover a new type of loss or interest: that may be an indication that the instant case is 'novel'.

The main purpose of this chapter has been to introduce the operation of policy reasoning in the duty context. Previously much less confined, the question of fairness, justness and reasonableness has a very specific role in the modern law, arising only when the court is taking a decision as to whether to extend the duty of care to cover the situation presently before. Again, the sheer variety of different policy contentions mean that we cannot exhaustively state all potentially relevant arguments. However, from the above cases, we can see that policy arguments which favour the recognition of a duty include the absence of an alternative remedy and the fact that a legal duty of care would simply reflect best practice. Going the other way, the fact that imposition of a duty of care would conflict with statutory regimes, or place the defender in a situation involving an unresolvable conflict of interests, or burden a valuable activity with so much risk as to jeopardise its pursuit, will be factors precluding the existence of a duty.

CHAPTER 8

Breach of a Duty of Care

INTRODUCTION

8.1 In Chapter 3, we started our discussion of the duty of care by identifying the four elements required to claim compensation for loss or damage resulting from a negligent act:

(1) that the defender owes a duty of care to the pursuer;

(2) that the defender breached that duty of care;

(3) that the pursuer suffered a legally recoverable loss or injury; and

(4) that there is a causal link between the loss or injury and the breach of the duty of care.

In this chapter, we turn our attention to the second element, asking the simple question: what specific conduct is required to fulfil the duty of care?

THREE COMMON MISTAKES

8.2 First, it is important to underscore an obvious, yet often overlooked, point: the law of delict only seeks to impose liability where the defender's conduct falls below a legally required standard of care; it is not concerned with imposing liability for each and every accident. In simple terms, the law expects a defender's conduct to match the standard of the reasonable person in the position of the defender. The law does not expect the defender to go beyond this standard and prevent every conceivable accident. This point was forcibly made in *Muir v Glasgow Corporation*.[1]

Second, and relatedly, there is a difference between questions about the *scope* of the duty of care and specific issues relating to the *standard* of that care. Both inquires may lead, by different routes, to a conclusion that there was no delictual wrongdoing.[2] However, as we explained in Chapter 3, the conventional approach today is to first state whether there is a duty of care, and then determine, second, what is the standard of care. In stating what the duty of care is, courts must be careful not to conflate that stage of inquiry with the second stage. Such a mistake is understandable, as at the duty stage you ask what a reasonable person could *foresee* and then at the breach stage you ask what the reasonable person would *do*. In practice, it can be tempting to be too precise when stating the duty of care. And, it is not always straightforward to distinguish these questions, especially in complex cases.[3] Yet, for our purposes, the key point is to ensure that such determinations are made on the correct basis, ie are we considering the overall scope of the duty of care, or are we investigating what is reasonable to expect of the defender? Each question should be dealt with separately.[4]

It is worth recapping what was examined in Chapter 3 regarding the scope of the duty of care. Questions about whether there is a duty of care in the first place – and the *extent* of that duty of care – relate to an earlier stage of examination. Here, a court will investigate (usually by applying established authority) whether there is a sufficiently proximate relationship between A and B in relation to preventing a particular type of foreseeable loss to B. As the aforementioned *Hughes v Lord Advocate* demonstrates, duty and scope questions are about establishing the general *type of foreseeable harm* and the general *nature of the relationship* in question.[5] It should be borne in mind that, historically, Scots law would examinate this type of question by asking if the loss or injury was too remote, ie it was not reasonably foreseeable that the pursuer would suffer that type of loss.[6] Today, it is far more common to argue that the loss was beyond the scope of the duty of care rather than framing it as a question of remoteness.[7]

Cases relating to medical or financial advice are most likely to give rise to questions of scope. Take the following example: if an individual seeks medical advice due to concerns that a future child might develop a potential hereditary condition, such as haemophilia, the doctor's duty of care in this scenario involves providing guidance on the likelihood of the child being born with that condition. It is reasonably foreseeable in this scenario that any negligent advice given about the condition will result in a specific type of identifiable harm. The duty does not extend, in these circumstances to other conditions, such as autism, which the child may be born with which do not relate to the hereditary condition.[8] We shall return to this scenario when discussing professional negligence in Chapter 11.

Third, a pursuer must be mindful of the position of the defender when setting out the alleged standard of care. In this chapter, we will discuss the general default rules relating to the standard of care. In subsequent chapters, we will explain the tailored rules which apply in situations involving defenders who are professionals, such as doctors; occupiers of property; manufacturers; and employers. If the defender falls into one of these categories, then the pursuer should use different precedents or legislation to establish the standard of care. Hence, there are specific legal regimes setting out the standard of care required of defenders in particular positions, and care must be taken in selecting the right regime.

The existence of separate or overlapping regimes means that, frequently, the default common law rules, which are explained in this chapter, will be supplemented with, or displaced by, tailored rules that are more appropriately calibrated to the position of the defender. For example, in cases involving faulty consumer goods or injuries sustained due to the state of someone's property, utilising a pursuer may opt to plead the common law articulation of the standard of care *and* the statutory position. For now, we examine the general approach leaving later chapters to explore the tailored regimes.

1 1943 SC (HL) 3. See discussion at para 3.10 above.
2 See *Newcastle Building Society v Paterson Robertson & Graham* 2001 SC 734 (OH).
3 See the Inner House decision in *SA v Grampian Health Board* [2024] CSIH 7 at paras 80 to 81 per Lord Malcolm. Here the Inner House, rightly, cast doubt on the extent to which questions relating to the duty of care can solve issues relating to the standard of care.
4 On the importance of these distinctions, see James Goudkamp, 'Breach of duty: a disappearing element of the action in negligence' [2017] *Cambridge Law Journal* 480. Arguably, however, matters of structure have gone too far in some cases, see: *Khan v Meadows* [2021] UKSC 21, [2022] AC 852. For a helpful case comment, see John Macleod, 'Harm Is Where One Starts From: *Khan v Meadows* and *Manchester Building Society v Grant Thornton LLP*' (2022) 26(1) *Edinburgh Law Review* 123. Now see the clarification in *Armstead v Royal & Sun Alliance Insurance Company Ltd* [2024] UKSC 6, [2025] AC 406 at para 73.
5 1963 SC (HL) 31; see also *Cruickshanks v Glasgow City Council* [2024] CSOH 35, 2024 SLT 526 at para 30 per Lord Weir.
6 *Reavis v Clan Line Steamers Ltd* 1925 SC 725 (IH).
7 *Simmons v British Steel plc* [2004] UKHL 20, 2004 SC (HL) 94.
8 *Khan v Meadows; DD v NHS Fife Health Board* [2022] SAC (Civ) 27 at paras 34–38.

THE STANDARD OF CARE

(1) Objectivity of the test

8.3 Famously, Lord Macmillan in *Muir v Glasgow Corporation* described the standard of care as an 'impersonal test' which 'eliminates the personal equation and is independent of the idiosyncrasies of the particular person whose conduct is in question.'[1]. Courts, therefore, take an objective approach in determining what a reasonable person would do. Mustill LJ explained in *Wilsher v Essex AHA*,[2] the duty is tailored to the *act* performed not the *actor* performing it. So, if a trainee doctor undertakes a particularly difficult procedure, the standard of care expected of them is that of a qualified doctor rather than a trainee doctor.[3] The reasonable standard of care is not, therefore, subjective. It does not adjust according to the specific abilities and skills of the defender. The standard is determined according to the nature of the act undertaken by the defender. Hence, a learner driver whilst driving a car on a public road is judged according to the standards of a qualified driver.[4]

Some exceptions should be considered. First, if someone is acting in an emergency then the court will only expect a reasonable degree of control over one's actions. People can react instinctively and impulsively when faced with an imminent threat. For example, in *Ng Chun Pui v Lee Chuen Tat* a driver swerved to avoid a car which had unexpectedly cut in front of them.[5] The instinctive actions of the driver, which caused harm, could not be judged as negligent given the specific circumstances. However, in *Sutherland v Glasgow Corporation*,[6] such an argument was unsuccessful. Accepting that such a response is available to a defender in Scots law, the Inner House nevertheless concluded, in this case, that a tramway car driver who applied the brakes suddenly to avoid a small dog was negligent. Here, the defender had failed to demonstrate the existence of a sufficiently serious emergency to explain their actions. Likewise, it was found in *Woodhouse v Lochs and Glens (Transport) Ltd*[7] that adverse weather conditions in the Highlands of Scotland did not amount an unpredictable emergency upon which the defender, an otherwise negligent coach driver, could justify their actions.

Courts are prepared to depart from the objective approach when it comes to sporting activities. In such cases, the expectation is that the participant acts with the care of reasonable player in *similar circumstances* to the defender. Here then we find an evident departure from the objectivity expectation because an amateur in a sporting context is assessed according to a comparator, ie another amateur and not a professional who has a higher degree of skill and experience.[8] The decision of the defender is therefore not scrutinised as closely as if they were a reasonable person. If participants were expected to obtain a higher standard, some may decide not to participate in sport for fear of being sued after a momentary lapse in judgement or lack of desired skill. As Lord Macphail has explained, only 'errors of judgement or lapse of skill going beyond such as, in the stress of the circumstances, may reasonably be regarded as excusable.'[9] However, if instinctive action or quick decision making is not necessarily part of the sport, such as golf, a court will not depart from the objective approach.[10]

It is also important to consider the position of children. Unfortunately, however, there is scant authority on this question as it rarely arises in reported case law. Nonetheless, based on *obiter dicta* it is fair to suppose that courts, if called upon, will adjust the standard of care thereby departing from the objectivity test. Thus, when an 8-year-old boy was injured by another during boisterous play, the Inner House commented that: '[t]hey were just playing as children will, and blame can hardly be attributed to [the child] who caused the unfortunate results which happened.'[11] In *Hunter v Perth and Kinross Council*[12] the Outer House, considering the English case of *Mullin v Richards*,[13] confirmed that the standard of care owed by a child is 'to be viewed from the perspective of what might reasonably be expected of a child of similar age and experience.'[14] It has, however, been suggested that the standard of care will not be varied if children are engaged in 'more adult pursuits.'[15] For example, the use of motorised vehicles would be considered an adult activity thereby raising the standard expected back up to the objective level of a reasonable adult exercising due skill and care. Nevertheless, it is highly unlikely that a case involving the direct negligence of a child will come to court given the alternative courses of action available to pursuers, such as seeking to find parents, carers, and teachers etc directly liable, in most conceivable cases where a child may cause injury or damage.

1 1943 SC HL 3 at 11.
2 [1987] QB 730 (CA).
3 *Andrews v Greater Glasgow Health Board* [2019] CSOH 31, 2019 SLT 727.
4 *Nettleship v Weston* [1971] 2 QB 691 (CA).
5 [1988] RTR 298 (PC, Hong Kong).
6 1949 SC 563 (IH), affirmed by the House of Lords at 1951 SC (HL) 1.
7 *Woodhouse v Lochs and Glens (Transport) Ltd* [2019] CSOH 105, 2020 SLT 208, reversed on other grounds [2020] CSIH 67, 2020 SLT 1203.
8 *Sharp v Highland and Islands Fire Board* [2005] CSOH 111, 2005 SLT 855.
9 *Sharp* at para 26.
10 *McMahon v Dear* [2014] CSOH 100, 2014 SLT 823.
11 *Gow v Glasgow Education Authority* 1922 SC 260 (IH) at 277 per the Lord Justice-Clerk (Scott Dickson).
12 2001 SCLR 856 (OH).
13 [1998] 1 WLR 1304 (CA).
14 *Mullin* at para 46.
15 E Reid, *The Law of Delict in Scotland* (2022) at para 10.35.

(2) The calculus of risk

8.4 How, then, do we determine the standard of care of a reasonable person? In somewhat poetic terms, Lord Macmillan described the reasonable person as follows:[1]

> 'Some persons are by nature unduly timorous and imagine every path beset with lions. Others, of more robust temperament, fail to foresee or nonchalantly disregard even the most obvious dangers. The reasonable man is presumed to be free both from over-apprehension and from over-confidence, but there is a sense in which the standard of care of the reasonable man involves in its application a subjective element. It is still left to the judge to decide what, in the circumstances of the particular case, the reasonable man would have had in contemplation, and what, accordingly, the party sought to be made liable ought to have foreseen.'

Despite its lyrical appeal, Lord Macmillan's approach offers only general guidance. Over the years, courts have developed numerous individual questions, which help to calibrate the most appropriate standard to be applied in any given case. In *Phee v Gordon*, Lord Hodge explained:[2]

> 'The court in assessing what a reasonable man would do uses a calculus of risk. It weighs up: (i) the likelihood of causing injury; (ii) the seriousness of that injury; (iii) the difficulty, inconvenience and cost of preventive measures; and (iv) the value of the activity that gives rise to the risk. For an example of the court attaching weight to the social value of the activity that gives rise to the risk and the adverse effect which the preventive measures would have on that activity.'

This is a non-exhaustive list of relevant considerations. Some factors will be more relevant than others depending on the circumstances; the court does not always need utilise all these individual factors in determining what a reasonable person would do, only those which are pertinent to the risk under examination. Nonetheless, balancing these factors is something which a reasonable person ought to do when determining whether to take a course of action.[3] We shall, therefore, examine each in turn.

1 1943 SC (HL) 3 at 11.
2 [2013] CSIH 18, 2013 SC 379 at para 28.
3 *Tomlinson v Congleton BC* [2003] UKHL 47, [2004] 1 AC 46 (HL); *Phee*; *Warner v Scapa Flow Charters* [2022] CSIH 25, 2022 SLT 609.

(3) Probability or likelihood of injury to the pursuer

8.5 Even if some harm to the pursuer is foreseeable, a defender who causes such an injury is not negligent in failing to take precautions to avoid it if the risk of that particular injury is so improbable that a reasonable person in the position of the defender would not have taken any precautions. Thus, for example, in *Bolton v Stone*[1] the plaintiff was injured by a cricket ball which had been hit out of a cricket ground. This had happened on six occasions in the previous 30 years, and no one had been injured. Lord Reid explained:[2]

> 'In my judgment, the test to be applied here is whether the risk of damage to a person on the road was so small that a reasonable man in the position of the appellants [the defendants], considering the matter from the point of view of safety, would have thought it right to refrain from taking steps to prevent the damage. In considering the matter I think that it would be right to take into account, not only how remote is the chance that a person might be struck, but also how serious the consequences are likely to be if a person is struck, but I do not think that it would be right to take into account the difficulty of remedial measures. If cricket cannot be played on a ground without creating a substantial risk, then it should not be played there at all.'

The House of Lords held that the defendants had not been negligent in failing to take precautions since the risk of injury was so slight in the circumstances that a reasonable person in the position of the defendants would not have taken any precautions.

1 [1951] AC 850 (HL).
2 *Bolton* at 868.

(4) Seriousness of injury to potential pursuer

8.6 As Lord Reid indicated in the passage cited above, the seriousness of the consequences for a person if he is injured is a relevant factor. In *Paris v Stepney Borough Council*,[1] a mechanic who had the use of only one eye was not supplied with goggles. When he was removing a rusty bolt from a car with a hammer, a chip of metal flew into his good eye and as a result he became totally blind. The employer had known that the plaintiff had only one eye. It was accepted that it was not the practice in the industry to supply goggles to workers engaged on the plaintiff's tasks. The question, however, was whether the employer had been negligent in failing to provide goggles for an employee whom they knew was already partially sighted. In the Court of Appeal,[2] the plaintiff's claim failed. Asquith LJ took the view that while the greater risk of injury was a relevant factor, the risk of greater injury was not. The House of Lords held, however, that the seriousness of the consequences of an injury for a particular plaintiff was a relevant consideration. Lord Normand observed:[3]

> 'The court's task of deciding what precautions a reasonable and prudent man would take in the circumstances of a particular case may not be easy. Nevertheless, the judgment of the reasonable and prudent man should be allowed its common every day scope, and it should not be restrained from considering the foreseeable consequences of an accident and their seriousness for the person to whom the duty of care is owed … the seriousness of the injury or damage risked and the likelihood of its being in fact caused may not be the only relevant factors. For example, Asquith LJ in *Daborn v Bath Tramways Motor Co Ltd and Smithey*[4] pointed out that it is sometimes necessary to take account of the consequences of not assuming a risk.'

Since the consequences of an eye injury for an already partially sighted person could be total blindness, the court held that the employer had been negligent in failing to provide him with goggles. It was irrelevant that the defendants might not have been negligent in failing to provide goggles to two-eyed workers.

1 [1951] AC 367 (HL).
2 [1949] 2 All ER 843 (CA).

3 [1951] AC 367 at 381–382.
4 [1946] 2 All ER 333 at 336 (CA).

(5) Utility of the activity

8.7 *Daborn v Bath Tramways Motor Co Ltd and Smithey*,[1] cited in the quotation from *Stepney*, concerned an ambulance with a left-hand drive which was used during World War II. The plaintiff had put a sign at the back of the vehicle which said, 'Caution – Left hand drive – No signals'. When she was turning to the right, having given a hand signal, she collided with a bus which she could not see was trying to overtake her. The plaintiff was injured. The defendant argued that the plaintiff, as well as the bus driver, had been negligent and that her damages should be reduced on the grounds of her contributory negligence.[2] The Court of Appeal held that the plaintiff had not been negligent. In the course of his judgment Asquith LJ said:[3]

> 'I think that the plaintiff did all that in the circumstances she could reasonably be required to do if you include in those circumstances, as I think you should: (i) the necessity in time of national emergency of employing all transport resources which were available and (ii) the inherent limitations and incapacities of this particular form of transport. In considering whether reasonable care has been observed, one must balance the risk against the consequences of not assuming that risk, and in the present instance that calculation seems to me to work out in favour of the plaintiff.'

Thus, the social utility of the activities which it is foreseeable may cause injury must be taken into account. In *Watt v Hertfordshire County Council*[4] a woman was trapped under a vehicle. The fire service sent a lorry with a jack. During the attempt to rescue the woman, the jack slipped and a fireman was injured. He claimed that the defendants, his employers, were negligent in not using a specially adapted lorry. The court held that given the emergency the employers were justified in using the vehicle which was available, ie a reasonable employer would have used the vehicle. They had not therefore fallen below the standard of the reasonable person in their position and therefore had not broken the duty of care which they owed to their employee. In *French v Strathclyde Fire Board*[5] it was observed that when fighting a fire, it might be reasonable to take a risk to save a life which would not be reasonable to prevent damage to property.

There can also be a social value in not taking steps to prevent a foreseeable accident. In *Tomlinson v Congleton Borough Council*,[6] the House of Lords held that a local authority was not under an obligation to take steps to reduce or eliminate the dangers of swimming in a lake. It was enough that they had provided warning notices. To do more would hinder the general public from enjoying the amenities of the lakeside:

> 'The majority of people who went to the beaches to sunbathe, paddle and play with their children were enjoying themselves in a way which gave them pleasure and caused no risk to themselves or anyone else. This must be something to be taken into account in deciding whether it was reasonable to expect the council to destroy the beaches.'[7]

Conversely, if there is no social value in the defender's failure to take reasonable steps to eliminate or reduce a risk, the defender's omission to do so will be negligent.[8]

1 [1946] 2 All ER 333 (CA).
2 On contributory negligence, see paras 9.13–9.15 below.
3 [1946] 2 All ER 333 (CA) at 336.
4 [1954] 1 WLR 208 (CA).
5 [2013] CSOH 3, 2013 SLT 247.
6 [2003] UKHL 47, [2004] 1 AC 46.
7 *Tomlinson* per Lord Hoffmann at 84. His speech at 82–86 provides an excellent example of the calculus of risk. Lord Hoffmann also considered that. as a general rule. the owner or occupier of property did not owe a duty of care to prevent persons engaging in activities on their land such as swimming or mountaineering, which involved an inherent risk of personal harm: *Tomlinson* at 84.
8 *Jolley v Sutton Borough Council* [2000] 1 WLR 1082 (HL) (no social value in failing to remove a rotting boat from a council estate).

(6) Practicality of precautions

8.8 The hypothetical reasonable person in the position of the defender will – indeed, can – only take such precautions as are practicable to avoid the risk of harm. In *Quinn v Cameron and Roberton Ltd*,[1] for example, the pursuer developed pneumoconiosis as a result of prolonged exposure to silica dust where he was working. His case against his employers failed on the basis that since the danger to employees from silica dust in iron foundries was not appreciated during the period when the pursuer was working for the employer (nine years prior to 1951), the defenders were not in breach of their duty of care by not providing precautions. Another reason why they had not been negligent was that effective dust extraction appliances were not available to the employers until 1950. The Lord President (Clyde) explained:[2]

> 'The Lord Ordinary has held it proved that the provision of dust extraction appliances at plough buffs was not general practice between 1946 and 1951, and the expert evidence is really unanimously in favour of this conclusion. Indeed any apparatus to cope with the dangerous dust only seems to have come into the market in 1950, and went into general practice thereafter.'

1 1956 SC 224 (IH). See also *Smith v P & O Bulk Shipping Ltd* [1998] 2 Lloyd's Rep 81 (QBD) (employer could not have known about danger from asbestos when plaintiff was employee).

2 *Quinn* at 233.

(7) Cost of precautions

8.9 The hypothetical reasonable person in the position of the defender will consider the cost of precautions and balance this against the probability of risk of harm and the seriousness of any injuries likely to be sustained. The defender's duty is not to be negligent; it is not to act to eliminate all risks of injury to the pursuer. Thus, for example, in *Latimer v AEC Ltd*[1] a factory floor became slippery because of a phenomenal rainstorm. In an attempt to avoid accidents, the employer spread three tons of sawdust on the floor. Nevertheless, an employee slipped and was injured on a part of the floor *not* covered by sawdust.[2] The plaintiff argued that the employer should have closed the factory while the floor was properly cleaned, thus eliminating the risk of employees slipping. This would, of course, have involved loss of production. The House of Lords held that the employer did all that a reasonable person would have done and was therefore not negligent. For Lord Tucker the only question was:[3]

> 'Has it been proved that the floor was so slippery that, remedial steps not being possible, a reasonably prudent employer would have closed down the factory rather than allow his employees to run the risks involved in continuing work? … The absence of any evidence that anyone in the factory during the afternoon or night shift, other than the appellant, slipped, or experienced any difficulty, or that any complaint was made by or on behalf of the workers, all points to the conclusion that the danger was, in fact, not such as to impose on a reasonable employer the obligation [to close down the factory].'

In *Charlton v Forrest Printing Ink Co Ltd*[4] it was one of the tasks of a group of employees to collect the wages for the workforce from a bank and take them to the factory. The employer had warned them of the possibility of being robbed and advised them to vary the times – and the transport used – when they went to collect the wages. Nevertheless, there was a robbery, and the plaintiff was blinded by acid which had been thrown in his face. The Court of Appeal held that the employer had taken reasonable precautions and had not been negligent in failing to use the services of Securicor to uplift the wages, which could have been done at a very modest cost. On the other hand, if a risk can be eliminated or reduced at little cost, then the defender's failure to do so will be negligent.[5] In *Napier v Scottish Ministers*,[6] on the other hand, it was held that the defenders were in breach of their duty to take reasonable care for the health and safety of the pursuer who was in prison and still had to slop out. The cost of the improvements necessary to eliminate the need for slopping out did not prevent liability arising.

1 [1953] AC 643 (HL).
2 In spite of using three tons, some areas were left uncovered.
3 *Latimer* at 659.
4 [1980] IRLR 331 (CA). The case was concerned with an employer's *contractual* duty to take reasonable care for the safety of employees; but the point is also applicable in respect of the employer's *delictual* duty of care towards his employees.
5 *Jolley v Sutton Borough Council* [2000] 1 WLR 1082 (HL). It should be noted that in *Tomlinson v Congleton Borough Council* [2003] UKHL 47 [2004] 1 AC 46, Lord Hoffmann at 83 did not regard the cost of destroying the lakeside as an important factor as opposed to the loss of social utility which that would have involved.
6 2005 1 SC 229 (OH).

(8) Compliance with common practice

8.10 Nowadays, it is quite common to encounter practice notes, guidance materials, policy briefs, and risk assessments addressing safety concerns in workplaces, public areas, sports, and a wide variety of other activities. Whether these documents are produced by specific bodies – such as trade associations, local authorities, or employers' groups – and presented as industry standards, or developed independently by individual communities or organisations, such policies often carry significant practical influence.

Moreover, Health and Safety regulations determine the operations of many employers and others captured by the Health and Safety Act 1974. In addition, guidance and advisory notices prepared by the Health and Safety Executive are vital to the modern health and safety landscape in the UK.. Frequently, pursuers will rely on such documents or regulations to demonstrate that defenders were negligent. Defenders may also seek to use evidence of an accepted customary practice within the relevant field to demonstrate that their actions did not fall below the standard of care.

It is accepted that such guidance and practice is relevant to the judicial determination of the standard of care, but are not conclusive.[1] In this process, the existence of any pertinent health and safety regulations should not be conflated with the separate task of determining the standard of care.[2] Pursuers need to establish what the standard of care is, independently, and cannot simply rely on common practice, industry policies or health and safety regulations as a default demonstration of fault.[3] Courts will examine each case on an individual basis, considering the full context and circumstances, and will not simply adopt such documents or practice as the standard of care.[4] Nevertheless, a clear departure from a commonly accepted safety precaution regarding a well-recognised risk offers the pursuer strong evidence upon which to construct a breach of duty argument.

1 *Brown v Rolls Royce Limited* 1960 SC (HL) 22.
2 *Kennedy v Cordia (Services) LLP* [2016] UKSC 6, 2016 SC (UKSC) 59. For further consideration see Chapter 10.
3 As per s 16 of Enterprise and Regulatory Reform Act 2013, a breach of health and safety regulations does not give rise to civil liability. See also *Elizabeth Gilchrist v Asda Stores Limited* [2015] CSOH 77.
4 *John Strange v Wincanton Logistics Limited* [2011] CSIH 65.

CONCLUSION

8.11 In conclusion, there are some useful points to bear in mind.

First, it falls to the pursuer to specify the care or precautions that a person, acting reasonably, would have taken in the circumstances. This burden is not insignificant and contrasts with statutory regimes, such as the Consumer Protection Act 1987, which as we shall see in Chapter 13, redistributes the burden between the pursuer and defender. In a common law negligence action, however, the pursuer must state, in relatively precise terms, what the defender should have done.

Secondly, if the standard of care is inadequately specified, the claim will be challenged on relevancy at an early stage in the proceedings. Many of the reported cases which deal with breach of duty of care often originates in an initial objection by the defender to relevancy of the case, a lack of specification or on a point of law. In practice this often means that no evidence is proven by either party before the overall legal merits of the case are debated. It also means that a pursuer must be well-prepared in advance of raising proceedings as the expectation is that they will be able to state the entirety of their case on paper ahead of any subsequent trial of the facts.[1]

Third, in determining the standard of care, the scientific knowledge available to the hypothetical reasonable person at that time can be crucial. In *Roe v Minister of Health* a patient was given a spinal anaesthetic. As was ordinary practice at the time, the phials containing the anaesthetic were kept in a solution of phenol.[2] Unknown to the hospital, the phials developed invisible cracks, and the anaesthetic became impregnated with phenol. As a result of the phenol in the anaesthetic, the patient was paralysed. The court held that the defendant had not broken the duty of care owed to the plaintiff: given the state of scientific knowledge at the time, a reasonable medical practitioner could not have foreseen that paralysis of a patient was a reasonable and probable consequence of storing the phials in phenol.

Fourth, it is for the court to determine the standard of care. It is common today for parties to rely on reports prepared by health and safety experts, investigations carried out by experts, or to incorporate into their legal argument industry guidance documents. Of course, this is helpful to a court when it seeks to place itself into the position of the defender. Trial judges can gain a great deal from oral evidence given by experts or pre-prepared reports. But, importantly, it is for the court to make the decision, not the expert evidence.[3] It is open to the judge to depart from what experts advise as the final decision rests with the court.

Lastly, an appeal against a determination of a trial judge – who has heard the evidence and set the standard of care – can only be made if the decision is 'plainly wrong'.[4] If you therefore wish to challenge the decision of the court, the threshold for an appellant is high. As Lord Reed has explained, the plainly wrong test is only satisfied where no reasonable judge, presented with the facts, could have reached that decision.[5] A challenge to a decision on the standard of care requires, therefore, an appellant to show that the decision cannot reasonably be explained or justified. He added that there may also be a patent error which gives grounds for an appeal, such as:

> 'a material error of law, or the making of a critical finding of fact which has no basis in the evidence, or a demonstrable misunderstanding of relevant evidence, or a demonstrable failure to consider relevant evidence.'[6]

Although this sets the bar high, there can be instances where an appeal court in Scotland is prepared to review a decision regarding the standard of care.[7]

1 *Lamb v Wray* 2014 SLT (Sh Ct) 2.
2 [1954] 2 QB 66 (CA).
3 *Warner v Scapa Flow Charters* [2022] CSIH 25, 2020 SLT 609 at para 40 per the Lord President (Carloway).
4 *Clarke v Edinburgh and District Tramways Co* 1919 SC (HL) 35 at 37 per Lord Shaw.
5 *Henderson v Foxworth Investments Ltd* [2014] UKSC 41, 2014 SC (UKSC) 203.
6 *Henderson* at para 67.
7 See *Woodhouse v Lochs and Glens (Transport) Ltd* [2020] CSIH 67, 2020 SLT 1203.

CHAPTER 9

Causation and Defences in Negligence

9.1 Before there is liability in delict, the pursuer must prove on the balance of probabilities that the defender's wrongdoing was the cause of the harm sustained by the pursuer. Causation is an essential requirement of any form of delictual liability, but for the purposes of this book, we will only examine it separately in the context of negligence. But the same principles apply where the conduct is intentional. The concept of causation is a complex and difficult subject raising fundamental philosophical as well as legal issues. In a work of the present compass, only an outline of the relevant issues is given.[1]

1 See HLA Hart and AM Honoré, *Causation and the Law* (2nd edn, 1985); R Goldberg (ed), *Perspectives on Causation* (2011); S Green, *Causation in Negligence* (2015); S Steel, *Proof of Causation in Tort Law* (2016).

FACTUAL CAUSATION

9.2 The first essential is that the defender's acts or omissions are a cause of the harm suffered by the pursuer. This is a question of fact. If the defender's conduct is not a factual cause of the harm, there is no liability even if the defender has broken a duty of care which he owed to the pursuer. To use Latin terminology, the defender's breach of duty must be a *causa sine qua non* of the pursuer's material harm. In other words, 'but for' the defender's conduct, the pursuer would not have sustained the harm. If the pursuer would have suffered the same harm notwithstanding the defender's breach of duty, then the defender's conduct is not a factual cause of the harm, ie it is not a *causa sine qua non.*

Accordingly, to determine whether the defender's breach of duty is a factual cause of the harm suffered by the pursuer, we must ask ourselves whether 'but for' the breach of duty, the harm would have occurred. As with any other matter of proof in a civil court, the standard of proof is the balance of probabilities; ie whether or not it is more likely than not that the pursuer's account of what happened is true:[1]

- If the pursuer can establish that it is more likely than not that the harm would *not* have occurred absent the defender's breach of duty, then that breach is a factual cause of the pursuer's harm.

- If, however, it is more likely than not that the harm *still* would have occurred regardless of the defender's breach of duty, then the defender's conduct is *not* a factual cause of the pursuer's harm.

The onus of satisfying the 'but for' test on the balance of probabilities rests on the pursuer;[2] it is not for the defender to provide an alternative explanation.[3] The pursuer may also succeed partially on causation, ie to show that some but not all losses of which complaint is made were caused by the defender's negligence.[4]

Some simple examples will illustrate the operation of the 'but for' test. In *Barnett v Chelsea and Kensington Hospital Management Committee*,[5] for example, the plaintiff's husband drank a cup of tea and became violently ill because the tea had been poisoned. The hospital doctor refused to treat the husband telling him to see his own doctor. The husband died. It was held that although the defendant may have been in breach of a duty of care, the hospital was not liable because the husband would still have died of the poison even if he had been treated by the hospital doctor, ie the husband did not die 'but for' the hospital's negligence. His fate was sealed as soon as the poisoned tea was consumed. Accordingly, the breach of duty was not a *causa sine qua non* of the husband's death and the plaintiff's action failed.

In *Kay's Tutor v Ayrshire and Arran Health Board*,[6] a child was brought into hospital suffering from meningitis. He was given a massive overdose of penicillin. The child thereupon suffered severe convulsions but, as a result of treatment, recovered. However, the child was left deaf. In an action against the hospital, the defenders admitted that they were in breach of their duty of care in administering the overdose of penicillin but denied that this breach of duty had caused the child's deafness. The House of Lords held that the onus lay on the pursuer (the child's father) to prove that 'but for' the overdose the child would not be deaf. In the absence of evidence to show that an overdose of penicillin caused deafness in a patient, and given that deafness is common in patients who suffer meningitis, the pursuer failed to establish that 'but for' the breach of duty deafness would not have occurred. The breach was therefore not a *causa sine qua non* of the child's deafness and the pursuer's action failed.

The pursuer need not establish the exact mechanism which caused the harm; all they must show is that the mechanism of harm arose from the defender's negligence.[7] As factual causation is a question of fact, appellate courts will often defer to the judgement of the trial judge who heard all of the evidence. Decisions on factual causation will only be overturned if they are 'plainly wrong'.[8]

1 In other words, if the pursuer can establish that it is 51% or more likely that the defender's breach caused their loss, the pursuer will succeed on causation.

2 See, for example, *Dingley v Chief Constable of Strathclyde Police (No 1)* 2000 SC (HL) 77 (pursuer failed to establish on the balance of probabilities that a whiplash injury sustained in a road accident had triggered the onset of symptomatic multiple sclerosis); *McGlinchey v General Motors UK Ltd* [2012] CSIH 91 (pursuer failed to establish that an accident in which she was crushed by her car was caused by its handbrake being defective); *Nelson v John Lewis Plc* [2024] SC EDIN 10 (more likely than not that pursuer's hearing loss started before ear injury, so claim failed on causation); *McIlwraith v Bluevale Structures Ltd* [2024] CSOH 92 (pursuer could not establish infection which caused leg to be amputated was caused by employment which required him to stand in water, as opposed to pre-existing diabetes which substantially increased the risk of severe infection).

3 See eg *Thomson v Kvaerner Govan Ltd* 2004 SC (HL) 1 (pursuer failed to establish that plank supplied by the defender was not of adequate strength and caused him to fall when he stepped on it; it was not for the defenders to establish an alternative non-negligent cause). The court need not side with other party: it may conclude that both versions of events are improbable, with the result that the pursuer will not have discharged the burden of proof: *The Popi M* [1985] 1 WLR 948 (HL).

4 See eg *Thorvaldsen v Dundee City Council* [2021] CSOH 120 (pursuer could establish that head injury caused concussion; but could not establish that it exacerbated headaches and depression).

5 [1969] 1 QB 428 (CA).

6 1987 SC (HL) 145.

7 See eg *Drake v Harbour* [2008] EWCA Civ 25 at para 28 per Toulson LJ. This is sometimes termed 'common sense' or 'pursuer-benevolent' causation.

8 See eg *Thomson v Kvaerner* at paras 16–17 per Lord Hope of Craighead; *Simmons v British Steel plc* [2004] UKHL 20, 2004 SC (HL) 94 (where the House of Lords castigated the Inner House for interfering with a Lord Ordinary's finding in facts, before themselves holding he had applied the law to the facts incorrectly). Compare *McDonald v Indigo Sun Retail Ltd* [2022] SAC (Civ) 15 (sheriff entitled to reach conclusion based on his assessment of expert evidence) with *CDE v Surrey and Sussex Healthcare NHS Trust* [2023] EWCA Civ 1330 (trial judge had calculated birth time of baby incorrectly; in that context even a minute's error could make a material difference).

9.3 In *Bolitho v City and Hackney Health Authority*,[1] it was accepted that a doctor had been in breach of her duty of care by failing to attend her patient, a child. The child died. It was also accepted that the only way in which the child's life could have been saved was by intubation. However, evidence was led that a responsible body of medical opinion would not have intubated in the circumstances. In other words, if the doctor had attended her patient, she would not have been negligent if she had not attempted to save the child's life by intubating her. Consequently, the child would still have died even if the doctor had attended her. The logic appears strained, but it is nevertheless compelling. Since the patient would still have died even if she had received reasonable care, ie no intubation, the doctor's negligence in failing to attend her was not a factual cause of her death. This demonstrates that the factual causation enquiry involves investigating the hypothetical: what actually would have happened if the defender's breach of duty was taken out of the equation?

Another striking example of the 'but for' test is *McWilliams v Sir William Arrol & Co and Lithgows Ltd*.[2] The pursuer's husband, a steel erector, was killed. It was held that the defenders were in breach of their duty of care towards McWilliams in failing to provide him with a safety belt. But it was also established that even if they had provided him with a safety belt, McWilliams would not have worn it. In these circumstances, the pursuer failed to prove that 'but for' the defenders' breach of duty the accident would not have occurred. The defenders' breach was not a *causa sine qua non* of McWilliams' death and the pursuer's action failed. In *McTear v Imperial Tobacco Co Ltd*,[3] the pursuer failed to establish that her husband would not have contracted lung cancer 'but for' smoking the defenders' brand of cigarettes. The Lord Ordinary (Nimmo-Smith) was persuaded by the defenders' argument that had their own brand been unavailable he would have smoked a different brand and developed lung cancer anyway.

Where a pursuer is injured as a result of the defender's breach of duty but later suffers an accident or disease unrelated to the defender's conduct, the fact that he would have been debilitated by the later accident or disease is taken into account in assessing the pursuer's loss.[4] But this does not apply, it seems, where the later event is a delict caused by another party.[5]

The 'but for' test also applies when the pursuer's claim is for pure economic loss. For example, D provides P with information about C which P uses to decide whether to enter into a transaction with C. P sustains economic loss as a consequence of the transaction with C. In an action to recover the loss from D, P must prove that he would not have entered into the transaction with C 'but for' D's misrepresentation in respect of C. If P would have entered into the transaction with C in the absence of D's advice, the action will fail for lack of factual causation.[6]

1 [1998] AC 232 (HL).
2 1962 SC (HL) 70, 1962 SLT 121.
3 [2005] CSOH 69, 2005 2 SC 1. The case as reported runs to 569 pages and occupies a whole volume of the Session Cases on its own. The discussion of causation is at pages 425–489 of the Session Cases report.
4 See *Jobling v Associated Dairies Ltd* [1982] AC 794 (HL).
5 *Baker v Willoughby* [1970] AC 467 (HL).
6 See eg *Leeds & Holbeck Building Society v Alex Morison & Co (No 2)* 2001 SCLR 41 (OH).

9.4 The but for test, applied using the balance of probabilities, is not displaced where the pursuer argues that the defender's negligence has caused them to lose the chance of a better outcome. Where the treatment of a patient would have had less than a 50 per cent chance of success, the failure to treat is not regarded as the cause of the pursuer's injuries or illness: in other words, the chances of success must be more than 50 per cent before the failure will be causally relevant.[1] In *Gregg v Scott*,[2] owing to the negligence of his GP, the treatment of the claimant's cancer was delayed by nine months. He argued that had he been referred to hospital when he first saw his GP there would have been a high likelihood of cure, whereas by the time treatment commenced his chances of recovery had fallen to below 50 per cent. Chances of recovery were defined as surviving for a period of ten years. At the trial it was established that even if he had been diagnosed and treated promptly, his chances of surviving for ten years would have been only 42 per cent: now they were only 25 per cent. Because his chances of surviving ten years were never 50 per cent or more, the trial judge held that on a balance of probability the complainant would not have survived for ten years even if treated promptly; therefore he had failed to establish that the negligent misdiagnosis would cause him to die prematurely. A majority of the House of Lords agreed. The claimant had to establish that the clinical negligence was the cause of the adverse consequences which had befallen him. Since the claimant would only have had a 42 per cent chance of surviving had he been treated immediately, he was unable to prove on the balance of probabilities that the failure to survive for ten years was the result of the negligent misdiagnosis rather than the cancer. The majority of their Lordships also held that the reduction in his chances of a cure – from 42 per cent to 25 per cent – was not a recoverable head of damage. Put another way, their Lordships refused to award damages for the increased risk of suffering harm in the future as opposed to the lost chance of avoiding a result which has in fact occurred. The notion of a 'loss of a chance' is also relevant to claims against solicitors or other professional advisers, where it is alleged that the negligent advice caused the pursuer to lose the chance of eg a successful claim against a third party.[3]

1 See *Kenyon v Bell* 1953 SC 125 (OH); *Hotson v East Berkshire Area Health Authority* [1987] AC 750 (HL).
2 [2005] 2 AC 176 (HL).
3 See eg *Gough v Cannons Law Practice* [2025] CSOH 28.

9.5 Further difficulties arise where there is more than one potential cause of the pursuer's injuries, ie (i) the defender's breach of a duty of care and (ii) another source of danger which is not the responsibility of the defender. The starting point of the discussion is *Wardlaw v Bonnington Castings Ltd*.[1] A workman contracted pneumoconiosis from breathing dust in the atmosphere of his workplace. Some of the dust was caused by a hammer in relation to which there were no known or available precautions which could be taken to prevent the employee breathing contaminated air. Therefore, the defender was not in breach of the duty of care owed to the pursuer in respect of the dust caused by the hammer. The dust from the hammer was a non-negligent potential cause. However, there were other machines in the workshop which also produced dust for which adequate extraction plant was available, and the employers were held responsible for not adequately maintaining the extracting plant in relation to those machines.[2] The dust from the machines was a negligent potential cause.

There were therefore two possible sources of the dust which had caused the pursuer's illness, but the defender was only negligent in respect of one of those sources, ie the dust from the machines. The House of Lords held that the onus lay on the pursuer to show that on the balance of probabilities the dust from the machines was a *causa sine qua non* of his illness. In the situation of two potential sources of danger, the pursuer would discharge the onus if he could show that the source for which the defender was responsible had materially contributed to his injury. Lord Reid observed:[3]

> 'It appears to me that the source of his [the pursuer's] disease was the dust from both sources, and the real question is whether the dust from the swing grinders [the other machines] materially contributed to the disease. What is a material contribution must be a question of degree. A contribution which comes within the exception *de minimis non curat lex* is not material but I think that any contribution which does not fall within that exception must be material.'

In this case, the dust from the machines did materially contribute to the pursuer's illness and the pursuer was successful. Thus, where there are two or more sources of harm to the pursuer which operate concurrently, the source for which the defender is responsible will be regarded as a *causa sine qua non* of the pursuer's injury if it materially contributed to the injury. This approach has been applied in the medical negligence context.[4]

1 1956 SC (HL) 26.
2 This was a breach by the employer of their statutory duty under the Grinding of Metals (Miscellaneous Industries) Regulations 1925, SR & O 1925/904.
3 *Wardlaw v Bonnington Castings Ltd* 1956 SC (HL) 26 at 32.
4 *Williams v Bermuda Hospitals Board* [2016] UKPC 4, [2016] AC 888 (Bermuda).

9.6 The concept of factual causation was taken a considerable step further in *McGhee v National Coal Board*.[1] The pursuer worked all day in a hot and dusty kiln. He had to cycle home unwashed because the defender failed to provide on-site washing facilities. After several days, the pursuer contracted dermatitis. It was admitted that the dermatitis was attributable to the work the pursuer did in the brick kiln, but the defender was not in breach of a duty of care in allowing the pursuer to work there. The breach of duty was the failure to provide on-site washing facilities. This omission only resulted in the pursuer cycling home unwashed: clearly, it did not relate to the hours he spent working in the kiln. Common sense would suggest that it was far more likely that the dermatitis was contracted when he was working in the kiln, for which the employer was not delictually liable, rather than during the short time he cycled home. But the expert evidence could not establish how dermatitis was contracted. *Wardlaw v Bonnington Castings Ltd*[2] could therefore not provide a solution since it could not be proven that the additional exposure to injury caused by cycling home unwashed had materially contributed to his injury. *Wardlaw v Bonnington Castings Ltd* is concerned with two sources of danger operating *concurrently*; but *McGhee v National Coal Board* is concerned with two sources of danger operating *consecutively* where the defender was responsible only for the later one. Therefore, it can be argued that the pursuer in *McGhee* would have to prove – which on the evidence he could not – that the later source of danger had caused, or at least materially contributed to, his dermatitis.

However, the House of Lords was prepared to take a broader view of causation. The medical evidence suggested that the fact that the pursuer had to cycle home caked with grime and sweat added materially to *the risk* that the disease might develop, although it could not explain why this was so. In the view of the House, materially to increase the risk of the pursuer's injuries was to be regarded as a material contribution to the injury. Lord Reid opined:[3]

> 'But it has often been said that the legal concept of causation is not based on logic or philosophy. It is based on the practical way in which the ordinary man's mind works in the every-day affairs of life. From a broad and practical viewpoint I can see no substantial difference between saying that what the defender did materially increased the risk of injury to the pursuer and saying that what the defender did made a material contribution to his injury.'

Lord Salmon observed:[4]

> 'In the circumstances of the present case,[5] the possibility of a distinction existing between (a) having materially increased the risk of contracting the disease and (b) having materially contributed to causing the disease may no doubt be a fruitful source of interesting academic discussions between students of philosophy. Such a distinction is, however, far too unreal to be recognised by the common law.'

Thus, where there are two or more sources of danger, and the defender only is liable for one source, factual causation will be established if the pursuer can prove on the balance of probabilities *either* that the defender's breach of duty materially contributed to his injury *or* that the defender's breach of duty materially increased the risk of the pursuer sustaining injury. It does not matter if the sources of danger operate concurrently or consecutively.

1 1973 SC (HL) 37; see Lord Hope of Craighead 'James McGhee – A Second Mrs Donoghue?' [2003] *Cambridge Law Journal* 587.
2 1956 SC (HL) 26.
3 *McGhee v National Coal Board* 1973 SC (HL) 37 at 53–54.
4 *McGhee* at 62.
5 Given the defender's admitted breach of a duty of care.

9.7 *McGhee v National Coal Board* was approved and extended by the House of Lords in *Fairchild v Glenhaven Funeral Services Ltd*.[1] F was employed by E1 and E2 at different times and for different periods. Both E1 and E2 were in breach of a duty of care to F by allowing him to breathe asbestos dust. F contracted cancer. The medical evidence established that the disease was contracted by breathing asbestos dust but, because of the limits of scientific knowledge, it could not be established that the cancer was the result of inhaling asbestos dust during his employment with E1 or E2 or both employers. But it was also proven that once the disease had been contracted, F's condition would not deteriorate because of further exposure to asbestos dust. Thus, causation could not be established based on a material contribution to F's illness. However, it was accepted that the *risk* of contracting the cancer increased in relation to the total exposure to asbestos dust.

In these circumstances, their Lordships took the view that the normal 'but for' test should be suspended. Lord Nicholls of Birkenhead considered that the plaintiff should succeed as 'any other outcome would be deeply offensive to instinctive notions of what justice requires and fairness demands'.[2] Since both E1 and E2 were in breach of the duty of care they owed to F and these breaches had materially increased the risk of F contracting cancer, *McGhee* was applicable and the causal requirement was satisfied.[3] It should be noted that in *McGhee*, the pursuer sustained harm as a consequence of the defender's breach of duty or the defender's non-delictual conduct, both of which materially increased the risk of his contracting dermatitis: even if the illness was not contracted as a result of the defender's breach of duty, it was nevertheless caused by the defender's conduct – albeit conduct that might not have been negligent. *Fairchild* goes further in that by increasing the risk of the pursuer sustaining harm as a result of the defender's breach of duty, the defender may be held to have caused the pursuer's illness when it was in fact caused by the negligence of another person.

In *Sienkiewicz v Greif (UK) Ltd*,[4] the defendant's negligent exposure of the plaintiff to asbestos over her working life at their premises increased her risk of contracting mesothelioma by only 18 per cent. Although this case only involved one defendant, the Supreme Court nevertheless held that the *Fairchild* exception applied and the plaintiff was entitled to succeed as the defendant had materially increased the risk of her contracting the disease. There was no need for her to prove that the defendant's negligence had doubled the risk of her contracting mesothelioma.[5]

There are, however, important limitations. First, as the Supreme Court re-emphasised in *Sienkiewicz*, the principle in *McGhee* and *Fairchild* only applies when it is impossible to establish scientifically the cause of the pursuer's injury. Second, while the *sources* of danger may be different, it must be established that each source could have in fact been the cause of the pursuer's injuries. In *Wardlaw*, *McGhee* and *Fairchild* it was clear that dust caused the pursuers' diseases: the only question was whether the defenders' breach of duty had materially contributed to, or increased the risk of, the pursuers' illnesses. By way of contrast, in *Kay's Tutor v Ayrshire and Arran Health Board*,[6] there was no evidence that the defender's breach of duty in giving the overdose of penicillin could in fact have caused the child's deafness. In these circumstances, *Wardlaw*, *McGhee* and *Fairchild* are irrelevant. As Lord Griffiths explained:[7]

> 'The principle in *McGhee* would only fall for consideration if it was first proved that it was an accepted medical fact that penicillin in some cases caused or aggravated deafness. The question would then arise whether when there are two competing causes of deafness, namely meningitis and penicillin, the law should presume in favour of the [pursuer] that the [delictual] cause was responsible for the damage.'

Moreover, the departure from the ordinary 'but for' rule only applies when there are two or more sources of the *same* noxious agent which caused the pursuer's illness or injuries: if there is more than one noxious agent which could have caused the pursuer's injuries or illness, the threshold 'but for' test of causal connection will not be relaxed. In *Wilsher v Essex Area Health Authority*,[8] a baby's medical condition could have been caused by a noxious agent (a) which arose because of the defendant's breach of duty: but there were another four different noxious agents – for which the defendant was not responsible – each of which could equally have harmed the child. The fact that the defendant's negligence materially increased the risk of the child from being harmed by noxious agent (a) was held not to be a sufficient causative link when the child's condition could have been caused by noxious agents (b), (c), (d) or (e).

The *Fairchild* exception seems to be viewed as a specific judicial response to conditions where science is not yet at a stage to allow us to determine with any certainty which exposure caused the pursuer's condition, or whether a particular exposure caused that condition to worsen:[9]

> 'The special rule devised in Fairchild is justified on grounds of policy and fairness by the inability of current medical science to identify which exposure to asbestos, whether environmental or occupational, caused the disease to take hold, rendering proof on traditional principles impossible for claimants. Thus it is understandable that it has not been applied where asbestos exposure is no more than one of a number of potential explanations …'

1 [2003] 1 AC 32 (HL). See JM Thomson 'The Raising of Lazarus: The Resurrection of *McGhee v National Coal Board*' (2003) 7 *Edinburgh Law Review* 80.

2 *Fairchild* at para 36. See also Lord Bingham of Cornhill at para 34 and Lord Hoffmann at paras 62–63.
3 If *in fact* F had contracted cancer while in the employment of E1, it is difficult to see how the exposure to asbestos dust while in the employment of E2 materially increased the risk of F contracting cancer.
4 [2011] UKSC 10, [2011] 2 AC 229.
5 The pursuer will fail if the increase in the risk of contracting the disease as a result of the defender's negligence is minimal: *Prescott v University of St Andrews* [2016] CSOH 3; *Kerr v Midlothian Council* [2024] CSOH 112, 2025 SLT 268.
6 1987 SC (HL) 145; discussed at para 9.1 above.
7 1987 SLT 577 at 168–169.
8 [1988] AC 1074 (HL), approved by the House of Lords in *Fairchild.*
9 *Kerr v Midlothian Council* at para 78 per Lord Malcolm. The same medical uncertainty has justified applying *Fairchild* to the causation of lung cancer by asbestos: *Heneghan v Manchester Dry Docks* [2016] EWCA Civ 816; [2016] 1 WLR 2036.

9.8 Another example of rules of causation being expanded for policy reasons is in the medical negligence context. In *Chester v Afshar*[1] the House of Lords was prepared to suspend the normal operation of the 'but for' test to ensure that a doctor's obligation to inform a patient of the risks inherent in a medical procedure would not be undermined. The purpose of the obligation was to enable a patient to make an informed decision on whether to agree to the procedure. This duty would be rendered almost obsolete if only those patients who would not have agreed to the procedure were able to sue when their doctor was in breach of this duty. This expansion of the rules of causation is justified by the importance of informed consent: if a patient undertakes a procedure which causes them an injury, and would not have at that time undertaken the procedure if they had been fully warned by the doctor, then they may sue in respect of that injury. Following *Chester*, it does not matter that they would, at a different time in future, have considered undertaking the procedure.[2]

1 [2005] 1 AC 134 (HL).
2 However, if, on the balance of probabilities, the doctor had fully advised the pursuer, and they still would have undertaken the procedure at that precise point in time, then their case will fail on causation: *Diamond v Royal Devon and Exeter NHS Foundation Trust* [2019] EWCA Civ 585.

LEGAL CAUSATION

9.9 For the purpose of liability in delict, it is not enough that the defender's breach of duty is a factual cause or *causa sine qua non* of the pursuer's harm. While factual causation is a necessary condition of delictual liability, it is not sufficient. In addition, the defender's breach of duty must be the *legal* cause of the pursuer's harm. To use Latin terminology, it must be the *causa causans*. Various terms are used to describe legal causation: these include the direct, decisive, proximate, real, dominant, efficient, effective and substantial cause of the pursuer's loss or harm.

For example, A drops a brick on B's foot, breaking his toe. B is taken to hospital in an ambulance. The ambulance is driven carelessly by C, and B is killed in a road accident. A's breach of duty is a *causa sine qua non* of B's death since 'but for' A's dropping the brick on his toe, B would not have been in the ambulance in which he died. But should A be delictually liable for B's death which was caused by the ambulance driver's careless driving? The answer is no. A's breach of duty, although a *causa sine qua non* of B's death, is not treated as the legal cause, ie it is not the *causa causans*. The *causa causans* is C's careless driving. We can say that the chain of causation between A's breach of duty and B's death has been broken because of the careless act of the ambulance driver, which prevents A's breach of duty from being the legal cause of B's death. To use legal terminology, C's conduct is a *novus actus interveniens* which breaks the chain of causation so that A is not delictually liable for B's death, although A remains liable for B's broken toe.

In this example, the *novus actus interveniens* was the conduct of a third party: C, the ambulance driver. But the conduct of the victim may also break the chain of causation. So, for example, if A drops a brick on B's foot, breaking his toe, whereupon B chooses to die by suicide to put himself out of pain, A will not be delictually liable for B's death. B's action has broken the chain of causation and, as a result, A's breach of duty is not regarded as the legal cause, the *causa causans*, of B's death.[1]

When, then, will an act of a third party or the act of the victim constitute *a novus actus interveniens*, breaking the chain of causation? Since we are concerned with determining legal causation, this is ultimately a question for the courts: the judges will *evaluate* whether in the circumstances it is fair to relieve the defender of his delictual liability. At one time, this was a crucial decision where the victim had contributed to his own injuries: for if the court decided that the pursuer's conduct was a *novus actus interveniens* so that the defender's breach of duty was not the *causa causans*, the pursuer was denied any compensation. However, as a result of the Law Reform (Contributory Negligence) Act 1945, the court now has the power to reduce the damages awarded to the pursuer in proportion to the pursuer's responsibility for her own injuries.[2] Although the 1945 Act has, in so far as the pursuer's conduct is concerned, reduced the importance of determining a single cause or *causa causans*, the court still retains the power of limiting a defender's delictual liability for breach of a duty of care. It does this by deciding that the breach is not the legal cause of the pursuer's injuries, for example because of the intervention of a third party. Therefore, the determination of legal causation remains important.

The decision as to whether a breach of duty constitutes the *causa causans* of the pursuer's injuries 'must be dealt with broadly and upon common sense principles as a jury would probably deal with it'.[3] Two factors are important, as we shall now see.

1 The victim's death by suicide will not break the chain of causation if the purpose of the defender's duty of care was to look after the victim (*Reeves v Commissioner of Police of the Metropolis* [2001] 1 AC 360 (HL); *Paterson v Lanarkshire Health Board* [2023] CSOH 1, 2023 SLT 67) or the defender's conduct caused the victim physical harm which led to depression which resulted in the victim's death by suicide (*Corr v IBC Vehicles* [2008] 1 AC 884 (HL)). Of course, the defender's negligence must be a factual cause of, or make a material contribution to, the pursuer's death by suicide: *Zgonec-Rozej v Pereira* [2025] EWCA Civ 171.

2 On contributory negligence, see paras 9.13–9.15 below.

3 *Admiralty Commissioners v SS Volute* [1922] 1 AC 129 (HL) at 144 per Lord Birkenhead LC. See also eg *Stapley v Gypsum Mines Ltd* [1953] AC 663 at 681 per Lord Reid.

(1) Foreseeability

9.10 Where there has been a breach of duty by the defender, the act of a third party or the victim will not generally break the chain of causation if it was reasonably foreseeable that the subsequent act would take place. In *Sayers v Harlow Urban District Council*,[1] for example, the plaintiff entered a cubicle in a public lavatory maintained by the defendant. Owing to a fault in the lock, she could not reopen the door. She banged on the door and put her hand out of the window in unsuccessful attempts to attract attention. After 15 minutes, she tried to escape through the space between the top of the door and the roof. She put her left foot on the lavatory seat, her right foot on the toilet roll holder, one hand on the lavatory cistern and the other hand on the top of the door. When she found it impossible to squeeze through the space, she proceeded to come down but, because of her weight, the toilet roll holder rotated, she lost her balance and fell. The court held that it was reasonably foreseeable that a person in Mrs Sayers' position would try to escape and that this was not a hazardous enterprise. Accordingly, her attempted escape was not a *novus actus interveniens* and the defendant's breach of duty was the *causa causans* of the accident. However, when she found she could not escape, she was careless in putting so much weight on the toilet roll holder: although this did not break the chain of causation, it did constitute contributory negligence and her damages were reduced by 25 per cent.[2]

Even if the subsequent act of a third party or the pursuer is reasonably foreseeable, it may break the chain of causation if it was hazardous for the third party or the pursuer to act in such a way. In *McKew v Holland and Hannen and Cubitts (Scotland) Ltd*,[3] the pursuer injured his ankle as a result of the defender's breach of duty. Because of the fracture, his leg was liable to 'give way' from time to time. After the accident, the pursuer went to view a flat. The stairway leading to the fiat had no handrail. Although he knew that his leg was likely to give way at any time, after visiting the flat the pursuer went down the stairs in a normal manner ie he did not go down slowly so that he could sit on a step if his leg 'gave way'. His leg gave way and in panic the pursuer jumped down ten steps and was injured. The court held that the defender was not liable for the second injury. Although it was reasonably foreseeable that the pursuer might climb stairs which had no handrail, he had acted in a hazardous manner in walking down the stairs in the normal way without assistance. The defender's breach of duty which had caused the injury to the pursuer's ankle was not the *causa causans* of the pursuer's second injury. Instead, the pursuer's carelessness in walking down the stairs without assistance constituted hazardous conduct on the pursuer's part which broke the chain of causation between the defender's breach of duty and the pursuer's second injuries.

McKew was distinguished in *Spencer v Wincanton Holdings Ltd (Wincanton Logistics Ltd)*.[4] Here the defendant admitted liability for the injuries the plaintiff had suffered from an accident at work which led to the amputation of his leg. Eight months after the amputation, he tripped and fell when he was filling his car at a garage without summoning help or steadying himself using his sticks or his prosthesis. As a result of this fall, he was confined to a wheelchair. The Court of Appeal held that the second accident was an unexpected but real consequence of the first accident. Whether an intervening event should be treated as breaking the chain of causation was ultimately a question of fairness, ie whether it was fair to relieve the defendant of liability for the subsequent event. The plaintiff's act of filling his car without any help fell far below the unreasonableness of the pursuer's behaviour in *McKew*. The defendant was therefore liable with a reduction of a third to reflect the plaintiff's contributory negligence. This case illustrates how legal causation is ultimately an evaluative judgment by the court on the extent of the defender's liability and whether it is fair that he should be liable for the full extent of the pursuer's injuries.[5] A 'high degree of unreasonableness' is required for the conduct to constitute a *novus actus interveniens*.[6]

In *Sabri-Tabrizi v Lothian Health Board*,[7] the pursuer became pregnant because of a failed sterilisation. She had a termination. Knowing that she was fertile, she had sexual intercourse with her husband on several occasions. She fell pregnant again. Although the defenders admitted liability for the first pregnancy, they denied liability for the second. The Lord Ordinary (Nimmo-Smith) agreed:[8]

> 'The alleged negligence resulted in the pursuer's being still fertile, just as she would have been had the failed sterilisation operation never been carried out. The pursuer knew this, and consequently knew that there

was a risk of her becoming pregnant if she had sexual intercourse with her husband … She avers that she took precautions, but in so far as there remained a residual risk, in a question between her and the defenders I think that it is unreasonable of her to expose herself to that risk. Accordingly I regard her decision to have sexual intercourse in the knowledge that she was not sterile as constituting a *novus actus interveniens*, breaking the chain of causation, with the result that the defenders cannot be held liable for the second pregnancy and the consequences thereof'.

1 [1958] 1 WLR 623 (CA).
2 On contributory negligence, see paras 9.15–9.17 below. Compare *Sayers* with *Clay v TUI UK Ltd* [2018] EWCA Civ 1177 (claimant locked on hotel balcony; attempted to climb onto the adjoining balcony when ledge gave way; claimant's actions had turned inconvenient situation into a dangerous one, breaking the chain of causation).
3 1970 SC (HL) 20.
4 [2009] EWCA Civ 1404.
5 See eg *Chubb Fire Ltd v Vicar of Spalding* [2010] EWCA Civ 981 (any liability of the defendant was broken as a result of the intervening acts of vandals); *Scott v Gavigan* [2016] EWCA Civ 544 (claimant's act of drunkenly running out into road into the path of the defendant was not so unreasonable as to amount to a *novus actus interveniens*; the frequency with which pedestrians run out on the road would make it unpalatable to say that they should bear total responsibility for any resulting injury); *Tsetvanova v Walden* [2020] SC EDIN 37, 2021 SLT (Sh Ct) 3 (pursuer's act of jumping out of window to escape defender who broke into property not sufficient to break causal chain).
6 *Raybould v T&N Gilmartin (Contractors) Ltd* [2018] SAC Civ 31, 2019 SLT (Sh Ct) 1 at para 27 per Sheriff Principal M Stephen.
7 1998 SC 373 (OH).
8 *Sabri-Tabrizi* at 378.

(2) The order of events

9.11 The order of events may be important in determining whether the defender's breach of duty is the *causa causans* of the pursuer's injuries. In *Donaghy v National Coal Board*,[1] the defender broke the duty of care which was owed to the pursuer by leaving a detonator lying around the workplace. The pursuer took the detonator home and hit it with a hammer. As a result, he was injured. The court held that the pursuer's conduct amounted to a *novus actus interveniens*: it was unforeseeable, unreasonable, ie hazardous, and was the last act which had led to the accident. However, in *Davidson v City of Glasgow District Council*,[2] the second defender supplied the pursuer's employer, the first defender, with planks which were too short for a particular task. The employer rejected the planks, but, owing to the employer's alleged carelessness, one of the short planks was not rejected. As a result of the plank being too short, there was an accident in which the pursuer was injured. The pursuer sued the employer (first defender) and the supplier (the second defender). The second defender argued that the employer's failure to reject all the planks constituted a *novus actus interveniens*. The court held that merely because the employer's conduct was the 'last act' that led to the accident, this did not necessarily mean that it amounted to a *novus actus interveniens*:[3]

> 'Even although there was in effect an intermediate inspection, and assuming in the alternative that the first defenders [the employer] failed to discover that one of the planks remained and was inadvertently used, it does not follow that that was negligence or that it broke the chain of causation and was the sole cause of the accident.'

Thus, where an accident is caused to A as a result of a breach of duty by B *and* a breach of duty by C, the mere fact that B's breach of duty arose after C's breach of duty will not necessarily break the chain of causation to exonerate C from delictual liability. In *Grant v Sun Shipping Co Ltd*,[4] ship repairers working on a ship left hatches uncovered. By doing so, they were in breach of a duty of care owed to dock labourers on the ship. The ship owners also failed to ensure that the hatches were covered and did not provide an adequate system of lighting: this also constituted a breach of their duty of care to dock labourers on the ship. The pursuer, a dock labourer, fell through an unlit hatch. The House of Lords held that the shipowner's breach of duty did not constitute a *novus actus interveniens* breaking the chain of causation between the accident and the ship repairers' breach of duty of care towards the pursuer by leaving the hatches uncovered. Instead, both the ship owners and the ship repairers were jointly liable in delict.

1 1957 SLT (Notes) 35 (OH).
2 1993 SLT 479 (OH).
3 *Davidson* at 482 per Temporary Judge D B Robertson QC.
4 1948 SC (HL) 73.

(3) Conclusion

9.12 Where A's breach of a duty of care is a *causa sine qua non* of B's injuries, the courts appear unwilling to be persuaded that a subsequent act – even if careless – constitutes a *novus actus interveniens* unless it is so unusual or unexpected that it could not have been reasonably foreseeable, or so hazardous on the part of B, that it would be unreasonable to hold A liable. Although this will be the usual result, there can, of course, still be exceptional cases where the chain of causation is broken and A's breach of duty is not treated as the *causa causans* of B's injuries. So, for example, if A injured B's foot and B suffered an infection in hospital, the chain of causation would not be broken as it is reasonably foreseeable that B might get an infection in hospital. But if the surgeon in the hospital is careless and amputates B's uninjured foot, the chain of causation is broken since the surgeon's conduct is so unusual and unexpected that it is not reasonably foreseeable and therefore it constitutes a *novus actus interveniens*. This exonerates A from delictual liability in respect of the amputation, but not, of course, in respect of the original injury to B's foot.

Where it is established that multiple wrongdoers have caused, or contributed, to the injury (or risk of injury) suffered by the pursuer, those wrongdoers will be jointly and severally liable.[1] This means that the pursuer can sue any one of them and recover in full;[2] the wrongdoer held liable may then (if possible) take contribution proceedings against the other wrongdoers to recover their share of the total liability.[3]

1 See eg *Anderson v Ayr & South Ayrshire Local Committee of St Andrew's Ambulance Association* 1943 SC 248 (IH) (pursuer injured in ambulance crash where both ambulance driver and driver of other vehicle negligent); *Lyons v QBE UK Ltd* [2025] SC EDIN 20.

2 Note that, in cases of material contribution to risk, where the *Fairchild* exception applies, the House of Lords in *Barker v Corus* [2006] UKHL 20, [2006] 2 AC 572 held that it would be unfair to have a solvent employer shoulder the liability of insolvent employers or employers before the court, and held that the employers would only be liable to the extent of their contribution. This was swiftly reversed by statute for mesothelioma cases (Compensation Act 2006, s 3). The decision has not been followed in Scotland: *Wright v Stoddard International Plc* 2008 Rep LR 2 (OH); *Dickie v Flexcon Glenrothes Ltd* 2009 WL 2848187 (Sh Ct).

3 Law Reform (Miscellaneous Provisions) (Scotland) Act 1940, s 3. See eg *Phee v Gordon* [2013] CSIH 18, 2013 SC 369 (pursuer was injured by a stray golf ball. The golfer who hit the shot was 20 per cent liable and the golf club 80 per cent liable in view of the hazardous layout of the course); *A-R v Eljamel* [2022] CSIH 34, 2022 SLT 881 (consultant neurosurgeon 100% liable and hospital 0% liable in medical negligence case; surgery carried out when neurosurgeon working privately, hospital's delay did not cause significant harm to pursuer).

DEFENCES TO NEGLIGENCE

(1) Volenti non fit injuria

9.13 It is often said that the defender will escape liability if the pursuer has voluntarily and fully undertaken the risk of harm created by the defender's breach of duty. This is the doctrine of *volenti non fit injuria*. The doctrine of *volenti* provides the defender with a complete defence to an action in delict. The theoretical basis of *volenti* is that by knowing acceptance of the risk, the pursuer has absolved the defender of the consequences of the defender's breach of the duty of care owed to the pursuer. However, the requirements of the doctrine are stringent.[1] This is because it 'amounts to a waiver by the pursuer of the defenders' liability to her in damages'.[2] Two matters must be established by the defender:[3]

(a) *Sciens*: that the pursuer was aware of the particular risk.

(b) *Volens*: that the pursuer accepted or voluntarily assumed that risk entirely at its own expense.

Successful invocations of *volenti non fit injuria* in response to claims in negligence are rare.[4] The plea is specifically excluded where a passenger is injured when travelling in a car driven by a driver with comprehensive insurance.[5] The plea does not arise where a rescuer attends a dangerous scene and attempts to rescue a person in peril.[6] The courts will be extremely slow to apply it in a claim brought by an employee against an employer.[7]

Where the risk of physical injury is brought home to a prospective participant in an dangerous activity via a 'consent form' or waiver, statute provides that any express exclusion of liability for death or personal injury is void.[8] While, strictly, that does not remove the argument that the participant has implicitly agreed to run the risk, a judge likely will not look upon such an argument favourably.[9] While it sometimes is said that *volenti* offers participants in sports a defence to negligence actions arising from risks inherent in the sport, it is probably more accurate to say that no breach of a duty of care occurs where the risk is inherent in the sport.[10]

1 See eg *James v White Lion Hotel* [2021] EWCA Civ 31, [2021] QB 1153 at para 91. On *volenti* generally, see Reid, *The Law of Delict in Scotland* at paras 29.02–29.23.
2 *Raybould v T&N Gilmartin (Contractors) Ltd* [2018] SAC (Civ) 31, 2019 SLT (Sh Ct) 1 at para 16.
3 *Raybould* at para 16.
4 For a case demonstrating the extreme facts on which *volenti* may succeed, see *Morris v Murray* [1991] 2 QB 6 (CA) (plaintiff in pub with friend who consumed equivalent of 17 whiskies, then agreed to go on a flight piloted by the friend, which crashed. Defence of *volenti* established as the risk of being flown in a light aircraft by an extremely drunk pilot obvious, even taking into account the plaintiff's drunken state).
5 Road Traffic Act 1988, s 149.
6 See eg *Steel v Glasgow Iron and Steel Co* 1944 SC 237 (IH).
7 See eg *Keenan v The City Line Ltd* 1953 SLT 128 (OH) (albeit allowing the defence in that case to go to trial). The defence may apply more readily in the case of deliberate disobedience of orders by an employee: *Shatwell v ICI Ltd* [1965] AC 656 (HL) (a case on breach of statutory regulations).
8 Consumer Rights Act 2015, ss 65–66; Unfair Contract Terms 1977, s 16(1)(a).
9 See eg *Byrne v Motorsport Vision Racing Ltd* [2024] EWHC 2966 (KB).
10 As a corollary, conduct which goes beyond the risks inherent in the game may well amount to a breach of duty: *Czernuszka v King* [2023] EWHC 380 (KB), [2023] 4 WLR 26.

9.14 The practical operation of *volenti*, therefore, is limited. However, it should be noted that s 2(3) of the Occupiers' Liability (Scotland) Act 1960 provides for a *volenti* defence.[1] In *Titchener v British Railways Board*[2] the defender failed to maintain a fence made of sleepers which was positioned along a railway track. A 15-year-old girl climbed through the fence and went up the embankment to take a short cut across the railway line to a piece of waste ground. She was injured by a train when she was crossing the line. The House indicated, in *obiter dicta*, that the defender would have succeeded in raising a plea of *volenti*. The pursuer was aware that trains ran along the track (and therefore, at 15, could be taken to be *sciens* of the risk involved). Significantly, in cross-examination, she admitted that crossing the track was 'just a chance [she] took', which established the necessary *sciens*. But the primary basis for the decision was that no duty of care as the nature of the danger posed by the railway line was obvious and well-known to the pursuer, emphasising that the plea of *volenti* may be redundant in many occupiers' liability cases.[3]

The practical significance of *volenti* further has been much reduced by the availability of the defence of contributory negligence, which provides a more nuanced manner of attaching responsibility for recklessness or carelessness on the part of the pursuer.[4]

1 On occupiers' liability, see paras 12.13–12.19 below.
2 1984 SC (HL) 34.
3 See too *Devlin v Strathclyde Regional Council* 1993 SLT 699 (OH). For a clear judicial recognition on the facts of the redundancy of *volenti*, in the context of a claim brought in respect of the death of a smoker against cigarette producers, see *McTear v Imperial Tobacco* 2005 2 SC 1 at paras 7.207–7.208 (p 559–560 of the Session Cases report).
4 For a compelling argument that the defence of *volenti* should simply be abolished, see J Gardner, 'Rethinking Risk-Taking: The Death of *Volenti*' [2023] *Cambridge Law Journal* 110.

(2) Contributory negligence[1]

9.15 At common law, if causative potency was to be attributed to the pursuer's actions, then its claim would fail.[2] Such an all-or-nothing rule was thought unpalatable, and the modern notion of contributory negligence was introduced by s 1(1) of the Law Reform (Contributory Negligence) Act 1945, which provides:

> 'Where any person suffers *damage as the result partly of his own fault* and *partly due to the fault of any other person or persons*, a claim in respect of that damage shall not be defeated by reason of the fault of the person suffering the damage, but the *damages recoverable* in respect thereof *shall be reduced* to such an extent as the *court thinks just and equitable* having regard to the *claimant's share in the responsibility* for the damage.' [Emphasis added]

The effect of a finding of contributory negligence is to permit the court to reduce the damages which would otherwise have been awarded to the pursuer, to reflect the pursuer's responsibility for the damage or injury sustained.

There are two stages to interrogating any allegation by a defender that a pursuer is contributorily negligent:

(a) Did the pursuer fail to take reasonable care in looking after its own safety or interests, and, if so, did that lack of reasonable care contribute to the damage suffered by the pursuer?

(b) If so, what is the comparative blameworthiness of the pursuer's failure to take reasonable care?

The first stage effectively asks whether the pursuer is guilty of contributory negligence; the second stage asks what reduction to the damages to be awarded to the pursuer would be 'just and equitable' in light of the pursuer's contributory negligence. The notion of 'fault' is broad:[3] it may, for instance, include a deliberate decision by a pursuer to take acts which would result in death by suicide.[4]

Here, we will focus on the application of contributory negligence as a defence to claims in negligence. It seems unlikely that the defence would operate in the context of the intentional delicts.[5]

1 See generally E Reid, *The Law of Delict in Scotland* (2022) at paras 29.54–29.67; D Nolan and J Goudkamp, *Contributory Negligence* (2nd edn, OUP, 2023); J Goudkamp and D Nolan, *Contributory Negligence in the Twenty-First Century* (OUP, 2019).

2 See eg *McNaughton v Caledonian Railway Co Ltd* (1858) 21 D 160 (IH).

3 'Fault' is defined in s 4(1) of the 1945 Act as meaning 'negligence, breach of statutory duty or other act or omission which gives rise to a liability in tort or would, apart from this Act, give rise to the defence of contributory negligent'.

4 See eg *Reeves v Commissioner of Police of the Metropolis* [2000] 1 AC 360 (HL); *Corr v IBC Vehicles Ltd* [2008] UKHL 13, [2008] 1 AC 884.

5 See *Standard Chartered Bank v Pakistan National Shipping Corporation* [2002] UKHL 43, [2003] 1 AC 959 at paras 42–45 per Lord Rodger of Earlsferry, followed in Scotland in the fraudulent misrepresentation case of *Kidd v Paull & Williamsons LLP* [2017] CSOH 16, 2018 SC 193 at para 66. The point was left open in relation to assault in *McLaughin v Morrison* [2014] CSOH 123, 2014 SLT 862.

9.16 The assessment of whether a pursuer fails to take reasonable care is a familiar one: it is an objective question, asking whether the pursuer has exercised 'all such precautions' for her own safety or other interests as a person of 'ordinary prudence' would observe.[1] Allowances will be made for the age of the pursuer.[2] The assessment as to whether or not the pursuer has reasonably looked after its own interests is holistic. For instance, while normally it can be said that a pursuer travelling in a car without wearing a seatbelt does not take reasonable care,[3] that may not be the case for a pursuer with an abdominal injury which makes the wearing of a seatbelt painful,[4] or for a taxi driver following police advice not to wear a seatbelt in case of a violent attack by a passenger.[5] A momentary lapse of reason, resulting in injury via inattention or inadvertence, will be unlikely to amount to contributory negligence.[6]

A failure by the pursuer to take reasonable care will not, however, be relevant unless the defender can show that the pursuer's failure contributed to the damage suffered. The focus is on contribution to the particular damage suffered by the pursuer, not solely on the contribution to any events or accidents leading up to that damage.[7] For example, while the wearing by the pursuer of a seatbelt would not prevent a collision caused by another driver's negligence, it may reduce the extent of the injuries suffered by the pursuer, and therefore such failure contributes to the overall damage suffered in the event of a collision. A claimant who died from lung cancer was held to have contributed to that damage by being a life-long smoker, and the damages awarded to his estate from an employer who negligently exposed him to asbestosis was reduced accordingly.[8]

For the pursuer's negligence to be contributory, it must expose her to an increased risk of the type of damage suffered as a result of the defender's negligence.[9] For instance, if the pursuer's defective car explodes while she is not wearing a seatbelt, while she may be said to be lacking reasonable care, that lack of reasonable care has not contributed to the particular damage suffered by the pursuer: the wearing of a seatbelt does not protect one from an explosion. The failure to wear a seatbelt is not a 'potent cause' in this example. Similarly, where a prisoner with a known drug and alcohol addiction suffered a withdrawal seizure, falling from the top prisoner bunk he had been allocated, the claimant's 'fault' in developing an addiction was not a 'potent cause' of his injury: it was so divorced in time, place, and circumstances from his fall that it did not amount to contributory negligence.[10]

1 *Froom v Butcher* [1976] QB 286 (CA) at 294G per Lord Denning MR. See, however, *Ashton v City of Liverpool Young Men's Christian Association* [2023] EWHC 707 (KB), which seems to take account of the claimant's vulnerability in assessing her blameworthiness. See D Brodie, 'Contribution and Vulnerable Adults' [2023] *Reparation Bulletin* 6.
2 See eg *Jackson v Murray* [2015] UKSC 5, 2015 SC (UKSC) 105.
3 See eg *Froom*.
4 *Mackay v Borthwick* 1982 SLT 265 (OH).
5 *Pace v Cully* 1992 SLT 1073 (OH).
6 *McGowan v W&JR Watson Ltd* [2006] CSIH 62, 2007 SC 272.
7 See *Bowes v Highland Council* [2018] CSIH 38, 2018 SC 499 at paras 59–60 (Inner House overturned Lord Ordinary's finding of no contributory negligence, as his reasoning focussed too much on the hazard which the pursuer collided into, and not the pursuer's negligent driving which led him to leave the road and collide with that hazard).
8 See eg *Blackmore v Department for Communities and Local Government* [2017] EWCA Civ 1136, [2018] QB 471 (30% reduction).
9 *Jones v Livox Quarriers Ltd* [1952] 2 QB 608 (CA) (plaintiff's standing on back of vehicle contributed to risk of being crushed, as well as being knocked off).
10 *St George v Home Office* [2008] EWCA Civ 1068, [2009] 1 WLR 1670.

9.17 When contributory negligence is established, the proportion to be deducted from the damages is a matter for the discretion of the judge, ie what the judge considers just and equitable having regard to the pursuer's share in the responsibility for the damage. This involves considering the 'causative potency' and 'blameworthiness' of the relative fault of the pursuer and the defender.[1] The approach to apportionment may be influenced by the policy of the rule imposing liability on the defender,[2] or the context of the relationship between the parties.[3]

It has been observed that this is a 'rough and ready', as opposed to scientific, process, with a preference for round figures.[4] Minute, granular deductions should not be encouraged. An empirical study of 368 English and Welsh first instance judgments between 2000 and 2014 found that the average discount made by those courts was 40%, with the lowest being 10% and the highest being 90%.[5] Similar research has not been conducted in Scotland,[6] but the lowest[7] and highest[8] discounts made in the same period are identical to those observed in England and Wales. As s 1(1) of the 1945 Act depends on there being fault on the part of the pursuer and 'any other person or persons', 100% contributory negligence should be a logical impossibility[9] but some Scottish cases have thought such deductions to be possible.[10] The better view in such cases is that the pursuer's own conduct is such as to break the chain of causation, and the question of contributory negligence therefore need not arise.

It would be unproductive to attempt to more precisely state what discount will be thought 'just and equitable' in a particular case. Occasionally, the courts will develop a tariff to use in certain types of case: for example, in seatbelt cases, courts have broadly applied the guidelines set out in *Froom v Butcher*:[11] a 25% discount if the wearing of a seatbelt would have completed avoided injury; 15% if it would have reduced the injury; and 0% if wearing the seatbelt would not have prevented or reduced the injury in any event.[12]

Because of this imprecision, and the discretionary nature of the 'just and equitable' exercise, an appellate court will be slow to interfere with a trial judge's finding of a particular amount to be discounted. As Lord Reed stated in *Jackson v Murray*:[13]

> 'The question, therefore, is whether the court below went wrong. In the absence of an identifiable error, such as an error of law, or the taking into account of an irrelevant matter, or the failure to take account of a relevant matter, it is only a difference of view as to the apportionment of responsibility which exceeds the ambit of reasonable disagreement that warrants the conclusion that the court below has gone wrong. In other words, in the absence of an identifiable error, the appellate court must be satisfied that the apportionment made by the court below was not one which was reasonably open to it, within the limits of reasonable disagreement.'

In that case, the Inner House had found that the causative potency of the defender was higher than the pursuer's, and had discussed factors which suggested both were equally to blame. Nevertheless, it made a 70% discount, which suggested, on the contrary, that it thought the pursuer's causative potency and blameworthiness were higher than the defender's.

A majority of the UK Supreme Court[14] could not discern a reasonable basis for this conclusion, and instead substituted a discount of 50%.

1 *Davies v Swan Motor Company (Swansea) Ltd* [1949] 2 KB 291 (CA) at 326 per Denning LJ.
2 *Reeves v Commissioner of Police of the Metropolis* [2000] 1 AC 360 (HL) at 371 per Lord Hoffmann.
3 For instance, the employer-employee context may influence how the court weights the blameworthiness of each party's fault, but this does not prevent substantial deductions where the employee's fault is so egregious (see eg *Stapley v Gypsum Mines Ltd* [1953] AC 663 (HL)). Where a pedestrian is hit by a car, the court will also take account of the 'destructive disparity' between the driver of a car and a pedestrian: *Eagle v Chambers* [2003] EWCA Civ 1107 at para 15 per Hale LJ, applied *Jackson v Murray* [2015] UKSC 5, 2015 SC (UKSC) 105 at para 40.
4 *Jackson v Murray* at para 28 per Lord Reed.
5 J Goudkamp and D Nolan, 'Contributory Negligence in the Twenty-First Century: An Empirical Study of First Instance Decisions' (2016) 79 *Modern Law Review* 575. Only in one case was a deduction of 90% made by the court, with five cases opting for 80%. The authors excluded two cases with a finding of 100% discount, for reasons discussed below.
6 But see the helpful collation of cases in The Hon Lady Paton (ed), *McEwan and Paton on Damages for Personal Injuries in Scotland* (Release 69, 2025) at para 14-05.
7 *Delaney v McGregor Construction (Highlands) Ltd* 2003 Rep LR 56 (OH) (10% discount: rash decision to stand near jammed iron rod and attempt to dislodge it manually from forklift, causing rod to fall on top of pursuer, but employer bore brunt of responsibility for breaches of workplace regulations).
8 *Stephen v Peters* 2005 SCLR 513 (OH) (90% discount: improperly calibrated tachometer and speed limiter meant that lorry driver could drive 10% faster than should have been possible, but his excessive speed was by far the preponderant cause of his injuries). See too *Jackson v Murray* [2012] CSOH 100, which was reduced to 70% by the Inner House and then 50% by the UK Supreme Court.
9 See *Anderson v Newham College of Further Education* [2002] EWCA Civ 505.
10 *Anderson* was not followed in *McEwan v Lothian Buses plc* 2006 SCLR 592 (OH), but the Lord Ordinary (Emslie) did not think a 100% discount appropriate on the facts. See, possibly, *Till v Tayside Public Transport Company Ltd* [2017] CSOH 6, where the accident was said to be completely the fault of the pursuer's, but it is unclear if the court is analysing the matter as one of causation or contributory negligence.
11 [1976] QB 286 (CA). The Court of Appeal did not respond to an invitation to revise these figures in *Stanton v Collinson* [2010] EWCA Civ 81. These figures should also apply where a motorcyclist fails to wear a helmet: *Capps v Miller* [1989] 1 WLR 839 (CA). *Capps* was followed (albeit *obiter*) in *McFarlane v Thain* [2007] CSOH 176.
12 Of course, if the non-wearing of the seatbelt made no difference, then the pursuer's fault cannot be said to have made any contribution to its injury, so technically the court does not even get to the 'just and equitable' discount enquiry. See *Baker v Murdoch* 1977 SLT (Notes) 75, reversed on other grounds at 1979 SLT 145 (IH).
13 *Jackson v Murray* at para 35.
14 Lords Hodge and Wilson dissented, arguing that sufficient basis for a greater finding of blameworthiness on the part of the pursuer existed on the facts as found at first instance.

(3) Illegality[1]

9.18 The pursuer's illegality may feature in at least three respects in relation to a claim in delict:

(a) the pursuer alone may have been acting illegally when the injury occurred;

(b) the pursuer and the defender may have been acting illegally jointly when the injury occurred; and

(c) the pursuer's injury may result in them going on to commit a crime, and the question arises whether the defender is liable for any consequences arising from that crime.

The modern approach to all three situations is a flexible, policy-based one.[2] First, the court will evaluate the policy reasons which favour the application of the illegality defence. This will include the policy behind the (criminal or quasi-criminal) rule which the pursuer's conduct allegedly has violated and considerations of consistency and integrity of the legal system. Secondly, the court will evaluate the policy reasons against application of the defence and favouring the upholding of the pursuer's claim. This may include the policy behind the (civil) rule which the defender's conduct has violated. If, at this stage, the policy reasons against the application of the defence clearly outweigh those favouring it, then the defence will fail. If, however, the reasons favouring the application of the defence appear weightier, the court will then turn to a third stage, asking whether denial of the pursuer's claim is a disproportionate means of serving those policy objectives. Here, the court may consider 'the seriousness of the conduct, its centrality [to the pursuer's claim], whether it was intentional and whether there was marked disparity in the parties' respective culpability.'[3] Previous cases which do not follow this approach may not be reliable guides.

The most illuminating Scottish decision is that of *D v NHS Fife Health Board*, which falls into the third situation identified above.[4] The pursuer in that case suffered from bipolar disorder and presented to a hospital as manic. The pursuer was then allegedly negligently discharged, and was arrested and later convicted after pleading guilty to assaulting a police officer and for abusive behaviour towards his partner. He contended that these convictions would not have arisen but for the defender's negligence in discharging him from hospital, and the defender raised the illegality defence in response to the claim for damages arising from those convictions. The Sheriff Appeal Court upheld the defence.[5] First, weighty policy factors favoured denying the pursuer's claim: to do otherwise would undermine the finality of the acceptance of his guilty plea by the criminal courts in finding another party civilly liable for his actions; the offences were not trivial and were committed intentionally (if at a time when the pursuer was affected by his bipolar disorder); and rejecting the defence would sacrifice scarce NHS resources to compensate the pursuer for his own criminal actions. Secondly, the policy justifications favouring the success of the pursuer's claim – that there should be reparation for wrongdoing and that allowances should be made for the pursuer's bipolarism – were weak. Thirdly, while the court did not expressly conduct the proportionality exercise, it clearly thought the case to be materially indistinguishable from the decision of the UK Supreme Court in *Henderson v Dorset Healthcare University NHS Foundation Trust*. In line with that case, the pursuer's criminal conduct was serious, lay at the centre of this aspect of his claim in negligence, there was intent (without, perhaps, significant personal responsibility), and this was not a case where there was a marked disparity in the culpability of the parties.[6] Therefore, upholding the defence and denying this aspect of the pursuer's claim was a proportionate response. The decision may be different if the pursuer suffered from a mental disorder which rendered them unable to appreciate the nature or wrongfulness of their conduct.[7]

Most Scottish judgments concern the situation of joint illegality, particularly involving the theft or the taking of motor vehicles without the owner's consent. While some cases have envisaged a flexible approach which may be accommodated within the modern policy-based determination of the illegality defence,[8] other cases have taken a strict line which precludes a claim by a passenger injured in such circumstances.[9] It is suggested that contributory negligence is a more proportionate mechanism for the courts to express its disapproval of the pursuer's involvement in such cases.[10]

1 See B Lindsay and M Campbell, 'Illegality in the Scots Law of Delict' in M Dyson (ed), *Illegal Tort Claims* (Hart Publishing, 2025); Reid, *The Law of Delict in Scotland*, paras 29.24–29.53. The defence applies across the law of delict, but here is considered only in respect of negligence.

2 See *D v NHS Fife Health Board* [2022] SAC Civ 27, adopting *Henderson v Dorset University NHS Trust* [2020] UKSC 43, [2021] AC 563 at para 113–124 and *Grondona v Stoffel & Co* [2020] UKSC 42, [2021] AC 540, themselves applying in the delictual/tortious context the approach adopted in *Patel v Mirza* [2016] UKSC 42, [2017] AC 467.

3 *Henderson* at para 124, referring to *Patel* at para 107 per Lord Toulson.

4 This situation is sometimes referred to as a 'sanctions-shifting case', as it involves an attempt by the pursuer to shift a sanction imposed on them by the criminal law. For cases considering the application of the defence to quasi-criminal or regulatory fines in such circumstances, see eg *Geddes (Contractors) Ltd v Neil Johnson Health & Safety Services Ltd* [2017] CSOH 42; *Khan v Hussain* [2019] CSOH 11, 2019 SC 322.

5 *D v NHS Fife* at paras 40–41.

6 These factors were considered in *Henderson* at paras 138–144.

7 See *Lewis-Ranwell* [2024] EWCA Civ 138, [2024] KB 745 (illegality defence not triggered by criminal conduct in respect of which claimant had defence of insanity under English criminal law). Permission to appeal this decision was granted by the UK Supreme Court in May 2024, and that appeal is pending at the time of writing.

8 See eg *Weir v Wyper* 1992 SLT 579 (OH), *Taylor v Leslie* 1998 SLT 1248 (OH); *Currie v Clamp's Executor* 2002 SLT 196 (OH).

9 See eg *Lindsay v Poole* 1984 SLT 269 (OH); *Sloan v Triplett* 1985 SLT 294 (OH); *Ashcroft's Curator Bonis v Stewart* 1988 SLT 163 (OH); *Wilson v Price* 1989 SLT 484 (OH); *Duncan v Ross Harper & Murphy* 1993 SLT 105 (OH); *Andersen v Hameed* [2010] CSOH 99.

10 See eg *Taylor v Leslie* (illegality defence failed, but pursuer's damages discounted by 50% on account of contributory negligence); *Currie v Clamp's Executors* (damages discounted by one-third).

CHAPTER 10

Employers' Liability

EMPLOYERS' LIABILITY

10.1 In this chapter, we investigate the duty of care owed by an employer to their employee. Workplace accidents are still common, particularly in sectors such as construction, agriculture, and manufacturing. Whether it is a slip, trip, being struck by a falling object, or lifting heavy loads, accidents unfortunately happen. Of course, Scotland today is far less industrialised than it was a hundred years ago, making workplace accidents less frequent. Moreover, the introduction of the Health and Safety at Work etc Act 1974 raised safety standards across workplaces, with its implementation underscored by criminal penalties. Nevertheless, accidents still occur, and in some instances, they are the fault of the employer. Indeed, employees remain vulnerable in the workplace. Often, they do not choose what tasks they perform, who they work with, or how the work is carried out. It is the employer who determines the tasks, colleagues, and methods. For these reasons – and others – this topic deserves special attention.

It is essential to recognise that the safety relationship between employer and employee is shaped by a range of interrelated and overlapping responsibilities. Thus, it is an implied term of the contract of employment that an employer will take reasonable care for the safety of its employees. If an employer does not take reasonable care, it will be in material breach of contract. In these circumstances, an employee may withdraw their labour and sue for damages, as discussed below. An employer may be in breach of his contractual obligations even if the employee has not suffered any harm.

In addition to its contractual obligations, an employer owes a duty of care to its employees to prevent them from suffering physical or psychiatric harm as a result of the employer's negligent conduct.[1] Accordingly, an employee who is injured may sue their employer in delict as well as for breach of contract; but the employee cannot be compensated twice for the same loss. If the employee does not suffer any harm, there can be no liability in delict though there might still be a remedy for breach of contract.[2]

The obligation to take reasonable care for the safety of his employees is personal to the employer, ie legal liability for workplace safety cannot be shifted by the employer to senior employees or a third party.[3] However, in a modern industrial context, in order to *fulfil* the obligation of reasonable care, an employer may have to appoint a safety officer and/or safety committee. The scope of the duty incumbent on an employer includes taking reasonable care to supply the employee with proper plant and equipment, to select competent fellow workers and to provide a safe system of working.[4]

For example, an employer can be liable for failure to *devise* a safe system of working.[5] Where an employer fails to instruct an employee to use protective devices or clothes, or fails to provide adequate training, a breach of the duty to take reasonable care can arise. Equally, if an employee refuses to follow a safe system of working, it may be necessary for disciplinary action to be taken including, in some cases, dismissal of the employee. In one case, the refusal to wear a face mask during the coronavirus pandemic, as mandated by legislation, and in line with the employer's reasonable perception of potential harm, gave sufficient grounds for the employee's dismissal.[6]

On the other hand, if an employer fails to remedy an unsafe system of working or ignores reasonable requests from employees to render such systems safe, an employee may leave their employment and seek remedy for, *inter alia*, unfair dismissal.[7] During the coronavirus pandemic, for instance, an employer insisted that their employee attend the office despite legitimate concerns that physical socialising at that time would be unsafe. The employee won their employment tribunal case, establishing that they left their employment due to the unsafe system of working, which, in effect, was an unfair dismissal by the employer.[8]

Although an employer is expected to maintain the standards of the reasonable employer in their position, more is required of an employer than is expected of an ordinary person. Thus, in *Kennedy v Cordia*[9] the Supreme Court stressed that employers must be proactive in seeking out knowledge of potential risks to employees. Modern employers must, therefore, take positive, forward-looking steps to ensure against reasonably foreseeable injury. Nonetheless, bearing this proactive attitude in mind, in assessing whether a particular *employer* has taken reasonable care, the familiar criteria found in the calculus of risk will be relevant.[10] The court will therefore consider such factors as the nature of the danger, the employer's knowledge of the danger, the extent of the harm, the probability of the harm arising and the cost of eliminating the risk.[11]

1 *Wilsons and Clyde Coal Co Ltd v English* 1937 SC (HL) 46; *Stokes v Guest Keen & Nettlefold (Bolt & Nuts) Ltd* [1968] 1 WLR 1776; *Barber v Somerset County Council* [2004] UKHL 13, [2004] 1 WLR 1089; *Baker v Quantum Group Clothing Ltd* [2011] UKSC 17, [2011] 1 WLR 1003.

2 *Rothwell v Chemical and Insulating Co* [2007] UKHL 39, [2008] 1 AC 281 (pleural plaques do not constitute harm and therefore no delictual liability).
3 *Hislop v Durham* (1842) 4 D 1168 (IH); *Wilsons and Clyde Coal Co Ltd v English* 1937 SC (HL) 46; *MacIver v J & A Gardner Ltd* 2001 SLT 585 (OH).
4 *Pickford v ICI plc* [1998] 1 WLR 1189 (HL); *Kennedy v Cordia (Services) LLP (Scotland)* [2016] UKSC 6, 2016 SC (UKSC) 59.
5 *McGregor v AAH Pharmaceuticals Ltd* 1996 SLT 1161 (OH).
6 *Shanks v Lothian Health Board* 2023 SLT (Tr) 121.
7 Employment Rights Act 1996, s 100.
8 *Abraham Goldstein v Marie-Pierre Herve* [2024] EAT 35.
9 *Kennedy v Cordia* at para 110 per Lords Hodge and Reed, endorsing the formulation of an employer's duty of care in *Baker v Quantum* at para 9 per Lord Mance.
10 *Brisco v Secretary of State for Scotland* 1997 SC 14; *McErlean v J & B Scotland Ltd* 1997 SLT 1326 (OH); *McGinnes v Endeva Service Ltd* 2006 SLT 638 (OH).
11 *Latimer v AEC Ltd* [1953] AC 643 (HL); *Hatton v Sutherland* [2002] EWCA Civ 76, [2002] ICR 613 *Barber v Somerset; Baker v Quantum.*

10.2 From a policy perspective, however, the common law calculus of risk may not always lead to the most desirable outcome. In *Davie v New Merton Board Mills Ltd*,[1] for example, an employee was injured when a piece of a chisel he was using broke off and a splinter went into his eye. The defect in the chisel was latent and arose because the metal used for the chisel had not been tempered properly by the manufacturer. The employer had bought the chisel from a reputable retailer who had in turn bought it from a reputable wholesaler who had purchased it from the manufacturer. In these circumstances, the House of Lords held that the employer had taken reasonable care and the employee's action against the *employer* failed. The employee could, of course, have sued the manufacturer in delict for breach of the manufacturer's *Donoghue v Stevenson* duty of care which he owed to the ultimate consumer of the product.[2]

Parliament, however, subsequently took the view that this placed too heavy an onus on an employee. Accordingly, under the Employers' Liability (Defective Equipment) Act 1969,[3] if an employee suffers physical harm caused by a defect in equipment[4] provided by the employer and the defect is attributable wholly or partly to the fault of a third party,[5] for example the manufacturer, then the defect is deemed to be also attributable to negligence on the part of the employer. In other words, the employee can sue the employer without the need to prove that the employer was negligent. The *employer* will then seek redress against the third party either in contract or, theoretically at least, in delict.

The employer must take reasonable care in selecting competent workers who will not cause harm to the other employees. Once hired, the employer's duty of care also requires diligent management of employees' behaviour towards each other, ensuring any foreseeable physical or psychiatric injury does not result from poor workplace relationships.[6] If the employer fails to hire competent employees, or monitor their competence, and an employee is injured as a result, the employee can sue the employer for breach of the duty of care.[7] Before the employer can be negligent, he must know that the employee he has appointed could be a danger to fellow workers or that they now present a risk to fellow employees.[8] For example, the employer should ask whether an applicant for a job as a van driver has a clean driving licence and whether he has been convicted of careless or reckless driving.[9] Yet on the other hand, employers are not expected to prevent employees from exposure to normal frustrations, emotions and difficulties that naturally occur when working with others; such would be unreasonable, and beyond the duty of care.[10]

Traditionally, many injuries in the workplace were attributable to failures to provide safe systems of work, which resulted in physical injury. For example, the lack of a system to ensure that stepladders were available where they were needed placed employers in breach when an employee lost her footing climbing shelves to retrieve a box from the topmost one.[11] A delivery man who injured his back carrying a 48kg television should have been provided with a small trolly.[12] A harbour operator failed to provide a safe system for loading lorries onto a ferry. An employee, who was struck by a reversing trailer, suffered a serious injury to his arm.[13] The duty to provide a safe system of working is varied according to what the particular situation requires with regard to the employee. So, if an employer knows that an employee is an epileptic or has only one eye, the standards required to constitute reasonable care may be greater in respect of that employee than the other workers. Accordingly, the employer may be negligent vis-à-vis that employee even if his conduct would not amount to negligence if the employee were not epileptic or had two eyes.[14]

1 [1959] AC 604 (HL).
2 See *Donoghue v Stevenson* 1932 SC (HL) 31. On product liability generally, see Chapter 13 below.
3 Employers' Liability (Defective Equipment) Act 1969, s 1(1).
4 The courts have taken a wide view of the meaning of 'equipment' to protect employees: see, for example, *Knowles v Liverpool City Council* [1993] 1 WLR 1428 (HL) (council employee injured by a defective flagstone: flagstone held to constitute equipment).
5 The pursuer is not obliged to identify the third party who was at fault: *Edwards v Butlins Ltd* 1998 SLT 500 (IH).
6 *K v Chief Constable, Police Scotland* [2020] CSIH 18, 2020 SC 399 at para 66 per Lord President Carloway.
7 The duty extends to providing adequate supervision of employees whose behaviour at work might injure a fellow worker: *Gibson v British Rail Maintenance* 1995 SC 7 (IH); *Ward v Scotrail Railways Ltd* 1999 SC 255 (OH); *Waters v Commissioner of Police of the Metropolis* [2000] 1 WLR 1607 (HL).
8 See eg *Hudson v Ridge Manufacturing Co Ltd* [1957] 2 QB 348.
9 Subject to the offences being spent under the Rehabilitation of Offenders Act 1974.
10 *Rorrison v West Lothian College* 2000 SCLR 245 (OH) at 255 per Lord Reed; *Fraser v State Hospitals Board for Scotland* 2001 SLT 1051 (OH) at para 105 per Lord Carloway.
11 *McGregor v AAH Pharmaceuticals Ltd* 1996 SLT 1161 (OH).
12 *Lindsay v TNT Express (UK) Ltd* 1996 GWD 38-2231 (OH).
13 *Lee v Ardrossan Harbour Co Ltd* 1992 SLT 340 (OH).
14 *Paris v Stepney Borough Council* [1951] AC 367 (HL).

10.3 Today, many actions raised against an employer relate to an employee's mental health. Although there is no doubt that the employer's general duty includes taking reasonable steps to prevent the employee suffering psychiatric or psychological harm[1] the extent of this duty with regard to mental health continues to be litigated by parties.[2] The key case in this area remains *Hatton v Sutherland*.[3] In *Hatton*, the Court of Appeal held that where an employee has sustained psychiatric harm there are no special control mechanisms as developed in *Alcock*[4] and that the ordinary principles of employers' liability apply. Or a better way to view it is to say that within the context of employment, foreseeability operates differently. The general principles remain the same – foreseeability is key – yet the application to the specific context necessitates a refinement of the court's approach.

Hence, therefore, as with other areas, there will be no breach of the duty of care unless it can be shown that the harm sustained by the pursuer was a reasonably foreseeable consequence of the employer's conduct. But by its nature psychiatric or psychological harm is less foreseeable within the workplace than physical harm. To put it another way, in *Hatton* the court took the view that a reasonable employer is usually entitled to assume that an employee can withstand the normal pressures of work unless the employer knows that the employee is particularly vulnerable. This could arise, for example, where the employer was aware that the employee had had a nervous breakdown before[5] or the employee's doctor had informed him that the working conditions were causing the employee to suffer depression[6] or there have been unexplained and uncharacteristic absences from work. There can be liability if the psychiatric injury was caused by an excessive workload, ie where the employee was required to perform duties far beyond those agreed in her contract.[7] However, even when an employee was able to demonstrate the poor handling of a workplace complaint that amounted to a breach of the employer's duty of care they failed to establish that this was the cause of their depression.[8] Causation remains one of the biggest hurdles for workplace stress claims.

Following *Hatton*, the rule of thumb is that an employer does not have a general duty to monitor employees to see whether they are at risk of suffering psychiatric harm.[9] But even if psychiatric harm was reasonably foreseeable, there is no liability unless the employee can show that there were reasonable steps which the employer should have taken to prevent him suffering mental harm.[10] Striking the balance between what is reasonable and unreasonable can be difficult for an employer, particularly in situations where there are ongoing disciplinary or grievance processes which relate to employees who are known to be struggling with their mental health.[11] Aside from the principles articulated in *Hatton*, such cases will continue to be determined with regard to the specific fact pattern of the case before the court. In many instances, the reality will be that while an employer's general duty of care to protect his employees includes psychiatric harm it continues to be very difficult for pursuers to establish a breach of duty in respect of psychiatric harm caused by stressful work conditions, including bullying, poor management, or overwork. Unless the employer knew that the employee was particularly vulnerable or became aware of a vulnerability and there were reasonable – as opposed to difficult or expensive – steps to reduce the pressure on the employee, the default assumption is that employees can withstand the pressures of the job

We must be careful to distinguish between psychiatric injuries, which come about in the workplace due to an accident (ie a discrete event, which occurs in a particular manner at a specific time and place) and those injuries which are due to an ongoing system of working (ie the allocation of work, performance management of staff or day-to-day working relationships). When it comes to accidents which cause psychiatric injury, such as witnessing the physical – or mental – injuries of a third person, for example to a fellow employee,[12] different tests will be applied by the courts from those articulated in *Hatton*. In cases of accidents in the workplace, which cause psychiatric injury, the general rule is that the employer does not owe a duty of care unless the employee was within the area of risk of potential physical harm[13] or the *Alcock* criteria for liability in respect to psychiatric injury to secondary victims are satisfied.[14] In *Keen v Tayside Contractors*,[15] for example, a worker was instructed by his employer to assist the emergency services at the scene of a road accident where he saw the crushed and burned bodies of the victims. The pursuer's supervisor refused him permission to leave the scene of the accident even though he asked to do so. The pursuer claimed that the employer was negligent in (a) failing to instruct supervisors to let employees leave the scene of an accident where there were dead and mutilated bodies and (b) failing to provide post-incident support for employees who had been disturbed by seeing the victims. The Lord Ordinary (Lady Paton) dismissed the action. Although the employee suffered psychiatric harm caused by seeing the victims of the road accident, they failed to satisfy the *Alcock* criteria as there was no relationship of love and affection between the victims and the employee.[16]

1 Stress does not per se constitute psychiatric harm though it may lead to a psychiatric disorder such as acute stress reaction, PTSD or depression if allowed to continue unabated.

2 *Fraser v State Hospitals Board for Scotland* 2001 SLT 1051 (OH); *Cross v Highland and Islands Enterprise* 2001 SLT 1060 (OH); *Green v Argyll & Bute Council* 2002 WL 498950; *McCarthy v Highland Council* [2011] CSIH 51, 2012 SLT 95; *T v W* [2022] CSOH 44; *Frame v*

Abellio Scotrail Ltd [2024] SC EDIN 32 and *Carroll v Dumfries and Galloway Council* [2024] CSOH 81.

3 [2002] EWCA Civ 76, [2002] ICR 613 (CA), approved on this point (but reversing its application on the facts) by the House of Lords in *Barber v Somerset County Council* [2004] UKHL 13, [2004] 1 WLR 1089. See also *K v Chief Constable, Police Scotland* [2020] CSIH 18, 2020 SC 399 at para 90 per Lord Carloway.

4 *Alcock v Chief Constable of South Yorkshire Police* [1992] 1 AC 310 (HL), discussed at para 4.9–4.10 above.

5 *Walker v Northumberland CC* [1995] ICR 702 (QBD).

6 *Stevenson v East Dunbartonshire Council* 2003 SLT 97 (OH); *Barber.*

7 *Flood v University of Glasgow* [2010] CSIH 3, 2010 SLT 167. The excessive workload enabled the Inner House to distinguish the case from *Hatton.*

8 *Frame v Abellio Scotrail Limited* [2024] SC EDIN 32.

9 See *Barber.*

10 If the employer has taken reasonable steps there will be no breach of duty: see eg *Pratt v Scottish Ministers* [2013] CSIH 17, 2013 SLT 590.

11 See *Walker v Northumberland.*

12 See eg *Robertson v Forth Road Bridge Joint Board* 1995 SC 364 (IH); *Hunter v British Coal Corporation* [1999] QB 140 (CA).

13 In which case the employee is a primary victim and is protected by the employer's general duty to take reasonable care of his employees. It can be difficult to determine whether an employee has sufficient proximity to the accident which caused the harm to the third party to be regarded as a participant and therefore a primary victim. See *Robertson; Campbell v North Lanarkshire Council* 2000 SCLR 373 (OH); *Young v Charles Church (Southern) Ltd* (1998) 39 BMLR 146 (CA); *Salter v UB Frozen & Chilled Foods Ltd* 2004 SC 233 (OH).

14 Namely that there was a relationship of love and affection between the employee and the person who was injured, proximity to the accident or its immediate aftermath and direct visual observation of the accident or its aftermath.

15 2003 SLT 500 (OH).

16 This is consistent with *Frost v Chief Constable of South Yorkshire Police* [1999] 2 AC 455 (HL) where the injuries to the third parties witnessed by the plaintiffs were also caused by their employer. In *Donaldson v Scottish Ministers* [2009] CSOH 8, 2009 SLT 240 the pursuer suffered a psychiatric illness from watching one prisoner assaulting another prisoner. The Lord Ordinary (Woolman) held that the pursuer had not demonstrated what the employee should have done to avoid the incident.

10.4 The employer must provide a safe environment in which employees work.[1] Where an employee works at a place which is not under the control of his employer, the employer can still be liable for failing to inspect the premises to ensure that the employee is not exposed to unnecessary risks.[2] It has been held that there can be a breach of the duty if the employer has not taken reasonable steps to protect an employee from the risk of illness arising from passive smoking.[3]

At common law the onus lay on the employee to prove that the harm sustained was a breach of the employer's duty of care, ie that the employer was negligent. Since the nineteenth century, safety at work has been the subject of statutory regulations. These provide detailed safety requirements for machinery, particular processes and operations.

The Health and Safety at Work etc Act 1974 lays down the minimum standards required of employers for safety at the workplace. However, it is a criminal statute and it is expressly enacted that its breach does not give rise to a private law remedy for breach of statutory duty. Breach of these detailed regulations do not give rise to delictual liability.[4]

Nevertheless, where an employee is injured in circumstances that amount to a breach of health and safety regulations, it is important to remember that regulations may be utilised to demonstrate the employer's negligence under an equivalent duty at common law. Notably, the normalisation of risk assessments, under the expectations of modern health and safety regulations, has resulted in a concurrent common law expectation that a reasonably prudent employer will carry out risk assessments in appropriate circumstances and a failure to do so, can, when injury occurs, amount to a breach of the duty of care.[5] Nevertheless, pursuers seeking to rely on specific health and safety regulations in order to inform the substance of a separate common law duty must be mindful that regulatory expectations are only factually relevant to a court's overall consideration of the duty of care.[6] Regulations are not determinative of the common law standard of care, which remains a judicial question.[7]

An employer may owe the employee a separate duty under the Occupiers' Liability (Scotland) Act 1960, as well as the general duty of care owed to employees at common law.

1 For example, that the level of noise in the workplace will not cause deafness. The pursuer must establish the level of the noise: *Robinson v Midlothian Council* [2009] CSOH 109.

2 *Crombie v McDermott Scotland Ltd* 1996 SLT 1238 (OH); *Muir v North Ayrshire Council* 2005 SLT 963 (OH) (pursuer was a home help who was injured in the house of a client: employer could be liable as they knew the environment in which she was working).

3 *Rae v Strathclyde Joint Police Board* 1999 SCLR 793 (OH).

4 Health and Safety at Work Act 1974 s 47(1) and (2). As amended by the Enterprise and Regulatory Reform Act 2013, s 69. See also *Gilchrist v Asda Stores Ltd* [2015] CSOH 77 at para 14 per Lady Stacey.

5 *Kennedy v Cordia (Services) LLP* [2016] UKSC 6, 2016 SC (UKSC) 59 at para 110 per Lords Reed and Hodge.

6 *Rose v WNL Investments Limited* [2023] CSOH 49, 2023 SLT 829 at para 38 per Lord Sandison.

7 *Swierzko v Mathiesons Bakery Limited* [2024] SC EDIN 43 at para 37 per Sheriff Campbell.

CHAPTER 11

Professional Liability

11.1 This chapter examines the duty of care owed by a professional. In what follows, we will describe how to define a professional, the general principles which shape the legal expectations falling on a professional, before focusing on the medical and legal professions.

For reasons of policy and fairness, the standard expected of professionals is not fixed according to an objective reasonableness standard but rather varies depending on numerous factors, which we shall examine below.[1] There are sound reasons for varying the standard of care owed by a professional. By the nature of the role, professions are required to undertake tasks that are complex and demanding. Despite their best efforts, outcomes may not always be successful. Frequently, the factors influencing success lie beyond the professional's control. On this basis, it has long been accepted in the law that there can be a legitimate variation in opinions, judgements, and assessments of the best course of action.[2] Much of this, therefore, means a standard objective reasonableness test is inappropriate. Hence, acknowledging these challenges has a marked impact on how the standard of care of a professional is determined.

1 See para 11.3 below.
2 M Cannon KC et al, *Jackson and Powell on Professional Liability* (9th edn, Sweet & Maxwell, 2021) at para 2-001.

11.2 There is no fixed definition of a professional in the law of delict. Courts are prepared to extend the definition to ensure the law is flexible and adaptable to developments within wider society. However, several factors are considered when establishing if someone should be judged according to professional standards.[1] One factor is the existence of an institutional structure, which defines competencies, standards and required qualifications. Membership is restricted in professions to those who have attained educational outcomes and qualifications, such as diplomas or degrees, with an expectation that one's knowledge is routinely assessed, monitored and updated. The work will be specialist and require a degree of skill, knowledge, and experience which is not common to the public. Professions will often incorporate an ethical code, which requires adherence to community values. Relatedly, professions will enjoy a position of trust and respect within society. Specialist knowledge and recognition by some form of community, institution or legal body will be indicative of a person being a professional but not necessarily conclusive.[2]

Except in cases concerning the scope of the duty of care, which are mentioned below, often professional negligence cases will not engage the question of whether there is a duty of care. In most instances, it is beyond doubt. The central question is often: what *is* that duty. Hence, in determining whether there has been a breach of a duty of care, the defender's conduct is judged by the standard of care expected in his or her profession.[3] Put another way, in order to establish that the defender was negligent, the pursuer must prove that the defender's conduct fell below that of the reasonable accountant, architect, lawyer, medical practitioner or surveyor etc. While ultimately a question of law,[4] the usual practice of persons in the same trade, business or profession as the defender will be a significant, but not necessarily decisive, factor in determining whether the defender was negligent.

1 *ICL Tech Ltd v Johnston Oils Ltd* [2012] CSOH 62, 2012 SLT 667 at paras 14–23.

2 For discussion, see R Jackson, 'The Professions: Power, Privilege and Legal Liability' (2015) 31(3) *Professional Negligence* 122. See also *Dickson v Hygienic Institute* 1910 SC 352 (IH); *Atwal Enterprises Ltd v Toner t/a Donal Toner Associates* [2006] CSOH 76, 2006 SLT 537; *ICL Tech Ltd;* and *Frank Houlgate Investment Co Ltd v Biggart Baillie LLP* [2014] CSIH 79, 2014 SC 187.

3 In *Andrews v Greater Glasgow Health Board* [2019] CSOH 31, 2019 SLT 727 it was held that a junior doctor owes the patient the same standard of care as a more experienced doctor.

4 *Bolitho v City and Hackney Health Authority* [1998] AC 232 (HL).

THE TEST FOR PROFESSIONAL NEGLIGENCE

11.3 It can be particularly difficult to establish negligence where the defender's conduct involves an exercise of professional judgement. Often, there will be several courses of action open to the defender. In these circumstances, the defender will be considered negligent only if no reasonable professional in his or her position would have chosen the course of action that resulted in harm to the pursuer. Nor does it matter that the course of action chosen was *not* the normal practice in the profession. In the leading case of *Hunter v Hanley*[1] the pursuer alleged that the defender, a doctor, was negligent in using a needle which was unsuitable for treating the patient. In discussing the standard of care appropriate to a doctor, the Lord President (Clyde) observed:[2]

> '… in regard to deviation from ordinary professional practice … such deviation is not necessarily evidence of negligence. Indeed it would be disastrous if this were so, for all inducement to progress in medical science would then be destroyed. Even a substantial deviation from normal practice may be warranted by the particular circumstances. To

> establish liability by a doctor where deviation from normal practice is alleged, three facts require to be established. First of all it must be proved that there is a normal practice; secondly it must be proved that the defender has not adopted that practice; and thirdly (and this is of crucial importance) it must be established that the course which the doctor adopted is one which no professional man of ordinary skill would have taken if he had been acting with ordinary care'.

Thus, it is not enough that the defender's conduct deviated from normal practice: it must be demonstrated that no professional man of ordinary skill would have followed the course taken by the defender. However, a pursuer will not fail merely because she cannot establish that there was a normal practice which the defender did not follow: the crucial issue is the third, ie that the course that the defender followed was one no professional of ordinary skill would have taken if acting with ordinary care.[3] Even if the pursuer can establish that a responsible body of medical opinion regards the defender's decision or conduct as wrong, the defender will not be regarded as having been negligent if there is also a responsible body of medical opinion which regards the defender's decision or conduct as reasonable in the circumstances.[4]

1 1955 SC 200 (IH).
2 *Hunter v Hanley* at 206. Lord Clyde's approach was approved by McNair J in the leading English case, *Bolam v Friern Hospital Management Committee* [1957] 1 WLR 582 (QBD).
3 *Gerrard v Royal Infirmary of Edinburgh NHS Trust* [2005] CSIH 10, 2005 1 SC 192; *Atwal Enterprises Ltd v Toner t/a Donal Toner Associates* [2006] CSOH 76, 2006 SLT 537.
4 *Maynard v West Midlands Regional Health Authority* [1984] 1 WLR 634 (HL).

MEDICAL NEGLIGENCE

11.4 *Gordon v Wilson*[1] provides an illustration of the formidable difficulties facing a pursuer in an action of medical negligence, particularly where there are conflicting bodies of professional opinion. In that case, the pursuer argued that a doctor was negligent in delaying to refer a patient to a specialist.[2] Although the pursuer established that there was a responsible body of medical opinion which took the view that a reasonable doctor would have referred the patient to a specialist at an earlier stage, the court held that the defender was not negligent because the defender could show that there was also a responsible body of medical opinion to the effect that a reasonable doctor would not have referred the patient to a specialist until the defender had done so. Accordingly, the pursuer's action failed. Professional negligence cannot be established by preferring one body of professional opinion to another; instead, the pursuer must prove that no reasonable doctor exercising her ordinary clinical skills would have taken the defender's course of action in the circumstances of the case.[3]

The law was summarised by Lord Hodge in *Honisz v Lothian Health Board*:[4]

> 'First, as a general rule, where there are two opposing schools of thought among the relevant group of responsible medical practitioners as to the appropriateness of a particular practice, it is not the function of the court to prefer one school over the other … Secondly, however, the court does not defer to the opinion of the relevant professionals to the extent that, if a defender leads evidence that other responsible professionals among the relevant group of medical practitioners would have done what the impugned medical practitioner did, the judge must in all cases conclude that there has been no negligence. This is because, thirdly, in exceptional cases the court may conclude that a practice which responsible medical practitioners have perpetuated does not stand up to rational analysis … Where the judge is satisfied that the body of professional opinion, on which the defender relies, is not reasonable or responsible he may find the medical practitioner guilty of negligence, despite that body of opinion sanctioning his conduct. This will rarely occur as the assessment and balancing of risks and benefits are matters of clinical judgement. Thus it will normally require compelling expert evidence to demonstrate that an opinion of another medical expert is one which that other expert could not have held if he had taken care to examine the basis of the practice. Where experts have applied their minds to the comparative risks and benefits of a course of action and have reached a defensible conclusion, the court will have no basis for rejecting their view and concluding that the pursuer has proved negligence in terms of the *Hunter v Hanley* test. As Lord Browne-Wilkinson said in *Bolitho* (at p 243D–E) "it is only where the judge can be satisfied that the body of expert opinion cannot logically be supported at all that such opinion will not provide the benchmark by which the defendant's conduct falls to be assessed".'

These cases were concerned with the medical profession. But as indicated above, the test for establishing the requisite standard of care is applicable in relation to other professions where an exercise of professional judgement is involved.[5]

1 1992 SLT 849 (OH), See also, for example, *Hannigan v Lanarkshire Acute Hospitals NHS Trust* [2012] CSOH 152, 2013 SCLR 179; *JD v Lothian Health Board* [2017] CSIH 27, 2018 SCLR 1.

2 To prove causation, the pursuer must show that, but for the doctor's omission, the treatment had over a 50% chance of success: *Kenyon v Bell* 1953 SC 125 (OH); *Hotson v East Berkshire Area Health Authority* [1987] AC 750 (HL); *Gregg v Scott* [2005] UKHL 2, [2005] 2 AC 176. See para 9.4 above.

3 In *Bolitho v City and Hackney Health Authority* [1998] AC 232 (HL) it was stressed by the House of Lords that the body of medical opinion must be reasonable and responsible. In other words, there must be a logical basis for the opinion supported by the experts. Although this is ultimately a question of law, it would only be in rare cases that the court would reject the medical experts' views as unreasonable.

4 [2006] CSOH 24, 2008 SC 235 at para 39.

5 See, for example, *Campbell v Borders Health Board* [2012] CSIH 49; *Coyle v Lanarkshire Health Board* [2013] CSOH 167 (midwives); *Henderson v Merrett Syndicates Ltd (No 2)* [1996] PNLR 32 (Comm Ct) (underwriting agents); *Sneesby v Goldings* [1994] 12 WLUK 69 (CA) (surveyors); *Leeds & Holbeck Building Society v Alex Morison & Co (No 2)*

2001 SCLR 41 (OH); *McCrindle v Maclay, Murray & Spens* [2013] CSOH 72 (lawyers); *Atwal Enterprise Ltd v Toner t/a Donal Toner Associates* [2006] CSOH 76, 2006 SLT 537 (architects); *WTL International Ltd Retirement Benefits Scheme Trustees v Edwards* [2010] CSOH 34 (actuaries).

11.5 While the standard of care established in *Hunter v Hanley*[1] applies generally across those whose practice can be considered 'professional',[2] some of the most difficult complications arise in the medical context.

In *Darnley v Croydon Health Services NHS Trust*,[3] the claimant, who had been assaulted, attended an Accident and Emergency Unit with head injuries. Having been informed by the receptionist that he would face a four-to-five-hour wait, he left after 19 minutes and went home. Unfortunately, he developed permanent brain damage, which would not have occurred had he remained in the hospital. The receptionist had omitted to inform him that he would be triaged within 30 minutes of his arrival. The claim failed at first instance and in the Court of Appeal on the basis that there had been no assumption of responsibility and there was no duty on staff to provide accurate information about waiting times. The claimant was held responsible for his own injuries having chosen to leave against advice that he should wait. The decision was reversed in the Supreme Court. A hospital–patient relationship is established as soon as a patient presents for treatment. It is well established that this relationship imposes on the hospital a duty of care. The duty of the receptionist was not to provide misleading information. The standard applied was that of an averagely competent and reasonably well-informed person performing the function of an A&E receptionist. For the Supreme Court, this case was not about the standard of care owed by a medical professional assessed under the tests set out in *Hunter v Hanley*. This case confirmed that hospitals owe a duty of care to users of their services, regardless of whether staff like receptionists are considered professionals. The hospital had a basic duty to avoid giving misleading information. That duty was breached, leading the claimant to go home and suffer harm. The hospital was therefore liable.

1 1955 SC 200 (IH).
2 For judicial discussion on the meaning of professional, see *ICL Tech Ltd & Others v Johnston Oils Ltd* [2012] CSOH 62, 2012 SLT 667 at paras 14–23.
3 [2018] UKSC 50, [2019] AC 831.

11.6 Nevertheless, as *Darnley* demonstrates, patients are free to make their own decisions about their treatment. It is vital that such decisions are informed. A basic principle of the law of delict is that physical intervention without informed consent is an assault.[1] Medical treatment should proceed with the patient's consent but, given the complexities of human health and the highly specialised nature of modern medicine, the consent of a patient to a given course of action may be more or less meaningless unless it is informed by discussion between doctor and patient regarding any risks inherent in the proposed procedure, alternative courses of action, the consequences of taking no action and so on depending on the circumstances. The duty to inform patients then forms an important element of the duty of care owed by doctors to their patients. This is known as the doctrine of informed consent.

Prior to the Supreme Court decision in *Montgomery v Lanarkshire Health Board*[2] the failure of a doctor to disclose risks with a very low probability of materialising would not normally be negligent.[3] However, the Supreme Court refined the law in this area, drawing a distinction between diagnosis and advice on treatment. The facts of *Montgomery* are as follows. During her antenatal care, Mrs Montgomery's consultant had not informed her of several low probability risks associated with the vaginal delivery of a large baby from a small mother. Sadly, all these risks materialised, the child suffered hypoxia with consequent cerebral palsy affecting all four limbs. Mrs Mongomery's contention, that had she been informed of the risk of shoulder dystocia, she would have elected to have had the baby delivered by caesarean section, was accepted. It was held in the Supreme Court that the duty to disclose risks is not determined by the probability of the risk materialising, but by the significance which a reasonable person in the position of the patient would be likely to attach to the risk. Doctors, therefore, are under a duty to inform patients on risks which the patient would regard as significant.[4]

From the perspective of medical negligence, *Montgomery* is a significant case because the Supreme Court concluded that when it came to the advisory aspect of care, the professional practice test articulated in *Hunter v Hanley* did *not* apply.[5] Deciding whether to take a viable course of treatment was not simply a decision of professional judgement. In such situations, patients must be consulted, and alternatives and risks should be discussed. Failure to do so may amount to a breach of the duty of care. As the Supreme Court made clear:

> '[t]he doctor is therefore under a duty to take reasonable care to ensure that the patient is aware of any material risks involved in any recommended treatment, and of any reasonable alternative or variant treatments'.[6]

Montgomery, however, left several difficult questions for doctors, including when an alternative course of treatment should be discussed with a patient and to what extent a doctor should be mindful of unnecessarily alarming unqualified patients about remote risks.

1 See para 1.5 above.
2 [2015] UKSC 11, 2016 SC (UKSC) 63.
3 *Sidaway v Board of Governors of the Bethlem Royal Hospital and Maudsley Hospital* [1985] AC 871 (HL); followed in *Moyes v Lothian Health Board* 1990 SLT 444 (OH).
4 For discussion see E Reid, '*Montgomery v Lanarkshire Health Board* and the Rights of the Reasonable Patient' (2015) 19 *Edinburgh Law Review* 360.

5 *Montgomery* at para 86 per Lord Reed.
6 *Montgomery* at para 87 per Lord Reed.

11.7 In *McCulloch v Forth Valley Health Board*,[1] the Supreme Court returned to these questions, providing further guidance to medical professionals about the application of *Montgomery*. The pursuers in this case were the family of a patient who suffered a cardiac arrest and died. It was contended that the consultant cardiologist involved in the patient's treatment had failed, at an early stage, to give the patient adequate advice about their treatment options, one of which, they argued, would have saved his life. In response, it was argued by the defenders that the professional practice test applies when a doctor is considering what alternative treatments are viable options for the patient to consider. In omitting to advise on various treatment options, the doctor had exercised professional judgement, which was reasonable when considered against the practice of other professionals. The Inner House agreed with the hospital, explaining:[2]

> 'If alternative treatments are options reasonably available in the circumstances the patient is entitled to be informed of the risks of these accordingly. But where the doctor has rejected a particular treatment, not by taking on him or herself a decision more properly left to the patient, but upon the basis that it is not a treatment which is indicated in the circumstances of the case, then the [*Montgomery*] duty does not arise.'

On appeal to the Supreme Court, the pursuer failed to show that the Inner House had erred in its application of *Montgomery*. Lord Hamblen and Lord Burrows affirmed that a doctor does not breach their duty of care when they use their reasonable professional judgement to decide which alternatives to present to a patient.[3] Determining which options to discuss falls within the ambit of the doctor's clinical expertise and the merits of such a decision should be assessed according to a reasonable body of expert opinion, ie according to the *Hunter v Hanley* test.[4]

1 [2023] UKSC 26, 2023 SC (UKSC) 91.
2 [2021] CSIH 21, 2021 SLT 695 per Lady Dorrian at para 40.
3 [2023] UKSC 26, 2023 SC (UKSC) 91 at para 56–57 per Lords Hamblen and Burrows.
4 For discussion, see J Macleod, 'Double Duty: *McCulloch v Forth Valley Health Board*' (2024) 28(1) *Edinburgh Law Review* 130.

MEDICAL CASES: SCOPE OF THE DUTY

(1) Wrongful life

11.8 It is generally accepted that a person owes a duty of care not to harm a foetus, ie a child *in utero*. Where a foetus is injured in its mother's womb, if the child is subsequently born alive, the *child* can sue the defender in delict in respect of its physical harm even though the injuries were sustained when the child was a foetus. In *McKay v Essex Area Health Authority*,[1] a mother contracted rubella (German measles) during her pregnancy. When the child was born, the baby was severely physically impaired because of the mother's illness. The mother alleged that owing to the hospital's carelessness, she had not been informed that her baby might be born with malformations. Since no tests had been carried out, the mother had been denied the opportunity of a lawful termination of her pregnancy. The Court of Appeal held that the hospital may have been in breach of a duty of care towards the *mother* which would entitle her to damages for having to bring up a physically impaired child. But the hospital did not owe a duty of care towards the *child* to allow the child's mother the opportunity to terminate the pregnancy. A foetus has no right to be born whole or not at all. This denial of the existence of a duty of care towards a foetus to terminate the pregnancy if the foetus is malformed is clearly based on principles of public policy.[2] Accordingly, the law has refused to recognise wrongful life actions by denying the existence of a duty of care.

1 [1982] QB 1166 (CA).
2 Moreover, even if such a duty existed, the child's malformations were not caused by the careless conduct of the hospital but by the rubella; on the necessity for causation. Of course, if the hospital had caused the child's impairments, it *would* have been liable to the child, if born alive; see discussion beyond.

(2) Wrongful birth

11.9 While there will be no duty of care towards a foetus to terminate the pregnancy because it might be born with impairments, the Court of Appeal emphasised that the defendant could have been in breach of its duty towards the *mother* in not allowing her the opportunity of a termination. This is known as a wrongful birth action. In *McLelland v Greater Glasgow Health Board*,[1] an Extra Division accepted that wrongful birth actions can be pursued in Scots law. Thus, a hospital owes a duty of care to the parents of a child to provide the mother with an opportunity to terminate her pregnancy if her child is likely to be born physically or mentally disabled. While both parents can recover solatium for the distress of having a disabled child and the mother can recover solatium in respect of the pregnancy and birth, the basic economic cost of maintaining the child cannot be recovered: but any additional costs stemming from the special needs of a disabled child can be recovered.

1 2001 SLT 446 (IH).

(3) Wrongful conception

11.10 In *McFarlane v Tayside Health Board*,[1] the pursuers sought damages for the birth of a healthy child who had been born as a result of a failed sterilisation on the father. The Lord Ordinary (Gill) admitted that the defenders owed a duty of care to the pursuers who were their patients but denied the pursuers' action of damages. Lord Gill argued that the parents had not sustained any reparable loss. He refused to classify pregnancy and labour as physical injury to the mother and he did not regard the cost of rearing the child as economic loss, since such loss was outweighed by the inestimable benefits of being the parents of a healthy child. This decision was reversed by the Second Division.[2] There it was held that the parents' right not to have a child had been infringed, ie that the unplanned conception constituted the harm (*damnum*). This was a reparable interest in modern Scots law.[3] Consequently in a wrongful conception action the mother could recover damages for pain and suffering caused by the pregnancy and birth; and both parents could recover compensation for the economic costs of bringing up the child whose birth had not been planned. Moreover, their damages would not be reduced because the mother had refused to terminate the pregnancy.

This decision was in turn appealed to the House of Lords. There it was accepted that a doctor does owe a duty of care to a man or a woman who undergoes sterilisation and if as a result of medical negligence an unplanned conception occurs then there is a breach of that duty of care. The House agreed that the mother could recover solatium for pain and suffering caused by the pregnancy and birth as well as any derivative economic loss of earnings during that period. But their Lordships held that it was contrary to contemporary values of distributive justice that the parents should be able to recover for the economic cost of maintaining a healthy and normal child.[4] The principle of non-recoverability for the cost of bringing up a normal and healthy child was reaffirmed by the House of Lords in *Rees v Darlington Memorial Hospital NHS Trust*.[5] However, a majority of their Lordships felt that an award of solatium did not adequately recognise the wrongful infringement of the mother's freedom to limit the size of her family and made her a conventional non-compensatory award of £15,000 to afford some measure of recognition of the wrongful conception of her child.

1 1997 SLT 211 (OH), 2000 SC (HL) 1.
2 2000 SC (HL) 1.
3 In England, wrongful conception actions had been recognised for a long time. See eg *Thake v Maurice* [1986] QB 644 (CA); *Gold v Haringey Health Authority* [1988] QB 481 (CA). In *Goodwill v British Pregnancy Advisory Service* [1996] 1 WLR 1397 (CA), the Court of

Appeal held that the duty of care did not extend to advising the future sexual partners of male patients that their vasectomy could undergo a spontaneous reversal. *Sed quaere*?.

4 See also J Thomson 'Abandoning the Law of Delict' 2000 SLT (News) 43.

5 [2003] UKHL 52, [2004] 1 AC 309 (HL). *McFarlane* was followed even although the mother in *Rees* was blind.

(4) Harm beyond the scope of care

11.11 Even if a doctor is found to be negligent by the court, it does not always follow that the losses suffered fall within the scope of the duty of care. Some consequences of negligence are said to be too remote to be reasonably considered the responsibility of the defender. In *Khan v Meadows*,[1] the patient, Mrs Meadows, sought advice on whether she carried the gene for haemophilia. Her doctor arranged for her to be tested for haemophilia but neglected to inform her that she would require further genetic testing to affirm whether she carried the gene. She subsequently gave birth to a boy with both haemophilia and autism. Mrs Meadows established that she would have terminated her pregnancy had she known that she was indeed a carrier. In the High Court, she was awarded damages based on the additional costs of raising a child with both conditions. The Court of Appeal reversed this decision so far as costs associated with autism were concerned. This was affirmed in the Supreme Court. Dr Khan was under a duty to provide the patient with sufficient information to enable her to make an informed decision on continuing or terminating her pregnancy based on the risk of haemophilia. That duty was breached, but there was no duty with regard to autism and so no breach. The child's autism was not connected in any way to the risk of haemophilia. The risk of autism, therefore, was not within the scope of the duty owed to the patient.[2]

1 [2021] UKSC 21, [2022] AC 852. For consideration of *Khan* and its application in Scotland, see *D v Grampian Health Board* [2022] CSOH 63; *D v NHS Fife Health Board* [2022] SAC (Civ) 27.

2 For discussion, see John MacLeod, 'Harm is Where One Starts From: *Khan v Meadows* and *Manchester Building Society v Grant Thornton LLP*' (2022) 26(1) *Edinburgh Law Review* 123.

NEGLIGENCE OF LEGAL PROFESSIONALS

11.12 The position of the legal professions requires further treatment, albeit there are common themes raised here which apply to other professions which facilitate and manage financial transactions or projects with economic consequences for clients (eg accountants, surveyors, architects and auditors). Cases in this area can be complex because of the intricate fact patterns involved in commercial transactions, which often cut across different areas of private law. For example, where a solicitor takes instructions from her client, liability arises in contract and delict.[1] Courts refer to this as concurrent liability. Liability therefore coexists within two separate areas of law, often providing a client the option to sue under the contract or the law of delict. Yet these two areas of liability can also interact with each other. That is, the extent of the professional's delictual liability must be determined with regard to the terms of the contract.[2] Even when expectations are well-defined by the contract, arguments about the extent of the professional's duty to repair the losses suffered arise, which requires careful examination of the contract.[3] Debates in these cases concern the scope and purpose of the duty that the professional owed to their client; and, by consequence, in the event of breach, how much of the client's losses must the professional compensate, by way of damages, to discharge their obligation of reparation.[4] Questions about the scope of the duty of care are frequently important in cases involving solicitors, where the losses suffered are normally economic and have the potential, therefore, to be substantial.

For example, in the case of *Newcastle Building Society v Paterson Roberston and Graham*, a solicitor negligently prepared a report for their client, a building society.[5] Relying on the report's supposed accuracy, the building society had lent money to finance a flat purchase in return for which they gained a mortgage over the property. The report was inaccurate, and the borrower had, in fact, defrauded the building society on numerous matters. None of this was identified by the solicitor in their report, which amounted, *prima facie*, to negligence. Hence, the borrower defaulted on the repayments. The building society sued the solicitor for the sums due under the mortgage minus the value they would obtain via the sale of the repossessed property. In addition, they sought the value of potential interest they could have gained on the sum loaned if they had invested it rather than lent the money to the borrowers. In determining if the solicitor owed the building society a duty of care, the Outer House rejected the defender's argument that the losses flowed from the borrower's actions, not that of the solicitor. According to the Outer House, the proper valuation of the building society's losses – and the appropriate formulation of the solicitor's duty of care – required an investigation into the losses directly attributable to the inaccurate information. To do this required an evaluation of what losses the defender could foresee at the point they prepared the report. In this instance, therefore, the Outer House addressed the issue by assessing the scope of the solicitor's duty of care and identifying the specific interests they were responsible to protect.[6] Yet the court concluded the same analysis was applicable if examined via the law of contract. Accepting that, in general, the losses suffered by the building society did fall within the scope of the duty of care, both under the contract and the law of delict, the Lord Ordinary allowed the building society to proceed to a proof to demonstrate their losses and substantiate their argument regarding the solicitor's liability.

Regardless of what the solicitor is being asked to do, normally, the contract between a client and solicitor, known as the 'Letter of Engagement', will include an express contractual duty. It will state what the solicitor is instructed to do and how they will do that. Here the contract generally requires the solicitor to use reasonable skill and care in the performance of their services.[7] In interpreting what this means, the court will ask 'what the reasonably competent practitioner would do having regard to the standards normally adopted in his [or her] profession.'[8] The courts approach the question in an analogous way to the professional practice test set out in *Hunter v Hanley*. Although the contract may tailor the extent of the professional's duties, ie the range of activities considered to fall within the scope of the relationship, the criteria by which the solicitor's actions are judged are the same under the law of contract or delict: whether the course adopted was one which no ordinarily skilled solicitor exercising ordinary care would have taken.[9]

As a general rule, the solicitor owes a duty of care to her client: she does not owe a duty of care to a third party, for example a person who would benefit from an *inter vivos* transaction.[10] However, where a solicitor gives advice or information to a person who is not a client, ie who does not have a contractual relationship with the solicitor, the solicitor may be liable in delict provided the *Henderson v Merrett* criteria for a duty of care exists.[11] In other words, there must be voluntary assumption of responsibility by the solicitor and concomitant reliance on the third party's part or where the situation is novel, the pursuer must demonstrate that it is fair, just and reasonable to impose the duty. Nevertheless, where the pursuer is successful in establishing that such a duty exists, they will only succeed if it can be established that the solicitor was negligent in giving the advice, ie that a reasonable solicitor would not have given that advice in the circumstances.[12]

1 *Robertson v Bannigan* 1965 SC 20 (IH) at 31 per Lord Wheatley.
2 *McMahon v Grant Thornton UK LLP* [2020] CSOH 50, 2020 SLT 908 at para 75 per Lord Doherty.
3 *Dale House Developments Limited v Brian C Ronnie, Ryden LLP* [2024] CSOH 99.
4 *Manchester Building Society v Grant Thornton UK LLP* [2021] UKSC 20, [2022] AC 783.
5 2001 SC 734 (OH) approved in *Preferred Mortgages Ltd v Shanks* [2008] CSOH 23; *Henderson (t/a Henderson Group Development) v Wotherspoon* [2013] CSOH 113.
6 *Newcastle Building Society* at para 23 per Lord Reed.
7 M Cannon KC et al (eds), *Jackson & Powell on Professional Liability* (9th edn, 2021) para 11-004.
8 *Midland Bank Trust Co Limited v Hett, Stubbs and Kemp (a firm)* [1979] Ch 384 (Ch D) at 402 per Oliver J applied in *McMahon*.
9 *Ronnie O'Neill Freight Solutions Limited v MacRoberts LLP* [2023] CSOH 75, 2023 SLT 1196 at para 40 per Lord Braid; *McMahon* at para 104 per Lord Doherty.

10 *Tait v Brown & McRae* 1997 SLT (Sh Ct) 63.
11 See eg *Newcastle Building Society*.
12 When the client is an experienced businessman and a transaction does not involve any hidden legal pitfalls, a solicitor is not obliged to investigate matters outwith his instructions or warn the client of the commercial risks in the transaction: *Pickersgill v Riley* [2004] UKPC 14 (Jersey). See also *Keith v Chalmers* 2004 SC 287 (IH).

11.13 What of the situation where a solicitor acts on the instructions of a client but carelessly does not give effect to the client's instructions resulting in loss to a third party? Normally, no duty of care is owed to the third party.[1] An important exception exists, however, when the third party is a 'disappointed legatee'. Consider the following problem.

A instructs a solicitor to draw up a will under which B is the principal beneficiary. As a result of the solicitor's carelessness, the will is invalid, and B does not obtain the legacy. There is no contractual relationship between B and the solicitor. Therefore, B's remedy, if any, lies in delict against the solicitor. B has suffered pure economic loss and before there is delictual liability the solicitor must owe B a duty of care to prevent B suffering such loss.

Unlike the advice and information situations, B has not relied on the solicitor's expertise: B will probably *not* know the solicitor's identity. Even if the solicitor can be said to have assumed responsibility for B's interests, the duty of care will not normally arise because of the absence of concomitant reliance on B's part. We therefore have a situation where the courts must be prepared on policy grounds to impose a duty of care before the solicitor can be liable in delict.[2]

For many years, the Scottish courts refused to recognise such a duty of care.[3] However, in England, the issue was fully explored by the House of Lords in *White v Jones*.[4] After a family quarrel, a father struck his daughters out of his will. Later, they reconciled and he made it known he wanted to re-write his daughters into the will. In spite of the family's attempts to encourage their father's solicitor to fulfil the old man's instructions, the father died before the will was altered in favour of the daughters. By a majority,[5] the House of Lords held that the solicitor owed a duty of care to the disappointed legatees. For Lord Goff and Lord Browne-Wilkinson it was enough that the solicitor had assumed responsibility for the potential beneficiaries: this was implicit when accepting their father's instructions. Concomitant reliance was not necessary to impose a duty of care in the case of disappointed legatees. Lord Goff's reasoning was explicitly based on the 'impulse to do practical justice'.[6]

1 There are very rare cases where a duty can arise because of exceptional degrees of proximity between the parties and the solicitor has assumed responsibility for the third party: *Mortgage Corporation Ltd v Mitchells Roberton* 1997 SLT 1305 (OH).
2 See generally paras 5.10–5.20 above.

3 *Robertson v Fleming* (1861) 23 D (HL) 8 at 10 per Lord Chancellor Campbell; *Weir v J M Hodge & Son* 1990 SLT 266 (OH); *MacDougall v MacDougall's Executors* 1994 SLT 1178 (OH).
4 [1995] 2 AC 207 (HL).
5 Lord Goff of Chieveley, Lord Browne-Wilkinson and Lord Nolan; Lords Mustill and Keith of Kinkel dissented.
6 *White v Jones* at 259G–260H and 268–269.

11.14 It is quite clear that the majority in *White v Jones* felt that a negligent solicitor *should* be liable in this situation. But, although we may be sympathetic to the policy, the reasoning is less than happy. In particular, the absence of the need for reliance makes it impossible to fit *White v Jones* within the general duty of care to prevent economic loss. Lord Goff specifically recognised that the duty did not arise 'on ordinary principles' relating to an assumption of responsibility;[1] it was instead 'held in law' to extend to the intended beneficiary.[2] In other words, the assumption of responsibility was imposed by the court; it did not arise from the application of the general principles which apply to that concept.

In spite of its difficulties, *White v Jones* has been transplanted into Scots law.[3] Given that the potential pursuer falls into a restricted class, ie the 'legatee' named in the instructions and therefore known to the solicitor, it is thought that a duty of care can be justified in these circumstances.[4] For this reason, Scottish courts have not been prepared to extend *White v Jones* beyond disappointed legatees.[5] In *Fraser v McArthur Stewart*,[6] a solicitor advised his client that he could not divide the tenancy of a croft. Acting on that advice, the client nominated an individual as the tenant of the croft. After the client died, it was discovered that the advice was wrong and that the testator could have left the tenancy of the croft to be divided between his residuary legatees. The residuary legatees sued the solicitor in delict. The Lord Ordinary (Brailsford) held that while the solicitor had owed a duty of care to his client, he did not owe a duty of care to the residuary legatees. *White v Jones* should only apply where owing to the negligence of the solicitor the will did not represent the last stated intentions of the testator and the potential beneficiary was left disappointed. In *Matthews v Hunter & Robertson*[7] owing to the negligence of his solicitor, a man failed to evacuate a survivorship destination in favour of his former wife. As a result, when he died his estate was diminished by the value of the property which passed to his wife by virtue of the destination. The Lord Ordinary (Brodie) held that the deceased's executor could not recover damages in respect of the wrong advice given to the deceased because he did not sustain any loss while he was alive and there was therefore no actionable delictual claim which could transmit to the executor. Lord Brodie also considered that it would not be fair, just or reasonable to impose a duty of care on the solicitor vis-à-vis the executor, to take reasonable care to ensure that the estate was not diminished after the death of his client as a result of inaccurate advice that might have been given years before the executor had been nominated let alone confirmed. In *McLeod v Crawford*,[8] a solicitor advised a client to accept a full and final settlement rather than provisional damages. After the client died, his widow and children raised an action against the solicitor for professional negligence in respect of the advice he had given to the deceased. Lord Woolman held that the solicitor did not owe a duty of care to the widow or children. At the time the advice was given, there could have been a conflict of interests between the deceased and his family on the settlement he should choose. The solicitors had never assumed responsibility for the interests of the widow or the family. The necessary proximity was therefore absent and accordingly no duty of care arose. If there had been negligence the deceased's executor would have a remedy as the estate could sue.

1 [1995] 2 AC 207 (HL) at 268B.
2 *White v Jones* at 268D.
3 *Robertson v Watt & Co* (4 July 1995, unreported), a decision of the Second Division; *Holmes v Bank of Scotland* 2002 SLT 544 (OH); *McLeod v Crawford* [2010] CSOH 101, 2010 SLT 1035.
4 A better solution, perhaps, would be to allow the court to rectify the will so that it would correspond to the testator's final intentions, evidence of which would have to be very convincing!.
5 See eg *McLeod v Crawford*. In *McDonald v Grant-Sutherland* [2008] CSOH 150, the Lord Ordinary (Matthews) took the view (*obiter*) that *White v Jones* could apply to a disappointed liferenter if the liferent which he had purported to set up failed because of the solicitor's negligence.
6 [2009] CSOH 159, 2009 SLT 31.
7 [2008] CSOH 88, 2008 SLT 634.
8 [2010] CSOH 101, 2010 SLT 1035.

11.15 For policy reasons, there are some restrictions on the liability of legal professionals. Here, there may be some subtle differences between the law of Scotland and that of England & Wales. For example, in *Arthur J S Hall & Co v Simons*,[1] the House of Lords held that under English law barristers no longer had immunity from being sued for professional negligence in their conduct of civil or criminal cases. In his dissenting speech on the latter point, Lord Hope, one of the Scottish Lords of Appeal in Ordinary, considered that there should still be immunity in respect of the conduct of criminal proceedings. In *Wright v Paton Farrell*,[2] the First Division held that advocates and solicitors continued to have immunity under Scots law in respect of the conduct of criminal cases. The position in relation to the conduct of civil proceedings remains unclear,[3] however, it should be borne in mind that claims may be brought against the Lord Advocate for malicious prosecution.[4] It has always been accepted that an advocate can be liable for giving negligent advice, for example, an opinion on a point of law.[5]

1 [2002] 1 AC 615 (HL).
2 [2006] CSIH 7, 2006 SC 404. See G Gordon, 'Not Yet Dead: *Wright v Paton Farrell and Advocates' Immunity in Scotland*' (2007) 70(3) *Modern Law Review* 471.
3 The difficulty is that the House of Lords in *Hall* did not overrule *Rondel v Worsley* [1969] 1 AC 191 (HL), which had given barristers immunity in respect of both civil and criminal proceedings. *Hall* is technically not binding on the Scottish courts.
4 *Whitehouse v Lord Advocate* [2019] CSIH 52, 2020 SC 133; see para 1.8 above.
5 *Saif Ali v Sydney Mitchell & Co* [1980] AC 198 (HL). In *Jones v Kaney* [2011] UKSC 13, [2011] 2 AC 398, the Supreme Court held that there was no longer any justification for continuing to hold expert witnesses immune from being sued for professional negligence in relation to evidence they gave in court or for the views they expressed in anticipation of court proceedings.

CHAPTER 12

Delictual Liability Arising from Ownership or Occupation of Land

INTRODUCTION

12.1 Ownership, possession, or occupation of land or property comes with duties, not just rights. For example, if the use or neglect of land or property should cause damage to someone's person or property, damages may be payable. However, the law of delict is, of course, also concerned with protecting the rights of owners and occupiers. Hence, over the centuries numerous actions have been developed to provide remedies for owners and occupiers whose interests in their land or property has been infringed. Naturally, the ordinary principles of negligence may apply when property or land has been damaged, yet here our concern is with alternative actions. Thus, this chapter explains four specific regimes which place duties upon or give rights to an owner or occupier of land: trespass, malicious misuse of land (*aemulatio vicini*), nuisance, and the liability of occupiers of land or property to those who come onto the premises.

TRESPASS AND RELATED DELICTS

12.2 Under the common law of Scotland, trespass arises when a person deliberately enters another's land without permission or legal authority. They may be interdicted to prevent future entry, or, if damage is caused to the property, they may be made liable to pay damages.

The common law of trespass must, however, interact with modern legislative innovations. The Land Reform (Scotland) Act 2003 now confers extensive permissions on members of the public to cross property and to use property for recreational purposes. Section 5(1) expressly states that the exercise of access permissions under the 2003 Act does not constitute trespass, significantly modifying the common law of trespass in Scotland. However, this so-called 'right to roam' comes with restrictions: users must adhere to the Scottish Outdoor Access Code ensuring appropriate use of these access rights and, importantly, s 6 of the Act lists numerous types of land over which access rights are not exercisable. People cannot simply traipse over a private enclosed garden in an urban area; that would, in most cases, be trespass. Yet the appropriate exercise of these rights, in accordance with the 2003 Act, will provide an effective defence to any action grounded in trespass.[1]

Notwithstanding this right to roam, the common law position remains that trespass is a *temporary* intrusion into property owned by another without the permission of the owner: for example, playing football in the owner's field or taking a short cut through his garden. Because heritable property is owned *a coelo usque ad centrum* (from the heavens to the centre of the earth) trespass protects an owner's air space as well as his land and the ground below his property. Thus, for example, the owner of a house successfully obtained an interdict preventing the respondent's crane from sweeping over his property when the respondent was building on adjacent land.[2] Because of this, statute provides that aircraft may fly over a person's land without liability for trespass.[3]

The primary remedy for trespass is interdict. No compensation is available unless there has been actual damage to the property because of the intrusion.[4] There is therefore no liability for damages in Scots law merely for entering another's property. But the proprietor is entitled to use self-help to remove a trespasser provided it is reasonable in the circumstances; for example, the owner could ask a trespasser playing football in his field to leave but not threaten him with violence if the trespasser refuses to do so.[5] Interdict is an equitable remedy and is not granted automatically merely on proof of an unauthorised entry onto land. Before an interdict will be granted further intrusions must be likely and the intention of the trespasser is important. Any potential damage to the land because of the trespass will also be a relevant consideration. In *Winans v Macrae*,[6] for example, a shooting tenant of a lease of 200,000 acres was, perhaps understandably, refused an interdict to prevent a cottar's pet lamb from entering the property.

In summary, apart from specific statutory offences, in Scots law trespass is not per se criminal, does not give rise to an action in damages unless actual damage has been done to the property, and will only result in an interdict if likely to recur and any potential damage is not *de minimis*. However, the landowner is allowed a reasonable degree of self-help to remove the trespasser.

In this section, trespass has been defined as a *temporary* intrusion onto land. If a person enters onto another's property with the intention of occupying it for an indefinite period, for example a squatter, he does commit a criminal offence under the Trespass (Scotland) Act 1865. If the owner is not in possession at the time, the squatter is liable for the wrong of intrusion; if the owner is in possession and has been wrongfully removed by the squatter, the squatter is liable for the wrong of ejection. The rightful owner can seek summary ejection, violent profits[7] and compensation for actual losses incurred.

Sometimes property may intrude on a person's land without his consent, for example if a person builds beyond his boundaries and on his neighbour's land. This is an actionable wrong and is known as encroachment. The remedies are interdict, an order for removal or damages: self-help, while sometimes unwise, is nevertheless lawful.[8] Courts may refuse a removal order where the defender has acted in good faith, where there is no material detriment to the pursuer and where removal would cause a disproportionate loss to the defender compared to any benefit to be gained by the pursuer.[9]

1 For consideration of the right to roam and its restrictions, see *Gloag v Perth and Kinross Council* 2007 SCLR 530 (Sh Ct). See generally GL Gretton and AJM Steven, *Property, Trusts and Succession* (5th edn, Bloomsbury Professional, 2024), Chapter 20.
2 *Brown v Lee Constructions Ltd* 1977 SLT (Notes) 61 (OH).
3 Civil Aviation Act 1982, s 76.
4 See eg *Baird v Thomson* (1825) 3 S 448 (IH).
5 If the self-help is excessive and results in physical harm to the trespasser, the owner can be liable for assault or negligence: *Macdonald v Watson* (1883) 10 R 1079; *Revill v Newbery* [1996] QB 567 (CA).
6 (1885) 12 R 1051 (IH).
7 Violent profits are the greatest profits the owner could have made if he was in actual possession of the land. It is thought that this should have been the remedy awarded in *Saeed v Waheed* 1996 SLT (Sh Ct) 39 rather than damages for negligence.
8 For a discussion of encroachment, see GL Gretton and AJM Steven, *Property, Trusts and Succession* (2024) paras 18.10–18.16.
9 *Anderson v Brattisanni's* 1978 SLT (Notes) 42 (IH).

USE OF LAND IN *AEMULATIONEM VICINI*

12.3 Conflicts between neighbours are common and can stem from various issues like noise, fences, animals, or parking spaces. These disputes frequently turn personal, fuelled by feelings of grievance, anger, and hostility, and can persist as a result. Traditionally, it is said that an action of *aemulatio vicini* could be initiated in cases where the interference was driven by malice. Yet, as explained below, it is rare nowadays for a pursuer to choose this option to protect their interests. However, the essence of the action can be explained as follows. When A owns land (X) which adjoins B's land (Y), A will be liable to B if he uses his land (X) in a way that is detrimental to B's enjoyment of his land (Y). Before A is liable for using his land *in aemulationem vicini*, A must use his land with the predominant motive of harming B and not to further A's legitimate interests.[1] If A's predominant motive is not to harm B, then A cannot be liable for this wrong, but A's conduct may amount to nuisance.[2] Liability then, depends on malice.

In *Campbell v Muir*[3] where the defender spitefully exercised his right to fish from a boat in a river in such a way that it prevented anglers on the opposite bank from being able to cast their rods, the Lord President (Dunedin) held that the pursuer would have been entitled to interdict because 'the defender was on the particular occasion acting *in aemulationem vicini* against his neighbour's right, and that that was a just ground for complaint'.[4] In *More v Boyle*[5] it was accepted by the sheriff that the doctrine of *in aemulationem vicini* is still part of Scots law. Naturally, this case was decided in 1966, but the law has certainly evolved since then.

Today, in these situations, various statutes intervene to prevent the misuse of land,[6] which renders *aemulationem vicini* redundant in such cases. Nevertheless, it is still valuable to understand *aemulationem vicini*, if only to give us the chance to evaluate the effectiveness of alternative claims. For example, under *aemulationem vicini* liability arises only if it can be shown that the defender acted with the predominant motive of harming the pursuer. It is, of course, difficult to establish malice, so an objective assessment must be made of the defender's conduct to infer malice. In contrast, it is unnecessary to demonstrate malice, under contemporary legislation, such as modern planning law, which seeks to prevent and resolve neighbourhood disputes. The law will assess the matter according to the appropriateness of the act and the effect of the activity. It therefore is often better for an unhappy neighbour to use an alternative course of action, such as utilising antisocial behaviour legislation if they have a noisy neighbour.[7]

The only notable advantage to a pursuer is that liability under *aemulationem vicini* can arise from a single act of the defender provided the predominant motive of harm to the pursuer can be established. In the modern context, where the defender acts out of spite to harm or distress a neighbour, the expectation is that this occurs on more than one instance before a remedy will be offered. For instance, these sorts of fact scenarios, discussed here, may be actionable under the Protection from Harassment Act 1997 which avoids the difficult burden of proving malice, but, on the other hand, requires the pursuer to demonstrate a course of conduct, ie more than one incident.[8]

1 *Dewar v Fraser* (1767) Mor 12803.
2 On nuisance, see paras 12.4–12.11 below.
3 1908 SC 387 (IH).
4 *Campbell v Muir* at 393.
5 1967 SLT (Sh Ct) 38.
6 See eg the Protection from Harassment Act 1997, the Antisocial Behaviour etc (Scotland) Act 2012 (see eg *Moray Council v Debidin* 2012 GWD 32-643), and the High Hedges (Scotland) Act 2013.
7 The last reported case involving *aemulationem vicini* was *Canmore Housing Association Limited v Bairnsfather (t/a BR Autos)* 2004 SLT 673 (OH); the pursuers dropped this argument before proof.
8 See para 1.9 and eg *Green v Chalmers* [2017] SAC Civ 8, 2017 SLT (Sh Ct) 69.

NUISANCE

12.4 Nuisance is concerned with A's use of its land in a manner which interferes with B's use and enjoyment of theirs. Here we are still considering acts by a neighbour done on their land, such as noise, pollution or damage to the fabric of another's property situated on that land. However, with nuisance, in contrast to *aemulationem vicini*, the focus is on the effect of the action, not the motive of the defender. The basics of the claim are masterfully captured by Lord President Cooper in *Watt v Jamieson*.[1] It is an 'invasion of an interest in the private use and enjoyment of land' that amounts to 'disturbance or substantial inconvenience' to the owner or occupier's enjoyment of their property, which can amount to, in some circumstances, material damage to that land or buildings thereon.

Of note, however, is that in Scots law, the genus is divided into two subspecies: private and public. The distinction only really is relevant as it determines who is entitled to complain about the interference. Private nuisance relates to the interests of an owner or someone who has a rightful interest in the enjoyment of the land, whereas public nuisance offers the right to a wider category of parties who have an interest in the protection of the neighbourhood more generally.[2] Public nuisance is of greater significance historically.[3] Offensive or noxious states of affairs affecting public health or the community can usually be dealt with by Local Authorities exercising powers under the Environmental Protection Act 1990 or other legislation.[4] Our concern here, therefore, will be with private nuisance which continues to play an important role in the management of property interests between neighbours. There is an equivalent tort of private nuisance in English law, but care must be taken when relying on case law on that tort in Scotland.[5]

1 1954 SC 56 (IH) at 58. See generally NR Whitty, 'Nuisance' in *Stair Memorial Encyclopaedia* vol 14 (Reissue, 2001).
2 '[A]ny member or members of the public may bring an action for the stopping of a public danger or nuisance': DM Walker, *Delict*, (2nd edn, W. Green, 1981) at 96.
3 The most recent case where nuisance was invoked for the protection (from offensive fumes) of the neighbourhood generally appears to be *Farley & Ors v G Adam of Hillington* 1977 SLT (Sh Ct) 81.
4 See the Environmental Protection Act 1990, s 79(1) (as amended).
5 See eg *Fearn v Board of Trustees of Tate Gallery* [2023] UKSC 4, [2024] AC 1. For a discussion of key differences, see G Cameron, 'Cross-border Neighbour Law' [2014] *Juridical Review* 37. On the question of English influence on the origin of Scots nuisance, see G Cameron 'Scots and English Nuisance … Much the Same Thing?' (2005) 9 *Edinburgh Law Review* 98.

12.5 It is beneficial to return to Lord Cooper's definitive statement of nuisance in *Watt v Jamieson*:[1]

> 'I deduce that the proper angle of approach to a case of alleged nuisance is rather from the standpoint of the victim of the loss or inconvenience than from the standpoint of the alleged offender; and that if any person

> so uses his property as to occasion serious disturbance or substantial inconvenience to his neighbour or material damage to his neighbour's property, it is in the general case irrelevant to plead merely that he was making a normal and familiar use of his own property. The balance in all such cases has to be held between the freedom of a proprietor to use his property as he pleases and the duty on a proprietor not to inflict material loss or inconvenience on adjoining proprietors and adjoining property; and in every case the answer depends on considerations of fact and degree ... The critical question is whether what he was exposed to was *plus quam tolerabile* when due weight has been given to all the surrounding circumstances of the offensive conduct and its effects.'

Establishing nuisance does not turn on the reasonableness or otherwise of the defender's conduct, but whether the disturbance to the pursuer is more than a person ought reasonably to tolerate in the circumstances. Nuisance is seen from the standpoint of the victim. The key question is then to determine if the interference is material and assess whether that amounts to an unreasonable intrusion. Non-tangible interferences with a neighbour's ability to enjoy and use his or her land, disturbances or inconveniences, may be termed 'amenity nuisance'. This is nuisance in its classic form, but it is also common for it to be pleaded in circumstances where physical damage has occurred. In both situations, a pursuer must establish the key criteria identified by Lord Cooper.

1 1954 SC 56 (IH) at 58.

(1) Establishing nuisance

12.6 As is clear from Lord Cooper, to amount to nuisance the disturbance must be material, so its nature, extent and severity must be established in every case. These are matters of fact or degree; measurements of time, volume and so on will be necessary to establish a *prima facie* case.[1] Beyond that, the relevant circumstances to be weighed in the balance will vary. The possibility of remedial measures by either party will be taken into account. The nature of the locality may be relevant. Residents in a city may reasonably be expected to tolerate degrees of disturbance that would be intolerable, say in the Outer Isles. The Archbishop of Glasgow failed to interdict the use of drop hammers in a forge in a part of Glasgow with much heavy industry.[2] It will aid the defender if it can be established that the pursuer is more than usually sensitive to the disturbance complained of.[3] In *MacBean v Scottish Water*,[4] the Lord Ordinary (Woolman) found that the pursuer's residence was affected by smells from a nearby water treatment plant, but remedial measures having been put in place, on the evidence the remaining level of disturbance was not more than reasonably tolerable.

1 In *MacBean v Scottish Water* [2021] CSIH 36 findings relied in part on the evidence of 'smell assessors'. In *King v Advocate General for Scotland* [2009] CSOH 169 the pursuer's action at common law failed, evidence of low-flying aircraft over her property was sketchy and insufficient.
2 *Maguire v Charles McNeil Ltd* 1922 SC 174 (IH).
3 See eg *Simpson v Miller* (1863) 2 M 225 (IH) in which a woman complained of vibrations from a baker's dough mixing machine which did not appear to affect the other residents in the tenement.
4 [2020] CSOH 55, 2020 SLT 707; affirmed [2021] CSIH 36.

(2) Remedies for nuisance

12.7 Where the complaint concerns amenity nuisance, the object of the litigation is usually to put a stop to it or abate the nuisance. The primary remedy, therefore, is interdict although this is often accompanied by a plea for declarator.[1] An interdict need not necessarily put an end to the activity or operation, the terms of the interdict should be drafted no more widely than is required to put an end to its deleterious effects, in short, the activity can be allowed to continue provided the nuisance is abated. Interdict can also be awarded to prevent a nuisance from occurring. It must of course be clear that the activity will indeed cause more than reasonably tolerable disturbance.[2]

The public interest in the continuation of an activity or operation is not a basis for refusing interdict though of course, public interest will be taken into account in the balance. If the nuisance is relatively trivial then it may not pass the *plus quam tolerabile* test in any case. Public right does not trump private right. Having first determined that nuisance exists, where the public interest in continuation of the activity is overwhelming, the court may suspend the operation of interdict in order to allow remedial measures to be put in place.[3] Equally, the parties may agree that the defender should be given the opportunity to abate the nuisance.[4] In *Ben Nevis Distillery v The North British Aluminium Co Ltd*,[4] interdict was suspended to allow the defender to implement remedial measures to reduce the air pollution of which the pursuer complained. The public interest in the defender's operation was substantial, the company was a major employer in the area and contributed 72 per cent of the total aluminium production for the UK.[5]

Assuming general requirements for the grant of interdict are met, interdict will be granted where nuisance is established,[6] that is where the disturbance is determined to be *plus quam tolerabile*, more than reasonably tolerable in the circumstances. When interdict is sought there is no requirement to establish fault on the part of the defender.

1 Other remedies that may be sought include orders *ad factum praestandum* to enforce remedial action.

2 This contrasts with the position in England where the court may grant damages in lieu of injunction. The Scottish courts do not have an equivalent power.
3 As happened in *MacBean v Scottish Water* [2021] CSIH 55.
4 1948 SC 592 (IH).
5 See also *Webster v Lord Advocate* 1985 SC 173 (IH).
6 Interdict will be refused in the absence of reasonable apprehension that the activity or state of affairs objected to will continue or be repeated: *Hay's Trustees v Young* (1877) 4 R 398 (IH).

12.8 Where the loss suffered is physical harm to property,[1] interdict is most likely pointless unless the physical harm is continuing. Here then the pursuer will consider an action for damages instead. The most common claim for damages based on nuisance occurs when there has been a withdrawal of support within a tenement. Additionally, actions for damages arising from physical harm caused by flooding continue to be pursued. Of course, other fact scenarios not here mentioned arise, which justify a claim for damages.[2] It must be stressed, however, that if a pursuer wishes to claim damages, Scots law expects them to establish more than nuisance; that is, they must, in addition, show *culpa* on the part of the defender.

1 Which may include moveable property: *Ireland v Smith* (1895) 3 SLT 180 (IH).
2 See eg withdrawal of support within tenement (*Hamilton v Wahla* 1999 Rep LR 118 (Sh Ct)); flooding (*GA Estates Ltd v Caviapen Trustees Ltd* 1993 SLT 1037 (OH); *Viewpoint Housing Association v Edinburgh City Council* [2007] CSOH 114, 2007 SLT 772; *Sabet v Fife Council* [2019] CSOH 26, 2019 SLT 514); exposure of gable ends to the elements (*Powrie Castle Properties Ltd v Dundee City Council* 2001 SCLR 146 (Sheriff Principal); *Morris Amusements Ltd v Glasgow City Council* [2009] CSOH 84, 2009 SLT 697); water pollution (*Black Loch Angling Club v Tarmac Ltd* 2012 SCLR 501 (Sh Ct); *Devon Angling Association v Scottish Water* [2018] SAC Civ 7, 2018 SC (SAC) 35); fire in house (*Cunningham v Cameron* [2013] CSOH 193); fungal growth on house (*Chalmers v Diageo Scotland Ltd* [2017] CSOH 36).

(3) Nuisance, damages and culpa

12.9 In *RHM Bakeries Ltd v Strathclyde Regional Council*[1] the requirement for a pursuer seeking damages to establish *culpa* was affirmed. The pursuer must establish that the actions of their neighbour were either intentional or negligent. In such situations, negligence is established on the same basis of the standard of care; for example, taking into consideration the probability of harm, reasonable precautions, and standard practice. On this basis, a pursuer will first seek to establish that the harm amounted to *plus quam tolerabile*, ie a nuisance, and then demonstrate what the standard of care was and that it was breached.

This can be demanding for pursuers. Mindful of this, Lord Fraser in *RHM Bakers* noted that, while pursuers must 'aver the precise nature of the fault committed':[2]

> 'As a general rule it would, in my opinion, be relevant for a pursuer to make averments to the effect that his property has been damaged by a flood caused by an event on the defender's land, such as the collapse of a sewer which it was the defender's duty to maintain, that properly maintained sewers do not collapse, and that the collapse is evidence that the defender had failed in his duty to maintain the sewer. The onus will then be on the defender to explain the event in some way consistent with absence of fault on his part.'

Unfortunately, this *dictum* has been troublesome. For example, a formulation along these lines was pled unsuccessfully by the pursuers in *Argyll & Clyde Health Board v Strathclyde Regional Council*.[3] In that case, a water main in the control of the defenders had burst flooding the pursuers' premises. The pursuers pleadings were based on a failure on the part of the defender to maintain the pipe, but they had not specified the maintenance regime that ought to have been operated. Their contention then, was that the defenders had been negligent, but without specification of the standard of care they had failed to give the defenders due notice of the case against them. The action was held irrelevant and lacking in specification. Regardless of what Lord Fraser said in the House of Lords, courts were signalling that a pursuer needs to explain in detail what, in fact, they averred to be the fault of the defender. As it may already be clear, these developments have raised the question about the relationship between nuisance and general negligence.

Indeed, this uncertainty gave rise to the argument advanced by the defenders in *Kennedy v Glenbelle Ltd*,[4] that liability in damages for nuisance required proof of negligence. If the defenders could establish that, they hoped to demonstrate that the pursuer had failed to provide adequate evidence negligence and thus have the pursuer's case dismissed. In *Kennedy*, Lord President Hope confirmed that *culpa*, including negligence, was required if a pursuer sought damages based on nuisance. Lord Hope also stated that where *culpa* is established by demonstrating negligence 'the ordinary principles of negligence will provide an equivalent remedy'.[5] One way to understand this is to say that, in *Kennedy*, Lord Hope kept nuisance and the general principles of negligence conceptually separate. Therefore, His Lordship's approach to *culpa* in nuisance was to incorporate an analogous procedure for determining negligence-based fault from the general principles of negligence. In doing so, he sought to guide the determination of negligence-based-fault when it arose within the circumstances of nuisance.

Whatever the case, it is important to remember that negligence is just one manifestation of *culpa*. Lord Hope, in *Kennedy*, listed four other ways, apart from negligence, in which *culpa* could be established:[6] (1) malice, in which harm to the victim is intended; (2) intention, evidenced by a deliberate act done in the knowledge that harm will be the likely consequence; (3) recklessness, where the defender acts regardless of the likely consequences or is indifferent to them; and (4) conduct causing a special risk of abnormal damage which, Lord Hope conceded, might just be another form of recklessness. For example, in *Kennedy*, the damage caused by removing the basement wall, which, naturally, damaged the property above which belonged to the pursuer. Undertaking such activities as dismantling a supporting wall could be described as reckless or with intention as it would be obvious that such work would cause damage to the above property. Of note is that in *Kennedy*, the pursuer had also argued that the defender's *culpa* was, in fact, a deliberate act. In considering this, the court stated that proving the defender had knowledge that harm would result was sufficient to show a deliberate intention and, hence, *culpa*.[7]

1 1985 SC (HL) 17.
2 *RHM Bakeries* at 45.
3 1988 SLT 381 (OH).
4 1996 SC 95 (IH).
5 *Kennedy* at 100G–H.
6 *Kennedy* at 99C–F and 100G–H.
7 *Kennedy* at 100H.

12.10 Knowledge of likely consequences, however, is something which parties often litigate over when debating questions of *culpa*. The key question is: how far does the pursuer have to go in establishing the defender's knowledge of the likely consequences? In *Anderson v White*,[1] the Lord Ordinary (Philip) found that the defenders had actual or constructive knowledge of the damage to the pursuers' land caused by water backing up behind a dam in defenders' control, because of the complaints that had been made to them. In *Sabet v Fife Council*,[2] the common law case against the second defender, an upstream proprietor, was based on his failure to remove debris which had blocked a weir for four months before overflowing in heavy weather causing flooding to the pursuers' home. The Lord Ordinary (Ericht) held that the pursuers' averments, that the weir was prone to blockage, that it had been blocked for four months and that the defender ought to have known about the history of flooding at the weir and of the danger this posed to their property, were matters for the pursuer to establish at proof before answer.

Of course, *Sabet* did not involve a deliberate act, but a negligent omission. The pursuers contended that the defender was under a positive duty to protect them against an abnormal risk of flooding by removing debris from the weir, thus avoiding the pleading pitfall encountered in *Argyll & Clyde Health Board*.[3] The approach taken should hold good for intentional harm cases also. Knowledge which the defenders had or ought to have had must be established and if *culpa* is framed in terms of negligence there must be at least some specification of what it was the defender ought to have done that they did not, Lord Fraser's stipulation on not overburdening pursuers with precise averments of *culpa* notwithstanding. Indeed, taken together, Lord Fraser's approach to pleading (should we call this *culpa* lite?) and Lord Hope's ruling that negligence is only one form of culpable conduct with apparent acceptance that nuisance may be occasioned negligently, seem to serve the needs of litigation well.

Lord Fraser's relaxed approach was applied in *Black Loch Angling Club v Tarmac Ltd*,[4] in which Sheriff Sinclair said:

> 'Given the circumstances of such cases, the pursuer was not expected to give much notice to the defender of what was alleged to be the nature of the fault. He merely had to show that something had happened which should not have happened had the defender taken proper care.'[5]

The circumstances were that the water quality of the pursuers' loch was adversely affected by waste water which had drained from the defenders' quarry. This meant that fishing was not viable as the fish could not see the flies. The club lost revenue. The sheriff found that, in failing to inspect a leaking bund and in failing to take note of and respond to the presence of weathered rock on site, the defender's fault was more probably than not the source of contamination to the loch.

A similar approach to pleading *culpa* was taken in *McKenna v O'Hare*.[6] The foundations of the pursuers' property had been contaminated by kerosene which had seeped from the next-door garden, necessitating the demolition and rebuilding of the property. Following proof, it was not possible to determine whether the cause of the contamination had been a spill by the neighbour while moving an oil tank, which would have been negligence, or a deliberate act in emptying kerosene onto the ground, which would have been reckless at least. The point is that Lord Fraser's approach serves well where the pursuer cannot be expected to know the precise form of fault and suggests that nuisance and negligence cannot be entirely separated. This suggestion gains further strength from *Cunningham v Cameron*.[7] The case involved joint wrongdoers responsible for a house fire. The first defender, the upstairs neighbour, was at fault in having blocked the outlet to the pursuer's central heating flue by placing wood against it, a deliberate act with the obvious potential to case danger. The second defender, a gas engineer who had serviced the system, had, negligently and in breach of contract, failed to spot a fault in the installation. In apportionment, the Lord Ordinary (Tyre) did not make a decision on causative potency but held the first defender's conduct more blameworthy and so he was held to bear the greater part of liability.

1 2000 SLT 37 (OH).
2 [2019] CSOH 26, 2019 SLT 514. See also *Edwards v Fife Council* [2019] CSOH 27. These cases are reminiscent of the English case *Sedleigh-Denfield v O'Callaghan* [1940] AC 880 (HL), one of the authorities from which Lord President Cooper formulated his view on nuisance in *Watt v Jamieson*: see para 12.5 above.

3 Discussed in para 12.9 above.
4 2012 SCLR 501 (Sh Ct).
5 *McKenna* at 519.
6 [2017] SAC (Civ) 16, 2017 SC (SAC) 33.
7 [2013] CSOH 193.

12.11 Damages will be available for amenity nuisance but where the harm is restricted to disturbance or inconvenience, they may be difficult to quantify and fault must, of course, be proved. In *Shanlin v Collins*, damages were awarded in respect of illness caused by the barking of a neighbour's dogs.[1] In *Globe (Aberdeen) Ltd v North of Scotland Water Authority*,[2] the pursuers were allowed proof before answer when they sought to recover business losses consequent on road works outside the pub which continued for nine months rather than the six weeks for which they were originally scheduled. The pursuers alleged that the mess created by the operation, particularly mud on the pavements, made the pub unattractive to customers.

Where the harm takes the form of amenity nuisance, the niche occupied by this delict is clear. It is not possible to interdict harm caused negligently, because of course there is no wrong until the harm has taken place. One question that arises with physical harm to property is whether it should be necessary to satisfy the *plus quam tolerabile* requirement. It does not seem to make much sense to question how much flooding of one's home, or how much subsidence a person ought reasonably to bear. That said, physical harm is not always obviously material. In *Chalmers v Diageo Scotland Ltd*,[3] the pursuers sought damages for the growth of black fungus on the exterior of their house. This was a known effect of ethanol emitted from the defenders' bonded warehouses. Relying on *Kennedy v Glenbelle*,[4] the Lord Ordinary (Ericht) explained: 'In my view, the issue of whether something exceeds what is reasonably tolerable is by its very nature dependent on the facts and circumstances and should be decided after enquiry.'[5] In *Chalmers*, proof before answer was allowed. The *plus quam tolerabile* requirement then, is a test of materiality which must be established at proof in any action grounded on nuisance.

1 1973 SLT (Sh Ct) 21. See also *Chalmers v Dixon* (1876) 3 R 461 (IH). This is consistent with the statutory protection afforded to neighbours as well as neighbouring property and contrasts with the English position where it has been held that damages for personal injury cannot be recovered in private nuisance: *Transco Plc v Stockport MBC* [2003] UKHL 61, [2004] 2 AC 1. The position is different in public nuisance, see *Corby Group Litigation Claimants v Corby BC* [2008] EWCA Civ 463, [2009] QB 335.
2 2000 SC 392 (IH); see also *Hand v North of Scotland Water Authority* 2002 SLT 798 (OH).
3 [2017] CSOH 36.
4 *Chalmers* at para 13, citing *Kennedy v Glenbelle Ltd* 1996 SC 95 at 99B–C per Lord President Hope.
5 *Chalmers* at para 14. Further proceedings were still ongoing as of 2024: [2024] CSIH 2.

OCCUPIERS' LIABILITY

12.12 The Occupiers' Liability (Scotland) Act 1960 is a significant piece of legislation. Historically, it is important because it reversed the common law position set out in the House of Lords decision, *Dumbreck v Robert Addie & Sons.*[1]

Unlike the previous common law stance, the primary aim of the Act is to ensure that occupiers of land or property take responsibility for the safety of individuals entering their premises with respect to any dangers or risks on their property. It does not matter if the person entering is a lodger, family member, invitee, or even a trespasser. Each is owed a duty by an occupier under the Act; albeit, as we shall see, the expectations of that duty may be recalibrated depending upon whether someone was, for example, a trespasser rather than invited.

1 1929 SC (HL) 51.

(1) Defining an occupier

12.13 Determining who is an occupier is key; the statutory duty itself rests on the person 'occupying or having control of land or other premises'.[1] If the owner is not the occupier, they will not be liable under the 1960 Act but may incur liability at common law if they are in breach of a duty of care. A person occupies the land or other premises if they are in possession of the property, for example as a tenant. But a person will also be treated as the occupier if they have control of the land or other premises. A person has 'control' if they are legally entitled to take the steps in relation to the land or property which the statute requires to fulfil the duty of taking reasonable care of the premises.[2] So, for example, the owner of derelict property who is not *in fact* in possession is nevertheless the occupier because he has control of the premises. Similarly, an owner who moves out during building works, but who returns to her home each day has not relinquished control.[3] Deciding if a defender has enough possession or control to be considered an occupier depends on the specific facts and circumstances of each case.[4]

Under s 3 of the Act a landlord who is responsible for the maintenance or repair of premises remains the occupier.[5] Even if a tenant has physical control, it is the landlord who retains responsibility. Most private residential tenancies in Scotland will be regulated by the Housing (Scotland) Act 2006, which imposes a default obligation to repair and maintain the standard of the property. Usually, a landlord is prohibited by the 2006 Act from contracting out of this duty, ie passing it to their tenant. In short, private tenancies are unlikely to impose an occupier's duty on a tenant. Hence, s 3 of the 1960 Act is far more pertinent to commercial leases, where a tenant may often take on responsibility under the lease for repair and maintenance.

1 1960 Act, s 1(1). The common law rules for determining whether a person is an occupier for these purposes is expressly reserved in the Act: s 1(2).
2 *Gallagher v Kleinworth Benson (Trustees) Ltd* 2003 SCLR 384.
3 *Dawson v Page* [2012] CSOH 33, affirmed [2013] CSIH 24, 2013 SC 432.
4 *Feely v Co-operative Wholesale Society* 1990 SLT 547 (OH). On the difficulties of determining who is the relevant occupier when the property is in multi-occupation, see *Gallagher*.
5 1960 Act, s 3(1). See eg *Guy v Strathkelvin District Council* 1997 SCLR 405 (OH).

(2) Defining premises

12.14 While 'land' is self-explanatory, 'premises' are not defined in the 1960 Act. They would include houses, flats, sheds, garages, shops etc; land would include gardens. Moreover, the statutory duty to take such care as is reasonable in all the circumstances expressly applies to occupiers of 'any fixed or moveable structure, including any vessel, vehicle or aircraft'.[1] Thus the 1960 Act applies to a wide range of property: eg ships, barges, oil rigs, buses, caravans, cars, tractors, helicopters, planes and hovercraft. It is *not* therefore restricted to heritable property.

1 1960 Act, s 1(3)(a).

(3) Dangers on the premises

12.15 Section 2(1) of the 1960 Act lays down the nature and extent of the statutory duty:

> 'The care which an occupier of premises is required, by reason of his occupation or control of the premises, to show towards a person entering thereon in respect of dangers which are due to the state of the premises or to anything done or omitted to be done on them and for which the occupier is in law responsible shall … be such care as in all the circumstances of the case is reasonable to see that that person will not suffer injury or damage by reason of any such danger.'

Thus, the 1960 Act imposes a positive duty, meaning occupiers must be proactive in identifying dangers presented by their land or property.

Identifying any relevant risk or danger, therefore, is key to the approach taken by the Act. It is not enough for a defender to merely deny any knowledge of the danger or risk. To avoid liability, they must demonstrate that considering the circumstances it is not reasonable to expect knowledge of the danger or risk. In *Brown v Lakeland*, Lord Woolman considered it unreasonable to expect the defenders to anticipate the injury sustained by the defender when leaving their shop, noting that there had 'been no history of accidents among perhaps three million people who have visited the shop over the ten years of its existence.'[1] However, the lack of reported accidents itself does not automatically allow the defender to evade liability; if upon an accident occurring it becomes clear that there was a danger, and that the defender's approach was inadequate, it will be held accountable.[2] Under s 1, it is the occupiers' responsibility to be proactive and reasonable in assessing the risks and dangers on their premises.

Dangers 'due to the state of the premises' clearly cover obvious hazards such as, unstable footholds, concealed steps, or obscured obstructions on a pathway. Other dangers include things like uneven roads,[3] a sunken gulley beside a cycle path,[4] a ha-ha,[5] slippery floors and unsafe furniture or plenishings.[6] Some dangers can of course be temporary, such as exterior stairs at night which are unlight. During the day stairs can be safe yet when dark unsafe as per the Act. Note, dangers also include anything done or omitted to be done on the premises. For example, the failure to ensure that a pursuer would not enter a garden to clean windows while pugnacious West Highland terriers were also there has been held to be a breach of the 1960 Act.[7] More seriously, in *Honeybourne v Burgess*[8] it was held that hiring a bouncer who violently ejected a patron did not constitute a danger due to anything done or omitted to be done on the premises.

1 [2012] CSOH 105 at para 36.
2 See eg *Forrest v Iceland Foods Ltd* [2021] SC EDI 27; *Hodgson v Castlehill Housing Association* [2023] SC EDIN 5.
3 *Beggs v Motherwell Bridge Fabricators Ltd* 1998 SLT 1215 (OH) 4.
4 *Anderson v Scottish Ministers* [2009] CSOH 92.
5 *Cowan v Hopetoun House Preservation Trust* [2013] CSOH 9. A ha-ha is a sunken fence.
6 *Kerr v East Ayrshire Council* 2005 SLT (Sh Ct) 67 (glass pane in front door held to be a danger); *Bell v North Ayrshire Council* [2007] CSOH 144 (window that stuck held not to be a danger).
7 *Hill v Lovett* 1992 SLT 994 (OH).
8 [2005] CSOH 151, 2006 SLT 585.

(4) The occupier's duty

12.16 It is important to appreciate that the occupier's statutory obligation is only to take such care as is reasonable in all the circumstances to prevent injury or damage from such dangers: it is not to eliminate the risk that an accident might happen. In *Kirkham v Link Housing Group*, the Inner House observed that:

> '… the Occupiers' Liability (Scotland) Act 1960 does not impose a duty of insurance on the defenders. The defenders must have knowledge, actual

or deemed of any danger before they can be found liable in terms of the Act.'[1]

Hence, in determining whether the occupier has taken reasonable care, the calculus of risk is relevant.

As is familiar from Chapter 8, in determining whether the actions of the defender were reasonable the court will consider such factors as the nature of the danger, the occupier's knowledge of the danger,[2] the extent of the injury or harm, the probability of the injury or harm arising, the age of the person injured, whether the pursuer was permitted onto the premises and the cost of eliminating the danger. Thus, in *McGlone v British Railways Board*,[3] the defender was held to have taken reasonable care in respect of the danger of a 12-year-old child being burnt by a transformer. The defender had put up warnings and surrounded the transformer with a barbed wire fence which, nevertheless, had proved to be penetrable. Here, the House of Lords held that to provide an impenetrable and unclimbable fence went beyond what was reasonable in the circumstances, given that a 12-year-old child should have realised the danger he would incur if he climbed through the barbed wire. In the circumstances, the defender had discharged its duty of reasonable care by erecting an obstacle which a 12-year-old would take some trouble to overcome before he would be in danger. If the fence could have been penetrated by a three-year-old, then there might well have been a breach of the duty to take reasonable care in respect of a child of that age. The fact that the pursuer was a trespasser was also held to be a relevant factor in assessing whether reasonable care had been taken.[4]

A similar approach can be discerned in *Titchener v British Railways Board*.[5] A young man was killed by a train and his 15-year-old girlfriend was seriously injured. The couple had taken a short cut over the line to enter a derelict brickworks. The defender had provided a fence made of sleepers but there were gaps in the fence through which it was possible for persons to reach the railway line. It was argued that the Board had been in breach of its duty of reasonable care in failing to maintain the fence and thus ensure that there were no gaps providing access to the railway. The House of Lords held that the statutory duty was owed to the particular pursuer, ie a 15-year-old girl who knew the danger involved in crossing a railway line. Accordingly, in determining whether the defender had taken reasonable care, the pursuer's age and knowledge were relevant factors. In these circumstances, the fence – even with gaps – gave adequate warning to a girl of 15 who knew the danger of crossing the line. Indeed, Lord Fraser thought[6] that the defender would have taken reasonable care in respect of the pursuer if there had been no fence at all! It would therefore appear that the more obvious and greater the danger, the *less* by way of warning is required for the average person; conversely, *more* is required if the pursuer is, for example, a young child.

1 [2012] CSIH 58 at para 33 per the Lord Justice Clerk (Carloway).
2 As in *Kirkham*.
3 1966 SC (HL) 1.
4 See also *McLeod v British Railways Board* 2001 SC 534 (IH). In *Platt v Liverpool City Council* [1997] 5 WLUK 3 (CA) the court described as 'absurd' the contention that the defendant had not taken reasonable care to prevent children from entering dangerous premises, when it had put an eight-foot-high corrugated metal fence around the property.
5 1984 SC (HL) 34. See also *Devlin v Strathclyde Regional Council* 1993 SLT 699 (OH) (no breach of duty in respect of injuries to a 14-year-old child deliberately jumping on a skylight cover on a roof: the child was also a trespasser).
6 *Titchener* at 55.

12.17 It has been held that any duty on occupiers to fence off dangers does not apply to dangers inherent in the ordinary and familiar features of the landscape whether natural or man-made, for example a loch or reservoir.[1] This was recognised over a century ago:[2]

> '[I]n a town, as well as in the country, there are physical features which may be productive of injury to careless persons or to young children against which it is impossible to guard by protective measures. The situation of a town on the banks of a river is a familiar feature; and whether the stream be sluggish like the Clyde at Glasgow, or swift and variable like the Ness at Inverness, or the Tay at Perth, there is always danger to the individual who may be so unfortunate as to fall into the stream. But in none of these places has it been found necessary to fence the river to prevent children or careless persons from falling into the water.'

In *Tomlinson v Congleton Borough Council*,[3] the House of Lords reaffirmed the principle 'that it is contrary to common sense, and therefore not sound law, to expect [the occupier] to provide protection against an obvious danger on his land arising from a natural feature such as a lake or a cliff and to impose a duty on him to do so'.[4] Moreover, it was thought that it would be extremely rare for an occupier to be under a duty to prevent people taking risks inherent in the activities they chose to undertake on the occupier's land, for example swimming or mountaineering.[5] It was not the policy of the law 'to require the protection of the foolhardy or reckless few to deprive, or interfere with, the enjoyment by the remainder of society of the liberties and amenities to which they are rightly entitled'.[6] In other words, an individual should be allowed to engage in dangerous but otherwise harmless pastimes at her own risk, enabling the rest of society fully to enjoy the pleasures of the countryside and saving the occupier considerable expense.

1 *Graham v East of Scotland Water Authority* 2002 SCLR 340 (OH); *Fegan v Highland Council* [2007] CSIH 44, 2007 SC 723. However, in *Cowan v Hopetoun House Preservation Trust* [2013] CSOH 9.
2 *Stevenson v Glasgow Corporation* 1908 SC 1034 (IH) per Lord McLaren at 1039.

3 [2003] UKHL 47, [2004] 1 AC 46 (young man broke his neck when diving in a lake where swimming was prohibited).
4 *Tomlinson* at para 59 per Lord Hutton.
5 *Tomlinson* at para 45 per Lord Hoffmann.
6 *Tomlinson* at para 81 per Lord Hobhouse.

(5) Defences

12.18 The defence of *volenti non fit injuria* can be used by the defender.[1] Thus, if there had been a breach of duty in *Titchener*, the House of Lords indicated that *volenti* would have been a defence.[2] Damages may be reduced on the ground of contributory negligence.[3] The parties are free to vary the statutory duty by *agreement*.[4] This enables the occupier to undertake a more onerous or less onerous obligation. Where the premises are used for business, any exemption clause excluding or limiting the occupier's liability for death or personal injuries is void and any clause restricting liability for other kinds of damage is unenforceable unless it satisfies the requirement of reasonableness.[5]

1 1960 Act, s 2(1). See paras 9.13–9.14 above.
2 *Volenti* would also have been a defence in *Devlin v Strathclyde Regional Council* 1993 SLT 699 (OH).
3 See paras 9.15–9.17 above.
4 1960 Act, s 2(1). A non-contractual notice is therefore ineffective.
5 Unfair Contract Terms Act 1977, s 16; Consumer Rights Act 2015 s 65(1) and (4). Note the exception in s 66(4).

CHAPTER 13

Product Liability

INTRODUCTION

13.1 This chapter focuses on Part I of the Consumer Protection Act 1987, which adopts a distinct approach to product liability. We will explore how this Act safeguards consumers who suffer personal injuries from defective products or experience property damage caused by substandard consumer goods.

The common law position for product liability in the UK[1] was laid down in *Donoghue v Stevenson*.[2] It was held that a manufacturer owes a duty of care to the ultimate consumer where a product is intended to reach them in the same condition in which it left the manufacturer, with no opportunity for intermediate examination. If the product was manufactured carelessly with the result that the ultimate consumer suffered injury or harm to her property, the manufacturer is liable in negligence. However, the onus lies on the pursuer to prove that there was a breach of duty by the manufacturer, ie that the manufacturer was negligent.[3] If negligence cannot be established, the action fails. The 1987 Act takes a different approach, offering, in theory, a more consumer-friendly system for injured parties.

It must be borne in mind, however, that defective products engage several different areas of law, which interconnect. For example, when a consumer product is found to be faulty but has not caused damage to persons or other property, the loss is often purely economic, ie the value of the goods purchased. As explained in Chapter 5, such losses are generally not recoverable within the law of delict. However, importantly, for a consumer, several contractual remedies are available under the Consumer Rights Act 2015. Subject to the circumstances, such remedies include a right to reject, a right to repair or replacement or a right to price reduction.[4] Additionally, Part II of the Consumer Protection Act 1987 considers the adequacy of consumer products from the point of view of public safety in general, allowing for highly technical product specification rules, and imposing, in some situations, criminal sanctions for the circulation of unsafe goods within the UK marketplace.[5] Our focus here, however, is upon the private law aspects of Part I of the Consumer Protection Act 1987, which offers individuals remedies if their property or person is injured by a defective consumer product. It applies across the UK.

Part I of the Consumer Protection Act 1987 was a marked improvement on the common law position in the late 20th century.[6] For pursuers like Mrs Donoghue, there are many obstacles to establishing a common law case against a manufacturer. Apart from the difficulty of establishing negligence, other factors often operate to prevent the pursuer from succeeding. Where, for example, a manufacturer has provided an adequate warning that a product is potentially dangerous and this is ignored by the ultimate consumer, under the common law, there will be no liability because the pursuer's failure to heed the warning will constitute a *novus actus interveniens* which breaks the chain of causation.[7] Indeed, if it is well known that a product is dangerous, like alcohol or tobacco, if an adult of full age and capacity makes an informed decision to use it, there is no breach of the manufacturer's duty of care in merely making the product.[8] Today, however, regardless of the improvements found in the 1987 Act, the law is undoubtedly outdated and in need of reform.[9]

1 For a history and analysis of different product liability regimes in the US, EU and UK, see J Stapleton, *Product Liability* (Cambridge University Press, 1994). See also D Fairgrieve and RS Goldberg, *Product Liability* (3rd edn, OUP, 2020).
2 1932 SC (HL) 31.
3 If it is established that a product has failed because of a specified defect in the manufacturing process, it is open to a judge to hold that on the balance of probabilities this was due to the manufacturer's negligence: *Carroll v Fearon* [1998] PIQR P416 (CA).
4 Consumer Rights Act 2015.
5 Consumer Protection Act 1987, Part II.
6 For consideration of the pre-1987 position, see: The Law Commission and the Scottish Law Commission Report on the Liability for Defective Products (SLC No. 45) (1977), para 24–29.
7 *Kubach v Hollands* [1937] 3 All ER 907 (KBD). On causation generally, see Chapter 9 above.
8 *McTear v Imperial Tobacco* [2005] CSOH 69, 2005 2 SC 1. There could, of course, be a breach of duty if the alcohol or tobacco was contaminated by a different noxious substance.
9 At the time of writing the UK Parliament is considering The Product Regulation and Metrology Bill, which would grant powers to the UK Government to significantly update product safety.

STATUTORY PROTECTION

13.2 Because of difficulties found within the common law protection of consumers, a statutory regime of strict liability in respect of product liability was introduced under the Act. Provided the case falls within the statutory provisions, the defender is liable in delict to compensate the pursuer without the pursuer having to prove that the defender was negligent. The strict liability regime for defective products is to be found in Part I of the Act. The statute implements EC Directive No 85/374/EEC,[1] which represented a significant development in product safety standards across the European Union. Although the United Kingdom exited the EU on 31 December 2020, Part I of the 1987 Act now forms part of 'assimilated

EU law' which still applies in the UK legal system,[2] albeit UK courts are not bound to follow the guidance offered by the Court of Justice of the European Union on matters related to product safety.[3]

The policy behind the Act is simple, and is still relevant to UK courts: it is to place the primary responsibility for personal injury or damage to property caused by a defective product on the producer and to enable the consumer who has been injured by the defective product or whose property has been damaged by the defective product to obtain compensation from the producer without having to prove fault. From a juristic perspective, the Act reorientates the legal enquiry away from the actions of the defender to the product itself. As Hickinbottom J has explained:[4]

> '… whilst, in relation to a product, negligence focuses upon the acts and omissions of those involved in production etc, the Directive and the Act focus rather upon the condition or state of the product itself. This is fundamental to the move away from fault-based liability, heralded by the Directive'.

Before considering the legislation in more detail, it should be noted that a pursuer may raise a common law case alongside a claim based on the 1987 Act.[5] However, in most cases, the wisdom of this is questionable. While pursuers may bring an action based on a breach of the *Donoghue v Stevenson* duty of care, and there may be specific strategic reasons for doing so, the burdens placed upon them, and related costs, are considerable. In theory, the Consumer Protection Act 1987 provides a more consumer-friendly regime, yet it is also not without its limitations, some of which will be considered below.

1 In the EU, this Directive has now been repealed and replaced by Directive on Liability for Defective Products 2024/2853. But the CPA 1987 is still based on the 1985 Directive.
2 European Union (Withdrawal) Act 2018 s 2, as modified by the Retained EU Law (Revocation and Reform) Act 2023, s 5(1).
3 European Union (Withdrawal) Act 2018, s 6.
4 *Wilkes v DePuy International Limited* [2016] EWHC 3096 (QB) at para 63.
5 CPA 1987, s 2(6).

(1) Damage

13.3 The Consumer Protection Act 1987 imposes strict liability on the producer of a product 'where any damage is caused wholly or partly by a defect in a product'.[1] Damage is defined as 'death or personal injury or any loss of or damage to property (including land)'.[2] Thus, if a person is killed or injured by a defective product, or his land or other property is damaged by a defective product, the producer of the product is liable to pay compensation without proof of fault. In other words, the producer is strictly liable.

Damage to certain types of property is excluded from the statutory regime:

(a) Loss or damage to the defective product itself.[3] The cost of repair or the difference in value between a defective and a non-defective product is not recoverable under the Consumer Protection Act 1987. Nor is it recoverable in delict at common law since it is pure economic loss.[4] Where the product is a complex structure, loss or damage to the whole or part of the product caused by a defective component is also excluded. For example, if a motor car (complex product) is damaged as a result of a defective wheel (component), the damage to the car is excluded but not injury to the driver or damage to other property.

(b) Property damaged or lost as a result of a defective product where the property *damaged or lost* is not for private use.[5] Property is not for private use if it is not of a description of property ordinarily intended for private use, occupation or consumption *and* it is not intended by the person suffering the loss or damage mainly for his own private use, occupation or consumption. What this means is that before the Act applies and there is strict liability, the property damaged must be 'consumer' property, ie of a kind ordinarily intended for private use which the person suffering the loss or damage intended to be used for private use. For example, if A produces a defective vacuum cleaner, the Act will apply if the cleaner damages the carpet in B's home but not if it damages the carpet in B's office or factory. It is important to note that it is the property which is damaged which must be 'consumer' as opposed to 'business' property.[6] If A produces a defective lorry which is used in B's business, the Act *will* apply if the defective lorry damages C's family motor car but the Act will not apply if the defective lorry damages C's van which he uses for his business. When the Act is excluded because the property damaged is not 'consumer' property, resort will have to be made to delictual liability at common law when negligence will have to be established.

(c) Property damaged or lost as a result of a defective product, where the loss or damage does not exceed £275.[7] Where such loss or damage occurs, resort must again be made to delictual liability at common law when negligence will have to be established.[8] It should be noted that this exception only applies to damage to property. If, for example, A cuts his finger as a result of B's defective product, the Act still applies and B is strictly liable even if A's damages are less than £275.

1 CPA 1987, s 2(1).
2 CPA 1987, s 5(1).
3 CPA 1987, s 5(2).
4 See para 5.7 above.
5 CPA 1987, s 5(3).
6 See eg *Renfrew Golf Club v Motorcaddy Ltd* [2016] CSIH 57, 2016 SC 860.
7 CPA 1987, s 5(4). This includes interest.
8 Such an action would be brought under the small claims procedure.

(2) Definition of 'product'

13.4 Strict liability applies where damage is caused wholly or partly by a defect in a product. A 'product' is defined[1] as any goods or electricity. It includes – and this is important – components and raw materials which are parts of a complex product. So, if there is a complex product such as a motor car and a component of the car, for example a windscreen, is defective, that component, as well as the motor car, is regarded as a product for the purpose of the Consumer Protection Act 1987.

'Goods' also include 'substances, growing crops and things comprised in land by virtue of being attached to it and any ship, aircraft or vehicle'.[2] 'Substance' means any natural or artificial substance, whether in solid, liquid or gaseous form or in the form of vapour and includes substances which are comprised in or mixed with other goods, for example a cylinder of gas. Things comprised in land by virtue of being attached to it include, for example, the window frames of a house, a garden shed or a swing. 'Ship' includes any boat or vessel used for navigation; aircraft includes gliders, balloons and hovercraft; 'vehicle' is not defined. Game and agricultural produce constitute products for the purpose of the Act. Blood used for transfusions has been held to be a product for the purposes of the Act.[3]

It is still unclear whether software, such as a navigation app installed on an electronic device, qualifies as a product under the Act. The prevailing opinion suggests that it is unlikely to be considered a product.[4] However, there is an argument that if a physical product comes with pre-installed software then it may be defined as a product for the purposes of the Act.[5]

1 CPA 1987, s 1(2).
2 CPA 1987, s 45(1).
3 *A v National Blood Authority (No 1)* [2001] 3 All ER 289 (QBD).
4 That is, under other similar legislation 'goods' are generally not considered to be software: Sale of Goods Act 1979, Consumer Rights Act 2015, Commercial Agents (Council Directive) Regulations 1993. However, if pre-installed to the product there is an argument that it will fall within the ambit of the Act.
5 For consideration of this question regarding the definition of goods as per contracts of sale under the Sales of Goods Act 1979, see *St Albans City v International Computers*

Limited [1997] FSR 251 (CA). It is suggested a UK court would take a similar approach to the definition of a product under the Consumer Protection Act 1987, as it has under the 1993 Commercial Agents Regulations: *Computer Associates UK Ltd v Software Incubator Ltd* [2018] EWCA Civ 518.

(3) Parties liable

13.5 As mentioned above, *prima facie* strict liability is imposed on the producer of the product. A 'producer' is defined as the person who manufactured the product[1] or who won or abstracted the substance.[2] Where a product is not manufactured, won or abstracted but its essential characteristics are attributable to an industrial or other process, the producer is the person who carried out the process: for example, where the product is pasteurised milk, the producer is the person who carried out the pasteurisation process.[3] A person who merely packages goods is not a producer. Any person who puts her own name on a product, or uses a trade mark on a product, is liable under the Consumer Protection Act 1987 if by so doing he holds himself out to be the producer.[4] This provision brings 'own branders' within the strict liability regime. Similarly, any person who imports products from abroad with a view to distributing them within the UK is liable under the Act.[5] This clearly is to protect ultimate consumers from having to sue a producer outwith the UK. The importer may, of course, have a remedy, for example in contract, against the producer. The producer of a component or of raw materials used in a complex product is *prima facie* jointly and severally liable with the producer of the complex product if it is defective. Although strict liability falls on the producer, own brander or importer of a defective product, as a fall-back position the supplier of the product may also be liable. Thus, all parties in the distribution chain from the producer to the own brander or importer are potentially liable under the Act:

Producer ——— Wholesaler ——— Retailer ——— Purchaser

In this example, the wholesaler and retailer are suppliers within the meaning of the Act. However, a supplier will be liable only if the person who suffered the damage asked the supplier within a reasonable time of the damage being sustained to identify the producer or a supplier further up the chain of distribution and the supplier failed to provide the information within a reasonable time, provided it was not reasonably practicable for the person suffering the damage to identify the producer. In order to escape potential strict liability under the Act, a supplier must therefore keep records of his suppliers or producers.[6]

A supplier will not be strictly liable if the defective goods were not supplied in the course of business.[7] Accordingly, A will not be strictly liable if A sells his washing machine to his neighbour B in a private transaction or if A gives B the washing machine as a birthday present: but A will remain liable for breach of contract or in delict at common law if the washing machine is defective and injures B or damages B's property. Where we are dealing with a producer, own brander or importer, they will escape strict liability under the Act only if the goods were supplied otherwise than with a view to profit.[8] If, for example, A makes lemon curd which is *donated* to the local church sale of work, A is not liable, although he is a producer, because the goods were not supplied with a view to A's profit. But if A *sells* the lemon curd to the sale of work, A will remain liable under the Act. In both cases, the church will not be liable under the Act, since the only potential liability is as a supplier and the lemon curd was not sold in the course of a business. The church could, of course, be liable at common law.[9]

There remains considerable uncertainty regarding the legal status of online retailers that operate through non-traditional sales structures. For instance, it is unclear whether online retailers that engage in marketing of products, facilitate transactions, or participate in distribution within the supply chain fall within the scope of s 2 of the Act. Moreover, ambiguity persists as to whether intermediaries – those who enable third parties to market and distribute products via online platforms – should be classified as importers, branders, or retailers. These platforms often argue that they fall outside the ambit of s 1, as they typically do not hold or inspect the physical goods prior to distribution by third parties. Additionally, platforms that merely provide a marketplace without facilitating payment contend that their role does not constitute activity in the course of business. There is no reported case law addressing these specific issues. Until new legislation is enacted, it appears that courts will need to interpret and apply the existing legal framework to resolve such questions.

1 CPA 1987, s 2(2)(a).
2 CPA 1987, s 2(2)(b).
3 CPA 1987, s 2(2)(c).
4 CPA 1987, s 2(2)(b).
5 CPA 1987, s 2(2)(c) as amended by Sch 3 of the Product Safety and Metrology etc (Amendment etc) (EU Exit) Regulations 2019 (SI 2019/696).
6 CPA 1987, s 2(3). If the producer has the power to determine when the supplier should put the product on to the market, the supplier may be treated as the producer for the purposes of the CPA 1987: *O'Byrne v Aventis Pasteur MSD Ltd* [2010] UKSC 23, [2010] 1 WLR 1412.
7 CPA 1987, s 4(1)(c)(i). Where a product was supplied and used for a specific medical service which was financed entirely from public funds, the ECJ held that it was nevertheless supplied for an economic or business purpose and the producer remained strictly liable: *Veedfald v Arhus Amtskommune* [2003] 1 CMLR 41.

8 CPA 1987, s 4(1)(c)(ii).
9 If A supplies a 'free gift' when selling another product, A will be strictly liable under the Act if the gift is given away in the course of A's business.

(4) Meaning of 'defective product'

13.6 To attract strict liability, the damage must be caused 'wholly or partly' by a *defect* in the product.[1] What then is a defective product? A product is defective 'if the safety of the product is not such as persons generally are entitled to expect'.[2] For these purposes, 'safety shall include safety in the context of risks of damage to property as well as in the context of risks of death or personal injury'.[3] It will be noted that the test is what *consumers generally are* entitled to expect in terms of the safety of the product. The test is objective; if the product falls below the expectations of *consumers generally*, then it is defective.[4] This is in marked contrast to the concept of negligence at common law which is tested by the standards of the hypothetical reasonable person in the position of the manufacturer.[5] This reflects the focus of the CPA on the product itself, rather than on the conduct of the manufacturer (which is the concern of common law negligence).

Section 3 specifically gives guidance to the court as to how reasonable expectations are to be determined. It reads:

> '(2) In determining for the purposes of subsection (1) above what persons generally are entitled to expect in relation to a product all the circumstances shall be taken into account, including—
>
> (a) the manner in which, and purposes for which, the product has been marketed, its get-up, the use of any mark in relation to the product and any instructions for, or warnings with respect to, doing or refraining from doing anything with or in relation to the product;
>
> (b) what might reasonably be expected to be done with or in relation to the product; and
>
> (c) the time when the product was supplied by its producer to another;
>
> and nothing in this section shall require a defect to be inferred from the fact alone that the safety of a product which is supplied after that time is greater than the safety of the product in question.'

While each of these factors is considered by a court when assessing the reasonable expectations of a consumer, it is notable that the section 3 says 'all the circumstances shall be taken into account' which indicates that the above list is non-exhaustive. Thus, in *Hastings v Finsbury Orthopaedics Ltd*[6] it was stated that a product recall notice issued by the manufacturer in response to safety concerns did *not* immediately indicate that the product was defective. Context, therefore, is important in determining the defectiveness of a product.

Determining what a consumer is entitled to expect differs depending on the function and purpose of the product. For example, in *Abouzaid v Mothercare (UK) Ltd*,[7] the claimant was seeking to assist with fastening an elasticated strap to a pushchair, the plaintiff lost the sight in one of his eyes when the strap recoiled. Pill LJ concluded:

> 'The risk is in losing control of an elastic strap at a time when it is stretched and eyes are in the line of recoil. The product was defective because it was supplied with a design which permitted the risk to arise and without giving a warning that the user should not so position himself that the risk arose. Members of the public were entitled to expect better from the appellants. A factor in that expectation is the vulnerability of the eye and the serious consequences which may follow from a blunt injury to the eye. Expectations would be different if the worst which could occur was an impact of elastic on the hand. It is not necessary for the Court to determine precisely what more should have been done. It is clear that more could have been done, for example a non-elasticated method of attachment or instructions to fasten the straps from behind the seat unit, together with a warning.'

In *A v National Blood Authority (No 1)*,[8] the producer knew that some of their blood products might be infected but at the time there were no practical precautions that could be taken – no test could be used to identify the infected blood. It was argued by the defendants that a reasonable consumer would have understood that the blood product they received could not be fully tested for contamination. Further, it was contended that blood was the type of product which could not guarantee complete safety, therefore the ultimate consumer's reasonable expectation should be adjusted accordingly. The court rejected these arguments. It was held that the blood product was defective because a consumer was, in this instance, entitled to expect that blood transfused to them would be free from infection. Here, Burton J made a key distinction. The legitimate expectation to be assessed did not relate to whether sufficient blood tests could be carried out ahead of transfusion. Rather, what the court examined was the safety of the product itself. In this case, the reasonable expectation of the public was that the blood product would be safe, which in the court's opinion, was an appropriate expectation rendering the product in this instance defective.

On the other hand, the reasonable expectation of a consumer may sometimes include an acceptance of potential risks, which are otherwise, outweighed by the benefits of the product.[9] Where the risk is obvious, for example that coffee served in a polystyrene cup will be hot to hold, the product is not defective.[10] In the medical context, however, risks may not always be evident to the average consumer. However, given that the test applied is objective rather than subjective, the judicial interpretation of s 3 often infers that reasonable expectations include an understanding that where some products carry inherent risks as well as potential functional benefits, courts have concluded that risk of injury is not necessarily indicative of the product's defectiveness.[11] In *Wilkes*, the High Court found that medical products:

> 'will almost always involve design compromises, the effect of eliminating or reducing a particular risk can only be seen in the context of any adverse consequence of doing so, in the form of increased risks of a different sort or reduced benefit and utility.'[12]

In *Hastings v Finsbury Orthopaedics Ltd*, the pursuer's failed prosthesis was held not to be defective as the pursuer could not demonstrate on the balance of probabilities that the risk posed by the product in question was greater than that of available alternatives. *Hastings* raises questions, however, about the appropriate burdens now placed on a pursuer under the Act. In complex cases involving medical products, it is arguably unreasonably onerous for the pursuer to prove that alternative products available within the market carry no less risk than the defender's product. To demonstrate this, the pursuer required to present considerable technical and scientific material. In cases such as this, one might suppose that manufacturers will typically have greater expertise and access to information. Should they not therefore carry the burden to showing their product was not defective? Here is an example of whether UK law will now significantly depart from EU when it comes to product liability. Under the new Product Liability Directive, if excessive burdens of proof are placed upon a claimant, courts should consider a reversal of that burden if the claimant can demonstrate that the product was likely to be defective.[13]

1 CPA 1987, s 2(1). The onus rests on the pursuer to prove that the product was defective: *Foster v Biosil* (2001) 59 BMLR 178; *McGlinchey v General Motors UK Ltd* [2012] CSIH 91.
2 CPA 1987, s 3(1).
3 CPA 1987, s 3(1).
4 See *Wilkes v DuPuy International Ltd* [2016] EWHC 3096 (QB), [2018] QB 627.
5 For discussion of breach, see Chapter 8 above.
6 [2022] UKSC 19, 2022 SC (UKSC) 43.
7 [2000] 12 WLUK 627 (CA) at para 27.
8 [2001] 3 All ER 289 (QBD).
9 *Richardson v LRC Products* [2000] PIQR P164 (QBD) (condom failed but public knew that no form of contraception is 100 per cent effective and the manufacturer never claimed that the product was).
10 *B (A Child) v McDonald's Restaurants Ltd* [2002] EWHC 490 (QB).
11 *Wilkes; Gee v DePuy International Ltd* [2018] EWHC 1208 (QB) and *Hastings*.
12 *Wilkes* at 647.
13 Directive on Liability for Defective Products 2024/2853, Article 48.

13.7 Before there is liability under the Act, the pursuer has to show that the damage was '*caused* wholly or partly by a defect in a product'.[1] Therefore, as in the case of delictual liability at common law, the claim may fail unless there is a sufficient causative link between the damage and the defective product.[2] However, provided there are no causation problems, the pursuer who has suffered damage is entitled to compensation from the producer, own brander, importer or supplier without having to establish negligence. In other words, there is strict liability.

1 CPA 1987, s 2(1) (emphasis added); *Foster v Biosil* (2001) 59 BMLR 178; *McGlinchey v General Motors UK Ltd* [2012] CSIH 91.

2 Although CPA 1987 applies when a defective product causes psychiatric illness, it will probably not apply to secondary victims since their illnesses are caused by their reactions to the injuries of primary victims rather than by the defective product which injured the primary victim concerned. So, for example, persons who suffer mental harm by witnessing a plane crash caused by a defect in the plane's engines cannot recover damages under the CPA 1987 from the manufacturer of the plane. On delictual liability for mental harm, see Chapter 4 above.

(5) Defences to claim of strict liability

13.8 The Consumer Protection Act 1987 provides the defender with the following defences to a claim based on *strict* liability:

(a) The defect in the product is attributable to the defender's compliance with statutory or any retained EU obligations.[1]

(b) The defender did not at any time supply the product to another, for example the product was stolen.[2]

(c) The defect did not exist in the product at the relevant times.[3] In the case of a producer, own brander or importer this will be the time the product was supplied to another; in the case of a supplier, when the product was last supplied by a producer, an own brander or an importer into the UK. So, in the case of the producer etc, he will escape strict liability if the product was not defective when it entered circulation, but subsequently becomes defective.[4] There can, of course, still be delictual liability at common law. The supplier will escape strict liability if the product was not defective when it was last supplied by a producer etc even though the defect was subsequently caused by the supplier himself. For example, if a butcher keeps meat which was edible when he obtained it from the producer but sells it when it has gone off, the retailer will not be liable. This is, to say the least, an odd result but, of course, the retailer will be liable in contract to the purchaser and at common law in delict to the ultimate consumer when negligence will readily be inferred.

(d) The state of scientific and technical knowledge at the relevant time[5] was not such that a producer of products of the same description as the product in question, might have been expected to have discovered the defect if it had existed in his products while they were under his control.[6] This is known as the 'state of the art' defence. It is controversial in that a producer can escape *strict* liability if the defect in his product would not have been known by manufacturers of a similar product, given the state of scientific and technical knowledge at the time. It is important to stress that the defence is not what the producer actually knew but what he would have known if he had consulted those who might be expected to know the state of research and all the available literature etc.[7] It has been held that the defence is not available if the producer knows that his product might have harmful consequences.[8]

This defence is similar to the common law principle that a defender cannot be liable in delict if, as a result of the scientific knowledge available to the hypothetical reasonable person at the time, injury to the pursuer was not a reasonable and probable consequence of the defender's conduct.[9] Moreover, the defence expressly refers to the awareness of producers of similar products. This is similar to the important role that the practice of persons in the same trade, business or profession of the defender plays in establishing a breach of a duty of care at common law.[10] It can therefore be argued that the 'state of the art' defence re-introduces negligence into the regime of strict liability laid down in the Consumer Protection Act 1987.

In many cases, the defence will not be available to the producer simply because, given the state of scientific and technical knowledge at the time, he[11] should have known the product was defective. Where the defence could be used is in the production of drugs whose side effects could not have been discovered given the state of scientific knowledge which existed at the time they were produced; it may take years before the side effects of certain drugs become apparent in patients. In these circumstances, the defence could be used by the defender. It is somewhat ironic that one of the reasons for the move towards a strict liability regime for defective products was to avoid the shortcomings of the law of negligence which became apparent in the thalidomide tragedy. The European Court of Justice has held that the scope of the Consumer Protection Act 1987, s 4(1)(e) is not in conflict with EU law.[12]

(e) If the defective product is a complex product, the producer of a component or of any raw materials contained in the complex product has a defence if the defect in the complex product is wholly attributable to the design of the complex product or to the fact that he complied with the instructions of the producer of the complex product;[13] otherwise both the producer of the complex product and the producer of the component or raw materials are jointly and severally liable.

(f) Contributory negligence.[14]

Liability under the Consumer Protection Act 1987 cannot be excluded by an exemption clause.[15]

1 CPA 1987, s 4(1)(a).
2 CPA 1987, s 4(1)(b). *Veedfald v Arhus Amtskommune* [2003] 1 CMLR 41 (kidney flushing fluid used to prepare a kidney for transplantation had been 'supplied' in terms of the directive).
3 CPA 1987, s 4(1)(d). See eg *Piper v JRI Manufacturing Ltd* [2006] EWCA Civ 1344, (2006) 92 BMLR 141.
4 *Richardson v LRC Products Ltd* [2000] PIQR P164 (CA) (condom became damaged by ozone after it left the factory).
5 See discussion immediately above.
6 Consumer Protection Act 1987, s 4(1)(e).
7 *Richardson v LRC Products* [2000] PIQR P164 (CA). In *Abouzaid v Mothercare (UK) Ltd* [2000] 12 WLUK 627 (CA) the Court of Appeal doubted whether accident reports constituted 'technical knowledge'.
8 *A v National Blood Authority* [2001] 3 All ER 289 (QBD). This case provides a very full discussion of when a product is defective and the nature of the 'state of the art' defence: see in particular pp 334–342.
9 *Roe v Minister of Health* [1954] 2 QB 66 (CA).
10 See para 8.10 above.
11 Or, technically, producers of similar products.
12 *Commission of the European Communities v United Kingdom* (C300/95) [1997] All ER (EC) 481, ECJ.
13 Consumer Protection Act 1987, s 4(1)(f).
14 CPA 1987, s 6(4).
15 CPA 1987, s 7.

CONCLUSION

13.9 This discussion of product liability is significant as it highlights the inadequacy of the common law of delictual liability – based on the defender's *culpa* – in safeguarding the interests of consumers harmed by defective products. In response, a statutory regime of strict liability was introduced to relieve the ultimate consumer of the burden of proving fault in order to obtain compensation. However, the Consumer Protection Act 1987 is not exhaustive, providing considerable scope for defenders to defeat the supposed strict liability of the Act. Furthermore, the Act is now considerably outdated, failing to address the complexities of modern commerce, including online platform sales, software-related defects, and the evidentiary challenges faced by contemporary claimants in proving that goods were defective at the time of supply.[1]

1 For criticism of the 1987 Act from a different perspective, see D Nolan, *Questions of Liability: Essays on the Law of Tort* (Hart Publishing, 2023), Ch 14 ('Against Strict Product Liability').

CHAPTER 14

Defamation and Malicious Publication

INTRODUCTION

14.1 The law has long recognised a person's interest in his or her reputation. But the law also has recognised, for as long a time, the freedom of others to express thoughts and opinions. The law of defamation seeks to strike a balance between these two interests. In recent history, it has become acknowledged that even the mere threat of a defamation action may have a 'chilling effect' on free speech.

Historically, defamation was only one of a suite of principles of delictual liability which protected the reputation of the pursuer. A range of different 'verbal injuries' existed which could be called into aid where a pursuer perceived a slight on his honour or reputation. These separate wrongs retained a close link with Roman law, whereas the delict of defamation grew ever closer to English law. The Defamation and Malicious Publication (Scotland) Act 2021 abolished many of these separate verbal injuries, retaining only three concerned with the pursuer's business interests. At the same time, influenced by the perceived need to avert the 'chilling effect' of defamation litigation, the 2021 Act further aligned Scots law with English law on several points. But the 'chilling effect' appears to still exist, and future reforms are foreseeable.[1]

1 There has been much recent concern around so-called 'strategic litigation against public participation', or 'SLAPPs'. While defamation is not the only delict which may be used to stifle public participation, it is perhaps the paradigmatic example. At the time of writing, the Scottish Government is consulting on introducing an anti-SLAPP law.

DEFAMATION

(1) Elements of a claim

14.2 Where a pursuer wishes to raise a claim in defamation in relation to a particular statement, the following matters must be considered:

(1) What meaning would the reasonable audience member ascribe to the statement?

(2) Is that meaning defamatory of the pursuer?

(3) Has the making of that statement caused serious harm to the pursuer's reputation?

(4) Would the reasonable audience member take the statement to refer to the pursuer?

(5) Has the statement been published to a third party?

This section will also discuss the parties who can be sued, and who may sue, in defamation. Later sections will discuss defences and remedies.

Determining meaning

14.3 While a defamatory statement may take any form,[1] defamation most commonly arises in respect of the written or spoken word. Words may bear several different and distinct meanings, and the potential for varying interpretations multiplies when words are combined into a sentence. Moreover, the meaning of a statement may be considerably influenced by the context in which it is made. When presented with an allegedly defamatory statement, the court's first task is to work out the 'single meaning' which the statement objectively bears.

The court approaches this task from the perspective of the reasonable audience member (ie reader, viewer, or listener),[2] which may vary according to the medium or platform over which the statement was communicated.[3] The reasonable audience member is not 'naïve', 'overly analytical' or 'avid for scandal'.[4] They will consider a statement in its context: a defamatory sting created by a headline in a newspaper may be cured by the text of the accompanying article, and a reasonable reader will consider the whole publication before drawing their conclusions.[5] Statements made in the heat of an argument may be less likely to be taken seriously by a reasonable bystander,[6] and a reasonable person will not lightly consider the use of abusive language to have been intended to convey a factual allegation seriously.[7]

Scottish courts take a strict approach to the pleading of meaning: if the court finds that the statement cannot bear the meaning contended for by the pursuer, then its claim will be dismissed: the court will not substitute an alternative defamatory meaning not pleaded for by the pursuer.[8]

1 2021 Act, s 36(b): '"statement" means words, pictures, visual images, gestures or any other method of signifying meaning'. See eg *Monson v Tussauds Ltd* [1894] 1 QB 671 in which the placing of a waxwork of a man found 'not proven' in respect of a murder charge alongside others of those found guilty was held to constitute defamation.

2 See eg *Ashton Properties (Glasgow) Ltd v Unite the Union* [2024] SC GLA 37, 2025 SLT (Sh Ct) 1 at paras 39–42; *Gillespie v Wardrop* [2025] CSOH 46 at para 96.

3 See eg *Ashton Properties* (a 'tweet' on X); *Stocker v Stocker* [2019] UKSC 17, [2020] AC 593 (Facebook post).

4 *Macleod v Newsquest (Sunday Herald) Ltd* 2007 SCLR 555 (OH) at para 14, citing *Gillick v BBC* [1996] EMLR 267.

5 *Charlesworth v Mirror Group Newspapers* [1995] 2 AC 65 (HL).

6 Such statements are sometimes said to be made '*in rixa*'. See eg *Christie v Robertson* (1899) 1 F 1155 (OH).
7 On 'vulgar abuse', see eg *Vine v Barton* [2024] EWHC 1268 (KB) at paras 17–20.
8 See eg *James v Baird* 1916 SC (HL) 158.

14.4 A statement or action may appear to be harmless, yet when taken in the context of the facts and circumstances in which it was made, a defamatory meaning may be inferred. In this situation, Scots law allows a pursuer to plead the facts and circumstances from which the defamatory meaning of the statement or act can be drawn. This is known as 'the doctrine of innuendo'. For example, a statement that a Member of Parliament did not collect his parliamentary mail is, on the face of it, innocuous. However, when combined with the additional knowledge that the parliamentary post was (at least at the time) a key means of receiving concerns from constituents, the statement can be taken to give rise to an innuendo that the MP does not properly deal with the concerns of his constituents.[1] A post in a newspaper announcing the imminent birth of a child to a couple, when combined with the additional knowledge that the couple had married only the previous month, creates an innuendo that the child was conceived out of wedlock, which previously (but no longer) would be defamatory.[2]

The onus rests on the pursuer to state the meaning of the statement in the light of the relevant facts and circumstances. Any pleaded innuendo must be a 'reasonable, natural, or necessary inference from the words used, regard being had to the occasion and circumstances of their publication'.[3] Those circumstances may include facts which are general knowledge, or specific facts that the pursuer asserts are known to the statement's audience (which must be specifically averred).[4] The court's task first is to ascertain whether, on the basis of those facts, the statement reasonably can bear the innuendo meaning contended for by the pursuer. If so, the question becomes whether that innuendo meaning is the meaning which a reasonable person, with knowledge of the relevant facts, would derive from the statement.[5]

1 *Fairbairn v SNP* 1979 SC 393 (OH). For an example involving the use of an 'innocent face' emoticon, see *McAlpine v Bercow* [2013] EWHC 1342 (QB).
2 *Morrison v Ritchie & Co* (1902) 4 F 645 (IH).
3 *Russell v Stubbs* 1913 SC (HL) 14 at 24 per Lord Shaw of Dunfermline.
4 *Langlands v Leng* 1916 SC (HL) 102 at 105 per Viscount Haldane.
5 On these two questions, see eg *Russell v Stubbs* at 20 per Lord Kinnear (although, prior to the abolition of the presumption in favour of jury trials in defamation actions by s 20 of the 2021 Act, the second question was conceived as one for the jury).

Is that meaning defamatory? The consensus test

14.5 Not all statements which cause offence or insult are defamatory. The 2021 Act states that a 'statement about a person is defamatory if it causes harm to the person's reputation (that is, if it tends to lower the person's reputation in the estimation of ordinary persons).'[1] This is an objective question: it asks whether the statement attributes to the subject some quality, trait, or behaviour that the reasonable person would find objectionable in light of the shared values and standards of society.[2] This sometimes is known as the 'consensus test', reflecting the fact that the statement must have the effect of lowering the pursuer in the estimation of society generally. If the statement only would make a section of society think less of the pursuer, with a neutral (or positive) effect on the perception of the pursuer by everyone else, then it is not defamatory.[3] It is irrelevant for this test that a specific identified person thinks less of the pursuer as a result of the statement; or that a particular 'unreasonable' view can be demonstrated to be held in fact by a majority of members of society.[4]

1 2021 Act, s 1(4)(a). This effectively codifies the common law test adopted from *Sim v Stretch* [1936] 2 All ER 1237 (HL) at 1240 per Lord Atkin, albeit substituting 'ordinary persons' for 'right-thinking members of society'.
2 See *Cuthbert v Linklater* 1935 SLT 94 (IH) at 97 per the Lord Justice-Clerk (Aitchison), and, in more modern terms, *Hayden v Associated Newspapers* [2020] EWHC 540 (QB) at para 39.
3 See eg *Byrne v Deane* [1937] 1 KB 818 (CA) (although some would think less of a person for 'informing' on others to the police about the commission of an offence, the reasonable person would see such an act as virtuous and therefore such an allegation is not defamatory; cf *Winn v Quillan* (1900) 2 F 322 (IH)).
4 See eg *BrewDog v Frank Public Relations* [2020] EWHC 1276 (QB) (claiming that a business was a supporter of President Donald Trump was not defamatory, as a reasonable society is tolerant and should not think less of anyone else because of divergent political beliefs).

14.6 The clearest expression of common societal standards is the criminal law. It therefore is defamatory to accuse a person of committing a serious crime which ordinary people do not commit or condone, such as murder,[1] theft,[2] domestic abuse,[3] or being a paedophile.[4] It equally is defamatory to suggest that there are grounds to suspect that the pursuer has committed an offence, or that they should be investigated in relation to an offence.[5]

1 *Monson v Tussauds* [1894] 1 QB 94 (CA); *Waddell v British Broadcasting Corpn* 1973 SLT 246 (IH); *Berezovsky v Forbes Inc (No 2)* [2001] EMLR 45 (CA). See also *Mueen-Uddin v Secretary of State for the Home Department* [2024] UKSC 21 (crimes against humanity).
2 *Sutherland v British Telecommunications plc* 1989 SLT 531 (OH); *Yavuz v Tesco Stores* [2019] EWHC 1971 (QB).
3 *Wray v Associated Newspapers* 2000 SLT 869 (OH).
4 *Blake v Fox* [2024] EWHC 146 (KB).
5 *Chase v News Group Newspapers* [2003] EMLR 11 (CA).

14.7 Short of allegations of criminality, it has been held defamatory to undermine a person's moral character. For example, it is defamatory to accuse a person of condoning or celebrating an assault on another person.[1] So too may it be defamatory to accuse a person of being a 'homewrecker' and breaking up a family unit.[2] To state that a woman whose child had died was a heartless and uncaring mother is defamatory.[3] But the standards of morality are not fixed: for instance, at one time it was defamatory to state that a person was homosexual.[4] Nowadays, an allegation of homosexuality by itself would no longer be regarded as defamatory.[5] As a corollary, accusing someone of homophobic behaviour,[6] or using racist language,[7] would now be defamatory, even if such terms were unfortunately deemed acceptable in the past.

It is defamatory to call a person a hypocrite.[8] It may not be defamatory merely to call a person a liar or a 'stranger to the truth',[9] but it remains defamatory to allege specific acts of dishonesty,[10] perjury,[11] or to claim that someone is a pathological liar.[12]

1 *Riley v Murray* [2020] EWHC 977 (QB).
2 *Contostavlos v News Group Newspapers* [2014] EWHC 1339 (QB).
3 *McCabe v News Group Newspapers Ltd* 1992 SLT 707 (OH).
4 *AB v XY* 1917 SC 15 (IH).
5 *Cowan v Bennett* 2012 GWD 37-738 (Sh Ct). But, for instance, accusing a nun of being homosexual may be defamatory, because it alleges that she acts inconsistently with her vows: *Prophit v BBC* 1997 SLT 745 (OH).
6 *Campbell v Dugdale* [2020] CSIH 27, 2020 SC 481. However, to say that someone is 'homophobic' may give rise to considerations of honest opinion: see para 14.21 below.
7 *McAnulty v McCulloch* [2018] CSOH 121, 2019 SLT 449.
8 *Swinson v SNP* [2019] CSOH 98.
9 *Carroll v BBC* 1997 SLT (Sh Ct) 23; and see earlier *Watson v Duncan* (1890) 17 R 404 (IH).
10 *Packham v Wightman* [2023] EWHC 1256 (KB).
11 See eg the substantial award finally upheld in *Sheridan v Mirror Group Newspapers* [2018] CSIH 76, 2019 SC 203.
12 See the Australian case of *Wilson v Bauer Media* [2017] VSC 521.

14.8 Statements which disparage a person's professional competence or conduct are defamatory, for example, to accuse a doctor of gross professional negligence,[1] or a professor of their inability to teach,[2] or a dog-walker of mistreating animals in their care.[3] Allegations of conduct which is unprofessional in the circumstances are also defamatory: for example, to allege that an athlete refused to play a curling match for Scotland at an international competition,[4] to accuse a solicitor of conducting a case for his own – as opposed to his client's – interests,[5] or to say that a prison warden had sexual relations with a prisoner.[6] It is also defamatory to allege that a business's affairs are mixed up with organised crime.[7] It has also been held defamatory to write that an actor and director was 'notoriously ugly', but this conclusion can be doubted.[8]

It has been held defamatory falsely to allege that a person is insolvent[9] or is unwilling[10] or unable[11] to pay their debts. It therefore may be defamatory to claim that a person is using an unauthorised overdraft[12] or to provide a negative credit report in relation to a debtor.[13]

1 *Simmers v Morton* (1900) 8 SLT 285 (OH).
2 *Auld v Shairp* (1875) 2 R 940 (IH).
3 *Hiram v Mullen* 2020 SLT (Sh Ct) 135.
4 *Munro v Brown* [2011] CSOH 117.

5 *M'Rostie v Ironside* (1849) 12 D 74 (IH).
6 *Winter v News Scotland Ltd* 1991 SLT 828 (OH).
7 *Easdale v Henry* [2024] CSOH 17, 2024 SLT 545 (OH).
8 *Berkoff v Burchill* [1997] EMLR 139 (CA). As the dissenting judgment of Millett LJ contends, a director's appearance is irrelevant to their ability as a director. Moreover, a distinctive appearance may contribute to an actor's success. In any event, the case may employ a looser test what constitutes defamation than now must be used under s 1(4)(a) of the 2021 Act.
9 *AB v CD* (1904) 7 F 72 (IH).
10 *Outram v Reid* (1852) 14 D 577 (IH).
11 *Mazure v Stubbs Ltd* 1919 SC (HL) 112.
12 *Gatt v Barclays Bank* [2013] EWHC 2 (QB).
13 *Boyo v Lloyds Bank* [2019] EWHC 2279 (QB). However, in both this case and *Gatt*, the bank succeeded in a defence of truth and qualified privilege.

14.9 Establishing the defamatory nature of a statement has two important consequences:

(a) A defamatory statement is presumed to be false. This means that the pursuer need not establish the falsity of the statement: instead, the burden is on the defender to establish – if possible – the veracity of the statement through the defence of truth.[1]

(b) A defamatory statement is assumed to have been made with the intention to injure. This means that it is irrelevant that the defender did not intend to defame the pursuer.[2] The assumption of malice only is removed where the situation in which the communication was made attracts qualified privilege, which is discussed below.

1 *Mackellar v Duke of Sutherland* (1859) 21 D 222 (IH).
2 *Hulton v Jones* [1910] AC 20 (HL), accepted in Scotland in eg *Wragg v D C Thomson & Co Ltd* 1909 2 SLT 315 (OH). Averments of specific intention or malice will therefore not be relevant: *Stein v Beaverbrook Newspapers Ltd* 1968 SC 272 (IH).

The serious harm test

14.10 Prior to the 2021 Act, once the consensus test had been satisfied by the pursuer, damage to their reputation was implied from the defamatory meaning of the words.[1] The 2021 Act, influenced by English law,[2] has now introduced a 'serious harm' test. In addition to showing that the statement objectively conveyed a defamatory meaning, a pursuer must now also show that the 'publication of the statement caused (or is likely to cause) serious harm' to their reputation.[3]

The Explanatory Notes to the 2021 Act anticipate[4] that Scottish courts will find persuasive the approach of the UK Supreme Court, in respect of the English provision, in *Lachaux v Independent Print Ltd*.[5] Lord Sumption made it clear in this case that the serious harm test requires proof of 'the impact which the statement is shown actually to have had'. This must go beyond the meaning carried by the words themselves, and depends on 'a combination of the inherent tendency of the words and their actual impact on those to whom they were communicated.'[6] There are therefore two routes by which a pursuer can prove serious harm. First, if they can aver evidence about the actual real-life response of others to the statement, which evidences a substantially negative reception, then that may establish serious harm. For example, evidence that the pursuer's employer had requested a meeting with them to explain the defamatory allegation is actual proof that the statement has had a detrimental effect on the employer's perception of the pursuer.[7]

But courts recognise that it may be difficult for pursuers to bring forth real-life evidence of the effect of an allegedly defamatory statement, and therefore will be willing, in appropriate cases, to infer serious harm from the circumstances surrounding the making of the statement.[8] Here, the courts have been willing to take into account the 'meaning of the words', the 'situation of [the pursuer]', the 'circumstances of publication', and the 'inherent probabilities' in relation to the response to a statement of that nature.[9] The smaller the audience of a statement, the less likely a court will be willing to infer serious harm.[10] To take two contrasting examples: the court was unwilling to infer serious harm when a woman was accused of shoplifting by a supermarket security guard.[11] While theft was a serious accusation, the statement would only have been capable of being heard by a few other shoppers, who may have been too busy with their own shopping to pay any attention to the altercation. On the contrary, an inference of serious harm could be made when a defendant with 250,000 Twitter follows tweeted an allegation that the claimants were paedophiles.[12] The severity of the allegation, combined with the extent of publication and the fact that the claimants worked with children, allowed the inference to be made that the statement would have caused serious harm to their reputation.

The serious harm test requires a causative link to be established by the pursuer between the serious harm allegedly caused to its reputation and the particular statement made by the defender. This may make the test difficult to satisfy where the pursuer has a controversial or notorious persona, where it may be difficult to isolate that the harm complained of was caused by the defender's statement in particular.[13]

Where the pursuer is a non-natural person, the primary purpose of which is trading for profit, it must establish that the statement's publication has, or would, cause it 'serious financial loss'.[14]

1 *Bradley v Menley & James* 1913 SC 923 (IH) at 926 per the Lord Justice-Clerk (Macdonald).
2 Defamation Act 2013, s 1(1). On the judicial interpretation of the English test, which will guide the Scottish test, see S Bogle and B Lindsay, 'Serious Harm: Six Lessons Since *Lachaux*' (2024) 16(2) *Journal of Media Law* 417.

3 2021 Act, s 1(2)(b).
4 Explanatory Notes to the Defamation and Malicious Publication (Scotland) Act 2021 (asp 10) at para 11. See *Gillespie v Wardrop* [2025] CSOH 46 at paras 101–102.
5 [2019] UKSC 27, [2020] AC 612.
6 *Lachaux* at para 14.
7 *Davies v Carter* [2021] EWHC 3021 (QB). See also *Smith v Surridge* [2025] EWHC 74 (KB) (withdrawal of job offer evidence of serious harm).
8 See eg *Sivananthan v Vasikaran* [2022] EWHC 2938 (KB) and *Parsons v Garnett* [2022] EWHC 3017 (KB).
9 *Lachaux* at para 21.
10 See eg *Sivananthan*; *Amersi v Leslie* [2023] EWHC 1368 (KB).
11 *Yavuz v Tesco Stores Ltd* [2019] EWHC 1971 (QB).
12 *Blake v Fox* [2024] EWHC 146 (KB). But it is not a 'numbers game', and serious harm had been inferred from the publication of less serious allegations to a few hundred 'friends' on Facebook: *Miller v Peake* [2025] EWHC 453 (KB).
13 See *Miller v Turner* [2023] EWHC 2799 (KB), the counterclaim in *Blake v Fox*, and compare with *Bridgen v Hancock* [2025] EWHC 926 (KB).
14 2021 Act, s 1(3). It is not clear how this hurdle would have been cleared by the pursuer in the litigation in *Ashton Properties (Glasgow) Ltd v Unite the Union* [2024] SC GLA 37, 2025 SLT (Sh Ct) 1.

Identification

14.11 Often, it will be obvious that the statement refers to the pursuer. But even where the pursuer is not specifically named in the statement, they will be able to sue in defamation if they can establish that the words used are 'such as would reasonably lead persons acquainted' with them to believe that he or she 'was the person referred to'.[1] This may arise where the pursuer is not specifically named but referred to in vague terms,[2] or where the pursuer is the member of a small group which was the subject of the defamatory statement.[3]

1 *Knuppfer v London Express Newspaper* [1944] AC 116 (HL) at 119 per Viscount Simon LC.
2 See eg *Youssoupoff v MGM* (1934) 50 TLR 581 (CA) (character in movie would be taken to be a factual depiction of the plaintiff). In another context, the court will not be too legalistic in insisting upon distinctions being drawn between different companies in a corporate group: *Dyson Technology Ltd v Channel 4 Television Corp* [2023] EWCA Civ 884, [2023] 4 WLR 67.
3 See eg *Browne v DC Thomson Co Ltd* 1912 SC 359 (IH) (the 'Roman Catholic religious authorities in Queenstown', which consisted of a bishop and six clergymen).

Publication to a third party

14.12 Finally, under the 2021 Act, the offending statement must have been published to a third party before a claim in defamation may be brought.[1] This replaces the common law position, where a claim could be sustained if the statement had been communicated to the pursuer alone.[2] Publication under the Act means communication to another person by any means which they can access and understand, and takes place when it has been seen or heard by the recipient.[3]

1 2021 Act, s 1(2)(a).
2 See eg *Ramsay v MacLay & Co* (1890) 18 R 130 (IH) (poison pen letter sent to pursuer). Such 'two party' defamation claims were rare.
3 2021 Act, s 1(4)(b)–(c), read with s 36(a).

Parties to defamation

14.13 There are some limitations on who can pursue an action in defamation which briefly should be noted. There is no public interest in permitting a public authority to sue for defamation,[1] and this is reflected in the 2021 Act.[2] The definition of a public authority includes central and local government institutions, a court or tribunal, and 'person or office … whose functions include functions of a public nature'.[3] However, private sector organisations are not to be considered to be a public authority simply because they carry out 'functions of a public nature from time to time'.[4] A trade union likely can sue in defamation.[5] The death of the would-be pursuer raises difficult issues in Scotland.[6]

1 *Derbyshire County Council v Times Newspapers* [1993] AC 534 (HL).
2 2021 Act, s 2(1). 'Public authority' is defined in s 2 (2) of the 2021 Act.
3 2021 Act, 2(2). The Scottish Ministers may add to, or subtract from, this definition by regulations: s 2(6).
4 2021 Act, s 2(3).
5 See *Prospect v Evans* [2024] EWHC 1533 (KB), [2025] KB 127.
6 See E Reid, *The Law of Delict in Scotland* (2022), paras 18.64–18.67.

14.14 At common law, any person who repeats a defamatory allegation could themselves be liable for defamation.[1] This so-called 'repetition rule' must now be considered subject to s 3 of the 2021 Act. This provides that an action in defamation can only be brought against a person who is the author, editor, or publisher of the statement (or is an employee of such a person and was 'responsible for the statement's content or the decision to publish it').[2] The 'author' is the originator of the statement. An editor is a person bearing responsibility for content or the decision to publish, for example on a website or in a newspaper. Publishers are commercial operations in the business of issuing material to the public.[3] There are exceptions to the definition of an 'editor' in the case of online publications. Merely repeating the statement, or providing a link to its text, or expressing 'interest in, approval of, or disapproval of' the statement does not trigger liability.[4] However, if one of those actions materially increases the harm caused by publication of the statement, then the user may be considered an 'editor' of the statement who can be held liable in defamation.[5]

1 *Winn v Quillan* (1900) 2 F 322 (IH)
2 2021 Act, s 3(1).
3 'Author', 'editor' and 'publisher' are all defined in s 3(2) of the 2021 Act. Further categories may be added by the Scottish Ministers under regulations: s 4.

4 2021 Act, s 3(3)(a). The aim here is to avoid fixing parties for liability merely by eg retweeting or 'liking' a 'tweet' on X, or where a search engine displays a link to defamatory content published by another party. The courts are empowered to extend this provision by analogy, to provide similar protection in respect of new developments on social media and other online platforms: s 3(5).

5 2021 Act, s 3(3)(b). An X user with 200 followers who retweets a defamatory statement may therefore not be an 'editor', but a user with 500,000 followers who retweets the same statement may be considered as such.

(2) Defences

14.15 As we have seen, a pursuer who establishes the requirements for defamation generously receives the benefit of the presumption that the statement is false, and the assumption that the statement was made with the intention to injure.[1] Defenders, therefore, are in an unenviable position. The defences which exist to a claim in defamation are an important counterbalance to the generosity shown to pursuers and are fundamental in ensuring that appropriate protection is given to defenders' freedom of expression. No picture of the law of defamation is complete without giving some consideration to these defences.

Some defences have been placed on a statutory basis by the 2021 Act,[2] while some remain a matter for the common law.

1 See para 14.9 above.

2 2021 Act, s 8(1). However, cases on the common law variants of these defences remain relevant, to the extent they are compatible with the statutory versions. Case law on the equivalent provisions of the 2013 Act likely also will be persuasive: see *Gillespie v Wardrop* [2025] CSOH 46.

Truth

14.16 If the defender can rebut the presumption of falsity, by supplying evidence which establishes the truth of the imputation which the court has found the statement to convey, then that is a complete defence.[1] There therefore is a close relationship between the determination of meaning, and this defence: to succeed, the defender's evidence must substantially meet the meaning of the statement which the court has found the statement to bear.[2]

The statutory defence requires proof that the imputation conveyed by the statement is 'true or is substantially true': in other words, the 'sting' of the statement must be shown to be true.[3] If A accuses B of having murdered C on Sunday, A's defence of truth will not fail if it transpires that B in fact killed C on Monday. The exact date of B's crime does not detract from the 'sting' of the statement; B is no less a murderer for having committed the crime on the Monday instead of the Sunday.

If more than one imputation is conveyed, the defence will succeed only if all the facts which are defamatory are proved true.[4] But where the defender is able to establish the substantial truth of one or more imputations yet cannot establish the truth of other allegations which do not seriously harm the pursuer's reputation, then the defence of truth may still succeed.[5]

A defender who insists on the truth of allegations unrealistically throughout the trial may be met with an increased award of damages to reflect the additional distress thereby caused to the pursuer.[6]

1 2021 Act, s 5(1). The equivalent provision in the 2013 Act is s 2.
2 This may be quite a subtle exercise: *Riley v Murray* [2022] EWCA Civ 1146 at paras 28–37.
3 *Sarwar v News Group Newspapers* 1999 SLT 327 (OH).
4 *Fairbairn v Scottish National Party* 1979 SC 393 (OH).
5 2021 Act, s 5(2).
6 *Baigent v BBC* 2001 SC 281 (IH). Similarly, a court will not look kindly on a pursuer which takes outrageous steps to try and defeat a defence of truth: see *Vardy v Rooney* [2022] EWHC 2017 (QB).

Absolute privilege

14.17 Absolute privilege attaches to certain circumstances in or occasions on which a statement is made. Where a statement is protected by absolute privilege, it cannot form the basis of an action for defamation in any respect. As this is a complete defence, wholly ousting a pursuer's ability to bring an action in defamation, absolute privilege only arises in rare situations which are constitutionally mandated.

Statements made in the Westminster Parliament[1] and the Scottish Parliament[2] attract absolute privilege. This does not extend to statements made outside the formal settings of Parliament.[3] Reports of parliamentary proceedings are also absolutely privileged.[4]

Statements made in judicial proceedings by judges,[5] pleaders,[6] and witnesses[7] are absolutely privileged, although that privilege may not apply where the statements made are wholly and completely unconnected with the subject matter of the proceedings. Parties to litigation may, however, only have qualified privilege.[8] Contemporaneous and accurate reports of such proceedings also are absolutely privileged.[9] The Lord Advocate and those conducting prosecutions on her behalf also enjoys absolute privilege.[10]

1 Bill of Rights 1689, Article IX.
2 Scotland Act 1998, s 4(1)(a). For analysis of the more limited nature of absolute privilege in Holyrood (which, unlike at Westminster, does not apparently cover evidence given to committees by witnesses), see A Tickell, 'The Fragile Parliamentary Privilege of Devolved Legislatures: Feature or Bug?' [2022] *Public Law* 376.
3 *Buchanan v Jennings* [2004] UKPC 36, [2005] 1 AC 115 (New Zealand).

4 Parliamentary Papers Act 1840; Scotland Act 1998, s 41(2).
5 See eg *Watt v Thomson* (1870) 8 M (HL) 77. This also extends to other quasi-judicial bodies: *Thomson v Ross* 2001 SLT 807 (Scottish Solicitors Discipline Tribunal).
6 See eg *Rome v Watson* (1898) 25 R 733 (IH).
7 See eg *Watson v McEwan* (1905) 7 F (HL) 109; *B v Burns* 1993 SC 232 (IH).
8 *Williamson v Umphray and Robertson* (1890) 17 R 905 (IH). It would seem fair, however, to hold that, when a party acts in the capacity of a witness or a pleader, they enjoy absolute privilege to the same extent as would a non-party fulfilling those roles.
9 2021 Act, s 9.
10 *M'Murchy v Campbell* (1887) 14 R 725 (IH).

Qualified privilege

14.18 When a statement is protected by qualified privilege, an action of defamation will only succeed where privilege is lost, ie where the pursuer succeeds in establishing malice. If the defender establishes that their statement attracts qualified privilege, then the assumption that it was made with the intention to injure the pursuer falls away. To succeed, the pursuer must re-supply, through proof, that malice.[1]

The broadest category of qualified privilege is that which arises where the defender makes the statement pursuant to a moral, social, or legal duty. This privilege will arise where defender directs the statement to a recipient with a reciprocal interest in hearing that information: for instance, to the pursuer's superior, or to a regulatory body. So, for instance, complaints to the chief constable about the conduct of police officers attracts protection if an action of defamation is brought against the complainer by the officer who was the subject of the complaint.[2] Similarly, a letter to the deputy chief executive of the prison service about the unfitness of an employee to serve as an officer has been held to attract qualified privilege.[3] A party who responds to a request for information – for example, to provide a reference in relation to a former employee – usually will enjoy qualified privilege.[4] A complaint made by a councillor about a fellow councillor at a council meeting will attract qualified privilege.[5] But if communication is made to a party other than that deemed to have an interest in receiving the publication, qualified privilege will not arise.[6]

Another form of qualified privilege, sometimes discussed as a separate defence of 'fair retort', arises where the pursuer has verbally attacked the defender, and the defender has an interest in replying to undermine the validity of that attack. So, for example, where a prominent socialist politician was labelled a 'liar and a perjurer' by a former party comrade, and his response was to call her a 'scab', it was held that this was a 'fair retort' as it undermined the validity of the aspersions cast by the pursuer on his character.[7] However, where the defender oversteps the mark, and makes separate and distinct defamatory allegations regarding the pursuer, there will be no qualified privilege.[8]

There also exist some statutory provisions which confer qualified privilege in specific situations. For example, statements made in peer-reviewed scientific or academic journals attract qualified privilege.[9] Schedule 1 to the 2021 Act also contains a list of different types of statements which attract qualified privilege, if the publication of that statement is in the public interest.[10] These fall into two categories of privileged statements: those which can only be defeated by proving malice,[11] and those which also can be defeated by showing that the defender, having been requested by the pursuer to publish a reasonable explanatory or contradictory statement, refused or neglected to do so.[12]

1 *Massie v McCaig* [2013] CSIH 14, 2013 SC 343 at para 27.
2 *Fraser v Mirza* 1993 SC (HL) 27.
3 *Quilty v Windsor* 1999 SLT 346 (OH) See too *Pearson v Educational Institute of Scotland* 1997 SC 245, (OH) (report on the competency of the pursuer to be head of a college, sent by union to government department, attracted qualified privilege); *Lyons v Chief Constable of Strathclyde Police* [2013] CSIH 46 (qualified privilege attached to letters written by police to local authority licensing board that pursuer, who was seeking second hand dealer licence, was involved in organised crime).
4 *Farquhar v Neish* (1890) 17 R 716 (IH). However, even if not made maliciously, the writer of the reference may be liable in negligence: *Spring v Guardian Assurance plc* [1995] 2 AC 296 (HL).
5 *Horrocks v Lowe* [1975] AC 135 (HL).
6 *Watt v Longsdon* [1930] 1 KB 130 (CA) (disclosure to plaintiff's wife did not attract privilege).
7 *Curran v Scottish Daily Record* [2011] CSIH 86, 2012 SLT 359. The defence was not abolished by the 2021 Act: *Gillespie v Wardrop* [2025] CSOH 46 at para 131.
8 *Milne v Walker* (1893) 21 R 155 (IH) at 157. In this case, the pursuer had claimed that the defender's coffee was an inferior product. The defender's response, that the pursuer 'had no regard for the truth and was a liar', was protected by fair retort privilege.
9 2021 Act, s 10.
10 2021 Act, s 11(6).
11 2021 Act, s 11(2); see Sch 1, Part 1 for the list of statements falling into this category.
12 2021 Act, s 11(3) and (4); see Sch 1, Part 2 for the list of such statements.

14.19 Once the defender establishes that the statement was protected by qualified privilege, the pursuer must prove malice to succeed. Malice can be established if it can be shown that the defender abused the privileged occasion, or that there was intent to injure the pursuer.[1] But proof of malice is difficult. It may be inferred from extreme language,[2] a previous personal vendetta between the parties or the fact that the defender had no basis for any honest belief in the truth of the statement.[3]

1 See especially *Fraser v Mirza* 1993 SC (HL) 27.
2 See eg *Continental Tyre Group Ltd v Robertson* 2011 WL 1130227.
3 *Horrocks v Lowe* [1975] AC 135 (HL); *Kinley v Devine* [2014] CSOH 67.

Publication on a matter of public interest

14.20 The defence of qualified privilege was developed to give rise to a separate defence conferring protection on statements which were the product of responsible journalism.[1] This has since been statutorily re-orientated in s 6 of the 2021 Act as a defence which applies where the defender had a reasonable belief that publication of the statement was in the public interest.[2] The defence is not limited to journalists: it potentially may apply to anyone who publishes a statement which touches on a matter which is in the public interest. If the defender reasonably believes publication is in the public interest, that may furnish a defence if the publication contains factual inaccuracies that defame the pursuer.

The analysis under this defence has three stages. The first asks whether the 'statement complained of was, or formed part of, a statement on a matter of public interest'.[3] This considers the subject matter of the statement and asks whether, objectively, this would be in the public interest. The courts have taken a broad-brush approach to what is in the public interest.[4] If the court is so satisfied, the next question is whether the defender honestly believed that publication of that statement was in the public interest. This is a subjective question. If the defender cannot establish this, then the defence will fail.[5] Finally, there is the objective question of whether it was reasonable for the defender to believe that publication of the statement was in the public interest. In assessing this, the court must have regard to 'all the circumstances of the case',[6] giving appropriate leeway to editorial judgement.[7] This will usually be the most involved question when the defender seeks to invoke the defence.

The UK Supreme Court has suggested that a reasonable belief is 'one arrived at after conducting such enquiries and checks as it is reasonable to expect of the particular [defender] in all the circumstances of the case.'[8] As has been observed:[9]

> 'Attempts to confirm the truth of the specific imputation conveyed by the statement in issue are an important factor in the court's assessment. In this regard, records of research or the process undertaken by a defendant when drafting a publication may be significant. A court may require more in the way of research and investigation if allegations of dishonesty or criminal wrongdoing, as opposed to less serious allegations, have been made.'

The question whether or not the defender invited the pursuer to comment on the statement will be relevant to the question of reasonableness, but failure to seek comment does not necessarily make the defender's belief unreasonable.[10] Continued publication of a statement which is contrary to the published findings of an official investigation may render the defender's belief unreasonable.[11] If it can be established that the defender did not believe in the truth of what was published, then their belief that publishing it would be in the public interest is very likely to be unreasonable: '[n]o public interest is served by publishing or communicating misinformation'.[12]

1 The defence often was known as 'the *Reynolds* defence', after *Reynolds v Times Newspapers* [2001] 2 AC 127 (HL). The separate nature of the defence was confirmed in *Jameel v Wall Street Journal Europe* [2006] UKHL 44, [2007] 1 AC 359.
2 The defence is stated in substantially similar terms to s 4 of the Defamation Act 2013.
3 2021 Act, s 6(1)(a). 'Statement' includes a statement of opinion as well as fact: s 6(5).
4 See eg *Riley v Murray* [2023] EWCA Civ 1146 at para 71.
5 2021 Act, s 6(1)(b). The subjective element of the test is not expressly spelled out in this provision.
6 2021 Act, s 6(2).
7 2021 Act, s 6(4).
8 *Serafin v Malkiewicz* [2020] UKSC 23, [2020] 1 WLR 2455 at [72].
9 *Packham v Wightman* [2023] EWHC 1256 (KB) at para 31 per Saini J.
10 *Serafin* at para 76. See eg *Gillespie v Wardrop* [2025] CSOH 46 at paras 107–115.
11 *Banks v Cadwalladr* [2022] EWHC 1417 (QB), [2022] 1 WLR 5236; this aspect of the case was not disturbed when another part of the decision was reversed in [2023] EWCA Civ 219, [2023] KB 524.
12 *Reynolds* at 238 per Lord Hobhouse.

Honest opinion

14.21 Another defence of vital practical importance, and for holding the defender's freedom to express opinions, is that of honest opinion. This, contained in s 7 of the 2021 Act, replaces the old defence of 'fair comment'. This protects opinions which are honest deductions from a set of identified facts. There is now no need to demonstrate that the subject matter of the comment was in the public interest.

The first step in investigating the applicability of the defence is to distinguish matters of fact from matters of opinion; only the latter is protected by this defence.[1] This can be a very difficult task: the perspective adopted is that of a reasonable reader.[2] If the reasonable reader would recognise the statement as a value judgment, or a deduction from a set of facts, then that statement likely will be one of opinion. So, for example, a statement by a scientist that a chiropractic association promoted 'bogus treatment' was an opinion, as it was a value judgment that the state of scientific evidence did not support the promotion of such treatment.[3] Similarly, stating that the pursuer has said or done something which is homophobic[4] or racist[5] may well, in the circumstances, amount to opinion: they are expressions of views deduced from the pursuer's actions.

Next, for the defence to be engaged, the statement must identify the basis from which that opinion has been derived.[6] There must be an indication, either generally or specifically, of the evidence base from which the defender has formed that opinion. This may be drawn from facts, asserted facts in a privileged statement, or anything which the defender reasonably believed to be a fact at the time of publication.[7] For example, mention of statements made by the pursuer,[8] or published literature which contradict the pursuer's version of events,[9] will meet this criterion. But if the opinion is based on facts which turn out to be false, and the defender did not reasonably believe those facts to be true, the defence will not succeed.[10]

Thirdly, there is the objective question of whether an honest person could hold the stated opinion based on any part of the identified evidential basis.[11] If the opinion is a far-fetched or unrealistic deduction, then this requirement will not be met. But the 'honest commentator does not have to be logical' or 'evidence-based',[12] and the defence will protect opinions held by the 'prejudiced or obstinate' so long as the view could be honestly held.[13] Even a 'wounding and unbalanced' opinion may be protected.[14]

Finally, there is a subjective disqualification. Even if a reasonable person could hold the stated opinion on the basis of the identified evidence, the pursuer may still defeat the defence by showing that the defender did not 'genuinely hold' that opinion.[15]

1 2021 Act, s 7(2).
2 *Blake v Fox* [2023] EWCA Civ 1000 at para 23. See *Gillespie v Wardrop* [2025] CSOH 46 at paras 119–128.
3 *British Chiropractic Association v Singh* [2010] EWCA 350, [2011] 1 WLR 133.
4 *Campbell v Dugdale* [2020] CSIH 27, 2020 SC 481.
5 *Blake v Fox*.
6 2021 Act, s 7(3).
7 2021 Act, s 7(8). This is broader than s 3(4) of the 2013 Act, which does not permit the opinion to be based on something reasonably believed to be a fact.
8 As in *Campbell v Dugdale* (where there was reference to 'homophobic tweets' without needing to set out their exact content).
9 As in *Singh*.
10 See eg *Riley v Murray* [2022] EWCA Civ 1146. It is submitted that the decision in Scotland would be the same, as the defendant's belief in the truth of the fact (that the claimant had categorically tweeted that a political leader deserved to be attacked) was not reasonable.
11 2021 Act, s 7(4).
12 *Dyson v MGN Ltd* [2023] EWHC 3092 (KB) at para 137 per Jay J.
13 *Telnikoff v Matusevitch* [1992] 2 AC 343 (HL) at 354 per Lord Keith of Kinkell.
14 For instance, in *Dyson* the comment that the claimant had 'screwed the country' by, first, supporting a 'Leave' vote in the Brexit referendum, and then by moving the head office of his companies to Singapore, was held to be an honest opinion.
15 2021 Act, s 7(5).

(3) Remedies

Offer of amends

14.22 Much potentially expensive litigation has been avoided by the printing of a correction and apology. Under the 2021 Act, before lodging defences, the defender may make in writing an (unqualified) offer to correct the statement or a (qualified) offer to correct a specific defamatory meaning, to provide a sufficient apology, to pay compensation and expenses, or any other step (eg the making of a charitable donation).[1] The offer may be accepted or rejected by the pursuer. Acceptance of the offer by the pursuer ends further proceedings and, in the case of a qualified offer, ends proceedings so far as the defamatory meaning covered in the offer is concerned. The terms of the offer may be enforced.[2]

Where an unqualified offer is rejected, and the defender did not know, or have reason to believe, that the statement (a) referred to the pursuer and (b) was false and defamatory of them, then the rejection of its offer of amends provides a defence to any action brought by the pursuer.[3] The defender benefits from a presumption that it lacks such knowledge or reason to believe. This, in effect, provides a defence to innocent defamation: if the defender makes an offer of amends, and the pursuer rejects this but cannot establish that the defender knew or had reason to believe that the statement was false and defamatory of it, then the claim will fail.

1 2021 Act, s 13.
2 2021 Act, s 14. This section also makes provision for determination where parties cannot reach agreement on the form and substance of the correction and apology, on compensation to be paid or on expenses. See ss 14(4)–14(7).
3 2021 Act, s 16. Equivalent provisions in respect of the rejection of qualified offers are found in 2021 Act, s 17. Offers of amends where multiple persons are responsible for a defamatory statement are covered in s 15.

Statement in open court

14.23 The unsuccessful defender may be ordered to publish a summary of the judgment.[1] Where parties have reached an agreement in settlement of proceedings, whether or not this follows an offer of amends, the Act provides for a statement to be made in open court.[2] Furthermore, the court may order the display of a notice, for example on a website, to notify the fact that a statement is subject to proceedings or to remove a statement.[3] The court may also prevent, under s 30(2), persons who were not authors, editors or publishers from any further sale or distribution of material containing the statement complained of.[4]

1 2021 Act, s 28.
2 2021 Act, s 29.
3 2021 Act, s 30(1).
4 2021 Act, s 30(2).

Damages

14.24 In an action for defamation the individual pursuer is entitled to an award of solatium in respect of damage to reputation and distress and anxiety. Any patrimonial loss must be averred and proved. Although patrimonial loss, if it has been sustained, is relatively easy to assess, solatium is more difficult because it involves no little degree of speculation. In practice, solatium is usually a modest sum in Scots law.[1] Everyone is assumed to be of good character, so solatium is unlikely to be increased if the pursuer is particularly good. But the more eminent the pursuer, the greater the loss of reputation and more will consequently be awarded as solatium. In general, the worse the allegation, the greater the sum that will be awarded; in particular, the sum may be increased if the defender has persisted in the defamatory allegations against the pursuer.[2] However, at the end of the day, solatium is intended to compensate non-patrimonial loss:[3] a person who brings an action primarily to clear her name will receive only a nominal sum.[4]

A number of factors may serve to mitigate awards of solatium. First, if the pursuer's character or reputation is already tainted before the defamatory statement, evidence can be led by the defender to show that the pursuer did not therefore suffer as much as an ordinary person.[5] An immediate retraction of the statement and an apology will mitigate the loss.[6] This will also be the case if the pursuer provoked the defender into making the defamatory statement.[7] Where an offer of amends has been made, this may also mitigate damages.[8]

The pursuer may also seek an interdict preventing (re-)publication of the defamatory statement, if the ordinary requirements of seeking an interdict are met.[9]

It should be noted that actions in defamation now are subject to a one-year limitation period.[10]

1 See eg *Gilbert v Yorston* 1997 SLT 879 (OH) (no evidence that any third party believed the defamatory material: no effect on pursuer's career. Pursuer was awarded £1,500 as solatium).
2 *Baigent v British Broadcasting Corporation* 2001 SC 281 (IH) (awards of £60,000 and £50,000 were made against the BBC: the attack on the pursuers' personal integrity and professional ability was very vindictive); *Munro v Brown* [2011] CSOH 117: *Kinley v Devine* [2014] CSOH 67.
3 *Stein v Beaverbrook Newspapers Ltd* 1968 SC 272 (IH).
4 *Gilbert v Yorston*, as above.
5 *Corrigan v Monaghan* 1923 SC 1 (IH).
6 *Morrison v Ritchie & Co* (1902) 4 F 645 (IH).
7 *Paul v Jackson* (1884) 11 R 460 (IH).
8 2021 Act, s 16(6) and s 17(5).
9 See eg *Swinson v Scottish National Party* [2019] CSOH 98; *Easdale v Hendry* [2024] CSOH 17, 2024 SLT 545.
10 Prescription and Limitation Act 1973, s 18A (as amended).

MALICIOUS PUBLICATION

14.25 The 2021 Act also attempted to modernise the rules concerning the so-called 'verbal injuries'. It abolished most of these forms of wrongdoing, but retained and restated three distinct principles of 'malicious publication': (1) a false and malicious statement about the pursuer's business or business activities;[1] (2) a false and malicious statement about the pursuer's title to land or other property;[2] and (3) a false and malicious statement criticising or denigrating the quality, use or treatment of assets owned, possessed or controlled by the pursuer.[3] These correspond broadly to the old verbal injuries of falsehood causing business loss, slander of title and slander of property, all of which were abolished by s 27 of the 2021 Act (along with the problematic category of exposing the pursuer to public hatred, contempt and ridicule which has no new statutory equivalent).

In all forms of malicious publication, the statement must be communicated to a third party, and it must have caused (or be likely to cause) financial harm to the pursuer. While at common law, proof of sales opportunities lost presented a major hurdle to the recovery of damages,[4] a more generous approach is taken in the Act which stipulates that financial loss does not need to be shown if the statement is more likely than not to cause financial loss.[5]

There is still a considerable hurdle to surmount in terms of proving that the statement was malicious. It must be established in all three forms that:

> 'the false imputation conveyed by the statement complained of was presented as a statement of fact (rather than a statement of opinion) and was sufficiently credible so as to mislead a reasonable person … and that [the defender] knew that the imputation was false or was recklessly indifferent as to the truth of the imputation …'[6]

In addition, the pursuer must establish the defender's motivation for publication and this differs according to the form taken. Liability for statements causing harm to business interests requires that the defender's publication was 'motivated by a malicious intention to cause harm to [the pursuer's] business or business activities'.[7] Liability for statements causing doubt as to title to property requires that the defender's publication was 'motivated by a malicious intention to delay or jeopardise a transaction involving the [pursuer's] land or other property'.[8] Finally, liability for statements criticising assets requires that the defender's publication was 'motivated by a malicious intention to cause [the pursuer] financial loss'.[9]

1 2021 Act, s 21.
2 2021 Act, s 22.
3 2021 Act, s 23.
4 See eg *Philp v Morton* (1816) Hume 865; *McIrvine v McIrvine* [2012] CSOH 23.
5 2021 Act, s 24.
6 2021 Act, ss 21(2)(a) and (b)(i), 22(2)(a) and (b)(i) and 23(2)(a) and (b)(i), corresponding to the three forms of malicious publication, are identical.
7 2021 Act, s 21(2)(b)(ii).
8 2021 Act, s 22(2)(b)(ii).
9 2021 Act, s 23(2)(b)(ii).

CHAPTER 15

Vicarious Liability

INTRODUCTION

15.1 To this point, this book has discussed situations of personal liability: where the defender is liable to the pursuer for any loss caused by the defender's own wrongdoing. Vicarious liability – a general principle applying across the law of delict – is different.[1] It involves treating a defender ('D1') as liable for another defender's ('D2') wrong, regardless of whether D1 has itself committed any wrongdoing. If the criteria for the imposition of vicarious liability are met, then it matters not that D1 acted with the utmost care, or is entirely innocent of any blameworthy conduct.

For vicarious liability to apply, first, D2's conduct towards the pursuer must constitute a delict. This presents no unique difficulty: vicarious liability may arise for any form of wrongdoing discussed elsewhere in this book, be it intentional or unintentional.[2] Thereafter, two stages to the vicarious liability enquiry arise:

(1) Stage One: the relationship between D1 and D2 must be one of employment or be akin to employment.

(2) Stage Two: D2's conduct must be so closely connected to acts which it was authorised to do that it can fairly and properly be regarded as done by D2 while acting in the course of its employment or quasi-employment.

Stage One focuses on the relationship between D2 and D1: the paradigm case is that of employment, but other relationships which are 'akin to employment' may also suffice. Stage Two involves consideration of the relationship between D2's wrongful conduct and its relationship with D1: the D1 will only be liable for wrongful conduct which has a 'close connection' to its relationship with D2.

1 For more detailed discussion, see M Campbell and B Lindsay, 'Vicarious Liability in Scotland' in P Giliker (ed), *Vicarious Liability in the Common Law World* (Hart Publishing, 2022), Chapter 9; M Campbell and B Lindsay, 'Refining Vicarious Liability' (2024) 28(2) *Edinburgh Law Review* 174; E Reid, *The Law of Delict in Scotland* (2022), Chapter 3.

2 Where delictual liability is created by statute, it is theoretically possible that the statute may expressly or impliedly exclude the operation of vicarious liability. For a failed argument to this effect, see *Majrowski v Guy's and St Thomas's NHS Trust* [2006] UKHL 34, [2007] 1 AC 224 (Protection from Harassment Act 1997).

15.2 Where it is established that D2's delict has injured the pursuer, and D1 is vicariously liable for that delict, D1 and D2 are 'jointly and severally' liable. This means that the pursuer has the option of who to sue: D1, D2, or both. In practice, given that D1 often will be an employer or other organisation with resources and insurance coverage,[1] they alone will be pursued. As the liability is joint and several, there is no need for the pursuer to also bring a claim against D2. The pursuer can recover in full from D1, who can then, at least in theory, recover any compensation which has been paid out from D2.[2]

The pursuer may be a third party wholly unconnected to the relationship between D1 and D2. But sometimes the pursuer will be a fellow employee of the wrongdoer. Here, it is important to distinguish between D1's personal liability and vicarious liability.

(a) **Personal liability**: D2's conduct has resulted in a breach by D1 of the non-delegable duty it owes to its employees to ensure a safe system of working and provide competent fellow workers. Here, the focus is on what D1 has failed to do: in other words, it is an argument that D1 personally is liable for the pursuer's injuries.[3]

(b) **Vicarious liability**: D2's delictual conduct has injured the pursuer. If the pursuer can establish an employment-type relationship between D2 and D1, and that D2's conduct was closely connected with that relationship, then D1 will be vicariously liable for that conduct. The focus here is on D2's conduct and its connection to the employment-type relationship; there is no investigation into what D1 ought to have done differently.

Often, an employee injured by a fellow employee will frame their claim against the employer on both bases; the key difference to bear in mind is that vicarious liability does not depend on showing any fault on the part of the employer.

1 An employer is obliged to have insurance cover for injuries suffered by employees in the course of their employment: Employers' Liability (Compulsory Insurance) Act 1969. No civil liability lies for breach of the 1969 Act: see *Campbell v Gordon* [2016] UKSC 38, 2017 SC (UKSC) 13.

2 Law Reform (Miscellaneous Provisions) (Scotland) Act 1940, s 3(2). 'In theory' because (i) in practice, employer's liability insurers do not exercise their rights of contribution against an employee except in cases of wilful misconduct; and (ii) the employee's resources may mean they are not worth suing.

3 See generally Chapter 10 above. For a case failing to keep the two distinct, see *Nelson v John Lewis Plc* [2024] SC EDIN 10. Previous editions of this book discussed vicarious liability in the same chapter as employer's liability; given the importance of distinguishing the two forms of liability, and the extension of vicarious liability beyond the strict employment situation, this edition now treats them in separate chapters.

15.3 The practical aspects of vicarious liability are easy to state. The same cannot be said for its theoretical basis. In 1952, Lord President Cooper opined that no basis in theory for the law existed:[1]

> 'A mixture of ideas has inspired many unconvincing judicial efforts to find a scientific basis for the maxim, and I note that some of these have been dismissed in a recent work as "rhythmical inanities".[2] What was once presented as a legal principle has degenerated into a rule of expediency, imperfectly defined, and changing its shape before our eyes under the impact of changing social and political conditions.'

Nevertheless, a judicial menu of possible justifications for the imposition of vicarious liability has been provided, listing the following five factors as influential:[3]

> '(i) the employer is more likely to have the means to compensate the victim than the employee [including insurance];
>
> (ii) the [wrongdoing] will have been committed as a result of activity being undertaken by the employee on behalf of the employer;
>
> (iii) the employee's activity is likely to be part of the business activity of the employer;
>
> (iv) the employer, by employing the employee to carry on the activity will have created the risk of the [wrongdoing] committed by the employee;
>
> (v) the employee will, to a greater or lesser degree, have been under the control of the employer.'

Subsequent judgments have downplayed the importance of the first (the so-called 'deep pockets' argument) and the fifth (control).[4] The fourth factor – labelled as 'enterprise risk' – is thought to provide the most compelling justification for the principles of vicarious liability.[5] This is the idea that:[6]

> 'the employer or quasi-employer, who is taking the benefit of the activities carried on by a person integrated into its organisation, should bear the cost (or, one might say, should bear the risk) of the wrong committed by that person in the course of those activities'.

But while the principle provides a good explanation for some features of the present law, certain aspects of both Stage One[7] and Stage Two[8] of the vicarious liability enquiry would have to be refined to fully embrace the notion that the employer/quasi-employer should bear the risk of wrongs committed by those integrated into its operations. Nevertheless, the UK Supreme Court has suggested that bearing the principle of enterprise risk in mind can offer a useful cross-check on the justice of result in 'hard' vicarious liability cases.[9]

1 *Kilboy v South Eastern Fire Area Joint Committee* 1952 SC 280 (IH) at 285.
2 The reference here is to the 5th edn of Winfield's textbook on tort. The current edition (J Goudkamp and D Nolan, *Winfield and Jolowicz on Tort* (21st edn, Sweet & Maxwell,

2025) at para 24-006) is no less sceptical of the existence of a single explanation: 'the institution is probably to be explained not by reference to any single reason but by the cumulation of several'.

3 *Various Claimants v Catholic Child Welfare Society* [2012] UKSC 56, [2013] 2 AC 1 at para 35 per Lord Phillips of Worth Mantravers.

4 See eg *Armes v Nottinghamshire County Council* [2017] UKSC 60, [2018] AC 355 at paras 56–58.

5 See eg *Armes* at para 67; *BXB v Trustees of the Barry Congregation of Jehovah's Witnesses* [2023] UKSC 15, [2024] AC 567 at para 58(iv).

6 *BXB* at para 58(iv) per Lord Burrows. For fuller analysis, see D Brodie, *Enterprise Liability and the Common Law* (CUP, 2010).

7 For suggested refinements, see D Brodie, 'Enterprise Liability: the Consequences of a "Single Accepted Truth"' [2025] *Juridical Review* 25.

8 The approach of Singaporean law here might be instructive: *Skandinaviska Enskilda Banken AB v Asia Pacific Breweries (S) Pte Ltd* [2011] 3 SLR 540.

9 *BXB* at paras 58(iv) and 82. For application, see eg *JXJ v The Vicar of the Parish Church of Holcombe Rogus* [2023] EWHC 3221 (KB) at para 213.

STAGE ONE: THE RIGHT RELATIONSHIP?

(1) The employment paradigm

15.4 Once relevant wrongdoing has been identified, the next issue is to determine whether the relationship between the wrongdoer (D2) and the person alleged to be vicariously liable (D1) is one that gives rise to vicarious liability. The test 'is whether the relationship between' D1 and D2 'was one of employment or akin to employment'.[1]

Traditionally, this has involved an inquiry whether the person who committed the wrong is working under a contract of employment (which gives rise to vicarious liability) or is an independent contractor working under a contract for services (which does not). The traditional approach distinguished these two contrasting situations by using 'control' as a touchstone: unlike where engaging a party to provide a service, an employer has the power to control not only what the employee should do but also *how* he should do it.[2] But, although important, the absence of control does not preclude the finding of an employment relationship.[3]

The modern approach is multi-factorial,[4] with the following factors having been suggested (non-exclusively) as relevant:[5] the defender's control over the wrongdoer; whether or not the wrongdoer is integrated into (or is 'part and parcel' of) the defender's organisation; whether or not the wrongdoer depends economically on the defender to monetise their skill, labour, or talents; the intention of the parties;[6] whether the defender collects income tax and makes national insurance contributions on behalf of the wrongdoer; the renumeration structure between the defender and the wrongdoer; and whether the defender supplied the wrongdoer with necessary equipment.[7] Volunteers may, in some circumstances, be treated as employees[8] or (to similar effect as we shall see) as akin to employees.[9]

1 *BXB v Trustees of the Barry Congregation of Jehovah's Witnesses* [2023] UKSC 15, [2024] AC 567 at para 58(ii) per Lord Burrows.
2 See eg *Yewans v Nokes* (1880) 6 QBD 530.
3 See eg *Kilboy v South Eastern Fire Area Joint Committee* 1952 SLT 280 (IH), giving ship captains and underground mining officials as examples of employees free from employer interference.
4 See eg *Marshall v William Sharp & Sons Ltd* 1991 SLT 114 (IH). For application, see eg *United Wholesale Grocers Ltd v Sher* 1993 SLT 284 (OH); *Glossop v Wilson* 2010 WL 889419 (Sh Ct).
5 Campbell and Lindsay, 'Vicarious Liability in Scotland' at 198–199; Campbell and Lindsay, 'Refining Vicarious Liability' at 175–178.
6 See *Massey v Crown Life Insurance Co* [1978] ICR 590 (CA) at 594: the label used by parties may not be decisive, but may be indicative in ambiguous cases.
7 *Dignon v Irving* 1999 SCLR 601 (Sh Ct) (fact that wrongdoer brought own tools and materials pointed away from employment relationship).
8 See *Groom v Maritime and Coastguard Agency* [2024] EAT 71 (not a vicarious liability case).
9 As in eg *BXB*. See paras 15.7–15.8 below.

(2) *Pro hac vice* employment

15.5 In certain situations, an employee may be hired out to work under the instructions of another employer. This is referred to as '*pro hac vice*' employment.[1] For example, A, a general contractor, may hire equipment from B to be operated by an employee of B but under A's instruction. If the 'borrowed' employee is negligent and injures one of A's employees or a third party, who is vicariously liable, A or B?

The general rule is that B, the 'general' employer, remains vicariously liable even though the employee works under the general instructions of A.[2] To escape vicarious liability, B must establish that it has transferred to A not only the power to tell the employee *what* to do, but also the power to direct the employee *how* to perform that instructed task.[3] A more modern way of stating the test may be to ask whether there has been a transfer of responsibility for the employee's conduct in the discharge of the duties of employment.[4] Either formulation seems to involve a 'heavy burden' which is 'sensitive to the facts and circumstances of the case'.[5] It has been suggested such a transfer will be difficult to establish where the employee's role involves the application of some skill or expertise not possessed by A.[6] Whether the focus on control in these situations remains appropriate is a matter ripe for re-examination, especially in light of the recognition of 'dual vicarious liability'.

1 '*Pro hac vice*' translates as 'for this turn' or 'for this occasion', and refers to a form of 'limited or temporary employment'. *Lyell v Sun Microsystems Scotland* 2005 SCLR 786 (OH) at para 14 per the Lord Ordinary (Drummond Young).

2 *Mersey Docks and Harbour Board v Coggins and Griffith (Liverpool) Ltd* [1947] AC 1 (HL) at 10 per Viscount Simon.
3 *Mersey Docks* at 10–12 per Viscount Simon; at 13 per Lord Macmillan; at 17 per Lord Porter. For application, see eg *Park v Tractor Shovels Ltd* 1980 SLT 94 (OH); *Moir v Wide Arc Services Ltd* 1987 SLT 495 (OH) (no transfer); *Hawley v Luminar Leisure Plc* [2006] EWCA Civ 18 (transfer).
4 *King v Fife Council* 2004 Rep LR 33 (OH) at para 14.
5 *Royal Bank of Scotland v Bannerman Johnstone Maclay* [2005] CSIH 39, 2005 SC 437 at para 67 per the Lord Justice-Clerk (Gill).
6 See eg *Mersey Docks* at 22 per Lord Uthwatt.

(3) Dual vicarious liability

15.6 Where A's employee is temporarily seconded to B, an alternative to contending for *pro hac vice* employment is to argue for the existence of an employment relationship with both A and B. Slender authority in Scotland goes against so-called 'dual vicarious liability': 'it is not merely a tenet of the Christian faith that a man cannot serve two masters'.[1] But the matter has been considered more thoroughly in English law.

In *Viasystems (Tyneside) Ltd v Thermal Transfer (Northern) Ltd*,[2] the claimant's factory was damaged by a flood during repairs to its air conditioning system. The damage was caused by a fitter's mate, Strang. Strang, employed by A, had been provided to B who, in turn, had been sub-contracted to repair the ducts by C, the principal contractor. The claimants had a claim against C under their contract; the question then arose as to whether C could look to A or B for indemnification for Strang's negligence. It was accepted that no transfer of Strang's employment from A to B was envisaged. Rather than relying on this fact to absolve B, the Court of Appeal raised the issue as to whether dual vicarious liability was a legal possibility. It refuted the assumption that only one employer could be liable for an employee's negligence, and found that the situation before it was one where it properly could be said that both A and B were Strang's employers in relation to the duct repairs.

The UK Supreme Court, in an English appeal, subsequently has endorsed *Viasystems*, emphasising that the test is whether the wrongdoer is so integrated into the 'work, business, or organisation of both employers that it is just' to impose vicarious liability on both employers.[3]

While it has not yet been adopted in Scots law,[4] the endorsement of dual vicarious liability by the Supreme Court makes such adoption likely, and a Sheriff has remarked that dual vicarious liability might provide 'a more principled solution' to the issues presented by borrowed employees.[5] Nevertheless, assuming Scottish courts do adopt the concept, they should be cautious in being too eager to make findings of dual vicarious liability, as it may erode the general denial of vicarious liability for the acts of independent contractors.[6]

1 *Park v Tractor Shovels Ltd* 1980 SLT 94 at 101 per the Lord Ordinary (Cowie).
2 [2005] EWCA Civ 1155, [2006] QB 510.
3 *Various Claimants v Catholic Child Welfare Society v* [2012] UKSC 56, [2013] 1 AC 1 at paras 43–45, preferring the test adopted by Rix LJ in *Viasystems* at para 79. Dual vicarious liability was found on the facts of *CCWS*.
4 Although see *McTear Contracts Ltd v Bennet* 2021 WL 00827709, an Employment Appeal Tribunal case from Scotland where, at para 39, Lord Fairley discussed the 'exception' of dual vicarious liability.
5 *Grubb v Shannon* [2018] SC GLA 13, 2018 SLT (Sh Ct) 193 at para 55 per Sheriff Reid.
6 See *Kalma v African Minerals* [2018] EWHC 3506 (QB) at para 301(iii).

(4) Relationships 'akin to employment'

15.7 Once a relationship is characterised as one of employment then, leaving aside issues of transferred employees and dual vicarious liability, there is little doubt that Stage One is satisfied. However, there are relationships which share certain features with the employer/employee relationship, but which fall short of constituting full legal employment. Rather than exclude such circumstances from the operation of vicarious liability, courts will instead ask whether such relationships are sufficiently 'akin to employment' to justify the imposition of vicarious liability.[1] This has been justified in the following terms:[2]

> 'A relationship other than employment is in principle capable of giving rise to vicarious liability where harm is wrongfully done by an individual who carries on activities as an integral part of the business activities carried on by a defendant and for its benefit (rather than his activities being entirely attributable to the conduct of a recognisably independent business of his own or of a third party), and where the commission of the wrongful act is a risk created by the defendant by assigning those activities to the individual in question.'

The court therefore 'needs to consider carefully features of the relationship that are similar to, or different from, a contract of employment':[3]

> 'Depending on the facts, relevant features to consider may include: whether the work is being paid for in money or in kind, how integral to the organisation is the work carried out by [D2], the extent of [D1's] control over [D2] in carrying out the work, whether the work is being carried out for [D1's] benefit or in furtherance of the aims of the organisation, what the situation is with regard to appointment and termination, and whether there is a hierarchy of seniority into which the relevant role fits.'

Accordingly, courts have considered as sufficiently 'akin to employment' relationships between: a religious order and practitioners which it sent to teach at a school,[4] the Jehovah's Witness organisation and its elders who carried out its teachings,[5] a local authority and the foster parents into whose care it placed a child,[6] the Ministry of Justice and a prisoner assigned to work in a prison kitchen,[7] and a school and a former pupil undertaking work experience under close direction and supervision by its teachers.[8]

The UK Supreme Court has, however, re-affirmed the general principle that no vicarious liability exists for the acts of an independent contract; this should not be undermined by the growing recognition of relationships 'akin to employment'.[9] Nor is satisfaction of the test a foregone conclusion: the courts have held, for instance, that the relationship between an associate dentist and a dental practice,[10] and a football scout and a football club,[11] were not, on their facts, sufficiently 'akin to employment'.

It should be borne in mind, however, that cases turn on the facets of the particular relationship which arise for decision; future cases involving such parties may involve relationships structured differently from decided cases, which may justify different treatment on the facts.[12]

1 It is possible that statute might provide that such a relationship, although not formally one of employment, should give rise to vicarious liability. See eg Police and Fire Reform (Scotland) Act 2012, s 24 (chief constable vicariously liable for acts of constables).

2 *Cox v Ministry of Justice* [2016] UKSC 10, [2016] AC 660 at para 24 per Lord Reed.

3 *BXB v Trustees of the Barry Congregation of Jehovah's Witnesses* [2023] UKSC 15, [2024] AC 567 at para 58(ii) per Lord Burrows. While Lord Burrows suggests (at para 58(iv)) that policy reasoning may play some role in 'difficult' cases, the role of policy has been questioned: Campbell and Lindsay, 'Refining Vicarious Liability' at 182–188.

4 *Various Claimants v Catholic Child Welfare Society v* [2012] UKSC 56, [2013] 1 AC 1.

5 See *BXB*.

6 *Armes v Nottinghamshire County Council* [2017] UKSC 60, [2018] AC 355. See also *DJ v Barnsley Metropolitan Borough Council* [2024] EWCA Civ 148, [2025] 1 WLR 148 (relationship 'akin to employment' arose, under legislation in force at time, after council placed child into kinship care with aunt and uncle), and compare with *Cruickshanks v Glasgow City Council* 2024 SLT 526 (proof before answer allowed to ascertain extent of kinship carer arrangements).

7 See *Cox*.

8 *MXX v A Secondary School* [2023] EWCA Civ 996.

9 *Various Claimants v Barclays Bank Plc* [2020] UKSC 13, [2020] AC 973.

10 *Hughes v Rattan* [2022] EWCA Civ 107, [2022] 1 WLR 1680 (*obiter*, as breach of a non-delegable duty was found on the facts).

11 *DSN v Blackpool Football Club Ltd* [2021] EWCA Civ 1352; *TVZ v Manchester City Football Club Ltd* [2022] EWHC 7 (QB). In both cases, the scout operated independently; the conclusion would be different if the scout had a closer association with a limb of the football club.

12 See the cautionary words of the Court of Appeal of England and Wales in *DJ v Barnsley* at para 69.

15.8 Two Scottish decisions are worthy of further discussion. In *Grubb v Shannon*,[1] the pursuer suffered an allergic reaction to eyebrow tinting negligently applied by a self-employed beautician operating out of the defender's beauty parlour. The beautician rented a chair and room from the defender, had the authority to open and lock up the defender's salon, held access to the salon's social media accounts; appeared in promotional efforts using the salon's branding, and used a pricelist set by the defender. She kept all sums received from customers and had the discretion to offer promotions and discounts, used her own equipment, and was paid no money by the defender. Sheriff Reid concluded that the beautician:[2]

> 'did indeed carry on activities, entrusted to her by the defender, as an integral part of the defender's business activities, and for the benefit of the defender; that her activities were not attributable to the conduct of a recognisably independent business of her own, or of a third party …'.

The salon owner was therefore vicariously liable for the beautician's negligence, notwithstanding the fact that the beautician was not her employee.

The situation in *X v Brown*[3] was very different. There, the pursuer was a solicitor who alleged that a Sheriff had inappropriately touched and harassed her. She asserted that the Lord Advocate, as representative of the Scottish Ministers, was vicariously liable for the Sheriff's conduct as part of the Scottish Administration (as a manifestation of the Crown).[4] The Inner House reversed the Lord Ordinary's conclusion that the relationship between the Scottish Government and the Sheriff was 'akin to employment'. Sheriffs and other judicial officers were *sui generis*: they were neither employees nor independent contractors, nor could they be regarded as Crown servants.[5] While the Scottish Government ultimately provided the funds which paid judicial salaries and pensions, the level at which these are set is a matter for the UK Government.[6] The appointment, discipline, and removal of Sheriffs, while all involving some role for the First Minister, largely were a matter for an independent body.[7] This all demonstrated the lack of control held by the Scottish Government over judicial officers. While the Inner House was aware of the diminished role of control in establishing the existence of a relationship giving rise to vicarious liability, it suggested that the alternative approach of 'enterprise risk' was not appropriate; the judiciary could not be said to be 'integrated' into the business of the Scottish Government.[8] Even if integration could be established, the Inner House was clear that the policy of judicial independence was so potent that it would outweigh any indicia favouring the imposition of vicarious liability.[9] While the facts of *X v Brown* hopefully do not repeat themselves, the constitutional imperative of judicial independence would mean that vicarious liability never can arise for assaults, harassments, or other intentional wrongdoing by a judge falling outside the domain of their immunity from civil suit.

1 [2018] SC GLA 13, 2018 SLT (Sh Ct) 193.
2 *Grubb* at para 112.
3 [2024] CSIH 6, 2024 SC 309. The UK Supreme Court heard an appeal in this case in June 2025: what is said here necessarily must be read subject to the Supreme Court's judgment when it is issued.

4 At first instance, the Lord Ordinary concluded that it was the Lord Advocate, not the Advocate General for Scotland, who was the appropriate defender: *X v Y* [2023] CSOH 17; 2023 SC 235 at paras 60–67. This conclusion was not appealed: *X v Brown* at para 13.

5 *X v Brown* at paras 37–38.

6 *X v Brown* at para 39.

7 *X v Brown* at para 40.

8 *X v Brown* at para 41. It could be said that the judiciary is integrated into the wider state's administration of justice, which might raise the question of dual vicarious liability between the Scottish and UK Government. But this point was not argued, and in any event would have been countered by the policy of judicial independence.

9 *X v Brown* at paras 42–46. As for what is said at para 43, the fear that recognising the relationship between a judge and the state as one 'akin to employment' *for vicarious liability purposes* might cause the public to query judicial independence is, with respect, unconvincing. Given that there would be substantial overlap between delictual conduct falling outside of a judge's immunity, and the grounds for investigating a judge's fitness for office, there may well be a procedural solution to the concern (at para 44) that a pending delictual action, defended by the state, might affect how a judge decides cases.

STAGE TWO: THE RIGHT CONNECTION?

(1) The close connection test

15.9 Once it is established that the relationship between the defender ('D1') and wrongdoer ('D2') is one which gives rise to vicarious liability, we turn to Stage Two. This requires us to focus on D2's conduct and its connection to its relationship with D1. Here, the court must ask:[1]

> 'whether the wrongful conduct was so closely connected with acts that [D2] was authorised to do that it can fairly and properly be regarded as done by [D2] while acting in the course of [D2's] employment or quasi-employment'.

This requires the court 'to consider carefully on the facts the link between the wrongful conduct and [D2's] authorised activities.'[2] A 'sufficiently close connection' is what is required: the fact that D2's engagement by D1 was a 'but for' cause of D2's delict, or that it gave D2 the opportunity to commit the delict, is by itself insufficient. The fact that the wrongdoing occurred during working hours,[3] at the place of employment, does not automatically result in vicarious liability; nor does the fact that conduct occurs outside of working hours and off premises necessarily preclude vicarious liability.[4]

The 'close connection' test grew out of a test which enquired simply whether the conduct occurred in the course of the wrongdoer's employment.[5] While the old test was able to deal with cases of negligent performance of assigned duties, it struggled to deal with cases of intentional wrongdoing.[6] In *Lister v Hesley Hall Ltd*[7] – a case involving the infliction of historic child sex abuse by a warden at a boarding school – the House of Lords developed the 'close connection' test to deal with the facts of that case: while abuse of children could not be said to be something undertaken 'in the course' of a warden's employment, those acts had a 'close connection' to that employment.

Despite the context of *Lister*, the close connection test soon became accepted as the general test for establishing the connection between D2's wrongdoing and the relationship between D1 and D2.[8] However, its open-textured (some might say vague) nature has been judicially noted:[9]

> 'This "close connection" test focuses attention in the right direction. But it affords no guidance on the type or degree of connection which will normally be regarded as sufficiently close to prompt the legal conclusion that the risk of the wrongful act occurring, and any loss flowing from the wrongful act, should fall on the firm or employer rather than the third party who was wronged. It provides no clear assistance on when … an incident is to be regarded as sufficiently work-related, as distinct from personal … This lack of precision is inevitable, given the infinite range of circumstances where the issue arises. The crucial feature or features, either producing or negativing vicarious liability, vary widely from one case or type of case to the next. Essentially the court makes an evaluative judgment in each case, having regard to all the circumstances and, importantly, having regard also to the assistance provided by previous court decisions. In this field the latter form of assistance is particularly valuable.'

The adoption of the close connection test involves an 'evaluative judgement',[10] considering all of the circumstances of the case, and using previous cases as a guide. This test is wide enough so as to render any further consideration of policy redundant.[11]

1 *BXB v Trustees of the Barry Congregation of Jehovah's Witnesses* [2023] UKSC 15, [2024] AC 567 at para 58(iii) per Lord Burrows.
2 Ibid.
3 For cases where D2 is travelling to or from work, see *Smith v Stages* [1989] AC 928 (HL).
4 See eg *Bellman v Northampton Recruitment Ltd* [2018] EWCA Civ 2214, [2019] ICR 459 (company, fully controlled by its managing director, held vicariously liable for his punching of a subordinate who undermined his authority at drinks after work Christmas party).
5 See eg *Kirby v National Coal Board* 1958 SC 514 (IH).
6 See eg *Trotman v North Yorkshire County Council* [1999] IRLR 98 (local authority not vicariously liable for sexual assault of pupil by deputy headmaster).
7 [2001] UKHL 22, [2002] 1 AC 215, overruling *Trotman*.
8 It was adopted in Scotland by, eg, *Sharp v Highlands and Islands Fire Board* [2005] CSOH 111, 2005 SLT 855 (obiter). See generally S Bogle, 'Responsibility for Another's Wrong in Scotland: Stick with *Lister* or Twist with *Mohamud*?' [2019] *Juridical Review* 211.
9 *Dubai Aluminium Company Ltd v Saalam* [2002] UKHL 1, [2003] 2 AC 366 at paras 25–26 per Lord Nicholls of Birkenhead.
10 *Dubai Aluminium* at para 26.
11 *Various Claimants v Wm Morrison (Supermarkets) Plc* [2020] UKSC 12, [2020] AC 989 at para 24 per Lord Reed. Compare with *BXB* at paras 58(iv) and 82.

(2) Authorisation and prohibition

15.10 The analysis at Stage Two commences with the question:[1]

> '[W]hat functions or "field of activities" have been entrusted by the employer to the employee, or, in everyday language, what was the nature of his [or her] job ... this question must be addressed broadly.'

It is the closeness of the connection between those authorised functions and the wrongful conduct which must be interrogated.

Where the employer has specifically authorised (or ordered) the wrongdoer to commit the wrongful act, the connection between the wrongdoing and the relationship here is obviously extremely close. However, it is thought that cases of direct and specific authorisation are not truly cases of vicarious liability: the employer's authorisation of the wrongful act gives rise to primary liability.[2] Cases of direct authorisation are, in any event, rare.

Instead, authorisation likely will be implicit in the conferral of a certain role or responsibility on the employee, but may also be spelled out to some degree in their job description. For example, by appointing D2 as a shop assistant or manager, D1 confers on them responsibility to protect its stock from shoplifters.[3] If D2 accuses a customer of shoplifting, and physically restrains them pending the arrival of the police, then such conduct is closely connected to D2's authorised activities, and the shop owner therefore will be vicariously liable for any delict thereby committed by D2. But where a transport company employs D2 as a bus conductor, who then injures a fellow employee at a depot while driving a bus, then the negligent driving has no close connection to D2's authorised functions.[4]

Two cases, with superficially similar facts, illustrate the importance of keeping the focus sharp on what activities or functions specifically were authorised by D2. In *Lister v Hesley Hall Ltd*, D2 was a warden of a school boarding house, with responsibility for domestic supervision and maintaining discipline when the children were not at school. Broadly, his role was one of caring for the children in a domestic environment. His heinous abuse of the children, while in no sense authorised by D1, was nevertheless closely connected with the role into which D1 had placed him in respect of the children.[5] By contrast, in *C and S v Shaw*,[6] D1 had hired D2 as head caretaker for its sports centre. D2 used this position to groom two children he already knew as a family friend, resulting in alleged abuse. A key reason for the Inner House denying a close connection on the facts centred on D2's authorised functions: D2 'did not obtain any authority' over the children 'by virtue of his role as head caretaker'; he had 'no special responsibility towards child users of the sports centre'. His duties, centred on setting up equipment, conducting security rounds, and ensuring compliance with sports centre rules, did not authorise close personal individual contact with users of the sports centre.[7]

1 *Mohamud v Wm Morrison (Supermarkets) Plc* [2016] UKSC 11, [2016] AC 677 at para 44 per Lord Toulson.
2 *Lister v Helsey Hall Ltd* [2001] UKHL 22, [2002] 1 AC 215 at para 67 per Lord Millett.
3 See eg *Neville v C & A Modes Ltd* 1945 SC 175 (IH) (a claim in defamation).
4 *Iqbal v London Transport Executive*, available on bailii.org under the citation [1973] EWCA Civ 3.
5 See especially *Lister* at paras 20 and 28 per Lord Steyn; at para 82 per Lord Millett.
6 [2023] CSIH 36, 2024 SC 81 at para 21, affirming [2023] CSOH 11, 2023 SLT 359.
7 See too *MXX v A Secondary School* [2023] EWCA Civ 996 (former pupil on week's work experience held no position of authority and no caring or pastoral supervision over pupil that he groomed and assaulted).

15.11 The employers of the warden in *Lister* and the caretaker in *C & S v Shaw* clearly would have (at least implicitly) prohibited the abuse conducted by those employees. That did not, by itself, negate any 'close connection'. Consider the situation where an employee charged with transferring petrol from a tanker to an underground tanker lights a cigarette and causes an explosion. Such conduct, too, obviously would be prohibited by the employer if asked in advance whether the employee should spark up while transferring petrol. But the employee's act still retained a very close connection to the authorised action of ensuring the proper transfer of petrol, rendering the employer vicariously liable for his negligence:[1] in the old terminology, it was an 'unauthorised mode' of conducting authorised work.

Express prohibitions must be examined carefully. If the effect of the prohibition is to limit the scope of the employee's employment, then that may sever any close connection where conduct is carried out contrary to the prohibition. This arises where the effect of the prohibition effectively is to take the prohibited conduct well outside the employee's authorised functions. We gave above the example of a bus conductor: an express prohibition forbidding the driving of buses reinforces that the conductor's authorised functions relate to ticket checking, not the driving of buses.

But if the prohibition simply instructs the employee not to do its job in a particular way, then conduct which defies that prohibition will not, for that reason, lack a close connection to D2's authorised functions and duties. For instance, in *Rose v Plenty*,[2] a milkman was expressly instructed by his employer not to use boys to help him deliver milk. In breach of this order, he continued to use a 13-year-old boy to help him. The boy was injured because of the milkman's negligent driving of the float. The employers argued that they were not vicariously liable because the employee was acting outside the scope of his employment, having defied their express instruction. The Court of Appeal disagreed: the express prohibition did not take the conduct outside the scope of the milkman's employment. As Lord Denning MR explained:[3]

> 'In considering whether a prohibited act was within the course of the employment it depends very much on the purpose for which it is done … In the present case it seems to me that the course of [the milkman's] employment was to distribute the milk, collect the money and to bring back the bottles to the van. He got, or allowed, this young boy … to do part of that business which was the employer's business. It seems to me that although prohibited, it was conduct which was within the course of employment …'.

A similar approach was taken to a prohibition on employees using private vehicles without appropriate insurance coverage to conduct company business: the means of transport was 'incidental' to the employee's authorised functions, and therefore there remained a close connection between his employment and his negligent driving such as to make the employer liable.[4]

1 *Century Insurance Co Ltd v Northern Ireland Road Transport Board* [1942] AC 509 (HL).
2 [1976] 1 WLR 141 (CA). See similarly *Ilkiw v Williams* [1963] 1 WLR 991 (CA).
3 *Rose v Plenty* at 144.
4 *Canadian Pacific Railway Company v Lockhart* [1942] AC 591 (PC, Canada).

(3) Deviations and frolics

15.12 Difficulties also may arise where the employee deviates from the assigned task. This has frequently presented in cases where the employee has been tasked with driving a particular route, but elects to deviate from that route. What extent of deviation will reduce the connection between wrongdoing occurring on that deviation and the employee's authorised functions?

In *Williams v Hemphill (A & W) Ltd*,[1] members of the Boys' Brigade were at a camp at Benderloch, north of Oban. A company of Girl Guides was also at the camp. The girls were to return to Dollar by train. A lorry driver was instructed by his employer to take the boys back to Glasgow. He was persuaded by some of the boys to return to Glasgow via Connell, Stirling and Dollar railway stations so the boys could catch a glimpse of the girls. The shortest route back to Glasgow was via Loch Lomond. There was an accident and one of the boys (who had not instigated the change of route) was injured. The employers would not have authorised the route the driver had taken. The question was whether, by deviating from the authorised route, the driver was no longer acting within the scope of his employment, with the result that the employer would not have been vicariously liable. The House of Lords held that it was ultimately a question of degree whether, as a result of the deviation, the employee was no longer engaged on the employer's business, severing any close connection.[2] In this case, the dominant purpose of the journey was to transport the boys to Glasgow and the driver was still engaged in that task when the accident occurred, despite not having taken the most direct route. As Lord Pearce explained:[3]

> 'In weighing up, therefore, the question of degree whether the admittedly substantial deviation of progress the vehicle with its passengers and baggage was such as to make the lorry's progress a frolic of the servant unconnected with or in substitution for the master's business, the presence of the passengers is a decisive factor against regarding it as a mere frolic of the servant. In the present case the defenders remained liable, in spite of the deviation, for their driver's negligence.'

Lord Pearce acknowledged that there must be some limits on the extent of deviation (eg if the driver went to Glasgow via Inverness), and also opined that the outcome might be different if the injured party had initiated the deviation, or if the driver instead injured a third party while driving an empty lorry on a substantial detour.[4] The ultimate question is whether the deviation supersedes the authorised journey – ie forms a new journey entirely unconnected with the authorised functions – or whether it merely constitutes a detour from the prescribed route.[5]

1 1966 SC (HL) 31.
2 *Williams v Hemphill* at 45.
3 *Williams v Hemphill* at 46.
4 All these hypotheticals now would turn on application of the close connection test. First, Inverness. The deviation in *Williams* effectively involved the driver taking the route to the east of Loch Lomond instead of that to its west. Either route was a plausible way of getting to Glasgow, so negligence on either route would be closely connected to his authorised function of carrying the children to Glasgow. But driving to Inverness, around 100 miles in the opposite direction, would mean any wrongdoing en route would lack a close connection with the function of transporting the children *to Glasgow*. Secondly, it is submitted that the fact that the injured party was the one who convinced the driver to take the eastern route should not dislodge any close connection; the driver still is carrying out his authorised functions, even if he does so in a manner which bends to the unanimous will of his passengers. Thirdly, it is difficult to see why the presence of precious cargo or passengers affects the conclusion.
5 See eg *Angus v Glasgow Corporation* 1977 SLT 206 (IH) (detour of five miles to collect spectacles to ensure safe driving not so 'extravagant in time or distance' to constitute an independent journey); *RJ McLeod (Contractors) Ltd v South of Scotland Electricity Board* 1982 SLT 274 (OH) (detours to drive colleague home and visit mother in law, taking employee past home, did not wholly supersede original journey; detours essentially confined to various addresses in Cumbernauld, where employee also lived).

15.13 In both *Rose v Plenty* and *Williams v Hemphill* the court found in favour of vicarious liability because the wrongdoers could both be said to have been engaged on their employers' business and therefore the conduct was closely connected to their employment. The alternative, in both cases would have been a finding that the employee was off 'on a frolic of his own', that is, acting for his own purposes and therefore wholly unconnected with his employment.

In this context, 'frolic' does not connote triviality. Instead, the court must consider whether the employee's conduct amounts to 'an unrelated and independent venture of his own: a personal matter, rather than a matter connected to his authorised duties'.[1] But drawing this line is difficult. For example, in *Kirby v National Coal Board*,[2] a miner, during a temporary break, went to a prohibited place to smoke. When he struck a match, there was an explosion and the pursuer was injured. The Inner House held that by going to the prohibited area to smoke, he was no longer acting within the scope of his employment – mining – and consequently the defender was not vicariously liable: smoking in the prohibited area had no connection to the employee's authorised functions.

Contrastingly, in *Matthis v Pollock*,[3] a nightclub bouncer was chased from a club by patrons in response to the aggressive performance of his duties. Embarrassed by this, he went to his nearby home, picked up a knife, and returned to the area around the club, stabbing the claimant, who had attempted to intervene in an earlier incident within the club. Despite the attack being animated by personal animosity and a desire for revenge, the Court of Appeal held that the club owner was vicariously liable for the assault.[4] The bouncer was authorised to use force to keep order and discipline in the club, and was encouraged by the club owner to assert his powers vigorously to intimidate potentially troublesome customers. The stabbing was a response to a perceived undermining of that authority, and therefore was closely connected to his authorised role and functions.

The distinction is between unauthorised wrongful conduct which nevertheless is closely connected to the employee's authorised functions, and wrongful conduct which does not have a close connection to those functions, thus therefore constitutes an independent or selfish business, venture, or act by the employee. Drawing this distinction is the most difficult task at Stage Two of the vicarious liability enquiry. To assist, we will discuss some typical fact patterns which have arisen in the cases.

1 *Ward v Scotrail Railways* 1999 SC 255 (OH) per Lord Reed (then a Lord Ordinary) at 264.
2 1958 SC 514 (IH).
3 [2003] EWCA Civ 887, [2003] 1 WLR 2158.
4 *Matthis v Pollock* at paras 30–32. For other cases finding vicarious liability for the acts of bouncers, see *Vasey v Surrey Free Inns Plc* [1996] PIQR P373 (CA) and *Ashmore v Rock Steady Security Ltd* 2006 SLT 207 (OH) (where the point seems to have been conceded).

(4) Personal agendas, vendettas, and prejudice

15.14 Where D2 acts pursuant to a personal agenda, vendetta or prejudice, and the delict does not arise from the exercise of an authorised function, it will be difficult to find a close connection between the act and D2's employment.

Most obviously, where D2 embarks upon conduct which is targeted at undermining D1, D1 usually will not be vicariously liable for that conduct. In *Wm Morrison Supermarkets Plc v Various Claimants*,[1] Skelton, a member of Morrison's internal audit team had been given the job of collating Morrison's payroll data and transferring it to the company auditors, KPMG. Skelton recently had been reprimanded by Morrisons for minor misconduct. Aggrieved at his treatment, alongside transferring the data to KPMG as instructed, he also posted a copy of the payroll data on the internet and sent hard copies on CD-ROMs to three newspapers. Affected employees sued Morrisons for breaches of confidence and data protection rights, and misuse of private information. In the UK Supreme Court, Lord Reed held that the field of activities entrusted to Skelton did not extend to posting the data on the internet and so, given his motives were purely personal, his conduct was not sufficiently connected to his employment for his employers to incur vicarious liability.[2] It should be noted that this is a very focussed approach to Skelton's authorised functions: he had access to the data for the limited purpose of conveying it to KPMG, and was not empowered to disseminate it more widely. The analysis may be less straightforward if the employee instead was a data protection officer, but it is submitted that it still would be difficult to see how an act by the employee calculated to undermine the employer's business could be an act somehow in furtherance of that business.

More typical are cases where the employee's agenda, vendetta or prejudice results in an injury to a fellow employee or a third party. As we have seen from *Matthis v Pollock*, the fact that the employee acts pursuant to a personal vendetta while discharging their authorised functions does not prevent the finding of a close connection. For instance, workplace harassment by a supervisor who systematically traduces a lower-level colleague in the exercise of her supervisory functions may be closely connected to those authorised functions.[3] A punch thrown by a semi-professional rugby player in a brawl which ensued after a scrum, which spilt over after the end of a rugby match, was closely connected to the player's employment, despite it being prohibited by both the rules of the game and his contract with the club.[4]

An extreme case, which reached the UK Supreme Court, is *Mohamud v Wm Morrison (Supermarkets) Plc*.[5] Khan, a petrol station attendant, took offence at a request from a customer of Somali origin to print material from a USB stick. He racially abused the customer, ordered him never to return to the premises, then followed him out to his car, assaulting him on the garage forecourt. The UK Supreme Court held that his employer was vicariously liable for the assault.[6] Khan was entrusted to respond to customer enquiries. From his foulmouthed response to the initial enquiry, to ordering the customer to leave, to punching him on the garage forecourt, Khan abused the 'field of activities' assigned to him, but nevertheless still acted within his authorised functions by responding to the customer's request – albeit completely inappropriately.

Where the conduct does not arise out of the employee's 'field of activities', the chances of finding a close connection are slim. In *Vaickuviene v JS Sainsbury*,[7] a supermarket shelf stacker who harboured anti-immigrant and racist views harassed, and then murdered, another shelf stacker, who was from Lithuania. Despite the murder occurring on work premises during working hours, the course of conduct was held by the Inner House to lack a close connection with the assailant's employment with the supermarket.[8] His duties were to stack shelves and perform other retail stock related-duties. All that could be said was his employment put him in proximity to the deceased, and allowed him to manifest his prejudice against the deceased, which was insufficient.[9]

The application of the close connection test in the context of personal vendettas can further be seen by comparing two Privy Council cases brought by the victims of police shootings. In the first,[10] Kelvin Laurent was a probationer police officer in the British Virgin Islands, where officers do not routinely carry firearms. Nevertheless, he had a key which gave him access to a lock box which contained a pistol. Taking the pistol, he abandoned his post and duties to travel to a bar 14 miles away across sea and land where his ex-partner worked. Aggravated by the perception that she was associating with another man, he fired the pistol four times. One bullet struck the claimant, a British tourist, who claimed against the BVI police authority as vicariously liable for the assault. The Privy Council rejected that argument:[11] Laurent's wrongful use of the gun was not so closely connected with acts which he was authorised to do that it could be regarded as done in the course of his employment. His duties did not extend to the island on which the bar was located, he was not authorised to take the weapon out without the permission of his superior officer, and he was not responding to a call for assistance or investigating any reasonable suspicion related to his police duties. On the other hand, the police authority was held personally liable in negligently entrusting Laurent with the gun.[12]

By contrast, in the second case[13] from Jamaica, off-duty constable Morgan announced 'police!' and demanded immediate use of a public telephone from Bernard who was using it. The employer was vicariously liable when Bernard refused to surrender the phone and Morgan shot him, wounding him in the head. When Bernard recovered consciousness, he was in hospital and surrounded by officers. Constable Morgan promptly placed Bernard under arrest and handcuffed him to the bed. The connection between the wrongful act and employment was established because Morgan was purporting to be acting on police business and clearly (by effecting an arrest) took the view that Bernard had interfered with the execution of his duties as a police officer.[14]

1 [2020] UKSC 12, [2020] AC 989.
2 *Various Claimants v Morrisons* at paras 33–47. See too *Ali v Luton Borough Council* [2022] EHWC 132 (QB) (personal data relating to claimant leaked by ex-husband's lover who was employed by council's social work department and had low-level access to database; council not vicariously liable).
3 As countenanced in *Majrowski v Guy's and St Thomas's NHS Trust* [2006] UKHL 34, [2007] 1 AC 224. Bullying of a coworker in order to advance one's employment prospects may be sufficiently connected with the bully's assigned work to satisfy Stage Two: *Green v DB Group Services (UK) Ltd* [2006] EWHC 1898 (QB) at para 154.
4 *Gravil v Carroll* [2008] EWCA Civ 689, [2008] ICR 1222 at paras 23–30.
5 *Mohamud v Wm Morrison Supermarkets Plc* [2016] UKSC 11, [2016] AC 677.
6 *Mohamud* at paras 47–48. See, similarly, *Kennedy v Aviva Rail London Ltd* [2021] EWHC 2838 (QB) (railway revenue officer authorised to make reports to British Transport Police, so false report made out of spite against claimant was closely connected to authorised duties).
7 [2013] CSIH 67, 2014 SC 147.
8 *Vaickuviene* at paras 30–36.
9 In such circumstances, employers may be in breach of their common law duty of care to provide the victim with competent and non-dangerous fellow employees: see Chapter 11. Such a claim was not fully pled in *Vaickuviene*.
10 *Hartwell v Attorney General of the British Virgin Islands* [2004] UKPC 12, [2004] 1 WLR 1273.
11 *Hartwell* at paras 16–17.
12 See para 6.7 above.
13 *Bernard v Attorney General for Jamaica* [2004] UKPC 47. See too *Brown v Robinson* [2004] UKPC 56 (Jamaica) (employer vicariously liable for shooting by security guard).
14 *Bernard* at paras 25–28.

(5) Abuses of trust

15.15 As established by *Lister v Hesley Hall*,[1] D2's abuse of the trust reposed in it by D1 to care for vulnerable persons may render D1 vicariously liable for D2's abuse. If the field of activities assigned to D2 by D1 authorises them to look after vulnerable persons, then wrongdoing which takes advantage of that relationship may be said to be 'closely connected' to D1's assigned functions. No special or 'tailored' test applies in this context.[2]

There must be close focus on precisely which functions have been authorised by D1. Where D2 is entrusted to care for the pursuer in a residential setting, cases have tended to find a close connection between D2's relationship with D1 and abuse thereby commited.[3] More broadly, certain forms of religious leader may have such all-encompassing moral, pastoral, and evangelical responsibilities, necessitating alone time with vulnerable people, that the finding of a close connection between abuse and those responsibilities may be more likely.[4] But this may be less likely where, for instance, the abuse occurs in the context of a separate religious commune established for non-parishioners which falls beyond the usual responsibilities assigned to that form of religious leader.[5] In any event, it must always be shown that the abuse was connected to functions which the religious leader or clergy member have had bestowed on them by the organisation.[6]

Where a work experience student grooms and later sexually abuses a pupil, the absence of caring or pastoral responsibilities means that the abuse is not 'closely connected' to the limited functions entrusted to him by the school.[7] The same reasoning applies where the abuser is a kitchen porter at a boarding school.[8] The abuse in such a situation is not 'inextricably interwoven' with the carrying out of the wrongdoer's assigned functions.[9] Similarly, a medical doctor who abuses his position by religiously indoctrinating a patient does not render the surgery vicariously liable for that wrongdoing: the surgery authorised the doctor to give medical, not spiritual, guidance.[10]

Abuse which continues once the abuser's authorised functions towards the person have terminated (eg when a pupil has left school) may still be 'closely connected' with the abuser's role.[11] But where D2's association with the pursuer arises independently of D1, it may be difficult to say that the abusive conduct arises in connection with D2's involvement with D1.[12]

It has been held that the employer of a social worker who formed a relationship with a client in his care was not vicariously liable for any wrongdoing constituted by that relationship.[13] The better view is that such conduct may be closely connected to a carer's authorised caring responsibilities.[14]

1 [2001] UKHL 22, [2002] 1 AC 215.
2 *BXB v Trustees of the Barry Congregation of Jehovah's Witnesses* [2023] UKSC 15, [2024] AC 567 at para 58(iii) and (v).
3 See eg *Lister; Various Claimants v Catholic Child Welfare Society* [2012] UKSC 56, [2013] 2 AC 1; *AB v Chethams School of Music* [2021] EWHC 1419 (QB); *Kennedy v Bonnici* [2021] CSOH 106, 2022 SLT 63. But where the abuse is perpetrated other than by the person entrusted by D1 to look after the pursuer, there will be no close connection: *EL v The Children's Society* [2012] EWHC 365 (abuse by son of entrusted parents).
4 *Maga v Archbishop of Birmingham* [2010] EWCA Civ 256, [2010] PTSR 1618 (priest with wide authority to proselytise and with special responsibility for youth work).
5 *JXJ v The Vicar of the Parish Church of Holcombe Rogus* [2023] EWHC 3221 (KB) (abuse by reverend occurred in context of monastic community establishment of which was not authorised by Church of England).

6 Compare *BXB* at para 74 (abuse by Jehovah's Witness elder at his home while being comforted by friend and congregant not connected to ecclesiastical activity) with *A v Trustees of the Watchtower Bible and Tract Society* [2015] EWHC 1722 (QB) at paras 82–90 (abuse by Jehovah's Witness ministerial servant during or after home bible study and door-to-door proselytism closely connected to ecclesiastical activities).

7 *MXX v A Secondary School* [2023] EWCA Civ 996 at paras 85–88.

8 *EXE v Governors of the Royal Naval School* [2020] EWHC 596 (QB) at paras 125–130.

9 *MXX* at para 88, quoting *Lister* at para 28 per Lord Steyn. See too eg *GB v Stoke City Football Club Ltd* [2015] EWHC 2862 (QB).

10 *Brayshaw v Partners of Apsley Surgery* [2018] EWHC 3286 (QB).

11 *Haringey LBC v FZO* [2020] EWCA Civ 180.

12 See *BXB* at para 75 (D2 and claimant close friends) and *C & S v Shaw* [2023] CSIH 36, 2024 SC 81 (D2 a family friend of the pursuers' mother before employment with D1).

13 *Shields v Crossroads (Orkney)* [2013] CSOH 144, 2014 SLT 190. However, the primary basis for rejecting vicarious liability on the facts was that, as this was a consensual relationship, no delict had been committed by the carer.

14 See E Reid, 'Loose Connections: Matters of the Heart and Delictual Wrongdoing' (2014) 18(1) *Edinburgh Law Review* 93. In *NM v Henderson* [2024] CSOH 84, 2025 SLT 35, the Lord Ordinary (Clark) allowed proof before answer to establish whether an ambulance technician's campaign of sexual harassment and abuse against a patient was closely connected to his employment.

(6) Workplace pranks

15.16 Pranks in the workplace played by one employee on another have featured frequently in the case law. It is usually hard to find a close connection in such cases; a prank is the quintessential frolic of the employee's own. For instance, in *Wilson v EXEL UK Ltd*,[1] a supervisor pulled his colleague's ponytail and made a sexual remark. This was wholly unconnected with any supervisory responsibilities assigned to him, and therefore his employer was not vicariously liable for the assault. A similar negative conclusion often follows in workplace prank cases.[2] Two exceptions should briefly be discussed.

First, vicarious liability for a workplace prank may follow if the prank arises in the conduct of the prankster's authorised responsibilities or functions. In *Harrison v Michelin Tyre Co Ltd*,[3] an employee injured his back as the result of a fall caused by a prank. By means of a hand trolley, a fellow employee had raised and then dropped a duckboard on which the plaintiff was standing. Because the prankster's job was to push the trolley, his act was held to be reasonably incidental to the course of his employment and the employer was vicariously liable. Similarly, when a summer temp was instructed by his employer to follow the instructions of his fellow employees, who commanded him to place his hand in a machine, the employer was vicariously liable for the negligent act of accidentally turning on the machine to the temp's injury.[4] These decisions pre-date the close connection test, so, if similar facts arose today, they would need to be re-analysed using the modern law.[5]

Secondly, it has been suggested that, where the employer is aware of the employee's tendency to play pranks, that this means any delict arising from that employee's prank is closely connected to the employment relationship.[6] This confuses vicarious liability with the employer's primary liability: the knowledge of the employer is relevant to primary, not vicarious, liability.

1 [2010] CSIH 35, 2010 SLT 671.
2 See eg *Somerville v Harsco Infrastructure Ltd* 2015 GWD 38-607; *Graham v Commercial Bodyworks Ltd* [2015] EWCA Civ 47; *Chell v Tarmac Cement and Lime Ltd* [2022] EWCA Civ 7.
3 [1985] ICR 696 (QBD).
4 *Chapman v Oakleigh Animal Products Ltd*, Court of Appeal of England and Wales, reported in (1970) 8 *Managerial Law* 1063.
5 The prank in *Harrison* involved a momentary deviation from the employee's assigned functions, and the employer in *Chapman* authorised the negligent employee to give orders to the plaintiff, so it is suggested that such a connection would exist.
6 *Nelson v John Lewis Plc* [2024] SC EDIN 10 at para 69 and 74–75.

(7) Employee theft

15.17 Where an employee is tasked with looking after an item of property, and they misappropriate that item, then the employer might be vicariously liable for that theft or any ensuing damage to the property.[1] In *Central Motors (Glasgow) v Cessnock Garage and Motor Company*,[2] the pursuer entrusted a car to the defenders. A nightwatchman took the car for a joyride, damaging it in a crash. In the Inner House, Lord Cullen stated that:[3]

> 'An honest master does not employ or authorise his servant to commit crimes of dishonesty towards third parties; but nevertheless he may incur liability for a crime of dishonesty committed by the servant if it was committed by him within the field of activities which the employment assigned to him, and that although the crime was committed by the servant solely in pursuance of his own private advantage.'

The nightwatchman 'acted ill' in his assigned duty to take care of the car, and therefore the garage owner was vicariously liable for his theft and damage to the car.[4] An employer may be vicariously liable where an employee who is entrusted to carry out a particular process in relation to property misappropriates the property in the course of that process.[5] But where it cannot be shown that the devious employee had authorised functions in respect of the property, vicarious liability may be harder to establish.[6]

Where an employee's assigned functions includes administration of a tendering process, and they take a bribe in order to award the tender to a particular party, the employer may be vicariously liable to an unsuccessful bidder for the employee's wrongdoing in accepting the bribe.[7]

1 Where the stolen property later causes harm to a third party, it may be difficult to establish a close connection: *Vance v Bough* 2008 Rep LR 90 (OH).
2 1925 SC 796 (IH).
3 *Central Motors (Glasgow)* at 802.
4 See too *Morris v CW Martin & Sons* [1966] 1 QB 716 (CA) (theft of mink fur by employee of cleaning firm: firm vicariously liable).
5 *Brink's Global Services v Igrox* [2010] EWCA Civ 207, [2011] IRLR 343 (employee entrusted to fumigate cargo stole silver bars from that cargo; employer held vicariously liable).
6 *The Huntsworth Wine Company Ltd v London City Bond* [2021] EWHC 2831 (Comm) at paras 172–176 (a case where it could not be established which of the defendant's employees had passed on information about the location of valuable wine to thieves).
7 *Oil States Industries (UK) Ltd v S* [2022] CSOH 52, 2023 SC 209.

(8) Misrepresentation by an employee

15.18 It seems that the close connection test does not apply, however, where the employee's fraud induces a third party to enter into a particular course of action. Instead, the analysis turns into one from the law of agency: did the employee have actual or ostensible authority to make the representation, or enter into the fraudulent transaction?[1] If the answer is 'yes', then the employer will be liable as the employee's principal. Use of this separate test, confirmed post-*Lister*,[2] supposedly is justified on the basis that it applies only to wrongdoing where the pursuer has in some sense relied on the employee's representation, in situations where it always is possible for the pursuer to check with the principal as to the scope of the employee's authority before proceeding with any transaction.[3] That same logic should mean that the test also should apply for cases of negligent misstatement, but no conclusive authority exists on this point.[4]

1 See eg *Lloyd v Grace, Smith & Co* [1912] AC 716 (HL); *Armagas v Mundogas SA* [1986] AC 717; *Taylor v Glasgow District Council* 1997 SC 183 (IH).
2 *Winter v Hockley Mint Ltd* [2018] EWCA Civ 2480; [2019] 1 WLR 1617.
3 See eg *Armagas* at 739 per Robert Goff LJ. The House of Lords upheld the Court of Appeal's judgment on the vicarious liability point.
4 For discussion, see PG Watts and FMB Reynolds, *Bowstead & Reynolds on Agency* (23rd edn, Sweet & Maxwell, 2023) at para 8-180.

PRINCIPAL AND AGENT

15.19 It is often said that a principal is vicariously liable for the wrongs of its agent. But, as we have just seen, the law of agency does not use a close connection test but instead enquires into the authority possessed by the agent: actual authority, apparent/ostensible authority created by the conduct or representation of the principal, or post-facto authorisation through ratification. However, liability of the principal for delicts committed by an agent having authority either is a personal liability of the principal, or involves the attribution to the principal of the agent's wrongful act. It is not 'vicarious liability' in the sense discussed in this chapter, and no more will be said on the matter.[1] If an employment or employment-like relationship also exists between principal and agent, however, then vicarious liability in the terms discussed in this chapter may arise: but that arises out of the (quasi)-employment relationship, not the relationship of agent and principal.

1 For fuller discussion, see L McGregor, *The Law of Agency in Scotland* (SULI) (W. Green, 2013), Chapter 13; PG Watts and FMB Reynolds, *Bowstead & Reynolds on Agency* (Sweet & Maxwell, 2023), paras 8-178–204.

CHAPTER 16

Prescription and Limitation

INTRODUCTION

16.1 Practically speaking, one of the most important questions in the law of delict is determining when the right to sue comes into existence. If you fail to do this, you risk losing your right to claim damages, regardless of the legal merits of your case. In other words, if you delay too long, you may lose the opportunity to seek compensation from the defender.

In this chapter, we will examine the impact of the passage of time on a claim. Specifically, we will consider situations where someone's right to claim is either barred by the court, known as limitation, or completely extinguished by law due to the passage of time, known as prescription. Our main objective is to explain the key concepts that underpin this area of law.

It is important to note that prescription and limitation are notoriously complex topics, often subject to legislative amendments. Specific cases can give rise to fact-sensitive considerations, which must always be checked against the most recent legislative updates or judicial interpretations. Here, we aim to provide an overview of the concepts and their operation rather than an exhaustive account of the law.[1] Our approach assumes that loss or damage occurred on or after 1 June 2022.[2]

The highly technical nature of prescription and limitation can often obscure the fact that these rules implement fundamental principles of civil law. Various historical, political, moral, and policy factors have shaped the boundaries of the law of delict. Of course, the extent to which we can expect certain conduct from each other, and the ways in which we can practically realise those expectations, are profoundly influenced by doctrines of liability, such as the duty of care, which we have already covered in earlier chapters. Crucially, however, these expectations are also affected by rules that prohibit or restrict access to the resources of a court, that is prescription and limitation.

By barring or extinguishing claims, the rules of prescription and limitation fundamentally determine how questions of otherwise historical injustice are resolved. For example, for many years, claims for historical sexual abuse of children were refused due to the passage of time.[3] Although recent legislative amendments have attempted to correct this issue,[4] this episode starkly demonstrates the power of otherwise technical rules relating to so-called time-barred claims, regardless of the underlying merits of the legal case.

Numerous reasons can be offered in support of these rules. Prescription is an ancient concept, found in early texts of Roman law,[5] and has evolved throughout various periods of legal development in various European jurisdictions. Over the centuries, different reasons have been offered.[6] One reason, which still resonates today, is that civil law aims to resolve disputes and maintain a peaceful society.[7] Allowing historic cases could lead to endless disputes, creating a litigious and fractious society.

Similarly, limitation has an ancient history, and its rationale is much the same as that of prescription. However, limitation is particularly concerned with the process of litigation. From an early period, legislators and courts invoking the concept of limitation have often been concerned that evidence may no longer be viable after the passage of time. Witnesses' memories can fade, the authenticity of documents can become uncertain, and vital evidence may be lost. In other words, cases can become stale.[8] Courts, therefore, are reluctant to let such cases proceed.[9]

1 For more extensive accounts, see D Johnston, *Prescription and Limitation* (2nd edn, W. Green, 2012); DM Walker and EJ Russell, *Prescription and Limitation (Scotland) Act 1973* (7th edn, W. Green, 2021). See also E Reid, *The Law of Delict in Scotland* (2022) paras 30.01–30.22 and *Discussion Paper on Prescription* (Scot Law Com No 160, 2016).

2 Although this date appears arbitrary, it is significant as certain aspects of the rules applicable to prescription operate differently before this date as per the Prescription (Scotland) Act 2018 (Commencement, Saving and Transitional Provisions) Regulations 2022. For discussion see AR Taylor and J Stirling, 'A Changing Balance in Short Negative Prescription' 2023 SLT (News) 155–161. Litigation concerning the pre-1 June 2022 position regarding short negative prescription continues: *Tilbury Douglas Construction Limited v Ove Arup & Partners Scotland Limited* [2024] CSIH 15, 2024 SC 383 (appeal to UK Supreme Court outstanding at time of writing).

3 See M Campbell and B Lindsay, 'Vicarious Liability in Scotland' in P Giliker (ed), *Vicarious Liability in the Common Law World* (2022) at 215–217.

4 Limitation (Childhood Abuse) (Scotland) Act 2017.

5 *Institutes of Roman Law by Gaius, with a Translation and Commentary by the late Edward Poste* (4th edn, Clarendon Press, 1904) 2.44.

6 For a majestic summary, see D Johnston, *Prescription and Limitation* (W. Green, 2012) paras 1.31–164. See also H Dondorp, D Ibbeston and E Schrage (eds), *Limitation and Prescription: A Comparative Legal History* (Duncker & Humblot, 2019). In Scotland, the most serious attempt at justification can be found in the nineteenth century: M Napier, *Commentaries on the Law of Prescription in Scotland* (2nd edn, 1854) 1–7.

7 See *Brisbane Regional Health Authority v Taylor* (1996) 186 CLR 541 at 551–554 per McHugh J.

8 *AS v Poor Sisters of Nazareth* [2008] UKHL 32, 2008 SC (HL) 146 at para 5 per Lord Hope of Craighead.

9 See *B v Murray (No 2)* 2005 SLT 982 at paras 21-22, 28-29 per Lord Drummond Young.

PRESCRIPTION AND LIMITATION (SCOTLAND) ACT 1973

16.2 The primary legislation in this area is the Prescription and Limitation (Scotland) Act 1973. It is significant for several reasons. First, it consolidated the existing Scottish common law on prescription, which had evolved over centuries, and organised the older legislation into a unified system. It is now rarely necessary to consult earlier versions of the law to resolve issues relating to prescription or limitation. Secondly, it harmonised the Scottish and English conceptions of limitation, essentially utilising the English notion that it is a procedural bar against an action. However, it is important to note that it did not unify Scottish law with English law: the time periods and other related matters can be subtly but vitally different. Thirdly, the 1973 Act remains the anchor point for the law in this area regardless of subsequent updates or amendments, which are incorporated into the Act, and this also means that it covers a vast number of rights and obligations, which might not always be evident on first reading. For the most part, all necessary statutory guidance is contained within the 1973 Act, albeit one must refer sometimes to judicial interpretation of the Act. Naturally, therefore, the 1973 Act has undergone numerous amendments over the years, admittedly making it somewhat challenging to navigate. However, it is the central foundation for the law of prescription and limitation.

Prescription can either be positive or negative. Positive prescription is said to fortify 'doubtful titles by consuming existing ones.'[1] A classic example is when the ownership of a small strip of land at the end of a garden is uncertain. In such cases, a conveyancer typically drafts a title for the land in the name of the garden's owner and registers it with the Land Register of Scotland. According to the rules of *positive* prescription, if 10 years pass peacefully and without judicial interruption, the garden's owner becomes the owner of the small strip of land. In contrast negative prescription is said to 'consume rights and obligations.'[2] A common example of negative prescription occurs when someone fails to raise a negligence claim in time after their property is damaged. It is important to remember that negative prescription completely extinguishes the legal claim, unless parties agree to extend the period.[3] For instance, any obligation for reparation ceases to exist, and previously significant facts become legally irrelevant simply due to the lapse of time. This chapter focuses on negative prescription.

Limitation measures the passage of time and prevents someone from raising an action, but it does not extinguish the right or obligation. In theory, prescription is a rule of substantive law that goes to the very essence of the legal claim; thus, it is said to extinguish the right. Limitation, on the other hand, acknowledges that a legal right or obligation still exists but prevents the action from proceeding. It can be helpful to view limitation as a procedural rule of the court, aimed at ensuring the efficient use of its resources and the reliability of the evidence presented. The 1973 Act incorporates both concepts, with Part I addressing prescription and Part II addressing limitation.

1 D Johnston, *Prescription and Limitation* (W. Green, 2012) para 1.01.
2 Ibid.
3 1973 Act, s 13.

16.3 There are several important distinctions between limitation and prescription, some are mentioned here:

- The defender must raise limitation as a plea against the competency of the action. If they fail to do so, the court does not necessarily need to take notice of limitation. Prescription, however, is something which a court is bound to take notice of regardless of the parties' pleadings.
- In general, the court has the authority to override the time limits imposed by limitation. To do so the court needs to be persuaded that it is equitable and would not prejudice the defender in being able to defend the action.[1]
- Parties can voluntarily extend the prescription period by a maximum of one year at a time. However, with limitation, parties can waive their right to insist on limitation applying.[2]
- Often, the decision to waive a limitation period is made because the defender is eager to – and of course confident they will – obtain a favourable judgment on a point of law. There can be various strategic reasons as to why that matters to a defender. Prescription is not something that a defender can control.

It is worth also explaining some additional concepts which do not appear within the legislation, but which can be found in the reported case law. For example, the long prescription period refers to the time for which a claim remains viable regardless of whether the pursuer is aware they have a claim or not.[3] For example, if your property is damaged regardless of whether you are unaware of the cause of your injury and could not have known at that time, your right will prescribe after twenty years. Sometimes the end date for long prescription is called the long-stop date.

On the other hand, short prescription or sometimes short negative prescription refers to the period given to a person to raise an action following the date upon which they became aware or should have been aware that they had suffered damage or injury. For instance, if you become aware of what caused damage to your property then you have five years within which to raise your action.[4] This is an exception to the default rule for prescription – which will be examined further below – that, in an action for damages, the relevant time starts to run from the date the loss occurred, regardless of the pursuer's knowledge. Short prescription therefore is relevant when the date of knowledge is later than the date of loss, providing an important exception to the default rule in situations where it would be inequitable to the pursuer for their claim to be barred.

1 Johnston, *Prescription* at para 13.08.
2 1973 Act, s 13.
3 Johnston, *Prescription* at para 7.05.
4 The Prescription (Scotland) Act 2018 has now reserved the Supreme Court's interpretation of negative short prescription under the old law in *David T Morrison & Co Limited v ICL Plastics Limited* [2014] UKSC 48, 2014 SC (UKSC) 222. But that interpretation still applies to instances of injury or damage sustained prior to 1 June 2022. For discussion, see *Glasgow City Council v VFS Financial Services* [2022] CSIH 1, 2022 SC 133 at para 3 per Lord Tyre.

TYPES OF CLAIMS

16.4 It is important to grasp the types of claims for reparation that a pursuer may make, including how the 1973 Act characterises those claims. Section 6 of the 1973 Act refers to Sch 1, which identifies the following types of loss or damage, which give rise to a right of reparation:

- Death and personal injury, including psychological or psychiatric injury.
- Damages for personal injury following the death.
- Injury or damage covered by the Consumer Protection Act 1987.
- Damage to reputation.
- Damage to economic interests.
- Damage to property.

Identifying the type of claim is key to locating the relevant rules in the 1973 Act. There can be different limitation and prescription periods for different types of claims. For example, importantly, personal injury (including psychiatric/psychological injury) claims do *not* prescribe under the 1973 Act,[1] yet they are subject to a three-year limitation period.[2] On the other hand, a personal injury sustained due to a defective consumer product as per the Consumer Protection Act 1987 *does* prescribe after a 10-year period,[3] while at the same time has a limitation period of three years.[4] Moreover, limitation does not apply to damage to property or economic losses, yet of course, prescription does apply in these circumstances.

1 1973 Act, s 7(2); Sch 1, para 2(g).
2 1973 Act, ss 17 and 18.
3 1973 Act, s 22A.
4 1973 Act, s 22B.

DETERMINING THE START DATE

16.5 Once you know how your claim is classified, determining the start date is of the utmost importance. To begin, we shall outline the basics below, tackling more complex issues thereafter. It is easier to consider limitation and prescription side by side in this section, albeit there can be subtle differences in some instances.

(1) Identify the start date

16.6 Section 11(1) of the 1973 Act sets out the start date for prescription regarding the obligation to make reparation. It states plainly:

> 'any obligation to pay damages (whatever the source of the obligation) for loss, injury or damage caused by an act or omission shall be regarded for the purposes of section 6 of this Act as having become enforceable *on the date when the loss, injury or damage occurred*'.

If the act which has caused loss, injury or damage is continuing, s 11(2) confirms that the date will be 'deemed for the purposes of subsection (1) above to have occurred on the date when the act or omission ceased.'

In terms of limitation, different rules apply depending on the type of injury or damage. Part II of the 1973 Act, which covers limitation, needs to be carefully examined to ensure the right provisions are applied. However, s 17 is important as it applies to actions in respect of personal injuries not resulting in death, by far the most frequently raised action in Scotland. Here, the start date is stated under s 17(2)(a) to be:

> 'the date on which the injuries were sustained or, where the act or omission to which the injuries were attributable was a continuing one, that date or the date on which the act or omission ceased, whichever is the later'.

Although the statutory drafting of each is slightly different – eg the use of 'sustained' versus 'occurred' – courts are generally mindful when interpreting ss 11(1) and 17 (2)(a) that there is a degree of consistency between the two. The primary expectation is that there has been a legally recoverably type of loss or injury (sometimes referred to as *damnum*) which was caused by some form of wrongful act (sometimes referred to as *injuria* or default).[1]

1 *Dunlop v M'Gowans* 1980 SC (HL) 73; *David T Morrison & Co Limited v ICL Plastics Limited and others* [2014] UKSC 48, 2014 SC (UKSC) 222.

(2) Postponing the start date

16.7 The start date for limitation of personal injury claims can be postponed if the pursuer can demonstrate they were unaware that they had suffered a loss or injury. Section 17(2)(b) states:

'the date (if later than any date mentioned in paragraph (a) above) on which the pursuer in the action became, or on which, in the opinion of the court, it would have been reasonably practicable for him in all the circumstances to become, aware of all the following facts—

(i) that the injuries in question were sufficiently serious to justify his bringing an action of damages on the assumption that the person against whom the action was brought did not dispute liability and was able to satisfy a decree;

(ii) that the injuries were attributable in whole or in part to an act or omission; and

(iii) that the defender was a person to whose act or omission the injuries were attributable in whole or in part or the employer or principal of such a person'.

16.8 This section is generous to pursuers. Consequently, the reported case law often involves marginal cases that regularly fail to pass the threshold set by s 17(2)(b). For example, in *Agnew v Scott Lithgow Ltd No 2*,[1] the pursuer raised proceedings against his former employers for an injury caused whilst operating heavy machinery, known as vibration white finger (VWF). He had suffered symptoms since 1982, such as cold hands, but did not know the cause of it. Upon finishing his employment in September 1995, he continued to suffer symptoms, and towards the end of that year, he became aware of VWF. He was informed by the end of 1995 that his colleagues were raising court proceedings against their former employer for damages due to VWF, yet he did not seek medical treatment at this point to ascertain if he himself had VWF. For the pursuer, the starting date was February 1998, when he was informed that he did, in fact, have VWF and raised proceedings thereafter. However, his case failed to demonstrate that there was justification under s 17(2)(b) to stop the limitation clock. The Inner House concluded that:

'the pursuer ought to have been aware that he should make enquiry about his condition once he heard talk from his former colleagues about making claims arising out of having contracted VWF.'[2] (454)

It was at this point, he should have known his injuries were serious, attributable to an act or omission and that his former employer was, at least, in part responsible.

1 2003 SC 448 (IH).
2 *Agnew* at 453.

16.9 As noted, limitation does not apply to damage to property or economic interests. However, prescription does pertain here and hence there are specific rules set out in the 1973 Act with respect to postponement of prescription. Section 11(3) of the Act provides:

'In relation to a case where on the date referred to in subsection (1) above (or, as the case may be, that subsection as modified by subsection (2) above) the creditor was not aware, and could not with reasonable diligence have been aware, of each of the facts mentioned in subsection (3A), the said subsection (1) shall have effect as if for the reference therein to that date there were substituted a reference to the date when the creditor first became, or could with reasonable diligence have become, so aware.

(3A) The facts referred to in subsection (3) are—

(a) that loss, injury or damage has occurred,

(b) that the loss, injury or damage was caused by a person's act or omission, and

(c) the identity of that person.

(3B) It does not matter for the purposes of subsections (3) and (3A) whether the creditor is aware that the act or omission that caused the loss, injury or damage is actionable in law.'

Glasper v Rodger[1] offers a useful illustration of s 11(3)'s operation. In this case, the pursuer sought damages from their former solicitors, based on professional negligence. In 1984, the defender was acting on behalf of the pursuers in a property transaction. Following the successful purchase of the Atholl Arms Hotel by the pursuers, the defender wrongly registered the title to the hotel, giving sole ownership to the son of the pursuer. By giving exclusive ownership in the hotel to the son, the defender had acted contrary to the pursuer's instructions. The pursuer stated they only discovered this in August 1985, after their son disappeared, and a creditor sought to reclaim the hotel to satisfy the debts owed by their son. The defenders argued that the case was time-barred, as the loss occurred on the date the wrong title was registered. The pursuer argued that their ignorance of the loss was ongoing and not due to a lack of reasonable diligence, requesting a postponement of the date. On their analysis, prescription started from when the pursuers were aware of the solicitor's negligence. Therefore, they raised their action in 1990, exactly five-years after that date. The pursuers were eventually successful in persuading the Inner House that they should be allowed, on this basis, to prove they were not aware until a later date and on that basis their case had not prescribed.

1 1996 SLT 44 (IH).

EQUITABLE DISPENSATION OF LIMITATION

16.10 To recap: it will be recalled that there are no limitation rules on claims concerning damage or loss of property, as well as claims related to economic interests. For our purposes, this means that limitation applies to cases concerning (i) personal injury which did not result in death, (ii) actions where death resulted from personal injuries, (iii) actions for harassment; and (iv) actions relating to reputation. Of course, there are other types of action covered by Part II of the 1973 Act. Putting aside questions of prescription which have already been addressed above, in such cases involving, for example, personal injury, you may fail to surmount the limitation hurdle set out in s 17, ie you did not raise your case within three years. Furthermore, you may have been unable to convince the court to postpone the start date due to ignorance. In such a scenario, the 1973 Act offers pursuers one last opportunity to escape the effects of time upon their claim: the court's power to override time limits set under Part II.

Section 19A is a considerable power offered to the court to ensure that legitimate cases, which might otherwise fail the limitation hurdle, are given the opportunity to be examined by the court. Subsection (1) says:

> 'Where a person would be entitled, but for any of the provisions of section 17, 18, 18A or 18B of this Act, to bring an action, the court may, if it seems to it equitable to do so, allow him to bring the action notwithstanding that provision (but see section 19AA).'

This is an equitable power. In practice, it gives discretion to the judge to determine the matter. All the circumstances of the case are taken into consideration, including the length of time in bringing the action, whether the pursuer was responsible for the delay, whether there is an action available against the pursuer's solicitor if the solicitor was responsible for the delay, the inconvenience to the defender etc.[1] In practice, the power is used sparingly in claims for personal injuries or death from personal injuries because of the knowledge provisions which must be satisfied before the three-year limitation period begins to run

1 See *McCullough v Norwest Socea Ltd* 1981 SLT 201 (OH); *Carson v Howard Doris Ltd* 1981 SC 278 (OH); *Donald v Rutherford* 1984 SLT 70 (IH); *Whyte v Walker* 1983 SLT 441(OH); *Clark v McLean* 1994 SC 410 (IH); *Gorrie v Marist Brothers* 2002 SCLR 436 (OH); *Harrison v West of Scotland Kart Club* [2008] CSOH 33; *AS v Poor Sisters of Nazareth* [2008] UKHL 32, 2008 SC (HL) 146; *Sinclair v Morrison* [2009] CSOH 81; *Chinn v Cyclacel Ltd* [2013] CSOH 17, 2013 SLT 278; *A v N* [2013] CSOH 161.

CONCLUSION

16.11 In Scotland and elsewhere in the UK, it is now the legislator who determines what should and should not prescribe, what should be limited, and the respective time periods, yet it is the courts who apply the law and retain a reasonable amount of power to shape the development of the law in this area.

Given the political nature of these questions, and the significance of depriving otherwise legitimate claims for justice it is appropriate that the legislator should take the lead in this area. Nonetheless, limiting access to courts is controversial. For example, The Northern Ireland Troubles (Legacy and Reconciliation) Act 2023 contains provisions that affect civil liability related to the Troubles in Northern Ireland. Specifically, the Act restricts the initiation of new civil proceedings for Troubles-related offences. While the Act seeks to promote reconciliation, some may feel that it perpetuates injustice.[1] Or take, for example, claims for reparations which the ancestors of those enslaved on plantations may raise against modern-day beneficiaries.[2] Such claims are, for numerous reasons, incompetent under the law of delict, including the rules of prescription and limitation. Yet this does not mean that theoretical defenders do not feel a moral obligation to make reparation.[3]

This chapter provides only an overview of the key concepts and ideas around prescription and limitation. Because of the complexity of specific cases that lead to disputes in this field, only a brief outline has been possible. However, as demonstrated, prescription and limitation are far from being merely technical topics; they reveal much about the nature of the law of delict and can significantly impact the outcome of a pursuer's case.

1 A Deb and C Murray, 'An Unfortunate Legacy: Fixing the Northern Ireland Troubles (Legacy and Reconciliation) Act 2023', UK Constitutional Law Blog (29 July 2024) (available at https://ukconstitutionallaw.org/). Accessed 19 June 2025. The UK Government has signalled its intention to repeal the 2023 Act.

2 S Mullen and S Newman, *Slavery, Abolition and the University of Glasgow: Report and Recommendations of the University of Glasgow History of Slavery Steering Committee* (2018).

3 See eg the statement of the University of Glasgow's Senior Management Group (available at https://www.gla.ac.uk/explore/historicalslaveryinitiative/report/). Accessed 19 June 2025.

CHAPTER 17

Damages

17.1 In this chapter, we examine the principles governing the award of damages – a monetary sum paid to a pursuer as compensation. Damages are understood here as a judicial remedy granted in response to a civil wrong committed by the defender. We will also explore the methods used to assess the appropriate amount to be awarded.

From the perspective of delict, damages represent the conclusion of the legal process. However, for the pursuer, they mark the beginning: compensation for the occurrence of a loss or injury is usually what prompts the pursuit of a remedy. Legally, though, one must rewind the narrative to its origin before damages can be claimed. The pursuer must first establish: (1) the existence of a legal obligation or duty; (2) a breach of that obligation; (3) a causal link between the breach and the loss or injury; (4) that the defender is the party responsible; and (5) that the claim is not barred by prescription or limitation.

Only once these foundational elements are satisfied can the pursuer proceed to quantify the damages sought. The first half of this chapter will address these core principles, while the second half will focus on the calculation of damages and the identification of those entitled to claim them.

THE PURPOSE OF DAMAGES

17.2 In Scots law, a court will be guided by the principle that damages should restore the pursuer to the position they would have been in had they not suffered the wrongful loss or injury. Damages are, therefore, restorative, not punitive, in Scots law.[1] Defenders are not punished, and pursuers are not avenged, by the law of delict.[2] Pursuers' losses are repaired, and defenders' wrongs are righted by payment of monetary compensation.[3] In some situations, it is easy to know how much should be paid – replacing the bumper of a car involves the cost of the replacement part and the labour in fitting it. However, in other situations the award of damages can only offer a monetary representation of full reparation, but can never adequately replace what was lost – you cannot bring a deceased relative back to life or reverse blindness by a monetary payment.

Scottish courts are mindful that the award should not be any more than what is appropriate to restore the pursuer to their previous position.[4] Once this award is granted, the issue is considered closed from a civil law standpoint.[5]

Parties are free to settle the dispute without litigating the matter in court. The effect of any voluntary agreement, and whether it is a full and final settlement of the pursuer's claim will, however, depend on the terms of that agreement.[6] In some situations, a settlement agreement will not satisfy the full amount due to a pursuer, raising the question as to whether the defender can reinitiate proceedings or sue another joint wrongdoer to make up the shortfall.[7] If any subsequent claim is raised, courts will pay close attention to any prior contractual relationship between the pursuer and the defender and the context within which the agreement was concluded, before allowing any additional claim to be raised.[8]

Note, there are other situations where the award of damages serves a vindicatory purpose.[9] Here, a right, such as reputation, has been infringed and, regardless of a related loss (ie economic interests, such as to one's business activities) the award of damages aims to set the record straight, so to speak. Thus, the award of damages can, in some situations (particularly regarding intentional delicts) operate as an acknowledgement of the wrong itself, ie represent a monetary correction of the infraction of that right. There is, however, very little judicial examination of the meaning of vindicatory damages and, as a concept itself, is rarely utilised by the courts in Scotland.[10]

1 *Black v North British Railway Co* 1908 SC 444 (IH).
2 *Winter v News Scotland Ltd* 1991 SLT 828 (IH).
3 *Auld v Shairp* (1874) 2 R 191 (IH).
4 *Tang Man Sit (Deceased) v Capacious Investments Ltd* [1996] AC 514 (PC, Hong Kong) at 522, approved in *Kidd v Lime Rock Management LLP* [2021] CSIH 62, 2021 SLT 1499 at para 3.
5 *Balfour v Baird & Sons* 1959 SC 64 (IH).
6 *Ward v WM Morrison Supermarkets Plc* [2025] SC EDIN 17.
7 For a fuller account of the law, see *Heaton v Axa Equity & Law Life Assurance Society Plc* [2002] UKHL 15, [2002] 2 AC 329 at paras 64–83 per Lord Rodger of Earlsferry.
8 *Kidd v Lime Rock*.
9 See eg *Mackenzie v Cluny Hydropathic Co Ltd* 1908 SC 200 (IH).
10 For discussion, see E Reid, *The Law of Delict in Scotland* (2022) at para 3.04. See also J Brown, 'Obtaining the "main keys to wisdom": Distinguishing "Damages" from Other Pecuniary Remedies in Scots law' (2023) 27(1) *Edinburgh Law Review* 77.

IDENTIFYING RECOVERABLE LOSSES

(1) The basic problem

17.3 Given that the primary purpose of an award of damages is to provide compensation, a core principle of Scots law is that a defender is only liable to make reparation for losses that can reasonably be said to have resulted from the wrongful act. In other words, a defender is not expected to compensate the pursuer for every factual loss subsequently arising. Regardless of what a pursuer might consider to be connected to the defender's wrongdoing, the current law seeks to find the correct balance between the parties about the recovery of losses.[1] Underlying this is a basic problem of distributive justice: where should the line be drawn regarding the repair of the pursuer's losses?

For example, A, driving carelessly, knocks down a pedestrian, B. Here, if B sues, she will recover an award of *solatium*, for her pain and suffering, plus damages for any derivative economic loss, such as loss of earnings sustained during a period of recuperation. The latter includes loss of wages between the date of the accident and the date of the court action; future loss of earnings from the date of the action (if B is unable to work or can work only at a lower paid job); the cost of medical treatment and nursing up to the date of the action and the cost of such care in the future. So far, so good.

However, problems arise because the effect of the accident on B's life is not necessarily limited to these things. Courts must draw a line for the sake of finality. For instance, if because of the accident, B was unable to give instructions to their stockbroker to purchase shares which they had intended to buy or is unable to place a bet on a forthcoming football match because of the accident, the profits that B would have made on these things are said to be unrecoverable. Even though it could be reasonably said that they arise from the fact that B was incapacitated because of the accident, the law seeks to find an endpoint for the recovery of losses.

Of course, it may be natural for B to suppose that all of this is the responsibility of A, and for a period of time courts were generous in this manner towards pursuers, allowing claims for direct losses following from the constituent wrong, without necessarily calibrating what this might include.[2] However, the law of delict now takes a different approach to negligently-caused losses. As Viscount Simonds famously remarked:[3]

> '[a] man must be considered to be responsible for the probable consequences of his act. To demand more of him is too harsh a rule, to demand less is to ignore that civilised order requires the observance of a minimum standard of behaviour'.

For present purposes, this is the critical question: how do courts identify and exclude losses which a pursuer may wish to recover from a defender?

1 See eg *Simmons v British Steel plc* 2004 SC (HL) 94.
2 *Polemis and Furness, Withy & Co (Re)* [1921] 3 KB 560, applied by *McKillen v Barclay Curle & Co Ltd* 1967 SLT 41, yet not followed by *Cowan v National Coal Board* 1958 SLT (Notes) 19.
3 *Overseas Tankship (UK) Ltd v Morts Dock & Engineering Co Ltd (The Wagon Mound)* [1961] AC 388 at p 422–423, approved by Lord Rodger in *Simmons v British Steel Plc* 2004 SC (HL) 94 at para 63.

(2) The grand rule of damages

17.4 Traditionally, the approach of Scots courts to the basic problem of recoverability was to ask if the losses were too remote. The classic statement of the rule on remoteness of losses in Scots law was articulated by the Lord Ordinary (Kinloch) in *Allan v Barclay*:[1]

> 'The grand rule on the subject of damages is, that none can be claimed except such as naturally and directly arise out of the wrong done; and such, therefore, as may reasonably be supposed to have been in the contemplation of the wrongdoer.'

Although the grand rule of damages has an appealing simplicity, it can be difficult to know in practice how it will operate from case-to-case and, specifically, how it interacts with other doctrines, such as the duty of care and causation. In fact, it should be noted that *Allan v Barclay* was concerned with whether an employer could recover damages for the loss of his injured employee's services, ie a pure economic loss claim. In other words, it was concerned with the defender's liability in the first place rather than the remoteness of losses suffered.[2] Thus, today *Allan* would be analysed from the point of view of the duty of care; that is, *Allan* is an example of something falling beyond the duty of care owed by the defender. It is not about the remoteness of losses. What this means is that in the case of personal injuries, the remoteness test has been somewhat jettisoned and replaced by other doctrines. However, it still has an important role to play in cases where economic or property loss was suffered by the pursuer.[3]

1 (1864) 2 M 873.
2 As noted in *Simmons v British Steel Plc* [2004] UKHL 20, 2004 SC (HL) 94 at para 61 per Lord Rodger.
3 See eg *Manorgate Limited v First Scottish Property Services Limited* [2013] CSOH 108.

(3) The *Simmons* approach to recoverability

17.5 The modern law regarding recoverability was set out in the leading case of *Simmons v British Steel*.[1] Here, the House of Lords made evident that the law of Scotland no longer relied solely on the grand rule as a means by which to identify recoverable losses; nor was it the case a pursuer could simply sue for all direct losses which flowed from the constituent wrong.

In this case, the pursuer was employed as a steel worker. He sustained a severe head injury after tripping and falling, striking his head on a metal stanchion. Following the accident, his pre-existing skin condition worsened, and he developed a severe depressive illness due to personality changes. It was established that the system of working was inadequate, and the defenders were negligent. From a factual perspective, it was the delay between the pursuer's fall and the development of the subsequent skin condition and depression some weeks later which raised questions as to whether these losses related to the defender's wrongdoing.

Initially, the pursuer was awarded damages for the physical head injury he suffered, but the Lord Ordinary refused to award damages for the onset of his skin condition and depression. The Inner House, however, disagreed, and allowed the pursuer to claim for the skin condition and depression. Eventually, reaching the House of Lords, the pursuer was again successful, but the legal justification offered by the Inner House was re-examined by the Lords Hope and Rodger. Central to this case, therefore, was determining the correct principles upon which to determine what the pursuer could recover from the defender.

In dismissing the defender's appeal, Lord Rodger summarised the relevant principles:[2]

> 'These authorities suggest that, once liability is established, any question of the remoteness of damage is to be approached along the following lines which may, of course, be open to refinement and development.
>
> (1) The starting point is that a defender is not liable for a consequence of a kind which is not reasonably foreseeable.[3]
>
> (2) While a defender is not liable for damage that was not reasonably foreseeable, it does not follow that he is liable for all damage that was reasonably foreseeable: depending on the circumstances, the defender may not be liable for damage caused by a novus actus interveniens or unreasonable conduct on the part of the pursuer, even if it was reasonably foreseeable.[4]
>
> (3) Subject to the qualification in (2), if the pursuer's injury is of a kind that was foreseeable, the defender is liable, even if the damage is greater in extent than was foreseeable or it was caused in a way that could not have been foreseen.[5]
>
> (4) The defender must take his victim as he finds him.[6]
>
> (5) Subject again to the qualification in (2), where personal injury to the pursuer was reasonably foreseeable, the defender is liable for any personal injury, whether physical or psychiatric, which the pursuer suffers as a result of his wrongdoing.'[7]

Lord Rodger here summarises how losses are minimised, considering several doctrines which all play a functional role in limiting a claim for damages. Of course, these doctrines are not all strictly relevant to an assessment of damages itself. For example, questions relating to the existence of the duty of care in the first place and the scope of that duty, eg questions of liability, are different from questions of causation and *novus actus interveniens*, which are factual, which are different from inquiring into whether, after all these questions have been answered, the damages sought are too remote to be recoverable. These individual doctrines will play a role, at different stages, in determining the damages which a pursuer can claim.[8]

1 [2004] UKHL 20, 2004 SC (HL) 94.
2 *Simmons* at para 6.
3 Citing *M'Kew v Holland & Hannen & Cubitts (Scotland) Ltd* 1970 SC (HL) 20 at 25 per Lord Reid; *Bourhill v Young* 1942 SC (HL) 78 at 85 per Lord Russell of Killowen; and *Allan v Barclay* (1864) 2 M 873 (IH) at 874 per Lord Kinloch.
4 Citing *M'Kew* at 25 per Lord Reid; *Lamb v Camden London Borough Council* [1981] QB 625 (CA); and contrasting *Ward v Cannock Chase District Council* [1986] Ch 546 (Ch D).
5 Citing *Hughes v Lord Advocate* 1963 SC (HL) 31 at 38 and 40 per Lord Reid.
6 Citing *Bourhill* at 92 per Lord Wright and *M'Killen v Barclay Curle & Co Ltd* 1967 SLT 41 (IH) at 42 per Lord President Clyde.
7 Citing *Page v Smith* [1996] AC 155 (HL) at 197F–H per Lord Lloyd of Berwick.
8 Admittedly, there is an academic argument to be made that the duty of care stage is redundant in this process: PH Winfield, 'Duty in Tortious Negligence' (1934) 34 *Colombia Law Review* 14; WW Buckland, 'The Duty to Take Care' (1935) 51 *Law Quarterly Review* 637; WA Wilson 'The Analysis of Negligence' in *Introductory Essays in Scots Law* (2nd edn, W. Green, 1984); and D Nolan, 'Deconstructing the Duty of Care' (2013) 129 *Law Quarterly Review* 559. See, however, NJ McBride, 'Duties of Care – Do They Really Exist?' (2004) 24(3) *Oxford Journal of Legal Studies* 413. The courts show no appetite for removing the duty of care and allocating its functions elsewhere in the negligence enquiry.

(4) Thin skull exception

17.6 A key factor in reducing the role of remoteness in personal injury cases is the so-called thin skull exception. Provided the defender can be said to foresee that physical injury may occur, the foreseeability of the chain of events thereafter is irrelevant. Thus, even if the pursuer is found to have an abnormally thin skull, making them more susceptible to injury, or the type of injury they suffered was unusual, the defender remains fully liable for the consequences of their actions, provided it was foreseeable that their actions could cause some form of physical injury.[1] In effect, this means that, if a pursuer has an underlying physical or psychological condition, which is unforeseeable to the defender, but which is nonetheless triggered by the harm caused, the defender is liable for the extra, unexpected damage resulting from their negligence. Physical injury must be foreseeable, but not the specific consequences.

For example, if A negligently burns B, and B's predisposition to cancer is triggered by the burn, resulting in B's death, A is liable for B's death.[2] In this situation, the foreseeability of death is considered irrelevant, or alternatively, what is relevant is that the defender could foresee that their actions would cause the pursuer injury. The extent or particular consequences of the injury do not need to be foreseen, only the fact that the actions may cause physical harm. Furthermore, if the pursuer is a primary victim of physical harm, the defender is liable for causing mental or psychiatric illness, even if such illness was not reasonably foreseeable.[3]

Note, however, this exception only applies in cases of personal injury; it does not apply where the damage was negligently caused to property or economic interests. Hence, the thin skull exception deviates from the general rule: defenders are only responsible for losses which are reasonably foreseeable. Subject, therefore, to *novus actus interveniens*[4] and the scope of the duty itself,[5] a defender will be held liable for those losses which naturally arise from the breach of the duty, and which can be said to be reasonably foreseeable.[6]

1 *Hughes v Lord Advocate* 1963 SC (HL) 31.
2 *Smith v Leech Brain & Co Ltd* [1962] 2 QB 405 (QBD).
3 *Page v Smith* [1996] AC 155 (HL).
4 *M'Kew v Holland & Hannen & Cubitts (Scotland) Ltd* 1970 SC (HL) 20.
5 *Hughes.*
6 *Simmons v British Steel* 2004 SC (HL) 94; *Manorgate Limited v First Scottish Property Services* Limited [2013] CSOH 108.

(5) Mitigation

17.7 Pursuers are expected to act reasonably in managing the consequences of the injury or loss they have suffered.[1] They should not aggravate or exacerbate the situation, thereby increasing their losses. Pursuers are, therefore, expected to mitigate their losses; a failure to do so will result in a reduction of the level of damages available to them. In *Banco de Portugal v Waterlow & Sons*, Lord Macmillan explained:[2]

> 'The law is satisfied if the party placed in a difficult situation by reason of the breach of a duty owed to him has acted reasonably in the adoption of remedial measures, and he will not be held disentitled to recover the cost of such measures merely because the party in breach can suggest that other measures less burdensome to him might have been taken.'

Often characterised as a duty placed upon the pursuer to mitigate, procedurally, the burden rests on the defender to show how the pursuer should have mitigated their losses. Moreover, it is a factual question which must be assessed based on evidence produced rather than hypothetical arguments.

In *McFadden v Margiotta*,[3] the pursuer claimed £15,853 in car hire charges for the use of a Porsche Boxster for 44 days whilst his car, a seven-year-old Mercedes SL350, was being repaired following a road accident involving the defender. Reducing the pursuer's claim, Sheriff Kelly QC noted that the 'hire charges incurred can hardly be described as reasonable. The cost would have been sufficient for the pursuer to actually purchase a new car.'[4] Although the pursuer was entitled to claim for car hire costs, it was found that a local garage was offering a more suitable replacement car for the pursuer's Mercedes at the cost of £100 per day.

In contrast, the Lord Ordinary (Woolman) found in *Manorgate Ltd v First Scottish Property Services Limited*[5] that the pursuers had acted reasonably in proceeding with development plans, and so incurring costs, even after discovering that the defender had been negligent in failing to disclose that the property purchased by the pursuer had, in fact, been designated a site of archaeological significance. If the pursuer had known this, they would not have initially proceeded with the purchase. However, due to the negligence of the defender, it was only after completing the purchase of the property that the pursuer became aware of the official designation of the site. The pursuer was allowed to claim from the defender wasted expenditure on the site, including architect fees and the costs of archaeological investigations, which were carried out to determine the extent of archaeological material present on the site. It was found that '[u]ntil the full archaeological picture was known, there was a chance that its optimism would be found to be justified.'[6] The pursuer's actions were reasonable in the circumstances.

1 *Pomphrey v James A Cuthbertson Ltd* 1951 SC 147 (IH).
2 [1932] AC 452 (HL) at 506.
3 [2016] SC HAM 44.
4 *McFadden* at para 12.
5 [2013] CSOH 108.
6 *Manorgate* at para 73.

(6) Recoverability and intentional wrongs

17.8 Where the intentional wrongs are concerned, different principles apply, and the defender is liable to make reparation for all losses suffered by the pursuer which directly arise from the wrong – whether these losses are reasonably foreseeable. The intention to injure the pursuer or equivalent, ie recklessness, which is normally an essential requisite of these delicts, disposes of any question of remoteness of losses.[1]

1 *Barry v Sutherland* 2002 SLT 413.

(7) Summary on recoverability

17.9 In setting out the basic problem of recoverability, we asked: how do courts identify and exclude losses which a pursuer may wish to recover from a defender? As we have seen, *Simmons* was a significant case for its clarification of how courts should approach this issue. Misunderstanding any of these stages can lead to cases being poorly presented and dismissed early in the process.[1] Thus, a pursuer must address a series of questions, before they can formulate the losses which are legally recoverable. These questions are:

(a) Is there a duty of care regarding that specific loss? (the duty question)

(b) Did that loss fall within the scope of the duty of care? (the scope question)

(c) Can the loss be said to have been caused by the defender? (the factual causation question)

(d) Did any specific event or act intervene making it no longer reasonably possible to hold the pursuer responsible? (the *novus actus interveniens* question)

(e) Can you factually demonstrate that the loss or injury for which damages are claimed was a reasonably foreseeable consequence of the breach of duty? (the remoteness question)

Of course, these questions relate to topics already covered in this book, but a pursuer must be mindful of these questions, including when formulating their claim for damages. A key point to note is that today Scottish courts prefer to deal with issues of recoverability under the scope of the duty or causation, leaving the traditional remoteness test with a somewhat more muted role in the reported case law.[2]

1 See eg *Henderson Group Development v Wotherspoon* [2013] CSOH 113.
2 On scope of duty, see eg *Newcastle Building Society v Paterson Robertson & Graham* 2001 SC 734 (IH) at para 8; *Henderson* at paras 20–21; *Miller v North Lanarkshire Council* [2019] SC EDIN 61 at paras 34–36; *K v Chief Constable of Police Scotland* [2020] CSIH 18, 2020 SC 399 at paras 88–89; *DD v NHS Fife Health Board* [2022] SAC (Civ) 27 at para 34; and, on causation, *SD v Grampian Health Board* [2024] CSIH 7 at para 83.

CALCULATION OF DAMAGES

17.10 The purpose of an award of damages is to compensate the pursuer for those losses which arose because of the delict. It is intended, so far as money can, to place the pursuer in the financial position he would have been if the wrong had not occurred.[1] Where the claim is in respect of damage to property, damages are relatively simple to assess, ie the cost of repair or replacement of the property.[2] If, after repair, the property is worth less than before it was damaged the pursuer can recover the diminution in value.[3] It is now settled that if the cost of repair is greater than would reasonably be expected because of the owner's impecuniosity at the time the property was damaged, the pursuer can recover for the increased costs of repair.[4]

1 See, for example, *O'Brien's Curator Bonis v British Steel plc* 1991 SC 315 (IH) at 480 per the Lord President (Hope); *Cantwell v Criminal Injuries Compensation Board* 2002 SC (HL) 1.
2 The pursuer still incurs a reparable loss even though he could have pursued a contractual claim against a third party to repair the property: *Ford Motor Co Ltd v HLM Design Ltd* 1997 SLT 837 (OH).
3 *Hunter v National Specialist Steeplejacks* 2004 Rep LR 26 (Sheriff Principal).
4 *Alcoa Minerals of Jamaica v Herbert Broderick* [2002] 1 AC 371 (PC, Jamaica); *Lagden v O'Connor* [2003] UKHL 64, [2004] 1 AC 1067. In these circumstances, the pursuer is not in breach of his duty to mitigate the loss by waiting until he could afford the repairs.

PERSONAL INJURY CLAIMS

17.11 Where a party suffers personal injuries because of the delictual conduct of the defender, he is entitled to obtain solatium in respect of non-patrimonial losses such as pain and suffering and compensation for any derivative economic loss which he has sustained. Again, 'the objective' is, so far as money can, to compensate the injured party for the consequences of the wrongful act.[1] The pursuer can claim in respect of loss, injury and damage suffered. It is now the practice to divide the claim into various heads of losses. Although it is sensible and convenient to do so, it is always important to remember that these are not several discrete claims but a *single* claim which can be regarded as falling into several parts for the purposes of quantification.[2] Compensation for the pain and suffering as a result of physical injury is known as solatium; compensation in respect of derivative economic loss is known as damages.

1 *Admiralty Comrs v SS Susquehanna (Owners)* [1926] AC 655 (HL).
2 *Irving v Hiddleston* 1998 SC 759 (OH).

(1) Solatium

17.12 It is, of course, clear that no money sum can in effect compensate for non-patrimonial losses such as pain and suffering. In *Wright v British Railways Board*[1] Lord Diplock said that:

> 'such loss is not susceptible of *measurement* in money. Any figure at which the assessor of damages arrives cannot be other than artificial and, if the aim is that justice meted out to all litigants should be even handed instead of depending on idiosyncrasies of the assessor, whether jury or judge, the figure must be "basically a conventional figure derived from an experience of awards in comparable cases".'[2]

In *McMillan v McDowall*, the judge opined that:

> 'While the assessment of solatium is not a precise science and has frequently been called a jury question, the view of [a Lord Ordinary] in a similar case must be treated with respect.'[3]

The court therefore approaches the question of solatium based on comparing one case with another, taking into account the severity and nature of the injuries sustained by the pursuer. The court assesses solatium as at the date of the proof and does not attempt to assess solatium as it would have been at the date of the injury itself.

In making an award of solatium the court considers not only the extent of the injury but also the pursuer's awareness of pain.[4] No award can be made if, because of his injuries, the pursuer has been rendered permanently unconscious. Such awards are made not only in respect of physical injury.

A person who, for example, suffers from an identifiable psychological condition can be awarded damages where the condition arises because of a delict.[5] In *MacLean v Lothian and Borders Fire Brigade*, an award of solatium took into account the pursuer's loss of congenial employment.[6] Cases of historic child abuse raise difficult issues of quantification.[7]

In making its assessment of solatium, the court considers not only the pain and suffering which has been experienced by the pursuer but also the pain and suffering which he is likely to have in the future. A global award is made. The award also takes into account the pursuer's loss of amenity. Everything which reduces the pursuer's enjoyment of life, which has been sustained as a result of the accident, will be reflected in the award of solatium. It has been held in England that the important element in such a claim is the fact of deprivation of amenity and not whether the injured person is aware of such deprivation.[8] Also included in an award of solatium is the pain and suffering occasioned when the pursuer is, was, or at any time will be, likely to become aware that his expectancy of life has been shortened by his injuries.[9]

1 [1983] 2 AC 773 (HL).
2 *Wright* at 777, citing *Ward v James* [1966] 1 QB 273 (CA) at 303 per Lord Denning MR (Lord Diplock's emphasis). It is submitted that the position is the same in Scots law.
3 *McMillan v McDowall* 1993 SLT 311 (OH) at 312 per Temporary Judge T G Coutts QC.
4 *Lim Poh Choo v Camden and Islington Area Health Authority* [1980] AC 174 (HL).
5 *Clark v Scottish Power plc* 1994 SLT 924 (OH); *Lawson v Scotdem Ltd* 2000 SLT 543n. Distress has, on occasion, been the subject of an award of solatium even in the absence of physical injury or mental illness: *Fraser v D M Hall & Son* 1997 SLT 808 (OH); *McLelland v Greater Glasgow Health Board* 2001 SLT 446 (IH) (distress to a parent caused by the wrongful birth of a handicapped child).
6 1999 SLT 702 (OH).
7 See eg *J v Fife Council* 2009 SLT 160 (OH); *F v Chalmers* [2025] CSOH 23, 2025 SLT 569.
8 See eg *Lim Poh Choo*. Of course, if the person has been rendered unconscious, he will not obtain compensation for pain and suffering.
9 Damages (Scotland) Act 2011, s 1(2).

(2) Patrimonial loss

17.13 Having assessed damages in respect of solatium the court must then turn to the question of patrimonial loss. The court first assesses the pursuer's past loss, ie loss incurred between the date of the accident and the date of the proof. It then attempts to assess the pursuer's future loss.

(3) Damages for patrimonial loss to the date of proof

17.14 If the pursuer has been out of work since the date of his accident, he will be entitled to be compensated for his loss of income. This loss can take various forms such as loss of wages or salary, a reduction in a share of partnership profits or loss of a dividend in a single-employee company.[1] In addition, the pursuer will frequently have a claim for expenses. The general rule is that reasonable expenses are recoverable. Consequently, reasonable medical expenses can be recovered even if it is shown at a later stage that they are unnecessary.[2] Expenses need not be confined to medical or nursing services. By s 8 of the Administration of Justice Act 1982, when a person has sustained personal injuries or has died in consequence of the personal injuries he has sustained, the defender is liable to pay damages in respect of necessary services which have been, or will be, rendered to the injured person by a relative in consequence of the injuries in question. Section 9 of the Administration of Justice Act 1982 also imposes an obligation upon the wrongdoer to pay to the injured person a reasonable sum by way of damages when he is unable, as a result of the accident, to render gratuitous personal services to his family.

In calculating loss of earnings, the pursuer's income tax must be taken into account and his liability to pay National Insurance contributions.[3] Accordingly, in so far as past patrimonial loss is concerned, the wages which form the basis of the calculation are the pursuer's net earnings.

1 *Anthony v Brabbs* 1998 SC 894 (IH).
2 *Clippens Oil Co Ltd v Edinburgh and District Water Trustees* 1907 SC (HL) 9; *Rubens v Walker* 1946 SC 215 (OH).
3 *British Transport Commission v Gourley* [1956] AC 185 (HL); *Cooper v Firth Brown Ltd* [1963] 1 WLR 418.

(4) Damages for future patrimonial loss

17.15 This head of claim is by far the most important in assessing damages in respect of personal injury. The first stage is to assess damages in respect of future loss of earnings.[1] This is done by taking the loss of the pursuer's net earnings at the date of proof and calculating that on an annual basis. The courts do not attempt to speculate on future rates of taxes and National Insurance contributions but base their calculation on the rates current at the date of proof.[2] No allowance is made for possible increases in the pursuer's earnings if he had not been injured. The figure produced is known as the 'multiplicand'.

1 Future loss of earnings is a matter of chance, not a fact to be proved on the balance of probabilities and so the test is one of 'real and substantial chance': *Malcolm v Dundee City Council* [2017] CSIH 32, 2017 SLT 1008.
2 *British Transport Commission v Gourley* [1956] AC 185 (HL).

17.16 The second stage is to find a 'multiplier'. The Ogden tables provide actuarial calculations of lump sums which are required to provide incomes for different persons at different ages. In *Wells v Wells*,[1] the House of Lords laid down that the rate of return on the investment of the damages should be three per cent, and that the Ogden tables should be used as the *starting point* for finding the appropriate multiplier. The traditional Scottish approach was to use the Ogden tables as a check on the multiplier which was found by less scientific methods. Nevertheless, the guidelines laid down by the House of Lords in *Wells* have been followed by the Scottish courts.[2] After taking the appropriate multiplier for the tables, there will usually be a deduction to take into account contingencies relating to the pursuer other than death, for example early retirement or redundancy.[3]

In cases where the victim's expectation of life has been diminished, in assessing the amount of future patrimonial loss, the court is to assume that the pursuer will live until the date when his death would have been expected had he not been injured. This is known as the notional date of death. In other words, the multiplier is to be determined on the basis of the notional date of death rather than the date when it is expected that the pursuer will actually die. The period between the expected date of death and the notional date of death is known as the lost period. In calculating the multiplicand in respect of the lost years the court will consider what the pursuer would have earned had he not been injured and what benefits he would have received and then deduct from that amount 25 per cent of the total: the 25 per cent reduction represents what would have been the pursuer's living expenses during the lost period had the injuries not been sustained.[4]

1 [1999] 1 AC 345 (HL). The House of Lords felt empowered to lay down a three per cent return because the pursuer would be assumed to invest the damages in index-linked government stock rather than in equities which might give a higher return but which, of course, are a less safe investment. Under s 1 of the Damages Act 1996, the Lord Chancellor and the Secretary of State for Scotland have the power to prescribe the rate of return. This has now been reduced to minus 0.75 per cent: Damages (Personal Injury) (Scotland) Order 2017 (SI 2017/96), Article 3. Modifications have also been made by the Damages (Review of Rate of Return) (Scotland) Regulations 2024 (SI 2024/163).

2 *McNulty v Marshalls Food Group Ltd* 1999 SC 195 (OH); *McManus' Executrix v Babcock Energy Ltd* 1999 SC 569 (OH).

3 Sometimes the multiplier produced by the Ogden tables is not suitable in a particular case where, for example, the injured person may be able to return to relatively well-paid work after retraining: see for example *McGhee v Diageo plc* [2007] CSIH 68, 2007 SLT 1016 and [2008] CSOH 74; *Brand v Transocean North Sea Ltd* [2011] CSOH 57.

4 Damages (Scotland) Act 2011, s 1.

17.17 The third stage is for the court to multiply the multiplicand by the multiplier to give a lump sum. So, for example, if the multiplicand is £20,000 and the multiplier is 10, then the total sum awarded is £200,000. The pursuer is expected to live off the income and capital, the theory being that the lump sum will have been consumed by the date the pursuer dies!

Where a pursuer is severely injured, damages can be awarded for the cost of her maintenance, nursing and medical care in the future. Again, the multiplicand/multiplier method is adopted. The court assesses the cost of maintenance and care on an annual basis and then applies a multiplier based on the Ogden tables.[1]

Loss of pension rights can also be taken into account in assessing future patrimonial loss,[2] as can the pursuer's general loss of value in the labour market. In *Hill v Wilson*,[3] damages were awarded for impairment to earning capacity as opposed to loss of future wages. It is particularly difficult to assess damages when the injured person is a child. In such a case:

> 'it has never been suggested that damages should be assessed on such a basis, namely on a basis which provides not only reasonable compensation but in effect a guarantee of future financial security'.[4]

In some cases, the court will abandon the multiplicand/multiplier method of calculating future patrimonial loss. This would happen where, for example, the pursuer has been able to continue working albeit on light work at a reduced wage, or there is evidence that the pursuer will be able to resume employment in the very near future, even though the job may be lower paid than previously.[5]

Personal injury cases can be tried by jury. Juries tend to award higher damages than judges, particularly in relation to solatium. Although a court can order a new trial if the sum awarded is excessive, it will not do so unless the damages awarded are beyond what a reasonable jury would award and there is serious injustice: the fact that a judge would have awarded considerably less is not sufficient.[6] In complex cases, particularly those involving future loss of earnings special cause may be shown for withholding jury trial.[7]

1 For the courts' approach before *Wells v Wells* [1999] 1 AC 445 (HL), see *O'Brien's Curator Bonis v British Steel plc* 1991 SC 315 (IH).
2 *Mitchell v Glenrothes Development Corpn* 1991 SLT 284 (OH) (conventional multiplicand/multiplier method used); *Cantwell v Criminal Injuries Compensation Board* 2002 SC (HL) 1.
3 1998 SC 81 (OH).
4 *O'Connor v Matthews* 1996 SLT 408 (OH) at 412, per the Lord Ordinary (Marnoch).
5 *Stevenson v British Coal Corp* 1989 SLT 136 (OH); *McGhee v Diageo plc* [2008] CSOH 74.
6 *Girvan v Inverness Farmers Dairy (No 2)* 1998 SC (HL) 1. Differences between judge and jury awards are discussed in *Currie v Esure Services Ltd* [2014] CSIH 112, 2015 SC 351 and *Young v MacVean* [2015] CSIH 70, 2016 SC 135.
7 See eg *Lewendon v International Paper (UK) Ltd* [2011] CSOH 116.

(5) Interest

17.18 Having assessed the quantity of damages, the court is obliged to consider the question of interest. Interest is payable under the Interest on Damages (Scotland) Act 1958, as amended by the Interest on Damages (Scotland) Act 1971.

Although solatium is awarded as a lump sum, it is important for the purpose of awards of interest to distinguish past and future solatium. Interest is only awarded on past solatium.[1] Past solatium is a sum awarded for the pursuer's pain and suffering until the date of proof. But if the pursuer is experiencing pain and suffering and loss of amenities at the date of the proof, the court will estimate damages to compensate the pursuer for the fact that these may continue in the future. So, for example, a court might award a total sum of £10,000 by way of solatium, made up of £6,000 for past solatium and £4,000 for future solatium. Interest on past solatium is paid at the average court rate for the period between the date of the accident and when the 'pain' diminished: this could, of course, have occurred before the date of the proof. If the pursuer is still suffering pain at the date of proof, interest will be awarded on past solatium at half the average court rate.[2]

Subject to the court's discretion, interest on damages for patrimonial loss runs from the date of the accident.[3] Again, although a global sum is awarded, damages are divided between past and future loss. In the case of past losses, interest is awarded at one half of the average court rate from the date of the accident to the date of proof. There is no interest payable on awards in respect of future patrimonial loss.[4] The rules applicable to interest in respect of personal injuries operate without prejudice to the general rule which awards interest at the court rate from the date of decree until the date of payment by the defender.

1 *Smith v Middleton* 1972 SC 30 (OH); *J v Fife Council* 2009 SLT 160 (OH).
2 *Keicher v National Coal Board* 1988 SLT 318 (OH); *Preston v Grampian Health Board* 1988 SLT 435 (OH).
3 *Macrae v Reed & Mallik Ltd* 1961 SC 68 (IH).
4 *Hill v Wilson* 1998 SC 81 (IH).

(6) Deductions from awards

17.19 In personal injury cases, deductions can be made from the damages awarded for financial (patrimonial) losses. For instance, it is not uncommon for the pursuer to be unable to work for an extended period between the incident and the final award. During this time, they may receive social security benefits. The recovery scheme is designed to ensure that the State does not bear the cost of losses that should be covered by the defender. Additionally, it prevents the claimant from receiving compensation twice for the same loss. At present, under the Social Security (Recovery of Benefits) Act 1997, it is the responsibility of the defender to deduct this sum from the pursuer's compensation award and pay those sums directly to the Department of Work and Pensions.

It is important to note that, under devolution arrangements with the UK, some social security benefits are administered by the Department for

Work and Pensions (DWP), while others are delivered by Social Security Scotland. In essence, the Scottish Parliament now has the power to replace UK-wide social security benefits with a Scottish equivalent. However, until the Scottish system is fully implemented, the UK and Scottish Governments presently coordinate the delivery of social security, which in practice means, at the point of writing, many social security benefits remain UK-wide. The recovery of benefit payments from compensation, presently, is done under the UK-wide scheme, however, a Scottish system has been introduced, but is yet to commence at the time of writing.[1]

Importantly, therefore, for now, UK-wide social security payments, such as Universal Credit, Jobseeker's Allowance, and Employment and Support Allowance are recoverable under the Social Security (Benefits Recovery) Act 1997. As per s 3 of the Social Security (Recovery of Benefits) Act 1997, the 'relevant period' for calculation is five years from the date of the accident or five years from first claiming benefit because of a disease. Thus, benefits paid over that five-year period are recoverable from the relevant head of loss. Payments which are paid thereafter are not recoverable. When damages are paid *before* the end of five years, the relevant period ends at the date of payment; therefore, benefits paid after that date but before the five-year period ends are not recoverable.[2]

1 Social Security (Amendment) (Scotland) Act 2025, s 19.
2 1997 Act, s 3. See *Mitchell v Laing* 1998 SC 342 (IH).

17.20 Section 10 of the Administration of Justice Act 1982 prohibits reduction of damages regarding the following benefits received by the pursuer:

> '(a) any contractual pension or benefit;[1]
>
> (b) any pension or retirement benefit to which s 2(1) of the Law Reform (Personal Injuries) Act 1948 applied;
>
> (c) any benefit payable from public funds in respect of any period after the date of the award of damages which is designed to secure to the injured person or any relative of a minimum level of subsistence;
>
> (d) any statutory redundancy payment;[2]
>
> (e) any payment made to the injured person or to any relative of his by the injured person's employer following upon the injuries in question where the recipient is under an obligation to reimburse the employer in the event of damages being recovered in respect of his injuries; and
>
> (f) any payment of a benevolent character made to the injured person or to any relative by any person following upon the injuries in question.'

Section 10 directs, however, that any remuneration or earnings from employment, any unemployment benefit payable from public funds payable *prior* to the date of the award of damages, or any payment of a benevolent character made by the person responsible for the accident to the injured person, shall be taken into account. Any savings to the pursuer as a result of being maintained in hospital or accommodation provided by a care home service is deducted.[3]

1 *Lewicki v Brown & Root Wimpey Highland Fabricators Ltd* 1996 SC 200 (HL) (payment under employer's long-term disability scheme held to be a contractual benefit and not deducted: cf if it had been treated as earnings or remuneration from employment). Where the pursuer's claim is in respect of loss of earnings and loss of a contractual retirement pension, then s 10(a) applies to the claim for loss of earnings so that his ill-health pension is not deducted but s 10(a) does *not* apply to the claim for loss of a contractual retirement pension so that his ill-health pension has to be brought into account: *Cantwell v Criminal Injuries Compensation Board* 2002 SC (HL) 1.

2 Reversing *Wilson v National Coal Board* 1981 SC (HL) 9. An *ex-gratia* non-statutory payment falls to be deducted: *Duncan v Glacier Metal Co Ltd* 1988 SLT 479 (OH).

3 Administration of Justice Act 1982, s 11.

(7) NHS charges

17.21 Where a pursuer has received hospital treatment, ambulance services, or both from the National Health Service because of an injury caused by the defender's wrongful conduct, the defender is liable to pay the corresponding NHS charges involved in treating the pursuer. As is evident, the NHS injury recovery scheme aims to ensure a fair distribution of the costs involved in the pursuer's care. For instance, if the pursuer sustains injuries in a car accident – which, along with workplace incidents, ranks among the most common causes of negligence-related harm in the UK – it would be unreasonable to expect the NHS to bear the financial burden of treating such injuries.

Thus, the Health and Social Care (Community Health and Standards) Act 2003 allows the NHS Injury Costs Recovery scheme to claim costs related to road traffic accidents, workplace injuries or any other type of personal injury. The NHS regularly updates the tariff charges for various types of treatment, which is available to defenders. Under the scheme, the defender is liable to make the payment if they voluntarily accept liability or are found to be liable during litigation. Under the scheme, the defender applies to the Scottish Ministers for a certificate which determines the amount payable.

PROVISIONAL AND INTERIM DAMAGES

17.22 The normal rule in actions of damages for personal injuries is that the damages are assessed once and for all at the date of proof. Consequently, pursuers used to delay bringing proceedings for a considerable period until they could ascertain the full extent of their loss. Pursuers often suffered hardship during the period between the accident and the date of proof. The situation was particularly unfair if the pursuer's physical condition was likely to deteriorate because of the injuries at some time in the future after the date of the proof. In *Stevenson v Pontifex and Wood*[1] the Lord President (Inglis) observed:[2]

> 'I hold the true rule of practice based on sound principle to be, that though the delict ... be of such a nature that it will necessarily be followed by injurious consequences in the future, or though it may for this reason be impossible to ascertain with precise accuracy at the date of the action ... the amount of loss which will result, yet the whole damage must be recovered in one action.'[3]

A pursuer's position in these circumstances has, to some extent, been alleviated by s 12 of the Administration of Justice Act 1982, which provides that the court is entitled to make an award of provisional damages in respect of personal injuries. Such an award can be made when it is proved, or admitted, that there is a risk that at some definite or indefinite time in the future, the pursuer will, as a result of the act or omission of the defender, which gave rise to the cause of the action, develop some serious disease or some serious deterioration in his physical or mental condition.[4] Provisional damages can only be awarded where the defender was, at the time of the accident giving rise to the cause of action, either a public authority or an insured person.[5] The purpose of this provision is therefore to give the pursuer an opportunity to claim damages in circumstances where his position is likely to worsen but where he cannot assess the full extent of his loss because the condition will take some time to deteriorate.

Before an award of provisional damages can be made, the pursuer must establish that there is a risk[6] that at some time in the future he will develop some serious disease or some serious deterioration in his physical or mental condition. Although assessment of the risk may be difficult,[7] it is clear that the risk must be more than *de minimis*.[8] There must be evidence that there is the possibility of a *serious* deterioration in the pursuer's condition.[9] If, for example, the pursuer's health or disability will become worse incrementally, there are no grounds for an award of provisional damages because there is no 'clear cut and severable threshold' when the pursuer could apply for damages in the future on the basis that a serious deterioration had in fact taken place.[10] Although the deterioration must be as a consequence of the wrongful conduct of the defender that led to the pursuer's personal injuries in the first place, nevertheless in deciding whether or not the deterioration is serious, account must be taken of the effect of such deterioration upon the pursuer's physical abilities in the context of his ordinary life: '[s]eriousness cannot be assessed in a vacuum'.[11]

Damages can only be deferred in respect of the serious deterioration in the pursuer's condition.[12]

1 (1887) 15 R 125 (IH).
2 (1887) 15 R 125 at 129.
3 See also *Dunlop v McGowans* 1979 SC 22 (IH).
4 Administration of Justice Act 1982, s 12(1)(a).
5 1982 Act, s 12(1)(b).
6 Cf the approach of the Lord Ordinary (Dervaird) who suggested (*obiter*) that if there was no risk but a certainty that there would be a deterioration, this would not be a suitable case for provisional damages: *Prentice v William Thyne Ltd* 1989 SLT 336n (OH) at 337.
7 *Potter v McCulloch* 1987 SLT 308 (OH) at 310 per the Lord Ordinary (Weir).
8 *White v Inveresk Paper Co Ltd* 1987 SC 143 (OH) at 6 per the Lord Ordinary (Murray).
9 *White v Inveresk* at 5 per the Lord Ordinary (Murray). See also *Potter v McCulloch* 1987 SLT 308 (OH) at 310 per the Lord Ordinary (Weir); *Meek v Burton's Gold Medal Biscuits Ltd* 1989 SLT 338n (OH) at 339 per the Lord Ordinary (Prosser). In *Bonar v Trafalgar House Offshore Fabrication Ltd* 1996 SLT 548 (OH) the Lord Ordinary (Gill) held that the court must determine what the apprehended deterioration is: contingent liability cannot be imposed on a defender unless the nature and extent of that liability is clear.
10 See also *Prentice v William Thyne Ltd* 1989 SLT 336n (OH) ('clear and sensible threshold'); *Robertson v British Bakeries Ltd* 1991 SLT 434 (OH) ('recognisable threshold').
11 *Robertson v British Bakeries Ltd* 1991 SLT 434 (OH) at 439 per the Lord Ordinary (Osborne).
12 *Meek v Burton's Gold Medal Biscuits Ltd* 1989 SLT 338n (OH).

17.23 Even if the pursuer satisfies the statutory criteria, the court is not obliged to defer the award of damages. The interests of the defender in not being called upon to pay further damages at some indefinite time in the future must also be considered.[1] Accordingly, an application for provisional damages is unlikely to be successful unless the medical evidence establishes that the deterioration is likely to take place in, say, a period of not more than ten years. Moreover, the court has the discretion to stipulate a time limit after which the pursuer is unable to claim further damages for a deterioration in his condition.[2] In *McColl v Barnes*,[3] for example, where it was established that there was a risk that post-traumatic epilepsy might occur within seven years of the date of the accident, the pursuer was allowed to apply within that period for a further award of damages if the risk should in fact materialise. In the course of his judgment, the Lord Ordinary (Morison) said:[4]

> 'In my opinion this is a most appropriate case for such an order to be made. An assessment made to reflect the possibility of the condition occurring would be unrealistic and impracticable. If no assessment were made and the risk were to materialise, the pursuer would be unjustly deprived of compensation for a serious injury which would be a result of the accident. Since the additional risk becomes negligible after a period of seven years from the date of the accident I shall restrict the order … to that period …'.

The court is also entitled to award interim damages. Interim damages are to be distinguished from provisional damages in so far as they do not depend upon a pursuer suffering from a continuing disability, the eventual seriousness of which cannot be ascertained. Interim payments can be made in the Court of Session in terms of Rule of Court 43.11 and will be awarded if the court is satisfied that the defender or defenders have admitted liability or that if the action proceeded to proof the pursuer would succeed in a question of liability without any substantial finding of contributory negligence on his part.[5] The court must be satisfied that it is 'practically certain' that the pursuer will succeed on the question of liability and that any finding of contributory negligence will not be so large as to have a material effect on the assessment of the amount the pursuer is likely to recover as damages.[6] An interim award is taken into account in making the final award and will not be made against the defender unless that defender is either a person who is insured in respect of the pursuer's claim or is a public authority or 'is a person whose means and resources are such as to enable him to make interim payment'.[7]

Lump sum payments are particularly unsuitable in some cases of catastrophic injury, particularly when a child is seriously injured and requires constant care. The sums involved in these cases can run into millions. Yet the victim might live for a long time and the lump sum might prove inadequate to pay for his care. Conversely, the victim may die earlier than expected giving rise to a windfall to his family which in the case of medical negligence will have been at the taxpayer's expense. To avoid these outcomes, in cases of severe catastrophic injuries, the parties have been prepared to settle in agreements which include periodical payments.[8]

1 *Paterson v Costain Mining Ltd* 1988 SLT 413 (OH).
2 Administration of Justice Act 1982, s 12(2).
3 1992 SLT 1188 (OH) see also *Lappin v Britannia Airways Ltd* 1989 SLT 181 (OH) (five years).
4 *McColl v Barns* at 1190.
5 See eg *Herbertson v Ascosmit Co Ltd* 1992 SLT 1115 (OH).
6 *Cowie v Atlantic Drilling Co Ltd* 1995 SC 288 (IH); *Cleland v Campbell* 1998 SLT 642 (OH).
7 Rule of Court of Session, Ch 43, rule 43.11(5).
8 *D's Parent and Guardian v Greater Glasgow Health Board* [2011] CSOH 99.

DAMAGE TO PROPERTY CLAIMS

17.24 In circumstances where property has been harmed or destroyed, the general principles apply: the pursuer is entitled to be put back into the position they would have been in if not for the defender's wrongdoing. Of course, this also means: that the harm needs to fall within the scope of the duty of care, that the pursuer takes steps to mitigate their losses, and that the damages sought must be reasonably foreseeable to the defender. In most cases, this is a somewhat uncomplicated process; yet problems arise in two types of situations. First, when the property is functionally destroyed, and the cost of a like-for-like replacement is more than the market value of the property. Second, debates arise regarding the remedial costs or steps taken by the pursuer whilst their property is being repaired.

If property is damaged beyond repair, the loss should be calculated according to the market value of the goods immediately prior to being damaged. In *Pomphrey v James A Cuthbertson Ltd*,[1] the pursuer's vehicle, which was used for deliveries, had been specially adapted to their needs. Following a car accident with the defender, the car was significantly damaged, and the pursuer proceeded to scrap the damaged car and buy a new vehicle, which they modified to suit their requirements. They claimed these costs from the defender, who disputed the valuation, arguing that the defenders had inflated the losses by proceeding with this course of action. The Inner House agreed with the defenders, holding that the valuation of the losses, in this instance, should be the market value of the vehicle at the time and not the subsequent purchase and adaption costs.

A key point made in *Pomphrey*, which relates to not only valuation but also mitigation, is that the pursuer must take the most economically efficient approach. Thus, when property is significantly damaged rendering repair and temporary replacement more expensive than treating the property as a complete loss and claiming the market value, the pursuer should opt for the second, more efficient, approach rather than the more costly first approach. Yet an exception exists: if the property has no comparative market value (ie it is not feasible to determine an equivalent market price) then the pursuer is entitled to replace and adapt the property to their specific needs and claim the costs of this from the defender.[2]

Over the years, there has been a great deal of litigation regarding vehicle hire costs incurred by innocent motorists whilst their own vehicle is being repaired following negligently caused damage. For the most part, these cases have been considered under the general rubric of mitigation, ie did the pursuer take reasonable steps in response to the defender's wrongdoing to minimise the extent of their losses? Scottish courts follow the House of Lords decision of *Lagden v O'Connor*,[3] which allowed the claimant to recover the credit hire costs of obtaining a substitute car whilst theirs was being repaired.[4] In *Lagden*, the claimant could not afford to pay for a replacement car. Using a credit hire company, therefore, was his only chance of obtaining a substitute vehicle. Of course, this came at a higher cost to paying the hire charges up front given that it involved interest payments, which the defendant disputed. The House of Lords, however, allowed the recovery of the credit cost for the substitute car and rejected the argument that she had failed to mitigate her losses.

In the Supreme Court decision of *Armstead v Royal & Sun Alliance Insurance Company Ltd* similar issues re-emerged regarding hire car payments.[5] Through no fault of their own, the claimant was involved in two car accidents. One accident involved their own vehicle, the second involved the substitute hire vehicle they acquired whilst their own car was being repaired. Under the terms of the substitute hire agreement, significant costs were due to be paid by the claimant to the hire company for the second accident. The question was whether these charges should be covered by the negligent driver who caused the first accident. The Supreme Court decided that such losses should be recoverable from the first driver. They rejected the defendant's argument that the claimants were seeking to recover pure economic losses rather than losses related to damage to their property.

Importantly, the Supreme Court confirmed that in this instance the question should be dealt with as part of remoteness, concluding the loss here was reasonably foreseeable. It clarified that in this case, there was no doubt that the loss fell within the scope of the duty of care to avoid causing damage to other's property. This distinction is important; it has consequences for how litigation is conducted and how evidence is used by parties. That is, if the question remains one of scope, the burden falls on the injured party to demonstrate that the wrongdoer is responsible for this type of loss. Yet if accepted to fall within the scope of the duty of care, it is for the wrongdoer to prove, factually, that the loss was too remote or that the injured party failed to adequately mitigate their losses. From a procedural perspective, this is a difference which influences the distribution of the burden in litigation between the parties, and ultimately how much such disputes will cost the respective parties.

1 *Pomphrey v James A Cuthbertson Ltd* 1951 SC 147 (IH).
2 *Clyde Navigation Trs v Bowring Steamship Co* 1929 SC 715 (IH).
3 [2006] UKHL 64, [2004] 1 AC 1067.
4 *Clark v City of Edinburgh Council* [2010] CSOH 144; *Allan v Amlin* [2013] CSOH 156.
5 [2024] UKSC 6, [2025] AC 406.

PURE ECONOMIC LOSS CLAIMS

17.25 If the loss is purely economic then, *prima facie*, the calculation of what is recoverable is straightforward. For example, in the case of a disappointed legatee, the loss is the value of the lost legacy.[1] Where a surveyor has been negligent and failed to discover defects, the loss to the purchaser is either the cost of repair or the diminution in the value of the property.[2] But difficulties have arisen in quantifying loss when the pursuer claims for more than the defender understands as falling within the scope of their duty or beyond the losses they could foresee as natural arising from a breach of their duty.

It is well settled that when A has entered a transaction as a result of B's fraud, B is liable for all A's losses arising directly from the transaction, even though some of them might not be reasonably foreseeable.[3] This would include losses which A incurs because of a general fall in the market value of the assets involved in the transaction.

What is the position if A has entered a transaction because of B's negligence? Regardless of whether that negligence is in the performance of services, the provision of advice or the delivery of information, it is important that the defender can establish the type of loss suffered falls within the scope of the duty of care.[4] It is important to remember that questions of remoteness are factual questions whereas those relating to scope are legal. Hence, parties can argue questions of scope as part of a legal debate while questions relating to remoteness must be determined at proof according to the balance of probabilities. If you have established liability and can demonstrate that your economic losses were reasonably foreseeable to the defender, then you will be successful in recovering your losses.

For example, in *Henderson Group Development v Wotherspoon*,[5] the pursuer claimed for loss of profits following a solicitor's negligent handing of various property transactions. The pursuer bought land with a plan to develop it over two stages. Phase 1 included the construction and sale of 12 residential flats with parking spaces. Phase 2 involved the sale of the remaining land for further development, including commercial units. Fully aware of his plans, the defenders negligently transferred to shared ownership of the Phase 2 land to the individual purchases of the residential flats. This mistake was discovered when the pursuer tried to sell the Phase 2 land for £250,000. Because of the defender's negligence, the sale fell through. A legal fix had to be done, but by then, the land's value had dropped to £100,000. Rather than sue for this diminution and the costs of remedy, the pursuer also sought projected future profits from the commercial use of the Phase 2 development which amounted to £600,000.

The defender argued, *inter alia*, that such losses were irrecoverable and that the claim should be dismissed. However, Lady Wise decided that the question of remoteness could not be determined without key facts being established. In this case, the pursuer has specified in their initial claim details regarding their losses, including loss of profits, and were prepared to demonstrate that the breach of the defender's duty of care was directly linked to the loss they suffered, and that this loss was reasonably foreseeable to the defenders.

1 *White v Jones* [1995] 2 AC 207 (HL); *Holmes v Bank of Scotland* 2002 SLT 544 (OH).
2 *Patel v Hooper & Jackson* [1999] 1 WLR 1792 (CA).
3 *Smith New Court Securities Ltd v Scrimgeour Vickers (Asset Management) Ltd* [1997] AC 254 (HL); *Barry v Sutherland* 2002 SLT 413 (OH).
4 *Newcastle Building Society v Paterson Robertson & Graham* 2001 SC 734 (IH).
5 [2013] CSOH 113.

17.26 Difficulties can arise in determining when the pursuer has sustained the loss. In some cases, a loss is sustained as soon as the pursuer enters a transaction after being given negligent advice. For example, after consulting his solicitor, A agrees to guarantee her son's business debts. She grants a standard security over her house in favour of her son's creditor. The business fails and the creditor enforces the standard security. She sues the solicitor alleging that she had not been advised sufficiently on the nature of the transaction and the standard security. Following the English case of *Forster v Outred & Co*,[1] A's loss would be held to have arisen when she granted the standard security and not when the creditor enforced it: the loss would be the difference in value between an encumbered and unencumbered property. On the other hand, there is no reason to believe that the business will fail. Nevertheless, in *Osborne & Hunter Ltd v Hardie Caldwell*[2] the Second Division held that while as a general rule there may be no loss until there is default, each case turns on its own facts: in this case it was negligent to advise anyone to lend money to the borrower and accordingly the client sustained a loss as soon as he parted with his money. In *Law Society v Sephton & Co*,[3] the House of Lords, approving *Foster v Outred*, held that loss occurred when a contingent liability depressed the value of property or led a party to a bilateral transaction receiving less than he should have done, or to be worse off than if he had not entered into the transaction, but that the mere possibility of an obligation to pay money in the future does not of itself constitute loss until the contingency in fact occurs.

1 [1982] 1 WLR 86 (CA).
2 1999 SLT 153 (IH).
3 [2006] UKHL 22, [2006] 2 AC 543.

CLAIMS ON BEHALF OF RELATIVES

17.27 In personal injury cases, the defender is required to offer a degree of compensation to relatives who have suffered economic loss because of the injuries. By virtue of s 8 of the Administration of Justice Act 1982, the injured person can recover on behalf of their relative damages which amount to reasonable remuneration for necessary services rendered to the pursuer by that relative.[1] The services rendered by the relative must be physical services, such as nursing.[2] Thus it has been held that s 8 of the 1982 Act did not apply when a relative had donated bone marrow to the pursuer who would otherwise have died.[3] The quantification of damages by reference to the number of hours of providing services and a modest notional hourly rate is well established.[4] But the courts often take a broad view when reaching an appropriate figure.[5] The damages can be reduced to take into account the injured person's contributory negligence.[6]

The pursuer, ie the injured person, then accounts to the relative for any damages recovered under this provision.[7] Originally, damages could only be awarded in respect of services rendered up to the date of the action;[8] but now damages can be awarded for services likely to be rendered by a relative to the injured person in the future.[9] Damages are not available under s 8 of the 1982 Act if the relative expressly agreed that no payment should be made in respect of the services rendered or to be rendered.[10] Where the injured person has died before the action is concluded, the deceased's executor may recover damages for necessary services rendered by a relative before the victim died.[11]

Where a person who was not in employment was injured, at common law he had no right to sue for loss of earnings since *ex hypothesi* he was not earning. In the 1980s, this was viewed as being particularly unfair given the domestic arrangements of many families in the UK at this time. At this time, many wives had given up their jobs to look after the home or children; prior to the 1982 Act their incapacity did not generate a recoverable loss. Section 9(1) of the Administration of Justice Act 1982, therefore, gives an injured person who has been providing unpaid personal services to a relative[12] the right to sue for damages if the pursuer is unable to continue to do so as a result of the injuries sustained. The personal services must be services which (a) were or might have been expected to have been rendered by the pursuer before the injuries; (b) were of a kind which when rendered by a person other than a relative would ordinarily have been obtainable on payment; and (c) the injured person but for the injuries in question might have been expected to render gratuitously to a relative.[13]

In *Ingham v John G Russell (Transport) Ltd*[14] the Inner House refused to restrict the concept of personal services to services which were rendered to the person of the relative, such as nursing, as opposed to the relative's property, such as cleaning the relative's house. It was enough that the services had been rendered *in person* by the injured person and therefore included maintenance or DIY services rendered by the injured person to his spouse. It is therefore clear that an injured woman, for example, can recover damages if she is unable to provide unpaid housekeeping and child-rearing services for her spouse, cohabitant or children. Because the personal services must have been rendered gratuitously before s 9 applies, the Administration of Justice Act 1982 recognises the fact that work in the home is still *prima facie* unpaid but that its economic value is such that justice demands that the injured person should receive compensation for the inability to continue to provide it, even though technically the pursuer has not suffered any patrimonial loss, ie loss of earnings.

Where the injured person's expectation of life has been diminished as a result of her injuries, in assessing the amount of damages under s 9(1), the court must assume that the pursuer would have lived until the notional date of death.[15] In other words the pursuer can obtain damages for the inability to provide gratuitous personal services to a relative during the lost years.

Where the injured person has died, a relative may claim as a head of loss a reasonable sum in respect of the loss of gratuitous personal services rendered to the relative by the deceased.[16] Before he can do so, the pursuer must be a relative who has the right to claim damages for loss of support by the deceased under the Damages (Scotland) Act 2011. Accordingly, it is to the provisions of the 2011 Act that we shall now turn.

1 'Personal injuries' means (a) any disease and (b) any impairment of a person's physical or mental condition: s 13(1) of the 1982 Act. 'Relative' includes the injured person's spouse or divorced spouse, civil partner or former civil partner, opposite sex and same sex cohabitants, any ascendant or descendant, any brother, sister, uncle or aunt or their issue and any person accepted by the injured party as a child of the family: any relationship by affinity is treated as a relationship by consanguinity and the half blood is treated as a relationship of the whole blood; a stepchild is treated as a child and illegitimacy is irrelevant: s 13 (1) of the 1982 Act.

2 BNA nursing and home help rates can be useful but are by no means conclusive of what reasonable remuneration should be in a particular case. See, for example, *Kennedy v Lees of Scotland* 1997 SLT 510 (OH) (use of agency rates rejected as unsuitable where victim had not received substantial nursing, but only short visits from relatives).

3 *Duffy v Lanarkshire Health Board* 1998 SCLR 1142 (OH). In *Sturgeon v Gallacher* 2003 SLT 67 (OH), the pursuer ran a farm in partnership with his wife. After he had been injured in an accident, his son laboured on the farm for £50 a week. The Lord Ordinary (Emslie) held that the son's work did not constitute necessary services for the purpose of the 1982 Act, s 8 as they were rendered to the partnership, not the pursuer. The pursuer could, however, include the extra outlay (the son's wages) in his claim for loss of earnings.

4 *Wallace v Glasgow City Council* [2010] CSOH 88 at para 30 per Lord Tyre; reversed on another point at [2011] CSIH 57.

5 *Kerr v Stiell Facilities* [2009] CSOH 67, 2009 SLT 851 following *Clark v Chief Constable of Lothian and Borders* 1993 SC 320 (IH).

6 *Yule v Forbes* 2004 SLT (Sh Ct) 13.

7 1982 Act, s 8(2). But where the relative is the defender, it has been held that a claim under s 8 is incompetent: *Kozikowska v Kozikowski* 1996 SLT 386 (OH). It was thought contrary to public policy that the pursuer should remunerate the person she blamed for her injuries – *sed quaere?*.

8 *Forsyth's Curator Bonis v Govan Shipbuilders* 1989 SCLR 78, 1989 SLT 91.

9 1982 Act, s 8(3).

10 1982 Act, s 8(1) and (3). See *Denheen v British Railways Board* 1986 SLT 249, 1988 SLT 320 (OH).

11 See, for example, *McManus' Executrix v Babcock Energy Ltd* 1999 SC 569 (OH); *Murray's Executrix v Greenock Dockyard Co Ltd* 2004 SLT 346 (OH).

12 For the definition of 'relative', see the 1982 Act, s 13, discussed at note 5 above.

13 1982 Act, s 9(3).

14 1991 SC 201 (IH).

15 1982 Act, s 9(1A).

16 1982 Act, s 9(2); *Ingham v John G Russell (Transport) Ltd* 1991 SC 201 (IH). It can be difficult to quantify the value of such services, particularly when the deceased was simply 'a normal, average married man living in a family who did the correspondingly normal, average things which a father and husband does around the house, the garden and the family car': *Beggs v Motherwell Bridge Fabricators Ltd* 1998 SLT 1215 (OH) at 1223 per the Lord Ordinary (Eassie). See also *Farrelly v Yarrow Shipbuilders Ltd* 1994 SLT 1349n (OH); *McManus' Executrix v Babcock Energy Ltd* 1999 SC 569 (OH); *Murray's Executrix v Greenock Dockyard Co Ltd* 2004 SLT 346 (OH) (£2,100 awarded as deceased only occasionally helped out, not discussed when reversed on other grounds 2004 SLT 1004 (IH)).

DEATH OF A RELATIVE

17.28 If a person dies because of another's wrong, two potential claims arise. First, the deceased's own claim which can transmit to the deceased's executor who can pursue the action for the benefit of the deceased's estate. Second, an independent standalone claim can be raised by the deceased's relatives.

(1) The deceased's claim

17.29 Where a person is killed outright as a result of the defender's wrong, the deceased's executor cannot raise an action in delict in respect of the death.[1] In these circumstances, the only claims are those of the deceased's relatives. However, if a person is injured and subsequently dies because of the injuries, the deceased's right to sue in delict in respect of personal injuries transmits to the executor who can sue on behalf of the deceased's estate. This complex area of the law is now regulated by the Damages (Scotland) Act 2011.[2]

Where a person dies the rights which vested in the deceased immediately before his death to sue for damages in respect of personal injuries transmit to the executor.[3] As a result, the executor can raise an action or, if an action has been raised by the deceased before he died, continue the action on behalf of the deceased's estate.[4] The executor may sue in respect of patrimonial loss, for example loss of earnings sustained by the deceased, but only up to the date of death.[5] In other words, patrimonial loss attributable to any period after the deceased's death, for example loss of future earnings, is non-transmissible to the executor. This is necessary to prevent double compensation given that the defender may have to meet claims for loss of support brought by the deceased's relatives.

The deceased's right to damages for non-patrimonial loss by way of solatium is also transmissible to the executor,[6] but again in assessing damages for solatium the court is to have regard only to the period ending immediately before the deceased's death.[7] Solatium is damages for pain and suffering arising from the personal injuries. In assessing damages for solatium, the court is entitled to have regard to the extent to which the deceased suffered because he was aware that his expectation of life had been reduced as a result of the injuries.[8]

The effect of these provisions can be illustrated by the following example. A is seriously injured as a result of the negligent driving of B. A dies two years after the accident.[9] If A had begun an action against B, A's executor can continue the action provided it has not been concluded.[10] If A had not begun proceedings, A's executor can bring an action against B.[11] However, the executor's claims for patrimonial loss and solatium are restricted to losses incurred by the deceased at the date of death: any patrimonial loss referable to a period after the date of death cannot be recovered by the executor. If the action is successful,[12] the damages awarded become part of the deceased's estate. This means that they will be distributed to the deceased's legatees if there is a will or to a surviving spouse or civil partner and the deceased's heirs according to the rules of intestate succession where the deceased died without a will. If A has relatives, they may have a claim against B if A's death *was* as a result of the personal injuries A has sustained. It is to the relative's dependent claim that we now turn.

1 Where death is caused by a fatal accident, the deceased's executor can obtain damages for the deceased's fear of impending death. However, it has been questioned whether Parliament intended the court to carry out 'the difficult – and often distasteful – task of trying to assess the feelings of pain and apprehensions of mortality of someone so abruptly and severely injured as so be in the imminent and real danger of death within a period of minutes': *Beggs v Motherwell Bridge Fabricators Ltd* 1998 SLT 1215 (OH) at 1223–1224 per the Lord Ordinary (Eassie). The sum awarded was £250, but see now *McArthur v Timberbush Tours Ltd* [2021] CSOH 75, 2021 SLT 1021 at para 40 (award of £5000 for 50 minutes of suffering). In England no damages are awarded under this head: *Hicks v Chief Constable of South Yorkshire Police* [1992] 2 All ER 65 (HL).

2 References in this section are to the Damages (Scotland) Act 2011 unless otherwise stated.

3 Damages (Scotland) Act 2011, s 2(1)(a).

4 D(S)A 2011, s 10. Where the action was brought by the deceased it is not concluded while an appeal is competent or before any appeal taken has been disposed of: s 10(2).

5 D(S)A 2011, s 2(2).

6 Damages (Scotland) Act 2011, s 2(1). See eg *McManus' Executrix v Babcock Energy Ltd* 1999 SC 569 (OH). This case was distinguished in *Murray's Executrix v Greenock Dockyard Co Ltd* 2004 SLT 346 (OH) on the ground that the deceased, while dying of an insidious disease, had suffered less than McManus.

7 D(S)A 2011, s 2(2).

8 D(S)A 2011, s 1(1) and (2). Otherwise, no damages by way of solatium are recoverable in respect of loss of expectation of life: s 1(3). In an action in respect of personal injuries, damages can also be awarded in respect of patrimonial loss arising from the fact that the injured person's expectation of life has been reduced: s 1(1) and (2). Where the action is brought by the executor, however, only patrimonial loss arising before the date of death can be recovered: s 2(2). Where the injured person has no dependent relatives who could sue for loss of support should the victim die, the rule that patrimonial loss can only be claimed by an executor up until the date of death may tempt the defender to delay settling the claim until the victim dies.

9 It is irrelevant whether the death was a result of A's injuries.

10 Damages (Scotland) Act 2011, s 10(1)(b).

11 D(S)A 2011, s 10(1)(a).

12 Any defences, eg *volens*, which B could use in an action by A are good against an action brought by A's executor. Similarly, damages can be reduced as a result of A's contributory negligence.

(2) The dependent claims

17.30 Where a person dies in consequence of personal injuries sustained by him as a result of the defender's conduct, then if the defender would have been liable to pay damages to the deceased if he had lived, she is also liable to pay damages to a certain class of the deceased's relatives.[1] It will be seen that a relative's right to sue is *dependent* on the defender being liable to pay damages if an action had been brought by the deceased in respect of the personal injuries sustained. Accordingly, the relative's claim can be defeated if the deceased would not have succeeded against the defender, for example if the defender did not owe a duty of care to the deceased or had not broken the duty or the deceased was *volens*. The relative's damages can also be reduced on the grounds of the deceased's contributory negligence.[2]

By s 4(2) of the 2011 Act it is expressly enacted that the relative's claim cannot be brought if the defender had discharged his liability to the deceased before he died. In other words, if the deceased had settled his claim before he died, this automatically excludes the deceased's relative's dependent claim. But because of the amount of damages which can be awarded to the deceased's relatives for non-patrimonial loss, the dependent claims are often more valuable than the deceased's claim. This led to a cruel dilemma where the victim was diagnosed with mesothelioma and knew that he would die within a very short time: should he accept a settlement which would exclude his family's right to sue after he had died or refuse and lose the financial support which could make his last months more bearable? To ease this dilemma, the 2011 Act provides that where the personal injury is mesothelioma, a settlement does not exclude the deceased's relatives' rights to claim damages for non-patrimonial loss.[3]

The nature of the dependent claim turns on whether the pursuer is a member of the deceased's immediate family or a wider class of relative as specified in the Damages (Scotland) Act 2011.

1 D(S)A 2011, ss 3 and 4. Personal Injuries means any disease and any impairment of a person's physical or mental condition: s 14(1). Where a child who has been born alive dies from injuries sustained *in utero* the parents have title to sue as the child could have sued the defender when the child was born alive: *Hamilton v Fife Health Board* 1993 SC 369 (IH). There would be no claim under the 2011 Act if the child was not born alive.

2 See eg *Beggs v Motherwell Bridge Fabricators Ltd* 1998 SLT 1215 (OH) (deceased 20 per cent contributorily negligent).

3 D(S)A 2011, s 5. See *Crozier v Scottish Power UK Ltd* [2024] CSIH 14, 2024 SC 373.

The immediate family

17.31 The deceased's immediate family consists of the following relatives:[1]

(1) the deceased's spouse or civil partner;

(2) the deceased's cohabitant, ie any person not being the spouse or civil partner of the deceased who immediately before the death was living with the deceased as husband and wife or in a relationship which has the characteristics of the relationship between civil partners;

(3) the deceased's children: this includes children who have been accepted by the deceased as children of the family. A posthumous child is included;[2]

(4) the deceased's parents: this includes any person who accepted the deceased as a child of his or her family;

(5) the deceased's brothers and sisters: this includes any person brought up in the same household as the deceased and who was accepted as a child of the family in which the deceased was a child; and

(6) the deceased's grandparent or the deceased's grandchild.

It will be clear that relatives now include members of the deceased's de facto family, thus reflecting contemporary family structures.

Any relationship by affinity is treated as a relationship by consanguinity;[3] any relationship of the half blood is treated as a relationship of the whole blood; and the stepchild of any person is treated as his child.[4] But in a claim for damages for non-patrimonial loss persons who would qualify only by affinity, for example the deceased's mother-in-law or father-in-law or son-in-law or daughter-in-law are excluded and step-parents and step-children are excluded unless they qualify because they had accepted the deceased as a child of their family or the deceased had accepted them as a child of the deceased's family.[5]

Members of the deceased's immediate family may claim damages for the following:

(1) Damages for patrimonial loss.

(a) Loss of support–

A relative can claim damages to compensate the relative for any loss of support which the relative has sustained or is likely to sustain as a result of the deceased, A's, death. This covers both loss of support up until the date of proof and loss of support in the future. The loss of support constitutes the multiplicand and an appropriate multiplier is found by reference to the Ogden tables.[6] These claims can be substantial.

The 2011 Act introduces a set of rules by which a relative's loss of support – and consequently the multiplicand – is to be calculated. The total amount available to support the deceased, A's, relatives is an amount equivalent to 75 per cent of A's net income.[7] Where the relatives are A's surviving spouse, civil partner or cohabitant and/or a dependent child, the total 75 per cent constitutes the family's loss of support.[8] A dependent child is a child who, at the date of A's death, had not attained the age of 18 and to whom A owed an obligation of aliment, ie A's child or a child whom A had accepted as a child of A's family.[9] In the case of other members of A's immediate family, including A's child or accepted child who is 18 or over, the loss of support is the actual amount of that loss, ie what support the relative in fact received from A.[10] Where the pursuers are A's surviving spouse, civil partner or cohabitant and/or a dependent child and another immediate relative, the sum awarded to the last is deducted from the 75 per cent of A's income and the balance is the loss of support for the former. For example:

A's net income is £40K. The total available for loss of support is £30K. If A's only relative is A's wife, she will have the full £30K as loss of support. If A is survived by A's wife and a dependent child, the loss of support for A's wife and child is £30K. If A is survived by his wife, a dependent child and A's mother whom he has supported by giving her £5K a year, then A's mother's loss of support is £5K and the wife and child's loss is £25K.

While the 2011 Act does not expressly do so, it is submitted that in applying this formula as a general rule the income of the surviving immediate relative should be ignored. However, by s 7(2) of the 2011 Act, the court may apply a different percentage 'if satisfied that it is necessary to do so for the purpose of avoiding a manifestly and materially unfair result'. This discretion should be used only in exceptional circumstances: otherwise the courts could undermine the utility of the 75 per cent rule. But it might be used if A's surviving spouse or civil partner was very wealthy and A had not contributed much to the family expenses. Conversely, it could be used when A had many dependent children and could not have spent anything like 25 per cent of his net income on himself.

No account is taken of any patrimonial gains which accrue to the relative by way of succession or settlement as a result of A's death. Similarly, no account is taken of insurance monies, pensions etc which the relative may receive.[11] If the deceased had obtained a provisional award of damages before his death, in assessing the relative's loss of support the court takes into account such part of the provisional award as was intended to compensate the deceased for any period beyond the date when he died.[12]

Unless a claim falls under the provisions of the 2011 Act, no person can obtain damages by reason of relationship to the deceased.[13] For the purpose of the legislation, loss of support has been narrowly construed. In *Mackintosh v Morrice's Executors*,[14] H and W were killed in a car crash. Before they died, they had transferred large sums to their daughters who were the pursuers in the action. This had been done to avoid the incidence of inheritance tax when the couple died. H and W were in good health, and it was probable that they would have survived for seven years from the date of transfer so that no inheritance tax would have been payable. The accident took place within the seven years. The daughters claimed sums representing the inheritance tax which they had paid but which would not have been due if their parents had not died prematurely in the car crash. Their claims failed because such claims are restricted to any loss of support sustained by them as a result of their parents' deaths. A sum representing a diminution in the value of their parents' estates which the pursuers inherited as residuary legatees could not be regarded as support given to them by their parents while they were alive. Their claim as their parents' executrices also failed because executors can only recover patrimonial losses sustained by deceased persons during their lifetimes:[15] and since there was no liability to pay inheritance tax until they died, the loss to the parents' estates was sustained after they had died and therefore did not transmit to their executrices.

(b) Funeral expenses–

The relative can recover any reasonable expenses incurred by the relative in relation to A's funeral.[16]

(c) Loss of A's personal services–

The relative is entitled to include as a head of damages a reasonable sum in respect of the loss of gratuitous personal services rendered to the relative by A.[17] 'Personal services' has the same meaning as in s 9(1) of the Administration of Justice Act 1982.[18]

(2) Damages for non-patrimonial loss.

By section 4(3)(b) of the 2011 Act a member of the deceased's immediate family can claim such sum of damages as the court thinks just by way of compensation for all or any of the following:

(a) distress and anxiety endured by the relative in contemplation of the suffering of A before A's death;

(b) the grief and sorrow of the relative caused by A's death;[19]

(c) the loss of such non-patrimonial benefit as the relative might be expected to derive from A's society and guidance if A had not died.

In making such an award, the court is not obliged to ascribe any of the award to any of these heads of loss.

The amount of damages to be awarded for non-patrimonial loss is entirely a matter for the discretion of the court. There is no official tariff. Juries have tended to make more generous awards than judges sitting without a jury. In order to reduce the disparity between judicial and jury awards in *Hamilton v Ferguson Transport (Spean Bridge) Ltd*[20] the Inner House directed judges to consider the awards made by juries as well as judges in similar cases. In addition, the Inner House took the view that in jury trials the judge should suggest a spectrum of the level of damages for non-patrimonial loss which would be appropriate; this spectrum is for the assistance of the jury and is not binding on them.[21] It will be interesting to see whether as a consequence the level of damages for non-patrimonial loss awarded by judges and juries will converge.

What is clear is that in contemporary Scotland, life is considered to be more precious than it may have been thought to be by earlier generations. Consequently, the loss of a life of a close relative seems a greater loss than before. This change has resulted in higher awards of damages for loss than used to be the case. In *Ryder v Highland Council*,[22] for example, an award of £40,000 was thought to be appropriate for a son's loss of his mother.[23]

1 Damages (Scotland) Act 2011, ss 4(5)(a) and 14(1).
2 *Cohen v Shaw* 1992 SLT 1022 (OH).
3 See *Monteith v Cape Insulation Ltd* 1998 SC 903 (IH).
4 D(S)A 2011, s 14(2).
5 D(S)A 2011, s 4(5)(a) and (b).
6 *McManus' Executrix v Babcock Energy Ltd* 1999 SC 569 (OH). The multiplicand only applies to the calculation of future loss of support: D(S)A 2011, s 7(1)(d). On multiplicands and multipliers see para 17.15–17.17 above.
7 D(S)A 2011, s 7(1)(a).
8 D(S)A 2011, s 7(c)(i).
9 D(S)A 2011, s 7(3)
10 D(S)A 2011, s 7(1)(b).
11 D(S)A 2011, s 8(1).
12 D(S)A 2011, s 8(3).
13 D(S)A 2011, s 8(5).
14 [2006] CSIH 43, 2007 SC 6.
15 See also *Milligan's Executors v Hewats* [2013] CSOH 60, 2013 SLT 758 (executors could not sue the deceased's solicitors since the deceased had not sustained any loss before he died).
16 D(S)A 2011, s 4(3)(a).
17 D(S)A 2011, s 6(1).

18 D(S)A 2011, s 6(2). For discussion of s 9(1) of the 1982 Act see para 17.27 above. See eg *McGee v RJK Building Services Ltd* [2013] CSOH 10, 2013 SLT 428.

19 The pursuer is entitled to establish the gravity of her grief and sorrow by bringing evidence that she sustained a psychiatric disorder as a consequence of the death: *Gillies v Lynch* 2002 SLT 1420 (OH). However, damages for psychiatric disorder will only arise if the defender owed an independent duty of care to the pursuer to prevent her sustaining psychiatric harm: for discussion, see above Chapter 4. In *Cruickshank v Fairfield Rowan Ltd* 2005 SLT 462 (OH), the Lord Ordinary (Brodie) confessed at 466 'to some difficulty with the notion that it is possible to discern in the circumstances of one family, bonds of affection that are stronger or a degree of emotional investment in the future of a child that is more profound, than in the circumstances of another family, and so in the circumstances in the one case to be very special and in the other case not'.

20 [2012] CSIH 52, 2012 SC 486. See also *Currie v Esure Services Ltd* [2014] CSIH 112, 2015 SC 351 and *Young v MacVean* [2015] CSIH 13, 2016 SC 135.

21 See eg *Kelly v Upper Clyde Shipbuilders* 2 July 2012, OH.

22 [2013] CSOH 95, 2013 SLT 847.

23 See also *McGee v RJK Building Services Ltd* [2013] CSOH 10, 2013 SLT 428. In *Currie v Esure Services* [2014] CSOH 34 parents were awarded £42,000 each in respect of the loss of their son: the deceased's brother was awarded £22,500. See also *Gallagher v SC Cheadle Hume Ltd* [2014] CSOH 103 (including awards to grandchildren).

Specified relatives

17.32 The specified relatives include the deceased's ascendants and descendants (other than a parent or grandparent or a child or a grandchild), former spouse or civil partner, but not a former cohabitant, uncles and aunts, nephews and nieces and cousins. Such relatives include the appropriate 'in-laws', and half blood is to be treated as full blood. A stepchild who has not been accepted as a child of the deceased's family is to be treated as a child.[1]

Specified relatives can claim damages for patrimonial loss arising from A's death. In relation to loss of support, the relative must establish the actual value of the support he received from A. The relative cannot take advantage of the 75 per cent rule. Relatives can also claim for reasonable funeral expenses and loss of A's gratuitous personal services. A specified relative is not entitled to damages for non-patrimonial loss. The fact that the deceased had no legal obligation to support the specified relative is irrelevant: reparation is made for the loss of *de facto* financial support both before the date of death and in the future.

1 D(S)A 2011, ss 14(1)(e)–(g) and (2).

Transmission

17.33 The right of a relative of A to a dependent claim under the Damages (Scotland) Act 2011 can transmit to the executor of the relative if the relative dies before an award of damages is made.[1] For example, if A dies leaving his wife, B, B's right to sue as a member of A's immediate family transmits to her executor if she dies before an award of damages has been made to her. In determining the amount of damages payable to the relative's executor, the court can only have regard to the period ending immediately before the relative's death.[2] This proviso, while obviously important in respect of the relative's claim for loss of support, could also affect a claim for non-patrimonial loss under s 4(3) of the 2011 Act if the relative died shortly after the deceased person.

1 D(S)A 2011, s 9(2).
2 D(S)A 2011, s 9(2).

Index

[*all references are to paragraph number*]

www.ingramcontent.com/pod-product-compliance
Ingram Content Group UK Ltd.
Pitfield, Milton Keynes, MK11 3LW, UK
UKHW020132290926
15471UKWH00003B/434

9 781526 53229